GCSE History

2oth Century Studies

Aaron Wilkes

George

林少軍

OXFORD

UNIVERSITY PRESS

OXFORD
UNIVERSITY PRESS

Great Clarendon Street, Oxford OX2 6DP

Oxford University Press is a department of the University of Oxford.
It furthers the University's objective of excellence in research,
scholarship, and education by publishing worldwide in

Oxford   New York

Auckland   Cape Town   Dar es Salaam   Hong Kong   Karachi
Kuala Lumpur   Madrid   Melbourne   Mexico City   Nairobi
New Delhi   Shanghai   Taipei   Toronto

With offices in

Argentina   Austria   Brazil   Chile   Czech Republic   France   Greece
Guatemala   Hungary   Italy   Japan   Poland   Portugal   Singapore
South Korea   Switzerland   Thailand   Turkey   Ukraine   Vietnam

Oxford is a registered trade mark of Oxford University Press
in the UK and in certain other countries

British Library Cataloguing in Publication Data

Data available

ISBN 978-1-84303-981-5

10 9 8 7 6 5 4

FE9815

Printed in Singapore by KHL Printing Co Pte Ltd

Editors: Nina Randall and Dawn Booth

Page design and layout: Neil Sutton, Pumpkin House, Cambridge

Illustrations: Celia Hart

Cover design: Martin Cross

Cover image: Corbis

Acknowledgements

5D (Left) Liverpool Record Office; 5D (Right) Getty Images/Stereoscopic Company;
6F Corbis/Bettmann; 7G Corbis/Bettmann; 7H Corbis/Swim Ink 2, LLC; 10E
London Metropolitan Archives (IMA); 11H Getty Images/Hulton Archive; 12A
Mary Evans Picture Library; 12B Museum of London/HIP; 13E Getty
Images/Hulton Archive; 14G Mary Evans Picture Library; 14H Museum of
London; 15D Imperial War Museum; 17A & B Corbis/Hulton Archive; 18A Punch
Limited; 21D Mary Evans Picture Library; 23D PA Photos/Topham Picturepoint;
24G Getty Images/Kurt Hutton; 24H Getty Images/General Photographic Agency;
24I Getty Images/George W. Hales/Fox Photos; 25L Popperfoto; 31B Aaron Wilkes;
31C PA Photos; 33E Getty Images/MPI; 35F Getty Images/Picture Post/Hulton
Archive; 36A Aaron Wilkes; 38H Hulton/Deutsch Collection/Corbis; 39J Punch
Limited; 40N Blackadder: The Whole Damn Dynasty, the Penguin Group, 1999;
43B Art Archive/Biblioteque des Arts Decoratifs/Marc Charmet; 44A Imperial War
Museum; 44B Robert and Tony Robinson; 45C Getty Images/Hulton Archive; 46A
Punch Ltd; 49A PA Photos; 51B Wellcome Library London; 51C Imperial War
Museum; 53B Imperial War Museum; 54C Mary Evans Picture Library; 55D Mary
Evans Picture Library; 57D Robert Hunt Library; 58A © Hulton-Deutsch
Collection/Corbis; 61H Getty Images/Topical Press Agency; 64A Bridgeman Art
Library/The Road from Arras to Bapaume, 1918 (litho), Nevinson, Christopher
Richard Wynne (1889–1946)/Private Collection, © The Fine Art Society, London;
65B © Hulton-Deutsch Collection/Corbis; 67 Mary Evans Picture Library; 68A
Imperial War Museum; 73G Sidney George Strube, published in the Daily Express
7 May 1919/Centre for the Study of Cartoons and Caricature, University of Kent;
78B Hulton Archive/Getty Images London; 83 (Both) Punch Limited; 87 Punch
Limited; 90C Solo Syndication/Associated Newspapers/British Cartoon Archive,
University of Kent: David Low, Evening Standard, 19 January 1933; 92E Punch
Limited; 92H Collection of Tonie & Valami Hold; 93I Solo Syndication/Associated
Newspapers/British Cartoon Archive, University of Kent: David Low, Evening
Standard, 23 May 1934; 95B © Ullstein-Archiv Gerstenberg; 97A Getty Images;
104A (Top) Aaron Wilkes; 104B © Bettmann/Corbis; 104D © Bettmann/Corbis;
106A akg-images; 108B Mary Evans Picture Library; 111B Mary Evans Picture
Library; 111C Imperial War Museum; 113B Mary Evans Picture Library; 113C
Mary Evans Picture Library; 114E Popperfoto; 119B Suddeutscher Verlag
Bilderdienst; 122A Corbis/Hulton Archive; 123B United States Holocaust
Memorial Museum; 124–125A © Hulton-Deutsch Collection/Corbis; 126 (Top) ©
Hulton-Deutsch Collection/Corbis; 126 (Bottom) Sidney George Strube, published
in the Daily Express 7 May 1919/Centre for the Study of Cartoons and Caricature,
University of Kent; 134E The Coca-Cola Company/Image courtesy of the
Advertising Archives; 135G Corbis; 136A Bettmann/Corbis; 137E Underwood &
Underwood/Corbis; 137F Corbis; 139H Getty Images/First National Pictures; 140A
Mary Evans Picture Library; 141C Bettmann/Corbis; 142F Getty Images; 144B
Bettman/Corbis; 145C Mary Evans Picture Library; 147C Popperfoto; 148
Popperfoto; 150A Corbis; 151B Getty Images; 153I Culver Pictures; 154
Bettmann/Corbis; 155 (Top) Bettmann/Corbis; 155 (Bottom) Roosevelt Library
Collection; 160C Punch Limited; 163A © Bettmann/Corbis; 165B Corbis; 165C
FPG; 167B © Archivo Iconografico, SA/Corbis; 169B Mary Evans Picture Library;
169C Swim Inc./Corbis; 170B © Bettmann/Corbis; 171C Mary Evans Picture
Library; 175A Corbis/Hulton Archive; 175B © Bettmann/Corbis; 177C ©
Bettmann/Corbis; 178D Corbis; 178E Heritage Image Partnership; 182A
Corbis/Hulton Archive; 184F Getty Images/Time Magazine/Time & Life Pictures;
185G David King Collection; 186/187I David King Collection; 188 © Hulton-
Deutsch collection/Corbis; 192 G Time Life Pictures/Getty Images; 193J David
Low, published in the Evening Standard 8 July 1936/Centre for the Study of
Cartoons and Caricature, University of Kent; 194M © Ullstein Bild; 195B ©
Hulton-Deutsch Collection/Corbis; 200R Hulton-Deutsch Collection/Corbis; 204
Solo Syndication/Associated Newspapers/British Cartoon Archive, University of
Kent: David Low, Evening Standard, 10 May 1935; 205 (both) Solo
Syndication/Associated Newspapers/British Cartoon Archive, University of Kent:
David Low, Evening Standard, 1938; 207B Art Archive/Imperial War Museum;
207C Air Fight over Portland, 1940, Eurich, Richard Ernest (1903–92)/© Imperial
War Museum, London/The Bridgeman Art Library; 207D Mary Evans Picture
Library; 209F Corbis/Bettmann; 209G Mary Evans Picture Library; 201H Hulton
Archive/Getty; 210I AFP/Getty Images; 210J Getty Images; 211K Corbis/Bettmann;
212C Time & Life Pictures/Getty Images; 215C Imperial War Museum; 217G Peter
Newark's Military Pictures; 218B Corbis/Hulton-Deutsch Colllection; 221K
Imperial War Museum; 223D PA Photos; 223E Getty Images; 223F Getty Images;
223G Hulton Archive/Getty Images; 223H Getty Images; 227C Peter Newark's
Pictures; 229D Alamy/Brian Harris; 230G Imperial War Museum; 231K akg-
images; 233D Art Archive; 235J Centre for the Study of Cartoons and Caricature,
University of Kent/Vicky/Evening Standard/Solo; 236A Corbis/David Pollack; 237C
Corbis/Bettmann; 238A Corbis/Bettmann; 239C Hulton-Deutsch Collection/Corbis;
240D © Corbis; 243B Peter Newark's Pictures; 243C Corbis/Hulton Archive; 243D
Corbis/Bettmann; 244A Corbis; 245B © Bettmann/Corbis; 245C Aero Graphics,
Inc./Corbis; 246E Corbis/Bettmann; 248A Bettmann/Corbis; 247F
Corbis/Bettmann; 249B Corbis/Bettmann; 250C Science Photo Library; 250D
Corbis/Bettmann; 251E Corbis/NASA; 254E Corbis/Bettmann; 257B Corbis; 257C
Corbis; 266C © Bettmann/Corbis; 257D PA Photos/AP; 259B Corbis/Bettmann;
262C & D Corbis/Bettmann; 263E Corbis/Bettmann; 267D Corbis/Steve Raymer;
271A © Bettmann/Corbis; 271B Popperfoto; 273B Bettmann/Corbis; 273C
Bettmann/Corbis; 273D Corbis; 275C Topfoto/RIA Novosti; 277C Hulton-Deutsch
Collection/Corbis; 277D Hulton-Deutsch Collection/Corbis; 279B ©
Bettmann/Corbis; 279C © Bettmann/Corbis; 281B © Libor Hajsky/epa/Corbis; 283
Corbis/Fabian Cevallos; 285B Corbis/Robert Maass; 287B Imperial War Museum;
288E akg-images; 288F Hulton-Deutsch Collection/Corbis; 291B Corbis/Hulton
Archive; 292C Hulton-Deutsch Collection/Corbis; 294A © Francoise de
Mulder/CORBIS; 296G Popperfoto; 299C Reuters/Corbis; 301F Getty
Images/David Silverman

Contents

1 Britain 1900–51

What was Britain like at the start of the 20th century? 4
How was poverty attacked? 8
Did women win the vote? 12
Political change 16
Why was there a general strike in 1926? 18
The 'hungry thirties' 22
From the cradle to the grave 26
How did Britain change after the war? 30

2 Britain and the Great War

The stage is set for war 36
'Like a line of falling dominoes …' 42
How did the government get people to fight? 44
Why wasn't the war 'over by Christmas'? 46
Britain's bravest? 48
Winning the war 52
The Battle of the Somme 56
The Home Front 58
Was it really a WORLD war? 62
Counting the cost 64

3 Peace deals

Who were the 'Big Three'? 66
Was the peace settlement fair on Germany? 70
A new Europe 74

4 Different ways to run a country

Democracy and dictatorship 76

5 Keeping the peace in the 1920s

What was the League of Nations? 80
How successful was the League of Nations in
    the 1920s? 84

6 The League of Nations in the 1930s

Why did the League of Nations fail in the 1930s? 88

7 Germany 1919–45

Germany and the Great War 94
What was the Weimar Republic? 96
Germany and the Treaty of Versailles 100
1923: a year of crisis 102
Germany recovers 106
What was Adolf Hitler's early life like? 108
Why were the Nazis so popular? 110
What was it like to live in Nazi Germany? 112
How did the Nazis control Germany? 116
Did all Germans support the Nazis? 118
Hitler goes to war 120
The 'Final Solution' 122
Germany at war 124

Have you been learning? 126

8 The USA 1919–45

The melting pot 128
How is the USA governed? 130
How far did the US economy 'boom' in the 1920s? 132
What were the 'Roaring Twenties'? 136
How widespread was intolerance in the 1920s? 140
What was Prohibition and why did it fail? 144
Why did Wall Street 'crash'? 146
The impact of the Wall Street Crash 150
Why did FDR win the 1932 election? 154
The New Deal 156
America and World War II 162

9 From Russian Empire to Soviet Union

Russia at the beginning of the 20th century 164
The 1905 revolution 166
'From each according to his ability; to each according
    to his needs' 168
How did the Great War affect Russia? 170
'Peace, bread and land' 172
Life in Lenin's Russia 176
How did Stalin change the Soviet Union? 182

Have you been learning? 188

10 Why was there another World War?

Was it Hitler's war? 190
David Low: Hitler's hated cartoonist 204

11 World War II

An overview of World War II 206
Dunkirk: victory or disaster? 212
Who were the 'Few'? 214
'Mr and Mrs Jones would like a nice little boy' 218
Total war 222
'The only thing that ever really frightened me' 226
Should Dresden have been bombed? 228
The end of World War II: why were nuclear
    bombs used? 232
United Nations? 236

**12i Why did relations between the USA and the
    USSR turn 'cold'?**

What was the Cold War? 238
The Berlin Crisis, 1948 242
Cold War madness 244
Alternative battlefields: chess, sport and space 248

12ii How did the USA try to contain Communism?

America and the Communist threat 252
'The elephant and the grasshopper' 256
The 'undeclared war' 258
Masters of war? 260
Death from above 264
War in your living room 268
'Hey, hey, LBJ! How many kids did you kill today?' 270
Peace with honour? 272

12iii The Red Empire in Eastern Europe

The Soviet Union and the Eastern Bloc 274
Uprising in Hungary 276
Why was the Berlin Wall built? 278
The Prague Spring 280
Solidarity in Poland 282
The collapse of the Red Empire 284

13 The Middle East

Why is there conflict in the Middle East? 286
War in the Middle East 290
What was Skyjack Sunday? 294
The search for peace 298

Have you been learning? 302

Glossary 304

Index 314

What was Britain like at the start of the 20th century?

Queen Victoria died on the evening of Monday 22 January 1901. She had been queen for 63 years: Britain's longest serving monarch to date. Her son, Edward, took over from his mother and became King Edward VII.

So what was Edwardian Britain really like? These four pages, divided into four categories – 'Rich and poor', 'Britain's place in the world', 'New technology' and 'Amusements' – invite you to find out.

Rich and poor

In 1900, a writer claimed that the lives led by the rich and poor were so different that Britain was like two nations – a poor one and a rich one. About 3% were very rich (upper class), 25% were relatively wealthy (middle-class bankers, doctors, accountants, managers and so on) and the rest, the working class, were poor – very, very poor.

The richer side of Britain enjoyed a life of luxury and ease. They owned land, homes and many didn't even have to work at all because they made so much money out of investments and rents. On the other side, the vast majority of poor people lived miserable lives – some earning only enough money to get by, others earning nowhere near enough to feed their families. There was no state sick pay, pensions or unemployment benefit. The injured and sick paid for their own medical care (see **Source A**).

Some rich people were even beginning to study the poor at the start of the 20th century. In 1902, Charles Booth published his final report on 'Life and labour of the people of London'. He discovered that nearly one-third of Londoners were so poor that they didn't have enough money to eat properly, despite having full-time jobs. And the problems weren't just in London either! At around the same time, in York, Seebohm Rowntree (of the sweet family) found that 43% of the city's wage earners were not earning enough to live on.

<u>Source A</u> ▾ *The social classes in 1900.*

SOCIAL CLASSES 1900–14

UPPER CLASS
PUBLIC SCHOOL • UNIVERSITY • THE ARMY • COUNTRY HOUSE FOR THE HUNTING SEASON • LONDON HOUSE FOR THE BALL SEASON • SCOTTISH HOUSE FOR THE SHOOTING SEASON • ABROAD FOR THE WINTER

MIDDLE CLASS
SMALL PUBLIC OR GRAMMAR SCHOOL • TRAINING OF MR. BUSINESS • WORK HARD BUT NOT LONG HOURS • COMFORTABLE LIFE WITH SERVANTS • A MONTH'S HOLIDAY BY THE SEA

LOWER CLASS
BOARD SCHOOL UNTIL 12 (OR LATER) • START WORK AT 12–14 • LONG HOURS • LOW WAGES • POOR HOUSES • DREAD OF UNEMPLOYMENT, SICKNESS AND POVERTY IN OLD AGE

Source B ▼ *Taken from an interview in* Poverty: A Study of Town Life, *by S. Rowntree, 1901.*

> "If there's anything extra to buy, such as a pair of boots for one of the children, me and the children go without dinner — or maybe only 'as a cuppa tea and a bit of bread, but Jack 'ollers [shouts] to take his dinner to work and I give it to 'im as usual. He never knows we go without and I never tells 'im."

Source C ▼ *A popular British song from 1900.*

> "We don't want to fight,
> but by jingo if we do,
> we've got the ships,
> we've got the men,
> we've got the money too."

Source D ▼ *These two photographs highlight the contrast between rich and poor in 1900. They were taken only a few days and a few miles apart, yet the poor slum area is vastly different from the rich Park Lane region of London. How can you tell which one is poor and which is rich?*

FACT *How small?*

In 1900, 15 children out of every 100 were dying before their fifth birthday. Also, a poor child was, on average, 9cm shorter than a rich one.

Source E ▼ *The poor in 1900. In 1901, Seebohm Rowntree looked at the lives of poor people in York. In his report, he said that many people lived below the 'poverty line' (the minimum amount of money a person needed to buy enough food, clothing and shelter). Rowntree said that no matter how hard a person worked, there were certain times when they couldn't help falling below the 'poverty line'. Study the graph below carefully. It appeared in Rowntree's report,* Poverty: A Study of Town Live, *published in 1901.*

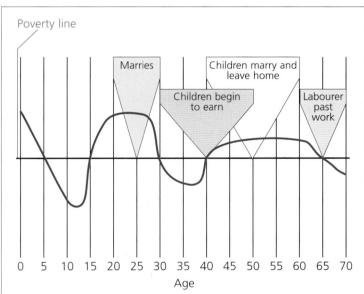

Poverty line

Marries

Children begin to earn

Children marry and leave home

Labourer past work

Age
0 5 10 15 20 25 30 35 40 45 50 55 60 65 70

Britain's place in the world

In 1900, the British people had every reason to be proud. For a start, most Brits were better fed, clothed, healthier and more educated than many of the people of other nations of the world. Cities were full of shops that contained a wide range of goods, either made in British factories or brought in from parts of their Empire. In 1900, Britain controlled over a quarter of the world (about 400 million people) and was the largest empire the world had ever seen.

Britain had been the first country in the world to have an industrial revolution. As a result, Britain became an industrial power and, by 1900, was the richest country in the world.

But there were signs that things wouldn't stay like this for long. The United States was making more goods than Britain, and Germany was quickly catching up. Canada was also making lots of their own goods – and buying less from Britain. The challenge for British businessmen, factory owners and entrepreneurs was to hold onto Britain's position as the country that did more trade (and made more money) than any other.

New technology

The start of the 20th century saw major development in four particular areas of discovery and invention. This new technology was to have a major impact on life after 1900. One historian went so far as to write that the new discoveries turned the 20th century into 'the age of the ordinary man'.

Transport

In 1884, Karl Benz, a German, made the first successful petrol-driven vehicle. It had three wheels and could reach speeds of up to ten miles per hour. In 1887, Gottlieb Daimler, another German, made the first four-wheeled petrol-driven car.

By 1900, car-making had become a big moneymaking industry but cars were still too expensive for most people. Then, in 1909, an American called Henry Ford began making what was to become one of the best-selling cars ever – the Model T Ford. Based in Detroit, USA, the Henry Ford Motor Company had made over one million by 1915. Ford used state-of-the-art techniques in his factory to **mass-produce** them on an **assembly line**. The cars would pass in front of the workers on a conveyor belt and each person would have an individual job to do. The cars were made quickly … and cheaply. In fact, in 1909, a Model T cost $900 to buy but, by 1927, Ford was making them so efficiently that the price dropped to $290.

FACT *Not so fast*

Along with the motor car came the motor driving offence. In 1896, Walter Arnold from Kent became the first British driver to be fined for speeding. He was caught doing eight miles per hour in a two miles per hour zone.

On 17 December 1903, in North Carolina, USA, Orville Wright made the first man-carrying powered flight. It lasted 12 seconds and he flew a distance of 37 metres. His brother, Wilbur, had helped to build the aeroplane. By 1905, the brothers had made nearly 300 flights, some lasting nearly 20 minutes. Flying became the latest craze and, in 1909, a Frenchman, Louis Bleriot, flew over the English Channel. By 1910, some countries were looking into the possibility of attaching bombs to planes so they could be dropped on an enemy!

Source F ▼ *An advert for the Ford car.*

Source G ▾ *The Wright Brothers' 'Model E' plane, at Ohio, in 1913.*

Source H ▸ *A film poster for a famous Charlie Chaplin comedy.*

Communications

The telephone, invented in 1876, rapidly grew in use between towns (and even countries) in the early 1900s. Radio would also become very popular after 1900 and by the 1920s would be the 'must have' household appliance. These inventions sped up the spread of news and enabled business to be done more quickly.

Consumer goods

New inventions, such as vacuum cleaners and electric irons, were based on the growing use of electricity. Other consumer goods, such as wristwatches, gramophones (ask your teacher!), telephones and cameras became popular after 1900, each helping to turn the old way of life upside-down.

Amusements

Sport remained a popular activity, as it had been in the previous century. Football, cricket, rugby, tennis and golf continued to attract thousands of spectators and participants. A trip to the cinema became as popular a pastime as any, and the early 1900s saw movie stars, such as Charlie Chaplin, Laurel and Hardy, and Buster Keaton become household names.

WISE UP WORDS

• mass-produce   assembly line

FACT *War clouds*

In the early 1900s, Britain had some serious military rivals. France had a very large army and Germany was beginning to build warships just as quickly (and just as good) as Britain's. Also, their army was one of the largest and best trained that Europe had ever seen.

WORK

1 Study **Sources A**, **B** and **D**. Choose a social class to belong to. Write a description of the class you have chosen, using as much description as you can about the lifestyle you have. Read your description to a classmate and see if he or she can guess which class you are describing.

2 Study **Source E** on page 5.
   a Draw you own version of this diagram.
   b According to Rowntree there were certain times when people couldn't help falling below the poverty line. Suggest three times when a person might do this and give reasons why.

3 Can you think of any new technology introduced in the 21st century that has had such an impact?

How was poverty attacked?

AIMS

Aim to learn:
- why poverty became a political issue after 1900;
- at least five ways in which the more vulnerable people in society were helped after 1906.

By 1900, the government was beginning to get involved in the lives of its citizens. There were laws limiting the amount of hours you worked and regulations on conditions in mines, factories, shops and offices. But you were very much on your own if you couldn't earn money for some reason. The government hadn't done much to help the old, the sick or the unemployed at all – they were mostly left to cope on their own.

So, why did this change? How were the most vulnerable people in society helped at the start of the 20th century? And what impact did this help have on their lives?

Meet William Wilkes, a 34-year-old factory worker from Stafford. This working-class man is typical of hundreds of thousands of British citizens living in towns and cities up and down the country at the beginning of the 20th century. So, what was life like for William?

The fear of sickness, accidents, unemployment and old age haunted them constantly. But change was on its way. By the beginning of the 20th century, a large number of people, including many politicians, were beginning to realise that the only way to help people such as William – and wipe out poverty – was through direct government action.

William lives with his wife, their three children and his wife's parents. Her mother and father are both over 70 and are too old to work.

William's wife works occasionally as a cleaner for some of the richer families in the area. However, she spends most of her time looking after the family.

William works at the Lotus Shoe Factory on Sandon Road. He has worked there since he was a teenager. He is paid about 20 shillings a week and one-third of this goes on rent.

William had a nasty fall two years ago and hurt his back. He couldn't work for three weeks and didn't get any money. He constantly worries about illness and accidents.

William's mother-in-law is very ill and stays in bed most days. He cannot afford to pay a doctor to visit her and the medicine to make her better would be too expensive.

William lives in a rented two-bedroomed terraced house in the central part of Stafford. He sleeps in his bedroom with his wife – his son shares their room too. His daughters share a bedroom with their grandparents.

So why help William and his family?

In 1901 and 1902, two reports were published that shocked Britain. Seebohm Rowntree made a survey in York, while Charles Booth studied poverty in London. They each found lots of evidence that many people were living below the poverty line. This meant they didn't have enough money to buy proper food, shelter and clothing. They even concluded that most people weren't poor because they drank too much or gambled – they were poor because of things they couldn't control, such as the ups and downs of Britain's economy.

Then another report hit the news-stands. In 1899, a big army recruiting campaign took place to find men to fight in the Boer War in Africa. But army chiefs were alarmed by the fact that 40 out of every 100 young men who volunteered were unfit to be soldiers and it wasn't due to the fact that the army had high entry standards! The government was shocked too and set up a special commission to find out why so many men failed the army medical exam. In 1904 the commission released its report (see **Source A**).

Source A ▼ *Some of the many conclusions of the Committee on Physical Deterioration, 1904.*

> "Bad health is not inherited; it can be improved by changes in food, hygiene and clothing.
>
> To further improve the health of the nation, the Committee believes we must:
> · get rid of overcrowded housing
> · make sure buildings are built correctly
> · control smoke pollution
> · ensure regular inspections of school children
> · set up day nurseries for the infants of working mothers, run by local councils
> · ban the sale of tobacco to children.
>
> Also, too many babies die due to poor feeding by the mother. This Committee believes we must teach young girls how to feed and look after babies properly."

These reports came at a time when more and more people were beginning to feel that one of the key responsibilities of any government was to look after the people who couldn't look after themselves. These people, including many politicians from the Liberal Party, believed that direct action was the only way to improve the health of the nation. One leading Liberal MP, David Lloyd George, even pointed to the fact that other countries were helping their poorest citizens – so why not Britain? German workers, for example, were better housed, better educated and healthier than British ones. Lloyd George argued that Britain would fall a long way behind Germany as an industrial power unless they took action (see **Source B**).

Source B ▼ *Lloyd George speaking about Germany in a newspaper interview.*

> "I never realised before on what a gigantic scale the German pension system is conducted. Nor had I any idea how successfully it works. It touches the great mass of German people in almost every walk of life. Old-age pensions form but a comparatively small part of the system. Does the German worker fall ill? State insurance comes to his aid. Is he permanently invalided from work? Again, he gets a regular grant whether he has reached the pension age or not."

In 1906, the Liberal Party won a huge victory in the General Election and set to work.

So *how* did the Liberals help William and his family?

Helping the children

The Liberal government felt that helping Britain's children was its main priority, as it was one of the most vulnerable groups in society.

Source C ▾ *Bradford was the first city to offer these meals. They introduced at a time when politicians were reeling from research which showed that a poor child was, on average, 9cm shorter than a rich one.*

THIS WEEK'S MENU

Monday: Tomato soup – Currant roly-poly pudding

Tuesday: Meat pudding – Rice pudding

Wednesday: Yorkshire pudding, gravy, peas – Rice pudding and sultanas

Thursday: Vegetable soup – Currant pastry or fruit tart

Friday: Stewed fish, parsley sauce, peas, mashed potatoes – Blancmange

Source D ▾ *Children's Charter (or the Children's Act, 1908). As you can see, many of these reforms are still in place today.*

- Children are 'protected persons' – parents can be prosecuted if they neglect or are cruel to them.

- Inspectors to regularly visit any children who have been neglected in the past.

- All children's homes to be regularly inspected.

- Youth courts and young offenders' homes set up to keep young criminals away from older ones.

- Children under 14 not allowed in pubs.

- Shopkeepers cannot sell cigarettes to children under 16.

Source G ▸ *A pensioner interviewed in 1909.*

Source E ▸
An anxious mother watches the doctor examine her son in one of Britain's first free medical checks.

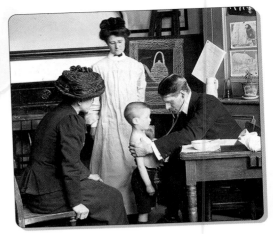

Source F ▾ *This graph shows how children gained (and lost) weight during parts of the year.*

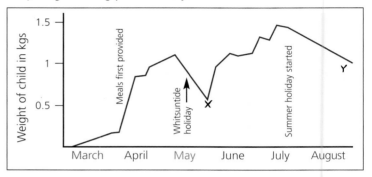

Helping the old

POST OFFICE

Most people dreaded old age. When you became too old to work, you either went to live with a member of your family – or went into the workhouse! These buildings, run as a charity by the local parish, were made deliberately unpleasant so that people would try to get out of them as soon as possible. They were almost a punishment for being old and poor!

In 1909 the Liberals brought in the Old Age Pensions Act – anyone over 70 who had no income was given 5 shillings a week. A married couple received 7 shillings and 6 pence. These amounts weren't a lot of money – but they clearly made a difference to people such as the 'pensioner' interviewed in **Source G**. In the first year of operation, 650 000 people collected a weekly pension from the post office.

"We was a burden to our children because they wouldn't let us go on the parish if they could help it. But now we want to go on livin' forever."

Helping the unemployed

In 1910, the first Labour Exchanges (job centres) were opened to help the unemployed find a job. A year later, unemployment pay of 7 shillings a week was available in some industries (shipbuilding and iron foundry to start with) for those who couldn't find work.

Helping the sick

In 1911, all low-paid workers were made to join a new National Health Insurance scheme. Workers paid 4 pence a week into a central fund, and the government and employers between them paid in 5 pence. Then, if workers were off work because of illness, the fund gave them money to live on (10 shillings a week) and provided medical care for 26 weeks.

Source H ▾ *A Liberal poster advertising National Health Insurance. Lloyd George is the doctor.*

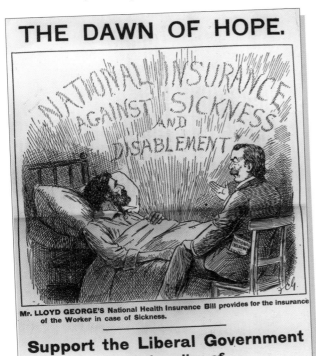

So how were these welfare reforms paid for?

Not surprisingly, there was plenty of opposition to the new **reforms**. Some based their objections on the cost of all these changes, while others thought it was wrong for the government to help people, as this might encourage them to be lazy.

But the Liberal Party pushed forward with its **welfare** reforms and even introduced ground-breaking tax plans to pay for the ideas. In 1909, what became known as the People's Budget was unveiled by the Liberals. New tax changes included:
*   increasing tax on tobacco and alcohol
*   introducing a licence fee on cars
*   raising income tax
*   increasing death duties (a tax paid when you die)
*   a new tax on the profit made when selling land.

The People's Budget was strongly opposed by the richer politicians but, after the Liberal Party won another General Election in 1910, the laws came into force.

WISE UP WORDS

*   welfare   reforms

WORK

1   The year is 1905. Imagine you are William Wilkes (the man on page 8). Write a short letter from William to his sister, in another town, explaining some of his the problems.

2   Look at **Source A**.
    a   Why was the Committee on Physical Deterioration set up?
    b   How did the report suggest that health could be improved?

3   Look at **Source F**.
    a   What was the result of introducing school meals?
    b   Why do you think children lost weight at points X and Y?

4   Look at **Source H**.
    a   How did the National Health Insurance scheme work?
    b   In your opinion, does the cartoonist support the Liberal reforms or not? Explain your answer.

5   The year is 1912. Imagine you are William Wilkes, write another short letter to a family member about how (or if) life has changed or improved since 1905!

Did women win the vote?

AIMS

Aim to understand:
- the difference between a suffragette and a suffragist;
- why women won the vote after 1919.

Look at **Source A** carefully. This poster appeared in 1900 and demonstrates how many men felt about the idea of giving women the right to vote. What is the poster trying to say about a woman's mind?

Source A ▾ *A woman's mind magnified.*

A WOMAN'S MIND MAGNIFIED

In 1900, no woman in Britain had the right to vote. Men ruled the nation from Parliament and women were expected to keep out of the way. It was widely believed (by men of course) that a woman's place was in the home, looking after her children and husband. If any woman had a job, it would always be lower paid than a man's ... and women were restricted to jobs as teachers, nannies, cleaners, nurses and factory workers.

Votes for women

By 1900, many people were beginning to think that the lowly status of women in British society was wrong. Increasingly, it was felt that the way to improve their status was to get women to vote. If they could vote, they might be able to elect politicians who promised to improve their lives and get them equal pay to men (for example – see **Source B**).

As early as 1867, an MP named John Stuart Mill tried to introduce a law allowing women to vote. He was defeated, but similar bills were introduced nearly every year after that ... and each time they were defeated!

Several groups even started campaigning to get women the vote. They were called suffrage groups because suffrage means the right to vote.

The suffragists

By 1900, the largest suffrage group was the National Union of Women's Suffrage Societies (NUWSS) led by Millicent Fawcett, who joined up 500 local suffrage groups. They were nicknamed the **suffragists** and used peaceful tactics to try to secure the vote. They organised petitions, held meetings, published posters and wrote letters to politicians (see **Source B**). At their most popular, they had 100 000 members, made up mostly of middle-class women who either had jobs or were wealthy. They didn't make much progress but they certainly turned women's suffrage into a hot political issue.

Source B ▾ *A postcard from 1912 produced by the NUWSS.*

What a Woman may be, and yet not have the Vote
MAYOR · NURSE · MOTHER · DOCTOR or TEACHER · FACTORY HAND

What a Man may have been, & yet not lose the Vote
CONVICT · LUNATIC · Proprietor of white Slaves · Unfit for Service · DRUNKARD

> Women don't join the army – so they don't fight to defend their land. Why should they vote then?

> Parliament's decisions affect both men AND women – so stopping women voting is unfair. Britain cannot be called a true democracy until all of its citizens can vote.

> Politics is for men – it always has been. Britain is the most powerful country in the world and it's the men who have created it.

> We are falling behind other countries – New Zealand let its women vote in 1893, for example.

> Women can vote in local council elections – so this proves they can be trusted to vote sensibly.

> Women are natural 'home-makers', not 'decision-makers'. And look how childish and bad-tempered they get at certain times of the month! Women are just too emotional to have the vote. Anyway, they are already represented by their husbands' vote.

Source C ▲ *The arguments for and against votes for women.*

The suffragettes

In 1903, a member of a suffrage group in Manchester got fed up at the lack of progress made by the suffragists. Her name was Emmeline Pankhurst and along with her daughters, Sylvia and Christable, they decided to change tactics. They felt that the only way to gain the country's attention was to get violent and become a nuisance. If enough people are annoyed, they thought, then Parliament might give in and give women the vote. Officially, the new **militant** (warlike) group was known as the Women's Social and Political Union (WSPU) – but they were more commonly known as the **suffragettes** ... and their tough new motto was 'deeds [action], not words' (see **Source D**).

Source D ▼ *A cartoon of a suffragette in her typical outfit, surrounded by the 'tools of her trade'.*

Source E ▼ *A suffragette being arrested after chaining herself to the railings.*

The suffragettes did all they could to get public attention. They smashed shop windows, threw eggs at politicians and chained themselves to the railings outside Buckingham Palace. They even sent themselves through the post to the houses of well-known politicians! Their slogan, 'Votes for women', was found everywhere – on dolls, clothes, badges, flags, banners and belts. Their magazine had over 40 000 readers and even the Prime Minister, Henry Campbell Bannerman, encouraged them 'to go on pestering'.

Source F ▼ *Millicent Fawcett, leader of the suffragists.*

> "In my opinion, far from having injured the movement, the suffragettes have done more during the last 12 months to bring women the vote than we have been able to accomplish in the same number of years."

The violence increases

Despite all the publicity, women were still not given the vote. Politicians who supported the idea of votes for women introduced bills in Parliament in 1907, 1908 and twice in 1910 – but they were all defeated.

The suffragettes' response to these setbacks was to get more violent. In April 1913, alone, they set fire to several schools, a lighthouse, dozens of post boxes, two churches, eight houses and three sports grounds. They let off four bombs and slashed famous paintings with knives. Someone even threw an axe at the Prime Minister. Most famously of all, suffragette Emily Davison was killed when she ran out in front of the King's horse at the Derby. Inside the dead woman's coat was sewn the suffragette colours of green, white and purple.

Source G ▼ *The front page of the* Daily Sketch, *published the day after Emily Davison threw herself in front of the King's horse.*

DAILY SKETCH.

HISTORY'S MOST WONDERFUL DERBY: FIRST HORSE DISQUALIFIED: A 100 TO 1 CHANCE WINS: SUFFRAGETTE NEARLY KILLED BY THE KING'S COLT.

Source H ▶ *A poster commenting on the suffragette campaign. Do you think the cartoonist supported the suffragettes or not?*

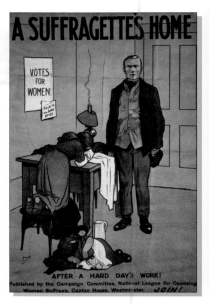

A SUFFRAGETTE'S HOME

The suffragettes believed the increase in violence worked – after all, they got loads of publicity. However, some believed the violence worked against their cause. It was argued that the suffragette violence made the government even more stubborn – they didn't want to be seen to give in to violence. If they did, perhaps other groups would use violence to get their way!

Source I ▼ *Millicent Fawcett speaking about the suffragettes in 1913.*

> "I think they would rather lose women's suffrage rather than give up their own way of demonstrating."

Hunger strikes

The suffragettes didn't mind getting arrested and imprisoned because it drew attention to their campaign. When in prison, they often went on hunger strike and refused to eat. The government reacted by ordering all hunger strikers to be force fed by pouring soup through a tube up their nose and down their throat.

In 1913, Parliament passed a new law – nicknamed the Cat and Mouse Act – which released weak hunger strikers until they were feeling better … then rearrested them and sent them back to jail.

WISE UP WORDS

• militant suffragettes suffragists munitions

Source J ▼ *A popular song from the early 1900s.*

"Put me on an island where the girls are few,
Put me with the most ferocious lions in the zoo,
Put me on a treadmill, and I'll never fret,
But for pity's sake, don't put me with a suffragette."

Women and war

In 1914, the Great War started and the suffragettes stopped their campaign of violence. Instead, they put their full support behind helping Britain to win the war. But the war brought women an unexpected opportunity. With more and more men leaving their jobs to become soldiers, women got the chance to do jobs they had never done before. They became bus drivers, milk deliverers, police officers, railway ticket collectors and car mechanics. Thousands worked in **munitions** factories (which were very unhealthy and dangerous), or became nurses or ambulance drivers near the front lines in France.

Source K ▶
A photograph of women mending a road during the Great War.

Source L ▼ *Prime Minister Herbert Asquith, speaking in August 1916. What do you think he means by women's 'special claim'?*

"It is true that women cannot fight with rifles, but they have aided in the most effective way in the war. What is more, when the war comes to an end, don't women have a special claim to be heard on the many questions which affect their interests? I cannot deny that claim."

Source M ▼ *A comparison of the quality and output in factories of men and women in 1918.*

Quantity

Metal – women's production equal to men's
Aircraft woodwork – women's production equal to men's
Bullet making – women's production equal to men's; in some cases, women produce 20% more than men
Shell making – women's production behind men

By the end of the war, many people felt that women had earned the right to vote – and many MPs didn't want the suffragettes to start their violent campaign again. In 1918, Parliament changed the voting laws and gave all men over 21 and all women over 30 the right to vote (as long as they owned their own house or were married to a man who did). Ten years later, Parliament reduced the voting age for women to 21, regardless of whether they owned a house or were married or not.

Source N ▼ *Men and women's wages in 1900.*

OCCUPATION	MEN'S PAY (per week)	WOMEN'S PAY (per week)
Carpet weaver	35 shillings	20 shillings
Clothing machinist	22 shillings	11 shillings
Typist	£3	£1

WORK

Look at **Source A**.
1 **a** What is the message of the cartoon?
   b Draw your own version of the cartoon to show how you feel women are considered in society today.
2 **a** Who were the suffragists?
   b Study **Source B**. What is the message of the cartoon?
   c Give four differences between a suffragist and a suffragette. Consider their tactics, attitude and behaviour in your answer.
   d Why do you think women wanted the right to vote? Give three reasons and explain your answers.
3 Read pages 13 and 14. Imagine you are a news reporter shadowing a passionate suffragette. You spend a week with her and were there when Emily Davison was killed. Write a news article describing the typical life of a suffragette and her efforts to raise awareness of 'votes for women.'
4 Read **Source J**. Do you think this song was written by a supporter of 'votes for women' or not?
5 What impact did the Great War have on the suffragette movement?

Political change

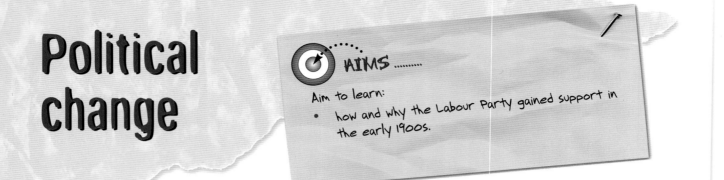

AIMS ....

Aim to learn:
- how and why the Labour Party gained support in the early 1900s.

In the late 1800s, British politics was dominated by two main political parties – the Liberals and the Conservatives. It had been this way for many years. But the two main parties soon came under heavy criticism for not understanding the needs of working-class people. Some felt a new political party was needed, a 'workers' party' that could fight for even better workers' rights, pay and conditions. One of these people was Keir Hardie, a Scottish miner who had started work as a young boy for just 12p a week! In 1893, in Bradford, Hardie and several others founded a new political party, the Independent Labour Party (ILP).

So what did the ILP stand for? Who supported it? And how did 'working-class politics' develop?

What did the Independent Labour Party stand for?

This new political party was based on **socialism**. Socialists believe that a country's wealth – such as its natural resources of coal and iron, for example, or its railways – should be owned by the state and run by the government for the good of all the people. Socialists also believe that governments should concentrate on welfare programmes in health care and education, as well as state help for vulnerable people such as the old, sick and unemployed. The ILP then sold itself as a working-class socialist party that claimed to stand up for the rights of ordinary people.

How did the ILP gain support?

In 1895, the ILP put up 25 candidates in the general election. They all lost! But support for them was growing in working-class areas, and ILP members were soon on school boards and local councils and committees. Then, in 1900, just over 100 people held a meeting in London. The mixed bunch of trade union leaders and ILP supporters all agreed on one thing – they wanted to get the working classes represented in Parliament. So they set up the Labour Representation Committee (LRC) to pay the wages of working-class candidates who were running for election. However, in the 1900 general election, only two working-class ILP candidates were elected – Keir Hardie and Richard Bell. But things were about to change.

Growing support

Trade unions (organisations in different industries that support their workers) felt they needed a political party that supported working people. So in the early 1900s, the largest and most powerful unions decided to help working-class candidates in elections and gave money to the LRC. In 1906, 29 LRC-sponsored candidates became MPs and set up as a separate party in Parliament. They called themselves the Labour Party and Keir Hardie was their leader. In 1910, 42 Labour MPs were elected – and the Liberal Party even asked the Labour MPs to support them on certain issues – it seemed that the two-party system of British politics had been broken!

The rise of the Labour Party

The Labour Party struggled during the Great War because they argued between themselves about whether to support the war or not. In 1918, the Party organised itself and published a **manifesto** (statement of aims and beliefs). Their new policy said members would work for a fairer distribution of wealth (in other words, even things out between the rich and poor a bit) and **nationalise** some industries. This meant that Britain's key industries – coalmines and railways, for example – should be taken over and run by the state. In the 1918 election, the Labour Party won 63 seats.

The Labour Party won 142 seats in the 1922 election and by 1924, after joining forces with the Liberal Party, managed to get enough seats in Parliament to form the government. Labour Prime Minister Ramsey MacDonald was the first Labour MP seat (see **Source B**).

Source A ▾ *A photo of Keir Hardie.*

Source B ▴ *A photo of Ramsey MacDonald.*

WORK

1. a Which were the two main political parties in the 19th century?
   b What were the main parties by the 1920s?
   c Why did workers want their own political party in the early 1900s?
   d Which are the main parties today?
   e Make a list of any other political parties you have heard of.

2. In your words, explain the following:
   a ILP; b LRC; c Labour Party; d socialism; e nationalise.

3. Look at **Source C**. Which do you think are the three most important factors that allowed the Labour Party to come into power in 1924?

WISE UP WORDS

• socialism   manifesto   nationalise

Source C ▾ *Why did Labour come to power in 1924? This diagram is a good example of how different factors can work together to bring about change.*

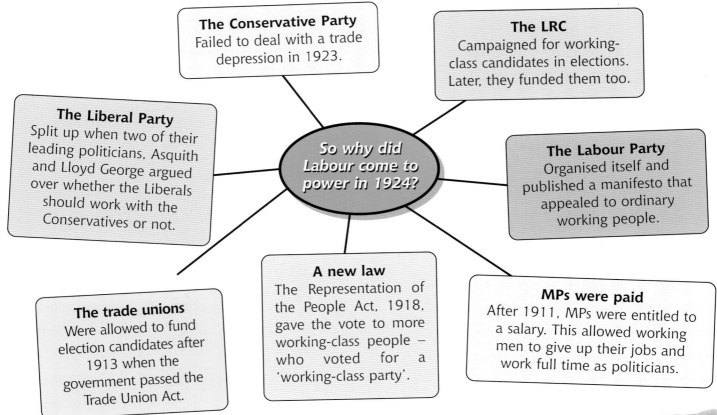

The Conservative Party
Failed to deal with a trade depression in 1923.

The LRC
Campaigned for working-class candidates in elections. Later, they funded them too.

The Liberal Party
Split up when two of their leading politicians, Asquith and Lloyd George argued over whether the Liberals should work with the Conservatives or not.

So why did Labour come to power in 1924?

The Labour Party
Organised itself and published a manifesto that appealed to ordinary working people.

The trade unions
Were allowed to fund election candidates after 1913 when the government passed the Trade Union Act.

A new law
The Representation of the People Act, 1918, gave the vote to more working-class people – who voted for a 'working-class party'.

MPs were paid
After 1911, MPs were entitled to a salary. This allowed working men to give up their jobs and work full time as politicians.

Why was there a general strike in 1926?

AIMS ....

Aim to know:
- What the term 'general strike' means;
- Why the general strike began;
- What the general strike achieved.

A general strike is when every worker in the country stops working. In May 1926, mine owners across Britain tried to increase miners' working hours and cut their pay! As you might guess, angry miners put down their pickaxes and went on strike. Soon, workers in other industries went on strike in sympathy for the mineworkers.

So what did the government do? Did the miners win? What happened in Britain during this first ever general strike? And how close was Britain to a full-scale revolution?

So why was there a general strike?

Before the Great War, there was a number of bitter disputes between workers and their employers. In 1912, for example, one million miners went on strike demanding a national minimum wage of 5 shillings (25p) per week … and the miners won! Six weeks into the strike, the government passed the Miners' Wage Act, which guaranteed them 5 shillings per week.

In 1913, all miners', railway workers' and transport workers' unions joined together to act as a united front. They were called the Triple Alliance.

Source A ▾ *A cartoon from 1913 about the threat of the Triple Alliance.*

BERNARD PARTRIDGE.

The three unions realised they had many common needs and could achieve more if they cooperated. Their 'deal' included a promise to support each other if there was a strike. However, on 15 April 1921 – **Black Friday** – the railway and transport unions failed to support mine workers and, when they went on strike on their own, mine owners increased their hours of work! Despite this, the Triple Alliance was still viewed by many as a powerful group (see **Source A**).

By 1925, the problems in the coal industry had still not been sorted. For a start, the industry itself was hopelessly out of date. Workers were still using pickaxes, for example, rather than the modern coal-cutting machines used in Germany and France. When the amount of coal sold to other countries fell again in July 1925, the mine owners tried to cut wages and increase hours again. When the Triple Alliance threatened a general strike, the government decided to give the mine owners the money to pay the miners. The payments started on Friday 31 July 1925 – known as **Red Friday**.

But coal exports continued to fall and, when the government cash stopped, the mine owners pressed forward with their plans to cut wages and increase hours. The miners' leader, A. J. Cook, famously replied, 'Not a penny off the pay, not a minute on the day' and talks between the miners' leaders and mine owners got nowhere.

A general strike starts

On Tuesday 4 May 1926 the Trade Union Congress (TUC – a council to represent trade unions), asked other workers to strike in sympathy with the miners. The government called it a general strike because huge numbers of road transport, bus, rail, truck, printing, gas, electricity, building, iron, steel and chemical workers stopped working. So how did the strike go?

Wednesday 5 May

The government sends a warship to Newcastle upon Tyne, where many of the strikers live. They also recruit nearly a quarter of a million new policemen.

The government immediately tries to control the media. They attempt to take over the BBC and publish a newspaper called *The British Gazette*.

Thursday 6 May

Fights break out between police and strikers in London, Glasgow and Edinburgh.

This strike is an attack on our democracy.

PM Stanley Baldwin calls the strike an attack on Britain's democracy.

Friday 7 May

The government sends the army to London and seizes all supplies of paper – this halts the publication of the TUC's paper *The British Worker*.

TO LONDON

Clashes between strikers and police continue in Liverpool, Hull and London.

Saturday 8 May

The army escorts food lorries from the London docks. Some buses, lorries and trains are now being driven by volunteers.

Rioting continues in Glasgow, Hull, Preston and Newcastle. Secretly, J. H. Thomas of the TUC has talks with the mine owners and the government.

Sunday 9 May

The Roman Catholic Church declares the strike 'a sin'.

Monday 10 May

Strikers in Northumberland derail a train and more workers join the strike.

THE FLYING SCOTSMAN SERVICE

The Prime Minister declares that 'Britain is threatened by revolution'. The government arrests over 300 Communists.

Tuesday 11 May

Suddenly, the TUC calls off the strike. Their 'strike fund' was running low and some feared a possible revolution – and strike leaders never wanted this.

The strikers drifted back to work but the miners fought on alone until November when they eventually returned to work – for less money and longer hours.

What did the general strike achieve?

The general strike is seen as a failure by most. The miners were defeated after all their efforts – and the TUC was ruined. Membership fell from 5.5 million in 1925 to only 375 000 in 1930. From 1927, a new law made general strikers illegal – a law that is still in force today.

> **FACT** *Arrests*
>
> Nearly 5000 arrests were made during the general strike, mainly for public disorder offences. Over 1000 people were sent to prison for between four and eight years when they derailed a train in Northumberland.

Source B ▼ *Lord Grey, writing in the* British Gazette, *May 1926.*

> "Neither in fact nor law is this a strike in the proper sense of the term this is an attempted revolution and if it succeeded, we would be ruled by a small body of extremists."

Source C ▼ *From* The British Worker, *May 1926.*

> "We are entering the second week of the general stoppage in support of the mine workers against the attack upon their standard of life by the coal workers. Nothing could be more wonderful than the magnificent response of millions."

WORK

1 Look at **Source A**.
   a What was the Triple Alliance?
   b What do you think the cartoonist was trying to say about the Triple Alliance?

2 Why was there not a general strike in April 1921 and July 1925?

3 So who was responsible for the General Strike?
   Choose two people from the following list and write a short answer which they might have given if asked who caused the General Strike.
   i   Mine worker
   ii Coalmine owner
   iii Trade Union leader
   iv Prime Minister.

4 Write out the following events from the General Strike in the correct chronological order.
   • A train is derailed by strikers
   • Volunteers begin to drive trams, lorries and buses
   • The Roman Catholic Church calls the strike 'a sin'
   • The Government sends a warship to Newcastle upon Tyne
   • The General Strike ends but the miners fight on
   • The TUC asks other workers to strike in sympathy for the miners
   • The miners return to work
   • The Prime Minister calls the strike 'an attack on Britain's democracy'
   • The army is sent to London and seizes all supplies of paper.

5 Look at **Sources B** and **C**.
   Identify which source was written by a supporter of the strike and which was written by an opponent. Give reasons for your answer.

6 'In history events don't always work out the way people hope.' Do the events of the General Strike support this statement or not?

Source D ▾ *A volunteer driver during the general strike protected by a police escort. Many middle-class Brits helped out during the strike in order to fulfil boyhood dreams of being a train or bus driver!*

The 'hungry thirties'

AIMS

Aim to understand:
- how the Great Depression affected Britain;
- the impact of the Jarrow Crusade.

To many people in Britain, the late 1920s was a time of hope. In some areas there were plenty of jobs, as new factories opened, making cars, aeroplanes and electrical goods. The international future looked brighter too when, in 1928, 65 countries signed a peace deal promising never to go to war again.

But just a few years into the 1930s, the world slumped into what became known as the Great Depression: companies went out of business, millions of people lost their jobs and even banks went bankrupt. And then another World War started in 1939.

So what caused this Great Depression? What was it like to live through? And how did it help lead to World War II?

The Great Depression

The **Great Depression**, or the 'slump' as it is sometimes called, started in America, a country that had grown rich in the 1920s. Its factories and businesses had done well selling goods, such as cars, refrigerators, radios, telephones, gramophones (ask your teacher) and watches, in America and all over the world. Some Americans had money to spare and bought shares in these companies, hoping to benefit from a share in the company profits. Some borrowed money from banks in order to join in this craze. But things started to go wrong in October 1929. Some people hadn't made as much money as they'd hoped and decided to sell their shares … fast. But the more they sold, the more the price dropped (try selling something no one wants). Millions of people couldn't sell their shares for as much as they'd paid for them. Some couldn't pay the banks back. Soon, many Americans couldn't afford to buy goods, and firms went out of business with millions loosing their jobs. America couldn't buy any foreign goods either – including those from countries such as Italy, Japan, Germany and Britain. Soon factories in all these countries also began to shut down.

By 1932 over 12 million Americans were out of work, nearly a quarter of the workforce. In Britain, about 3 million people lost their jobs. In Germany, it was 6 million. **Source A** illustrates how this Great Depression helped Hitler.

Source A ▼ *A modern historian describes how the Great Depression helped Hitler gain power in Germany. With Hitler in power the chance of world peace looked slim because Hitler promised to re-conquer land taken from Germany at the end of the Great War and create more 'living space' for Germans in Poland and Russia.*

"In 1929, world trade began to slow down. This means that countries stopped buying and selling to each other. German factories closed and people started to lose their jobs. Hitler took advantage of this and started to promise solutions to all Germany's problems. 'Vote for me' was Hitler's message, 'and I'll provide you with work and bread.' As more and more people lost their jobs, the Nazis got more and more votes."

By 1932 nearly one in five of the British workforce was out of a job. Worst hit were the industries that had made the country wealthy during the 1800s: 34% of coalminers were unemployed, 50% of steel workers and over 60% of shipbuilders. These industries were based mainly in the north of England, Wales, Scotland and Northern Ireland (see **Source C**).

However, some industries were doing well, mainly new ones, such as plastics, artificial fabrics and electrical goods. These industries were based in the Midlands and south of England. For workers in the new factories, the 1930s were not too bad. Their wages were steady and there were new consumer goods such as radios and cars to buy. Fairly cheap houses were built too … and people started to buy them rather than rent them.

Source B ▾ *Unemployment in Great Britain, 1921–40.*

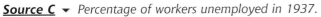

Source C ▾ *Percentage of workers unemployed in 1937.*

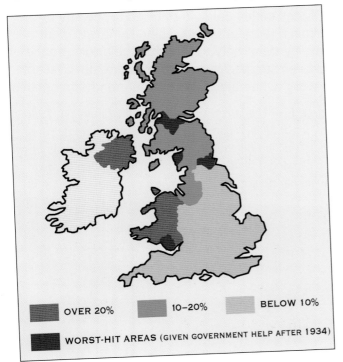

OVER 20%   10–20%   BELOW 10%

WORST-HIT AREAS (GIVEN GOVERNMENT HELP AFTER 1934)

Source D ▾ *A photograph of car production in the 1930s. Some towns, such as Coventry, thrived during this time.*

Source E ▾ *A modern historian.*

"[In the 1930s] there were almost two Britains: the expanding, busy towns of the southwest and Midlands, with their towns of 'semis', shops full of goods and almost full employment; and the run-down towns and cities of the north, Scotland, Wales and Northern Ireland, with slums, no money for improvements and unemployment blighting the lives of a quarter, a third or even half of the people."

Government action

Millions of families, mainly in the north of England, Wales, Scotland and Northern Ireland, suffered greatly during what became known to many as the 'hungry thirties'. Parents went without food so their children could eat and children went without schooling because their parents couldn't afford to buy shoes. People sold all they had – furniture, clothes, wedding rings – so they could buy coal for a fire to heat their rooms.

Source F ▼ *From a BBC radio interview, 1934.*

"If only he had work. Just imagine what it would be like. On the whole, my husband has worked about one year out of twelve and a half. His face was lovely when I married him, but now he's skin and bones. When I married, he was robust and he had a good job. He was earning eight to ten pounds a week. He's a left-handed ship's riveter, a craft which could be earning him a lot of money.

He fell out of work about four months after I was married, so I've hardly known what a week's wage was. Through all the struggling I've still not lost my respectability … We don't waste nothing. And there's no enjoyment comes out of our money — no pictures, no papers, no sport. Everything's patched and mended in our house."

Source G ▶ *An unemployed man in Wigan, 1939.*

The government was soon in crisis too. There was less money from taxes for them to spend on helping people because fewer people had jobs. They were also paying out a lot in 'dole' money! Their solution was to save money by cutting the wages of all government workers. They also cut dole money and introduced the hated Means Test. This meant that government officials investigated everyone who claimed dole money to see if they had any other money coming in. If you had an elderly relative living with you, for example, your dole was cut. If your children had part-time jobs, your dole was cut. As you might expect, people loathed this petty interference in their lives.

Source H ▶

A photograph of a man walking around London.

The Jarrow Crusade

One of the worst hit places during the Great Depression was the north-east of England.

Shipbuilding was one of the most common jobs in the area but, as world trade slowed down, there were less orders for ships. In 1934, one of the big shipbuilding yards in Jarrow closed down. Soon, nearly eight out of ten workers in the town were unemployed.

In 1936, 207 unemployed men, known as the Jarrow Marchers, walked from Jarrow to the Houses of Parliament in London, in an attempt to attract publicity and get the government to do something about their plight. The 280-mile march was led by local Jarrow MP, Ellen Wilkinson. They also collected over 12 000 signatures in a petition, which was handed to Parliament.

But the march achieved very little and the Prime Minister, Stanley Baldwin, refused to see any of the marchers' representatives. They eventually went home by train, only to find that their dole money had been stopped because they were 'not available for work' while they were on the month-long march!

Source I ▼ *The Jarrow Crusaders on their march in 1936. Look for: i) Ellen Wilkinson leading the march; ii) her dog, Paddy, walking behind her (you can just see his legs); iii) two men carrying a petition in a flat box; iv) a group of men playing harmonicas so the marchers can sing as they walk.*

Source J ▼ *Map showing the route of the Jarrow Crusade.*

NEWCASTLE
UPON TYNE — JARROW
12 MILES
— CHESTER-LE-STREET
12 MILES
— FERRYHILL
12 MILES
— DARLINGTON
16 MILES
— NORTHALLERTON
17 MILES
— RIPON
11½ MILES
— HARROGATE
15½ MILES
— LEEDS
9 MILES
— WAKEFIELD
9¾ MILES
— BARNSLEY
13½ MILES
— SHEFFIELD
— CHESTERFIELD
11¾ MILES
— MANSFIELD
12 MILES
— NOTTINGHAM
14½ MILES
— LOUGHBOROUGH
15 MILES
— LEICESTER
11¾ MILES
— MARKET HARBOROUGH
14½ MILES
— NORTHAMPTON
14½ MILES
— BEDFORD
21 MILES
— LUTON
19 MILES
— ST ALBANS
10¼ MILES
— EDMONTON
11 MILES
— MARBLE ARCH
8½ MILES
LONDON

Source K ▼ *The* Guardian *newspaper, 13 October 1936.*

"There is no political aspect to the march. It is simply the town of Jarrow saying 'Give us work'."

Politics in the 1930s

A succession of British Prime Ministers did little to improve the situation for those hardest hit by the Depression. However, in 1935 the cuts to dole money made in 1931 were removed and soon special loans were made to those areas in most trouble.

The unemployed in Britain made few serious protests and support for extreme political parties, such as the **Communists** or British Union of Fascists (BUF) (a party whose members had similar views to the Nazis) never really took hold. In 1936 BUF planned a march through the East End of London, an area full of working-class dockers and Jews. On the day of the march, the **Fascists'** route was blocked by people determined to prevent the BUF entering the East End. Soon the government gave

the police the right to ban political marches and the Fascist leader, Oswald Moseley, had his 'private army' of black-shirted soldiers disbanded.

Source L ▶ *Oswald Moseley and his black-shirts give the Nazi salute.*

Recovery

As stated earlier, there were two sides to Britain in the 1930s. Some areas prospered, such as the Midlands, while others suffered badly. This is how it stayed for most of the 1930s, until Neville Chamberlain, Prime Minister from 1937, began building up Britain's army, navy and air force. As you can see from **Source B**, unemployment dropped dramatically after 1937.

WISE UP WORDS

- Communists Fascists Great Depression

WORK

1 **a** Explain what is meant by the term 'Great Depression'.
   b In what ways did the Great Depression affect the chances of world peace?

2 Look at **Sources F**, **G** and **H**. What effect has the Great Depression and life on the dole had on the men in these sources?

3 **a** What was the reason for the 'Means Test'?
   b Explain how the Means Test worked.
   c Do you think it was a good system or not? Explain your answer.

4 **a** Why did the Jarrow Crusade take place?
   b Why do you think they chose a march as a way of getting publicity?

5 Look at **Source L.**
   a What was the BUF?
   b From which country have Moseley and his followers borrowed their salute?

From the cradle to the grave

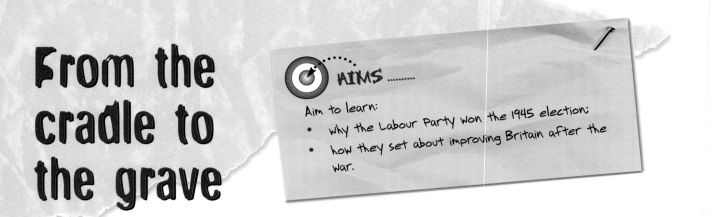

AIMS

Aim to learn:
- Why the Labour Party won the 1945 election;
- how they set about improving Britain after the war.

There is almost no one in Britain who isn't helped at some time or another by what is known as the **welfare state**. This is the name of the system by which the government aims to help those in need, mainly the old, sick, unemployed and children. It is sometimes called 'social security' and aims to ensure that nobody goes without food, shelter, clothing, medical care, education or any other basic need because they can't afford it.

Study **Source A** carefully; it gives a basic outline of the welfare state. You and your family will almost certainly have been helped out by this system at one time or another.

Although we take the things outlined in **Source A** for granted today, it is not a system that has been in place for many years. From 1906, the government had introduced some help for the most vulnerable sections of society – free school meals for poorer children, free school medical check-ups, small old-age pensions for the over 70s and basic sick and 'dole' pay – but nothing on the same scale as what was introduced after World War II.

Towards the end of the war, a man named Sir William Beveridge wrote a report about the state of Britain. It outlined some of the problems that Britain would have to face once the war was over; it became a surprise best-seller.

As the war ended, an election was held to decide who would run the country after the war. The Labour Party promised to follow Beveridge's advice but the Conservative Party, led by Winston Churchill, refused to make such a promise. The Labour Party won the election easily – and Winston Churchill, the man who had led Britain during the war, was out of power!

Almost immediately, the new government began to put Beveridge's plan into practice. It was a huge success:

- A National Health Service (NHS) was set up to provide health care for everyone. This made all medical treatment – doctors, hospitals, ambulances, dentists and opticians – free to all who wanted it.
- A weekly family allowance payment was introduced to help with childcare costs.
- The very poor received financial help or 'benefits'.
- Pensions for the elderly and disabled were increased.
- The school leaving age was raised to 15 to give children a greater chance of a decent education and more free university places were created.
- Twelve new towns were created. By 1948, 280 000 council homes were being built each year.

Of course, all this cost money. All workers would have to pay for the service through taxes and **National Insurance** contributions. This is how the welfare state is paid for today … and EVERYONE pays National Insurance when they get a job.

Despite the huge cost of the welfare state, it still remains a remarkable achievement. It didn't stay totally free for long – working people today have to pay for prescriptions, dental treatment and other things – but, on the whole, the welfare state ensures that no one is deprived of food, shelter, clothing, medical care, education or any other essentials because they can't afford them.

Source A ▶ The 20th century saw the government accept the need to care for its citizens 'from the cradle to the grave'. This diagram shows how this was attempted.

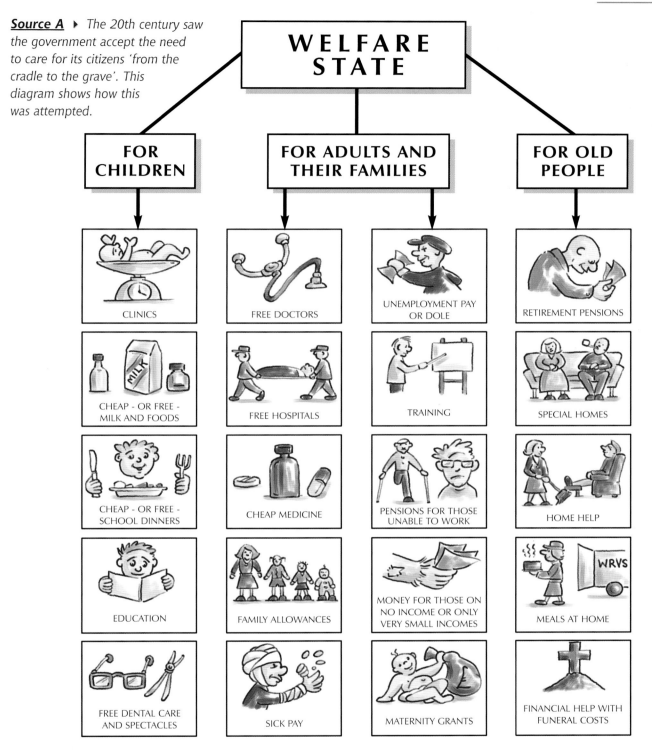

WELFARE STATE

FOR CHILDREN

- CLINICS
- CHEAP - OR FREE - MILK AND FOODS
- CHEAP - OR FREE - SCHOOL DINNERS
- EDUCATION
- FREE DENTAL CARE AND SPECTACLES

FOR ADULTS AND THEIR FAMILIES

- FREE DOCTORS
- FREE HOSPITALS
- CHEAP MEDICINE
- FAMILY ALLOWANCES
- SICK PAY

- UNEMPLOYMENT PAY OR DOLE
- TRAINING
- PENSIONS FOR THOSE UNABLE TO WORK
- MONEY FOR THOSE ON NO INCOME OR ONLY VERY SMALL INCOMES
- MATERNITY GRANTS

FOR OLD PEOPLE

- RETIREMENT PENSIONS
- SPECIAL HOMES
- HOME HELP
- MEALS AT HOME
- FINANCIAL HELP WITH FUNERAL COSTS

WORK

1 **a** Explain what is meant by the term 'welfare state'.

   b How has the welfare state helped you so far in life?

2 **a** What was the Beveridge Report?

   b In what ways was the Beveridge Report put into place?

The National Health Service

One of the major achievements of the new Labour government was the setting up of the National Health Service (NHS). This revolutionary new service ensured that:

- Everyone received free medical, dental, hospital and eye treatment.
- There was no charge for spectacles, false teeth or medicines.
- Most hospitals came under government control.
- Local councils provided midwives, home nursing, health visitors and ambulances.
- Doctors were paid by the government and encouraged to practice in poorer areas without fear of not getting paid because their patients could not afford the fees.

Source B ▾ *From a speech made by Nye Bevan, the man appointed by the government to introduce the NHS. It seems that Bevan's words hit home with health care providers – women's needs became a priority and they are now four times more likely to consult a doctor than ment. Life expectancy for women has risen from 66 to 78 since 1948.*

"A person ought not to be stopped from seeking medical assistance by the anxiety of doctors' bills … medical treatment should be made available to treat rich and poor alike in accordance with medical need and no other criteria. Worry about money in a time of sickness is a serious hindrance to recovery apart from its unnecessary cruelty. Records show that it is the mother in the average family who suffers most from the absence of a full health service. In trying to balance her budget she puts her own needs last."

The NHS brought lots of opposition at first – mainly from the doctors themselves. By 1947 only one in 100 doctors and surgeons in London was in favour of the scheme. They argued they would lose their independence, waste valuable time filling in forms and have their earning controlled by the government. Bevan eventually gave way and allowed doctors to treat private fee-paying patients if they wanted to and gave them a guaranteed income each year – not just payment each time they treated a patient. Eventually the opposition collapsed and the NHS formally came into being on 5 July 1948.

Source C ▾ *From an interview with Frederick Rebman, speaking in 2004, remembering the introduction of the NHS.*

"We were sorry to see Churchill voted out, he was our war leader, but he never promised to give the new ideas a go. The Labour Party did you see, and they publicised this in all the papers … servicemen [men in the army, navy and air force] like me expected so much after the war, perhaps Utopia [a perfect world], and the welfare state seemed to be a good start. I didn't mind the idea of paying a bit more of my salary to know that a doctor or a dentist was there if I needed them. I suppose … I think there was a bit of a rush when the NHS first started. There were stories of people going and getting whole new sets of teeth, new glasses, even wigs. Perhaps they'd have struggled on before with their short-sightedness or their painful teeth, but now they didn't have to."

BENEFITS OF THE NHS

- Brought immediate improvements in medical care such as a fall in infant death rate.

- Older people got better-fitting false teeth, good quality glasses and efficient hearing aids.

- Young mothers received proper medical care and were paid maternity benefit.

- There was a fall in deaths from diseases such as TB and diphtheria.

- It was the envy of the world – at first!

CRITICISMS OF THE NHS

- It was expensive to run – costing £400 million in its first year.

- Some said it encouraged people who wanted something for nothing, at the expense of the taxpayer.

- Some disliked that doctors were still allowed private patients. It was claimed this could lead to twin standards: better care for those who could afford it.

Source D ▼ *The cost of the NHS, 1950–2007.*

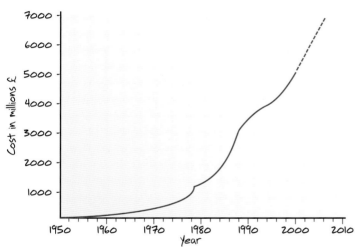

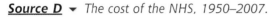

Source E ▼ *A letter to the* Daily Mail, *November 2006. The expense and organisation of the NHS still attracts fierce debate today.*

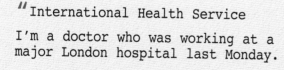

"International Health Service

I'm a doctor who was working at a major London hospital last Monday.

I treated patients from Portugal, Ecuador, Mexico, Albania, Peru, Algeria, Italy, Germany, Ethiopia, Eritrea, Iran and Iraq. There was also one from England.

The problem with the NHS isn't about too little money, but too many international patients who come here and get free treatment without any questions being asked of them."

The NHS is rarely out of the news, mainly due to the fact that it has problems: waiting lists are getting longer, while doctors and nurses are overworked. There is rarely a month that goes by without some big media scandal about 'dirty wards', 'crumbling hospitals' or 'nurses working long hours'. The main problem, of course, is money. Modern drugs are very expensive and modern medicine means that people are living longer … so there are more elderly people than ever before – and older people use the NHS more than younger people. The NHS has always been, and should continue to be, a really hot topic in British society!

WISE UP WORDS

- welfare state   National Insurance

WORK

1 In your own words, explain what the National Health Service was, when it was first set up in July 1948.

2 **a** Why did some doctors oppose the NHS at first?

   b How did the government eventually get the support of doctors?

3 Look at **Source C**.

   a According to this source, why did the Labour Party win the 1945 election?

   b Why do you think people rushed out to get 'whole new sets of teeth, new glasses, even wigs' when the NHS first started?

How did Britain change after the war?

Even before World War II came to an end, people were wondering about what they wanted Britain to be like afterwards. The two main political parties – Labour and the Conservatives – each knew they had to offer policies which would allow people to rebuild their lives and deal once and for all with the problems that they faced before the war.

As the war ended, an election was held to decide who would run the country. The Labour Party promised radical change in lots of areas, but the Conservatives seemed to spend their time criticising the Labour Party … and published very few details about their own ideas. The result of the election was a landslide victory for the Labour Party – 393 seats in Parliament, to the Conservatives' 213 and the Liberals' 12.

So what were their plans? How did Britain change? And how did Britain develop in the 1950s and 60s?

FACT *The Beveridge Report*

During the war, the government asked Sir William Beveridge to draw up a report on the state of Britain. He said that, when the war was over, the country had to do battle once more with five problems – want, disease, ignorance, squalor and idleness. He said that Britain would only progress as a nation once these 'giants' had been defeated. During the 1945 election campaign, the Labour Party claimed they would tackle the five 'giants' identified by Beveridge.

Nationalisation

The new Labour government believed in something called **nationalisation**. This means they wanted Britain's major services and industries – gas, coal mining, the railways – to be taken over and run by the state. The Labour Party believed it was wrong for private owners to profit from the country's most important industries; they thought that everyone should benefit instead.

So, from 1946 to 1950, Britain's key industries and services were nationalised. This means that the state bought up lots of different companies and different industries and joined them together as one (see **Source A**).

British Rail, for example, was formed in 1947 when the state bought the four major railway companies that served Britain. At a massive cost, the country's railway system was modernised – tracks were electrified and new streamlined trains were built. In an attempt to save money, 2000 stations were shut and thousands of miles of track were closed. However, British Rail continued to lose money, and was heavily criticised for poor service, expensive tickets and untidy trains, for years.

Source A ▾ *Nationalised industries*

Bank of England 1946

Coal mines (run by the National Coal Board) 1946

Telephones (became British Telecom)

Air transport (became British Aerospace) 1947

Railways, canals and roads 1947

Electricity (became the Electricity Board) 1947

Gas (became British Gas) 1948

Iron and steel (became British Steel) 1949

FACT *Privatisation*

After 1979 the Conservative government began a policy of privatisation. This meant that they began selling back industries for private ownership. In other words, ordinary citizens could buy shares in companies such as British Telecom and British Gas.

The welfare state

The Labour government's most ambitious plan was for 'social security from the cradle to the grave'. We call it the welfare state and it included:

National Insurance (1946): every person paid a small amount each week for a stamp that was stuck on a card. Employers and the government added money too. In return, everyone could claim benefits during times of unemployment, sickness, old age, pregnancy and so on.

National Assistance (1948): for anyone experiencing extra difficulty, it was possible for them to apply for National Assistance which meant money was given weekly with a special grant for items such as clothing or childcare goods. The name was changed to Social Security in 1974.

National Health Service (1948): this brand new system, paid for by taxpayers' money, gave medical attention to everyone – doctors, medicine, dental work, opticians, hospital care would all be free of charge. In later years there were basic charges for prescriptions, hearing aids, dental treatment and so on, although children, the elderly, and people on low incomes still get these for free.

Housing

By the end of World War II, Britain's housing crisis was huge. No new houses had been built during the war – and about 20% had been damaged, or even destroyed, by bombing raids.

One solution in the late 1940s was to build **prefabs**. These were small, one-storey homes made in pieces in factories which were put together on a site. Thousands of these 'temporary' houses were built – and some are even still lived in today (see **Source B**).

Source B ▾ *A photograph of temporary housing, built in the 1940s, which is still lived in today in Moseley, Birmingham.*

Another idea was to build whole new towns that could be properly planned and used to rehouse families from the slum areas of older towns. This new government policy saw the creation of towns such as Basildon, Corby, Crawley, Cwmbran, Hemel Hempstead and Stevenage. Indeed, by 1950 Britain was building more new houses than any other European country.

By the 1960s, town planners, who were running short of expensive land to build on, decided to build upwards instead. This resulted in hundreds of 'high-rise' blocks of flats being built all over the country in the main urban areas. These ugly, unpopular and sometimes unsafe buildings remained a common feature on Britain's landscape until many were pulled down in the early 1990s.

Source C ▾ *The demolition of two 19 storey blocks of flats at Queen Elizabeth Square, Gorbals in Glasgow, billed as the biggest controlled explosion in Europe since World War II.*

Education

Just before the end of the war a new Education Act of 1944 said that secondary education should be free, the same as primary education. The new law said that pupils should stay in school until they are 15 and local authorities should make meals, milk and medical services available at every school, all children had to have a test (the 11+) to decide what sort of school they should attend.

the age of 11, while the rest were condemned to second-rate schooling!

This system stayed in place until the mid-1960s, when the Labour government of the day instructed all local councils to make plans for 'comprehensive schooling'. This was designed for all youngsters, whatever their interests and abilities. In most parts of Britain, comprehensive has been the way most children have been educated since.

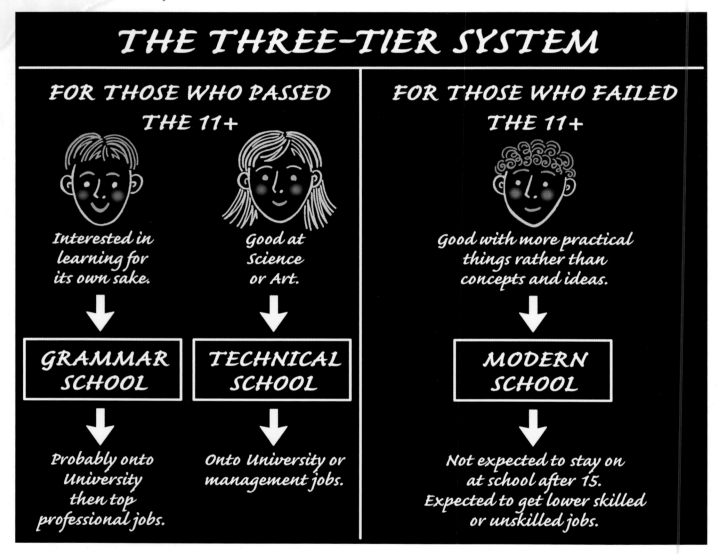

THE THREE-TIER SYSTEM

FOR THOSE WHO PASSED THE 11+

Interested in learning for its own sake.

GRAMMAR SCHOOL

Probably onto University then top professional jobs.

Good at Science or Art.

TECHNICAL SCHOOL

Onto University or management jobs.

FOR THOSE WHO FAILED THE 11+

Good with more practical things rather than concepts and ideas.

MODERN SCHOOL

Not expected to stay on at school after 15. Expected to get lower skilled or unskilled jobs.

The response to the new three-tier system was mixed. Those who supported it argued that it guaranteed an education for all students based on their ability rather than if their parents could afford one or not. Critics said that the new system was 'elitist', meaning that the children with lots of ability were educated at the 'better schools' from

Television and radio

Today, more and more people than ever before stay at home to be entertained. Going out to the cinema, for a 'pub meal', or a trip to the theatre are still popular, but 'staying in', in front of the TV, listening to music or using a home computer are more common than ever before. This great social shift in entertainment habits began at the start of the 20th century, but it was after World War II that things really started to change.

Radio and television had been invented before the war. Radio in particular was very popular, with nine out of every ten households owning a radio set: the BBC (there was only one channel to begin with) began regular TV broadcasts in 1936 but by 1939 there were still only 20 000 TV sets compared to nearly 9 million radios. Indeed, when Neville Chamberlain announced Britain was at war in 1939 he chose radio, not television, to tell everyone!

After the war, television gradually became more popular as TV sets became cheaper. Independent Television (ITV), funded by advertising, started in 1955, followed by BBC2 in 1964, Channel 4 in 1982 and Channel 5 in 1997. Colour television began in 1967 and by the late 1990s hundreds of channels were available via satellite communications.

Source D ▾ *An amazing prediction by James Burke in 1973.*

"Flat screen 3-D TV soon, certainly. And maybe I'm sticking my neck out here, but I think TV will be seen on two levels — one as we know now, the other a sort of information flow. Today, TV's a one-way system, we just look — the 'goggle box'!

In 50 years time, it could be a two-way communication device, so you can press a button to ask questions or switch over to your friends for a game. With Cablevision, there'll be hundreds of channels."

Source E ▾ *A 1950s advert for one of the first TVs.*

Source F ▾ *A modern historian*

"The effect has been huge. Many theatres and cinemas were forced to shut down. There was less point in paying to see stars when you could watch them on television for nothing. Above all, television has made the world a smaller place. In 1962, the satellite Telstar brought the first live pictures from America: in 1969 viewers watched live pictures of American astronauts on the moon."

Source G ▾ *Major events in radio and TV 1948–85.*

1948 Radio Luxemburg was the only station playing pop music – it launched the first show in this year.

1949 Cinema audiences reach their peak (over 500 million tickets sold) with one-third of the population going to cinema once a week.

1952 *The Archers*, Britain's longest running radio show, starts

1953 Coronation of Queen Elizabeth II televised, sparking a huge rush to buy TV sets

1954 First portable radio on sale

1955 ITV starts.

1958 *Blue Peter* starts.

1959 10.5 million TV sets in Britain

1960 *Coronation Street* starts

1961 75% of families had a TV

1962 First satellite pictures broadcast in Britain from America

1963 *Dr Who* first starts

1964 343 million cinema tickets sold

1967 Colour TV

1969 Viewers watch live pictures of US astronauts landing on the moon.

1970 176 million cinema tickets sold

1971 91% of families have TV

1972 *Newsround* starts

1974 First games console (made by Ataria) went on sale. The game it played was called PONG

1978 VHS video recorder goes on sale

1982 Channel 4 starts

1983 Breakfast TV starts

1984 53 million cinema tickets sold

1985 *Eastenders* starts

'Never had it so good'

After the war, Britain was in a pretty sorry state. The country owed a lot of money because millions had been borrowed (mainly from America) to pay for the war. Also, many things were still rationed: bread, sugar, bacon, butter and tea, for example. Gas and electricity supplies were low as well, forcing power cuts across the country for several hours a day during the winter months of 1946–47. In fact, this period in Britain's history is often called **austerity**, meaning there was a severe economy.

Then, during the 1950s, Britain's economy began to recover. At the 1951 general election, voters elected a Conservative government, led by Winston Churchill. The Conservatives stayed in power for the next 13 years. For most, these were years of growing prosperity – there was full employment and more money to spend on any number of new and exciting goods (see **Source H**). When new Prime Minister Harold Macmillan commented that British people had 'never had it so good', he was probably right: average wages rose from £6.40 per week in 1950 to nearly £12 in 1959!

But there were problems just around the corner. From 1957 onwards, Britain was buying more goods from abroad than it was selling to the other countries. This meant that more money was going out of the country than was coming in. In turn this led to other nations, such as America and Germany, getting far richer than Britain because we were buying more of *their* goods not our own … and during the 1970s and 1980s the poor sales of British cars, motorbikes and electrical goods, for example, would be a major headache for everyone and lead to higher and higher unemployment. For example, in 1965 95% of cars on British roads were made in Britain – by 1980 the figure had fallen to 40%.

WISE UP WORDS

- nationalisation   prefabs   austerity

"I'd never go back *from Electricity* to old-fashioned cooking now!"

Electric cookers have thermostat control on the oven, quick-heating boiling plates, and new, variable switches which give perfect heat-control from fast boiling to slow simmering—*and lower*, if you want it!

Go round and see one at your Electricity Service Centre. They are friendly, knowledgeable people there, and will be glad to help you. They can also let you have details about easy payments, and the new, free book, full of clever ideas for saving work, ELECTRICITY IN YOUR KITCHEN: or you are welcome to write for a copy to EDA, 2 Savoy Hill, London, W.C.2.

ELECTRICITY a Power of Good *for cooking!*
AND FOR WATER-HEATING TOO!

Source H ▲ *During pre-1950s, car ownership doubled and ownership of TV sets went up 30 times. Chain stores stocked fashionable clothing from all over the world and TV advertising (ITV started in 1955) made consumer goods, such as cookers, all the more desirable. Hire purchase (buy now, pay later in instalments) became very common too.*

Fact *End of an Empire*

After 1945, there were growing demands from more and more empire countries to govern themselves. The first to win independence was India in 1947, when Britain pulled out leaving two nations: India and Pakistan. In 1957, the first African colony got its independence when the Gold Coast (as it was known under British rule) became Ghana. Others followed, including Kenya, Nigeria and Rhodesia (now Zimbabwe). Today the British Empire consists of a few loyal islands.

WORK

1 a Which industries were nationalised after the war?
   b Why did the Labour government want to nationalise key industries?
   c Can you think of any disadvantages nationalisation may have?

2 Choose three of the 'five giants' (want, disease, ignorance, squalor and idleness), identified in the Beveridge Report. For each of your choices, explain how the Labour government took action to attack it.

3 a Explain what is meant by the three-tier school system.
   b Do you think all children fall into one of three groups? Give reasons for your answer.

4 a In your own words, write a paragraph explaining how TV has developed since World War II.
   b Write another paragraph, explaining the impact TV has on **your** life.

The stage is set for war

AIMS

- to identify both long- and short-term causes of the Great War.
- to identify key reasons for hostility between European countries in the years up to 1914.

Source A ▶ This one was built in Churchill, Worcestershire.

The memorial pictured in **Source A** is located in the small village of Churchill, Worcestershire, about 15 miles outside the Midland's cities of Wolverhampton and Birmingham. It was built in the early 1920s to honour the 43 villagers (41 men and two women) who contributed in some way towards the Great War of 1914–18. Seven out of the 43 are listed under the title 'Rest in peace', indicating that they were killed fighting. One of the men, Harold Bache, was an England cricketer before the war and played football for England amateurs and a local professional team, West Bromwich Albion. He was in his prime when he was shot dead by a sniper, while fighting in Belgium at the age of 26.

There is nothing particularly unusual about Churchill's war memorial – there are hundreds just like it all over Britain, most of them put up within five years of the Great War. They were intended as a reminder for future generations of the sacrifice made by ordinary British citizens at the beginning of the 20th century. Above all, the people who built them hoped that a war as horrific as the Great War would never happen again!

The Great War wasn't 'great' because the men who fought had a fantastic adventure. It was called the Great War because a war so big had never taken place before. Millions and millions of men, divided into two sides, or **alliances**, spent over four years trying to kill each other. In total about nine million people were killed – that's over 5000 deaths *per day*! Millions more were horrifically mutilated or mentally scarred for life.

So, why did the Great War start? How and where was if fought? What impact did it have on ordinary civilians? Who eventually won? And what plans were put in place when the war ended in the hope that the Great War of 1914–18 would be the war to end all wars?

FACT *Lessons learned?*

The Great War was not the 'war to end all wars'. Sadly, two more dates – 1939–45 – have been added to Churchill's memorial to commemorate a Second World War which killed approximately five times as many people as the Great War.

FACT *Impact*

The impact of the Great War on Churchill must have been huge. Local records show that the area's main employer, Churchill Forge, closed during the war because of its lack of labour. It took until 1920 to get it up and running again. The memorial also shows the impact on individual families – all five male members of the Vaughan family fought, one of whom died, while four members of the Bache family fought and one died.

Wars start because countries cannot solve their problems by talking. They are rarely started by ordinary people with regular jobs and regular lives – but by politicians, kings and queens. The irony of it all is that kings, queens and politicians are never the ones who end up fighting in them!

The Great War of 1914–18 started because people in power from several different countries couldn't sort out their disagreements properly. But the war didn't flare up suddenly. There was a long history of bad feeling that had built up over the years – and then one small incident suddenly turned the hatred into actual fighting.

Look through the following list of factors very carefully. They each outline one of the factors that combined to lead to the outbreak of war in August 1914.

FACTOR NO. 1: RIVALRY OVER EMPIRES

An empire means one country owns land in another part of the world. By 1914, Britain and France had large empires. They made money selling their goods to people in their areas of land – and helped themselves to any resources they wanted from these countries. Germany's emperor, Kaiser Wilhelm II, was determined that his country should have a big empire too. He wanted it as a status symbol, showing Germany's greatness and gaining it respect. This made Germany a rival of both Britain and France (see **Sources B**, **C** and **D**).

Source D  *A modern historian.*

"Britain and France had seized vast areas of land all over the world, and Holland, Spain, Portugal and Belgium also extended their colonies. By the time the new country of Germany [it had only become a united country under one ruler in 1871] was ready, most of the unoccupied land had already been taken, so that all she could get were some tiny islands in the Pacific Ocean and parts of Africa which were at the time unprofitable. Mighty Germany, the third largest country in Europe, had only half as many people in her colonies as tiny Holland had in hers."

Source B ▾ *Colonies – areas and number of people.*

COLONIES		KM²	PEOPLE
	British	31 000 000	400 000 000
	French	85 00 000	26 000 000
	German	25 00 000	12 000 000

Source C ▶ *The main European empires in 1914.*

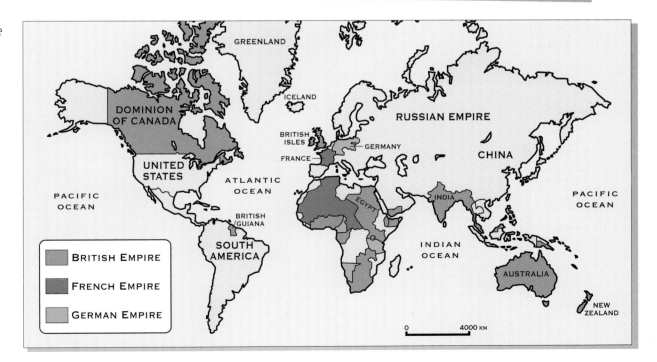

FACTOR NO. 2: RIVALRY OVER INDUSTRY

Since the 1880s, Germany had become a great industrial power with great coal mines, chemical works, steel factories and ironworks. They produced all types of goods too, so there was a great rivalry for trade, particularly with Britain. And production of everything soared and soared, year after year.

Source E ⊽ *German industrial production.*

	1872	1914
COAL	30 million tons	190 million tons
IRON	2 million tons	18 million tons

FACTOR NO. 3: RIVALRY OVER WEAPONS

Britain had a large navy to protect all the ships sailing to and from the countries in her empire. When Germany started to build a big navy, Britain was worried … so built bigger, faster and more heavily armed ships. Germany then did the same!

Germany also began a military race with France. They tried to outdo each other in the size of their armies, the number of guns and the strength of their fortresses. By 1914, all the larger countries in Europe were ready for war; all that was needed was something to start them fighting.

Source F ⊽ *European armies and their costs, 1914.*

	SOLDIERS	MONEY SPENT	
BRITAIN			EUROPEAN MILITARY SPENDING AND SIZE OF ARMIES 1913–14
FRANCE			
GERMANY			
AUSTRIA			
RUSSIA			= 500 000 SOLDIERS
ITALY			£ = £5 MILLION

Source G ⊽ *Number of Dreadnaughts built each year by Britain and Germany, 1906–14.*

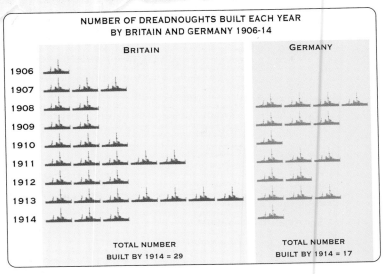

NUMBER OF DREADNOUGHTS BUILT EACH YEAR BY BRITAIN AND GERMANY 1906-14

BRITAIN — GERMANY
1906, 1907, 1908, 1909, 1910, 1911, 1912, 1913, 1914

TOTAL NUMBER BUILT BY 1914 = 29

TOTAL NUMBER BUILT BY 1914 = 17

Source H ⊽ *Britain's top ships were known as 'Dreadnaughts'. They were 152 metres (500ft) long, had 11-inch armour plating, ten 12-inch guns, eighteen 4-inch guns, five torpedo tubes … and were very fast. But Germany soon built their own version too.*

FACTOR NO. 4: RIVALRY OVER MOROCCO

In 1871, France and Germany fought a war against each other. Germany won and took two valuable French areas of land – Alsace and Lorraine. The French wanted these provinces back ... which led to tension between the two countries.

Then, in 1906, and again in 1911, France tried to take over the African country of Morocco. Germany wanted to control Morocco too and sent a warship to stop France. For a while, it looked like war would break out but Germany was forced to back down when Britain gave their support to the French. These incidents further increased British and French suspicion of Germany.

FACTOR NO. 5: RIVALRY OVER THE BALKANS

Today, Turkey is one of Europe's poorer countries. But for centuries she had a huge empire and ruled over many other countries. By 1900, though, the Turkish (or Ottoman) empire was breaking up and nations once ruled by the Turks – such as Serbia, Bulgaria and Romania – had become independent. Powerful nations such as Austria–Hungary and Russia were looking to have some control in this area too (known as the Balkans).

In 1908, Austria–Hungary unexpectedly took over Bosnia, a country that had once been under Turkish rule. Russia and its close ally, Serbia, protested against the invasion – but backed down when Germany said that they would support Austria–Hungary if there was a war. Russia and Serbia didn't fancy taking on Austria–Hungary *and* Germany together.

From then on, though, there was great suspicion between Russia and Austria-Hungary. Russia, in particular, began to build up its army on a massive scale.

Source I ▼ *A German view of Britain's empire.*

Source J ▼ *The Boiling Point from Punch magazine. This cartoon was published in October 1912. The figures on the pot represent the five great powers – Great Britain, France, Russia, Germany and Austria–Hungary. What message do you think the cartoonist was trying to get across?*

Source K ▾ *The Balkans in 1914. The map shows reasons why Austria–Hungary and Russia wanted to grab countries that had been Turkish (from Scott and Hillay Harrison text).*

Source L ▾ *Modern historian J. F. Aylett, In Search of History: Twentieth Century.*

"By 1914, all the major European powers were caught up in a web of agreements. But, instead of making the countries feel safer, it only increased their fears. If one country went to war, there was a risk that others would get dragged in. And that is what happened."

Source M ▾ *How the countries lined up for war.*

FACTOR NO. 6: THE ALLIANCE SYSTEM

From the early 1900s, the countries of Europe had been looking around for allies who would help them if ever any trouble started. Germany distrusted the two countries on either side of her (France and Russia) so formed an alliance with Austria–Hungary. This suited the Austrians because of their intense rivalry with Russia over the Balkans. Italy saw the benefit of joining an alliance with the two German countries next to her – so joined Austria–Hungary and formed a **Triple Alliance**.

France and Russia also formed their own alliance, promising to help each other if either were attacked. Britain, starting to feel a bit isolated, joined with France and Russia to form the **Triple Entente** ('Entente' means 'friendly understanding').

The scene was now set for a showdown. The two heavily armed groups were ready for war – all that was needed was a spark to 'set it off'!

Source N ▾ *Baldrick and Edmund in the television series 'Blackadder'.*

Baldrick: I heard that it started when a bloke called Archie Duke shot an ostrich 'cause he was hungry.

Edmund: I think you mean it started when the Archduke of Austro–Hungary got shot.

Baldrick: Nah, there was definitely an ostrich involved, sir.

Edmund: Well, possibly. But the real reason for the whole thing was that it was too much effort *not* to have a war.

George: By (Gum? [it's not `God']) this is interesting; I always loved history – the Battle of Hastings, Henry VIII and his six knives, all that.

Edmund: You see, Baldrick, in order to prevent war in Europe, two superblocs developed: us, the French and the Russians on one side, and the Germans and Austro–Hungary on the other. The idea was to have two vast opposing armies, each acting as the other's deterrent. That way there could never be a war.

Baldrick: But this is a sort of a war, isn't it, sir?

Edmund: Yes, that's right. You see, there was a tiny flaw in the plan.

George: What was that, sir?

Edmund: It was bollocks.

FACT *Plans*

There were even detailed attack plans drawn up if ever war started. The Germans, for example, feared an attack from France and Russia at the same time. So the man in charge of the German army, Count von Schlieffen, drew up a plan. The idea was to defeat France quickly and then face Russia. But one of the problems with Schlieffen's plan was the idea of passing through Belgium to attack France. Back in 1839, Britain had promised to help Belgium if she was attacked.

FACT *Family ties*

The kings of Russia, Great Britain and Germany were all cousins. They were grandsons of Queen Victoria!

WISE UP WORDS

alliances   Triple Alliance   Triple Entente

Source O ▾ *Which side looks most powerful in 1914 – the Triple Alliance or the Triple Entente?*

Country	Population (millions)	Population of overseas colonies (millions)	Size of army (millions of soldiers)	Size of navy (number of ships)
Germany	63	15	4.2	281
Austria–Hungary	50	–	0.8	67
Italy	35	2	0.7	36
Britain	41	390	0.7	388
France	40	63	3.7	207
Russia	139	–	1.2	166

WORK

1 **a** Make your own copy of this table (large enough to write a few sentences in each box).

Triple Alliance / Triple Entente	Germany	Austria–Hungary	Italy
Britain	Germany's Kaiser wanted an empire and a navy to rival Britain's – who felt threatened by this. There was also great competition between the two nations over trade.		
France			
Russia			

b Fill in as many boxes as you can with examples of tension between those countries. The causes of tension between Britain and Germany has been done for you to give you an example of the sort of detail required.

c In your opinion, between which two nations was the rivalry most intense?

d Explain how each of the following contributed to tensions between the European powers: i) colonies; ii) people wanting their independence; iii) weapons.

2 Look at **Source M**.

a Make a list of the countries in:
i) the Triple Alliance
ii) the Triple Entente.

b If the Triple Alliance attacked France, how could Russia's friendship help France?

c If Austria–Hungary attacked Russia, how could France's friendship help Russia?

d If Russia attacked Germany, how could Austria's friendship help Germany?

e The alliance system has been described as 'two sets of mountain climbers roped together'. What do you think is meant by this and what do you think the advantages and disadvantages of being 'roped' together are?

'Like a line of falling dominoes ...'

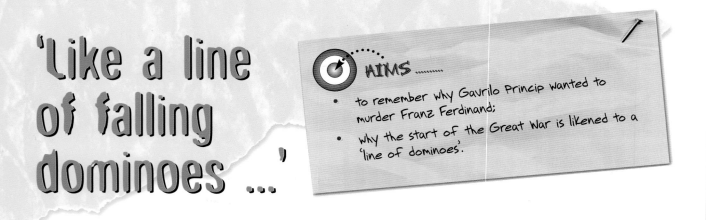

AIMS ....
- to remember why Gavrilo Princip wanted to murder Franz Ferdinand;
- why the start of the Great War is likened to a 'line of dominoes'.

So how did one man start a chain reaction that ended with the largest war the world had ever seen? And how did the pre-war alliances contribute to the start of the war?

In June 1914, Europe was close to war. In fact, it seemed as if some of the leaders in the Triple Alliance and the Triple Entente were *desperate* to try out their war plans and new weapons. All that was needed was a spark to make the whole of Europe explode into war. On 28 June 1914, the 'spark' arrived!

On 28 June 1914, Archduke Franz Ferdinand, an Austrian prince, arrived in Sarajevo with his wife, Sophie. Sarajevo was the capital city of Bosnia, a region which Austria–Hungary had conquered in 1908. Franz Josef, King of Austria–Hungary, was proud of his empire – sending his nephew, Franz, to Sarajevo on a visit was a way of letting his people know this!

Source A ▾ *Europe in June 1914.*

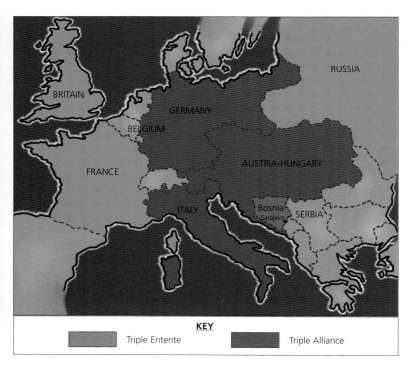

Many Bosnians didn't want to be part of Austria–Hungary at all. They wanted to join with their neighbour, Serbia, instead. Many Serbians wanted to join with Bosnia too. One gang of Serbians, led by a student called Gavrilo Princip, decided to take drastic action and strike a terrible blow to the country they hated ... they would kill Archduke Ferdinand, next in line to the Austro–Hungarian throne. On 28 June 1914, they would get their chance.

Archduke Franz Ferdinand arrived at Sarajevo Station at 9:28am. It was his wedding anniversary. As his car made its way to the town hall for a meeting with the mayor, Gavrilo Princip and five of his friends were waiting. As he slowly passed by, one of Gavrilo's gang threw a bomb at the Archduke's car. The Archduke caught the bomb and threw it on the floor. It blew up under the car behind, injuring eight people. The Archduke's car sped off to the town hall with the Archduke in a furious mood. He cancelled the rest of the visit. The bomb-thrower swallowed poison and jumped into a river.

At 11:00am, the Archduke and his wife left the town hall in their chauffeur-driven car. They were going to visit the people injured by the bomb. The car was travelling a lot faster this time! However, the driver took the wrong road and stopped to turn around. As the Archduke looked around to see if all was clear, he came face-to-face with Gavrilo Princip.

Princip fired two shots. The first hit the Archduke in the throat. The second hit his wife Sophie in the stomach. They both died. It was 11:00am. Princip swallowed poison but it failed to work. He was arrested and beaten up.

Source B ▼ *A drawing of the assassination, published on 12 July 1914.*

Source C ▼ *Timeline of events.*

28 July: Austria–Hungary blames Serbia for killing its Archduke. It attacks Serbia.

29 July: Russia, who has promised to protect Serbia against attack, gets its army ready to attack Austria–Hungary.

1 August: Germany, who supports Austria–Hungary, hears about Russian preparations for war. Germany declares war on Russia.

2 August: Britain prepares its warships.

3 August: Germany, whose plan is to defeat France BEFORE attacking Russia, declares war on France.

4 August: Germany asks Belgium to allow German soldiers to march through its country to attack France. Belgium says 'no'. Germany marches in anyway. Britain, who has a deal to protect Belgium from attack (dating back to 1839), declares war on Germany.

6 August: Austria–Hungary declares war on Russia.

12 August: Britain and France declare war on Austria–Hungary.

Although this was a terrible **assassination**, you might be wondering how this started a war. Read **Source C** to find out. The murders in Sarajevo on that Sunday morning in June 1914 started a whole chain of events that threw Europe into war: a war in which millions of people would die. One historian wrote, 'Like a line of falling dominoes, the nations of Europe toppled each other over into war.'

FACT *The final line-up*

Italy didn't join straight away. Instead, it waited until 1915 and joined in on the Britain, France and Russia side – not on the Germany and Austria–Hungary side as promised in the Triple Alliance. Although 28 countries joined in total, the major countries fought on these sides.

FACT *Gavrilo Princip*

Gavrilo Princip was 20 years old and a printer by trade. He was a member of the Black Hand Movement, a secret Serbian gang whose aim was to unite all Serbs, including those living all over the Austrian empire, into one nation.

WISE UP WORD

- assassination

WORK

1 Put the following events from 1914 in chronological order:
   - German troops invade Belgium
   - Russia prepares to attack Austria–Hungary
   - Britain declares war on Germany
   - Austria–Hungary declares war on Serbia
   - Germany declares war on Austria–Hungary
   - Germany declares war on Russia
   - Germany declares war on France.

2 Look at the following three statements made about the start of the Great War.
   A: 'The war was all Germany's fault.'
   B: 'The nations of Europe stumbled into war.'
   C: 'Some nations were more to blame than others.'

   a Write three short paragraphs supporting each of the statements. They should demonstrate how each statement could be correct.

   b Write one final paragraph, explaining which statement you think is most correct.

How did the government get people to fight?

AIMS
- to remember the main reasons why men joined up to fight;
- to understand key terms such as propaganda and conscription.

As soon as war broke out in August 1914, the British government asked for volunteers to fight. To begin with, there was a great rush to join up as men decided to 'do their bit for King and country'. By December 1914, one million men had enlisted, keen to get involved in a war they thought might be over soon. Army leaders, however, weren't so optimistic. Some felt the war would go on for at least three years – and knew the government would have to work very hard to get enough soldiers.

Britain's leaders used a number of techniques to encourage and persuade men to join up. To begin with, a huge **propaganda** campaign was started throughout the country. Leaflets and posters were issued that tried to persuade men to join up. They appealed to their patriotism and sense of honour, saying it was their duty to defend their country against the evil enemy. The posters always made any British soldiers look like heroes, while any enemy soldiers were made to look like cruel savages (see **Source A**). Newspapers carried long articles of battle victories, while defeats were hardly mentioned.

Source B ▼ *A Pals Battalion of friends from Accrington, Lancashire, who all joined up together in 1914. One of the men, who is lying down on the right, survived the war, despite being wounded on three occasions. Sadly, there is no record of who else survived.*

Source A ◄ *This poster shows a German nurse pouring water on the floor in front of a thirsty, injured British soldier. The Red Cross helped wounded soldiers on both sides – the Iron Cross is a German medal for bravery. Two fat Germans laugh in the background. How do you think this made some British men feel?*

The government also agreed to keep friends together who joined up at the same time. These units were called 'Pals Battalions' and sometimes whole football teams, orchestras, cricket teams or bus depots would sign up together, or perhaps groups of friends from the same school, street or village. Sadly, whole groups of friends would die together.

Women also played a major part in getting men to fight. The White Feather Campaign was a way of trying to shame men into joining up. Groups of women would patrol high streets and town centres handing out white feathers – a symbol of cowardice – to any man who seemed fit to fight and who was not in a military uniform. This sort of public humiliation was enough to see some men join immediately (see **Source C**)!

Source C ▾ *Women in the East End of London hoist the 'White Feather' flag, deriding those not enlisting in a time of war with the message 'Serve your country or wear this'.*

The recruitment campaign worked very well. By January 1916, about 2.5 million men had agreed to fight. But then the steady stream of volunteers began to dry up. People had begun to realise that war was not the big adventure that some had imagined – men were actually dying out there and many others were returning home wounded or crippled for life. The government responded to the lack of volunteers by introducing **conscription**. A new law said that any man aged between 18 and 41 could be forced to join the army if their name was randomly selected. Some refused to join when their 'call up' letter dropped through the letterbox but, by April 1918, an extra 2.5 million soldiers had been found through conscription.

FACT *'Conshies'*

Some men refused to fight because they thought it was wrong to kill or harm another human being. They were known as **conscientious objectors** (COs) or 'conshies'. There were nearly 20 000 COs in all, most of whom settled for non-fighting roles in the army, such as ambulance drivers, cooks, medical assistants or stretcher-bearers. Some, however, about 1000 in all, refused to do anything *at all* with the war. They were called **absolutists** and were sent to prison, where many were treated very badly. (In fact, 71 absolutists died in prison.) When the war finished they were kept in prison for an extra six months. On release, many failed to find work because shops and businesses put phrases such as 'COs and absolutists need not apply' in their job adverts!

WISE UP WORDS

- conscientious objectors   absolutists
  conscription   propaganda

WORK

1 Write a sentence or two to explain the following words or terms:
  - propaganda
  - Pals Battalion
  - White Feather Campaign
  - conscription
  - conscientious objector.

2 What were the advantages and disadvantages of Pals Battalions?

3 What was an absolutist and why were they treated so badly?

4 Look at **Source A**. Do you think this was an effective poster? In your answer make sure you comment on:
  - The message of the poster.
  - The contrast between Red Cross and Iron Cross.
  - The image of the two Germans.
  - The reaction of the German nurse to the wounded British soldier.
  - The possible response of British men and women on seeing this poster.

Why wasn't the war 'over by Christmas'?

AIMS

- to identify the major reasons why there was a stalemate on the Western front.

When the war started, people in Britain confidently expected that it would be over in months, even weeks. 'Over by Christmas' was a common saying in August 1914. After all, the last major war, between France and Prussia, had lasted just 32 weeks! So why did the war last so long?

Failing plans

Each fighting country had carefully prepared attack plans. Germany's plan was to defeat France in six weeks by invading at high speed through Belgium. Then the German army would turn around and march east to fight Russia. This was known as the Schlieffen Plan, after the German Minister of War thought it up.

But the Schlieffen Plan failed. The Germans thought the Belgian army would be easy to beat as they marched through their country on their way to France. They were wrong. The Belgians put up a fierce defence, helped by the British (who the Germans thought would never help Belgium). As a result, it took the Germans longer than expected to reach France. By September 1914, the German army was only 30 miles from Paris. There, however, along the River Marne, a million French and British troops stood in their way. As a battle began, both armies dug trenches in the soil to defend themselves. News then arrived that Russian troops in the east had attacked Germany. The Germans never imagined that the Russians could get their soldiers ready this quickly. In fact, German forces never got any closer to Paris than this – their Schlieffen Plan had failed. Even at this early stage, a high-ranking German general told the Kaiser, 'Your majesty, we have lost the war'.

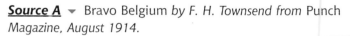

Source A ▼ Bravo Belgium *by F. H. Townsend from* Punch *Magazine, August 1914.*

NO THOROUGHFARE

F.H.Townsend Aug. 1914

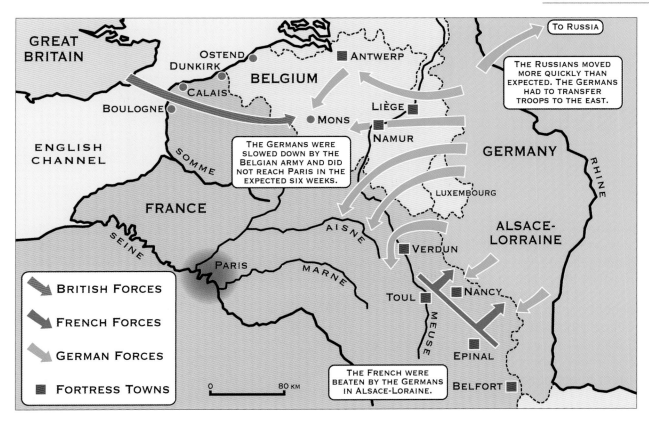

Source B ▲ *A map showing how the Schlieffen Plan failed.*

A stalemate develops

As neither side could go forward, each tried to outflank (move around) the other. As the armies marched north, trying to get around behind each other, they dug trenches as they went. By November 1914, both sides had reached the English Channel. The lines of trenches stretched the other way too, eventually reaching from the Channel to Switzerland, a distance of 400 miles.

In the east too, Russian troops faced Austrian and German forces. Each side dug trenches to stop the other side from advancing. These trenches were protected with sandbags and barbed wire. They were defended by millions of men with rifles, machine guns and hand grenades.

On both of the Western and Eastern fronts (a 'front' is an area where fighting takes place), the war was now at a stalemate – a complete inability to move forward and a solid determination not to be pushed back. In 1915, Britain's Minister of War, Earl Kitchener, summed up the stalemate when he said, 'I don't know what is to be done … but this isn't war!'

Source C ▼ *A description of trench warfare, taken from the 1979 film* All Quiet on the Western Front. *The film is based on a book by Erich Maria Remarque.*

> "For months now we have fought over a hundred yards of earth. They attack our trench, we attack their trench, then to keep the score even, they will attack our trench once again."

WORK

1. Look at **Source A**. Explain what the cartoonist is saying about Belgium and Germany.

2. It is Christmas 1914 and you work as a Government press officer. It is your job to prepare a press release for Britain's newspapers, which are eager to inform their readers why the war isn't over yet. In no more than 150 words explain:
   - Why the Schlieffen Plan failed.
   - How a stalemate developed on the Western and Eastern fronts.

Britain's bravest?

AIMS
- to have an idea of what life was like in a front line trench;
- what everyday difficulties the soldiers faced.

By the beginning of 1915, millions of men were dug into strong positions, facing each other in a long line of trenches across France and Belgium. Since each side's trenches were defended by barbed wire and sandbags, if one side attacked the other by charging across no man's land (the area between the two sets of trenches) they were picked off by enemy machine guns and snipers. This was stalemate.

Month after month, year after year, millions of men lived in appalling conditions in these trenches. Rats swarmed all over the place, lice bred in the men's uniforms, food arrived late and all the time there was the constant threat of enemy bombs.

One of the people who saw just how harsh trench life really was, was a 30 year old British medic and soldier named Noel Chavasse. He volunteered to join the army as soon as war broke out because he felt his medical training would be useful. This young man also happens to be Britain's most highly decorated soldier of the war. He won the Victoria Cross, Britain's highest award for bravery, twice. His amazing war story is told through his medical notebook and his personal letters home. They demonstrate the heroism of a remarkable man – and show the true horrors of trench warfare. As you read through Noel's notebook and letters, try to think about the following questions:

- What impression of trench warfare do you get from Noel Chavasse's notebook and letters?
- Why were conditions so bad?
- What was it like to fight?

18.8.14

If ever I get sent to the Front with a regiment I shall almost shed tears of joy ... I do envy Chris going off so soon, but I think this dog is going to have his day soon too.

Note: Chris was Noel's twin brother. They were both top athletes, competing for Britain in the 1908 Olympic Games at 400 metres.

5.12.14

At first the zip, zip of bullets hitting the sandbags by one's head is rather worrying, but then you get used to it. At one point, we had to get past a gate where a sniper lay in wait. I went by doing the 100 well within 10 seconds ... We had to rest five times while crossing a ploughed field as the Captain was very heavy on the improvised stretcher (two poles and a greatcoat). On the way, I saw a group of ten dead Frenchmen. Next evening, the men came out of the trenches. The young men were haggard, white and stooped like old men, but they had done gallantly ... two men have lost their nerve...

NOTEBOOK

18.8.14

I am really trying to train myself in every way I can to be useful, and am reading hard, all about the hygiene of a fighting army, and all about typhoid fever ... We pass from 50 to 100 recruits daily and vaccinate them afterwards. Two of us vaccinated 175 of them on Sunday.

NOTEBOOK

11.12.14

Just now we have several cripples with an interesting complaint of the feet, brought on by the men having their feet in water and mud for days at a time. The feet are very tender, and the men cannot walk, then when they take their boots off their feet swell like balloons.

Note: Here, Noel is describing trench foot (see **Source B**).

11.12.14

Our men have had a terrible experience of 72 hours in trenches, drenched through and in some places knee-deep in mud and water. To see them come out, and line up, and march off is almost terrible. They don't look like strong young men. They are muddied to the eyes. Their coats are plastered with mud and weigh an awful weight with the water which has soaked in. Their backs are bent, and they stagger and totter along the weight of their packs. Their faces are white and haggard and their eyes glare out from mud which with short, bristly beards give them an almost beastlike look. They look like wounded or sick wild things. I have seen nothing like it.

Note: The ordinary soldier would spend about a week in a front-line trench facing the enemy, four weeks in a support trench (about 100 metres behind the front line) and eight weeks in a reserve trench (about 300 metres behind the support trench).

16.12.14

NOTEBOOK

We found one of our men shot through the thigh. By the time I had got the muddy clothing out of the way my hands were filthy and I had no water to wash them. All I could do was to pour iodine into the wounds and put on clean dressings with forceps and give the poor fellow some morphia … Meanwhile, one of our officers was sniped through the forearm. It was a beautiful wound, just bad enough to send him home for Christmas. He went away very pleased with life, chuckling.

Note: Iodine is a liquid that is used as an antiseptic. Morphia – or morphine – is a painkiller. A wound that is serious enough to get you sent home – but not serious enough to threaten your life – was called a 'Blighty one'. 'Blighty' is a nickname for Britain.

19.12.14

NOTEBOOK

One could really do little for them. The wounds one had to dress were not the clean punctures I had imagined gunshot wounds to be, but because of the near range they at first made one think they had been made by explosive bullets … to take an instance of a wound in the fleshy part of the thigh, the entrance wound was neat and punctured, but the exit was a gaping burst, a big hole that I could put my fist into, with broken muscles hanging out.

12.1.15

NOTEBOOK

A constant change of vest is the only way to fight the constant plague of lice. By making friends with the cooks I have managed to give hot baths to about 100 men in the last two days. And whilst they were bathing, I soaked their clothes in petrol to kill the lice. They were dry by the time the wearer had finished his bath.

31.5.15

The striking of munitions workers for a half penny extra a day, while poor jaded and terrified boys of 18 years of age are shot for shirking the cruel hardships of winter trenches, fills us with dismay and rage. Why should trench-exhausted men be driven to collapse while boozy and cushy slackers at home are cajoled only? At the same time, we have a feeling that Germany is very hard pushed and that with proper ammunition, we shall soon win.

Note: Here, Noel refers to strikes back in England by workers in weapons factories.

FACT *Noel Chavasse*

Noel Chavasse was born in Oxford on 9 November 1884. His father was the Bishop of Liverpool. He was educated at Liverpool College and Oxford University, graduating with First Class Honours in Medicine in 1907. In 1909, he joined the Army Officer Medical Training Unit and in 1910 passed his surgery exams. He worked in Dublin and Liverpool before joining the army as a medic in 1913.

Source A ▶
Noel Chavasse.

5.6.15

I have now had four stretcher-bearers killed and one wounded, and one had had to go home with a strained heart and another because his nerves gave way after a very bad shelling. That is 7 out of 16 …

Last night I had a bad but necessary job. I had to crawl out behind part of the trench and bury three poor Englishmen who had been killed by a shell. I am going out after another tonight. This is the nasty side of war, but all is repaired in the feeling of comradeship and friendship made out there. It is a fine life and a man's job, but I think we shall all be glad to get home again.

20.6.15

At 2:00am a terrific bombardment began, and went on till 4:00am, but I was so tired that I dozed through it. But at 5:00am, I was woken up by the first batch of wounded coming down. Our Commanding Officer arrived with an artery bleeding in his head, which was troublesome to stop. Then news came that a Captain Cunningham was lying exhausted at the top end of the communication trench. So he had to be fetched down. I then found the trench blocked with men who had dropped exhausted trying to drag themselves along. The Huns [nickname for German soldiers] were putting big shells into the trench, and making direct hits, so that in places the trench was blown in, yet not a single wounded man was hit all day. It was a weary job helping poor Cunningham down the trench. He was hit in the leg and arm, and was very brave. We got some more men back at the same time, but when we arrived at our place we found that another bomb had burst just outside our dressing station, and wrecked it, and had killed four men next door.

NOTEBOOK

9.7.15

A poor young doctor had lice from a dugout. He rubbed himself over with petrol and then put on pyjamas and went to bed. There he set himself alight and rushed through the camp in flames. He has since died of his burns. He was only 23 years old.

24.9.15

Today a poor fellow was brought to me with a bad wound of the leg (most of his calf shot away). He dropped out on the way to the trenches (he comes from a first class Highland Bn. and crawled into a dugout where I am afraid he shot himself (he said he was cleaning his rifle – they all say that). When he gets well the poor chap will be court-martialled and either shot or given penal servitude, I fear. It seems like tending a dead man but it can't be helped. He seemed a poor specimen of humanity.

Note: Noel is referring to the way some men deliberately injured themselves to get out of fighting.

Letter: 26.12.15

Christmas Day was very quiet, hostilities seemed to stop by mutual consent, nobody seemed to have the heart to try to kill or maim each other on that day. I think it is a great tribute to the very firm though hidden hold Christianity has on every heart, that war has to cease on Christmas Day.

NOTEBOOK

26.9.16

We found a man bleeding badly from one arm. Then I found that the arm was all but off so I cut it off with a pair of scissors and did the stump up. The mud was fearful. While I and my Corporal were dressing a case we both sank up to our knees in the mud of the trench. Men had to be dug out and some poor wounded of another battalion perished in the mud. We had one sad casualty. A poor fellow was crouching at the bottom of the trench when there was a slip which buried him, and he was dead when he was dug out. Both his brothers have been in the Scottish and have been killed. His mother committed suicide after the death of the second. There is only a sister left.

14.3.17

It must be a military necessity, but our Higher Commanders are so aloof [uninvolved] that I doubt if they and their staff are really in touch with and understanding the battalions, and I get the impression myself of a want of organisation and full mastery of details. Anyway a doctor's job is rotten – for any attempts on our part to keep them well is so piffling against this constant overstrain (right and wrong). We do all sorts of things to defeat the disease germs and we whitewash cellars and spray dugouts … but against orders we are powerless.

Source B ▾ *A photo showing the nasty effects of trench foot.*

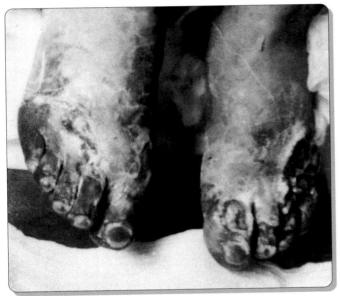

As you can see, Noel Chavasse was a remarkable medic and soldier. His notebook and letters home show the vivid reality of trench life. Noel's bravery was recognised at the highest level, when he received the Victoria Cross (VC) – Britain's highest award for bravery – in August 1916. In full view of the enemy, Noel spent 24 hours pulling wounded soldiers out of a shellhole, while a German machine gun sprayed his position. He was awarded a second VC a year later, when he spent two days and nights looking after wounded soldiers in no man's land. Noel was shot himself early in the rescue attempt but continued despite losing a lot of blood. He died of his wounds on 4 August 1917. Noel Chavasse is one of only three people awarded the VC twice.

Source C ▾ *A painting called* Repelling a German Counter-attack *by Frank Dadd. German soldiers run across no man's land to try to capture the British trenches. Look for: i) the different weapons used to stop the enemy; and ii) the soldiers who are not joining in with the defence – why do you think they have stopped fighting?*

WORK

1 Obituaries are pieces of writing, which appear in newspapers, about the lives and achievements of people who have just died. Write an obituary for Noel Chavasse using the following headings. You may want to add more.

OBITUARY FOR NOEL CHAUASSE
Born: Oxford 1884 Died: France 1917
Family
Education
Career
Achievements

2 **a** Imagine you are a medic, like Noel Chavasse, in the trenches. Write a short letter home, explaining about life and work in a front line trench. Remember you are writing as a medic so will probably focus on medical conditions such as trench foot, and the difficulties you have in your job. However you may also want to write about the dangers you face and the conditions you have to live in.

b All letters that soldiers sent home were censored. This means that a 'censor' would read them and cross out any information that might help the enemy or bad news that might upset people back home. With a pencil, underline any information in your letter that you think the censor would not allow.

Winning the war

AIMS

- to develop your own opinion on the effectiveness of different Great War weapons and battle techniques.

For nearly four years, each side tried to capture each other's trenches. They fought ferociously to hold on to their territory. Sometimes, for the loss of thousands of men, one side might move forward for a week or two and gain a few hundred metres of muddy, useless ground. A week later, for the loss of thousands more lives, they might be pushed back into their original trenches.

Throughout the war, the military generals tried lots of new ideas to break the stalemate. They tried out the latest in military technology, hoping to capture and keep the enemy's land.

Trying to win the war — the policy of attrition

One method used to win the war was the policy of **attrition**. Attrition means 'wearing away'. In other words, the military commanders tried to wear down the enemy. They attacked again and again, hoping that the other side would run out of soldiers and guns first. Sometimes an all-out attack would last months on end. During the Battle of the Somme,

British and French troops attacked from July to November 1916. By the end of the Battle, both the British and the French had lost over 620 000 men and had advanced by only ten miles! The Germans lost 450 000 soldiers. As you might expect, many people, both then and now, criticise the military leaders for their policy of attrition.

Source A 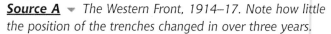 *The Western Front, 1914–17. Note how little the position of the trenches changed in over three years.*

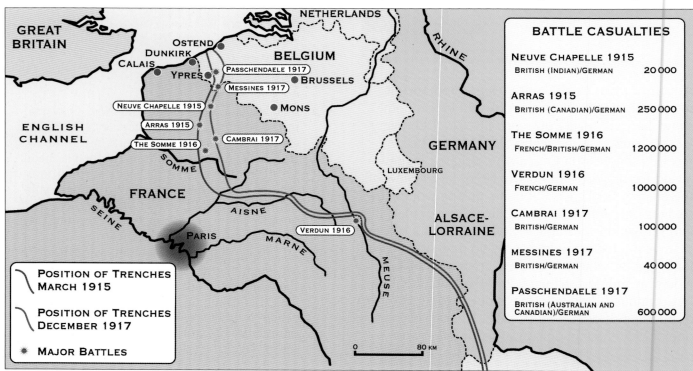

BATTLE CASUALTIES	
NEUVE CHAPELLE 1915	
BRITISH (INDIAN)/GERMAN	20 000
ARRAS 1915	
BRITISH (CANADIAN)/GERMAN	250 000
THE SOMME 1916	
FRENCH/BRITISH/GERMAN	1 200 000
VERDUN 1916	
FRENCH/GERMAN	1 000 000
CAMBRAI 1917	
BRITISH/GERMAN	100 000
MESSINES 1917	
BRITISH/GERMAN	40 000
PASSCHENDAELE 1917	
BRITISH (AUSTRALIAN AND CANADIAN)/GERMAN	600 000

Trying to win the war – gas

In 1915, the Germans used gas for the first time. One eyewitness wrote, 'a strange green mist, a running mass of men in agony, a four mile gap without a defender'. The gas attack managed to do what the soldiers hadn't – it broke through the trenches, killed the defenders and allowed the attacking German army to break through. But the Germans were quickly pushed back, and soon the British and French were using gas too.

But gas wasn't going to win the war – it was just too difficult to use. Often the wind changed direction and blew it back. Both sides developed good gas alarms and gas masks too. In fact, by the end of the war, both sides were hardly using gas at all.

Trying to win the war – artillery

Huge guns – known as artillery – were used to fire shells from behind the trenches, across no man's land and into the enemy's trenches. These bombardments, as they were known, sometimes lasted days and were meant to destroy the enemy trenches and allow for an easy crossing. But sometimes these mass bombings were ineffective – the enemy just got into their concrete bunkers dug deep below their trenches and waited for the shelling to stop. Later in the war, the 'creeping barrage' was devised – the artillery would fire in front of the soldiers as they crossed no man's land. But this tactic called for extreme accuracy and there were many examples of soldiers killed by their own shells.

Source B ▼ *Gassed by John Singer Sargent. There were two main types of gas bomb. Chlorine gas ate away at the lungs and caused a slow painful death. Mustard gas blinded the men and rotted their skin. Early gas masks consisted of a handkerchief dipped in urine tied over the face, but effective gas masks had been developed by 1916.*

Trying to win the war – tanks

The tank was a British invention. Many army generals thought that tanks were a waste of time but some people in the government liked them and decided to pay for some to be built. The tank worked very well on hard ground – in 1917, at the Battle of Cambras, almost 400 British tanks broke through German lines and pushed them back five miles. The problem was that the soldiers walking alongside the tanks couldn't keep up! However, the tanks were difficult to steer and more often than not, they broke down in the mud. They certainly caused alarm among German troops whenever the British used them, but historians still argue just how effective they really were.

Source C ▼ *The tank has gone on to become one of war's most decisive weapons – but they were not reliable enough in the Great War to make the impact that was hoped. In total, the British and French produced over 5000 tanks while the Germans made only 20.*

Trying to win the war – a new approach

In 1915, the Allies tried to break the stalemate on the Western Front by attacking in a different place – Turkey. The plan was to defeat the Turkish army (Turkey was allied with Germany), march through Turkey and attack Germany's other ally, Austria–Hungary. This meant that the enemy could be attacked from another direction.

A huge army, mainly from Australia, New Zealand and France, invaded Gallipoli in Turkey … but the Turks were waiting for them. Turkish machine guns mowed down thousands of men as they tried to get ashore (see **Source D**). In fact, the attacking troops didn't get much further than the top of the beaches and, after eight months of senseless slaughter, the decision was taken to pull out. The campaign was a complete failure and the man who thought it up, Winston Churchill, was humiliated.

Source D ▼ *A ship lands British troops, who came under heavy fire at Helles Heath. Many were wounded or killed.*

Breaking the stalemate

The giant battles and endless slaughter continued into 1917. But 1917 was a crucial year in the course of the war. Ordinary Russian people rebelled against their leader (they murdered their king and his entire family) and stopped fighting the Germans. Germany now concentrated all of its soldiers, guns, gas, ships and planes on fighting the British and the French.

However, by then, the USA had joined the war on the side of Britain and France. German submarines had been sinking hundreds of ships on their way from America to Britain. They had tried to starve Britain into surrender by sinking these supply ships. But many of the ships were American – and so many were destroyed that America joined the war against Germany in April 1917. The Germans now tried desperately to defeat the British and French before the fresh American soldiers arrived at the front lines. But, despite an all-out attack, the

Germans could not break through. The German soldiers started to **retreat**. Back home in Germany, the **civilians** had reached breaking point – they were starving and there were riots on the streets. Soon, the countries on Germany's side began to surrender – and German troops were exhausted. Eventually, Germany's king (Kaiser Wilhelm II) ran away to Holland and the government that replaced him called for a **ceasefire**. At 11:00am on 11 November 1918, the Great War was over.

FACT *The war at sea*

There was one great battle in which 110 German warships faced 145 British warships (the Battle of Jutland). The Brits lost more ships and sailors but the Germans stopped fighting first and sailed back to Germany. Both sides said they had won. Beneath the waves, German submarines prowled around looking to torpedo any enemy ship. Explosive mines bobbed around destroying anything – warships, food ships, passenger liners and hospital ships. But the Great War was not going to be one remembered for its sea battles. The Battle of Jutland had no clear winner and by 1918, British submarine-destroyer ships were protecting the food ships bringing supplies.

WISE UP WORDS

• ceasefire   retreat   civilians   attrition

WORK

1 **a** What is meant by the word 'stalemate'?

  b What was the policy of 'attrition'?

  c Why was it used?

2 Look at **Sources B**, **C** and **D**. Each of the pictures represents a different tactic used during the war in an attempt to break the stalemate. For each picture write your own label of no more than 50 words. Your label must not only describe what the picture shows but must also explain how it represents a new method to win the war.

3 **a** Why was 1917 such an important year in the war?

  b When exactly did the Great War end and how do we remember it today?

The Battle of the Somme

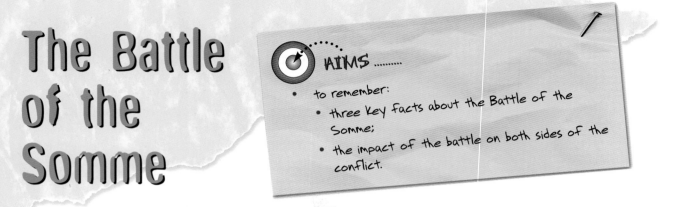

AIMS ....

- to remember:
  - three key facts about the Battle of the Somme;
  - the impact of the battle on both sides of the conflict.

A German army commander once described the British army as 'lions led by donkeys'. He admitted the great bravery of the ordinary British soldiers who went into battle, but felt that the generals who were in charge of them were fools. Field Marshall Sir Douglas Haig, who was in charge of the British army from 1915 to 1918, has even been called a 'butcher' for allowing so many men to die. But is this criticism of Haig and his generals fair? Were they 'donkeys' or just men who were trying their best to win a very difficult war? The evidence on this page focuses on one of the Great War's most famous battles – the Battle of the Somme. Use the evidence to form an opinion on the effectiveness of Field Marshall Haig and the impact of the battle.

Source A ▾ *Haig wrote this before the Battle of the Somme, 1916.*

> "The nation must be taught to bear losses … to see heavy casualty lists. Three years of war and the loss of one-tenth of Britain's men is not too great a price to pay."

Source B ▾ *Before the Battle of the Somme, the generals assured their troops that the shells would destroy the enemy before the men went into battle.*

> "You will be able to go over the top with a walking stick … you will find the Germans all dead, not even a rat will have survived."

Source C ▾ *From Brooman's* The Great War, *1991. The number of dead soldiers appears in* The Guinness Book of Records *as the 'greatest number of casualties in one battle'!*

> "On that first day of the Battle of the Somme, 20 000 British soldiers were killed and 35 000 wounded, but this did not make General Haig want to change his methods. He ordered more attacks but the same tragic story was repeated each time. Against the advice of experts who said he didn't have enough, he sent fifty tanks into the battle in September. Twenty-nine broke down before they even reached the battlefield and the rest soon got stuck in the mud. By the end of the battle, the British and French had lost 620 000 men and the Germans 450 000. The allies had advanced 15 kilometres at the furthest point."

Source D ▲ *Dead German soldiers at the Battle of the Somme, 1916. The British fired over a million shells at the German trenches for five days. Most escaped harm by digging very deep dugouts (German spy planes had seen men getting ready to attack) but this dugout suffered a direct hit.*

Source E ▼ *Haig believed that wearing the enemy down was the key to success. He said this after two weeks of the battle.*

> "In another six weeks the enemy will find it hard to get enough men."

Source F ▼ *This quote is taken from the autobiography of the German general Ludendorff, My War Memories, 1914–1918, written in 1919.*

> "We had heavy losses in men and material. As a result of the Somme, we were completely exhausted on the Western Front."

Source G ▼ *One of Haig's generals said this in 1915 when told that the Battle of Loos had cost 60 000 lives.*

> "What the hell does that matter? There are plenty more men in Britain."

Source H ▼ *From the official German Army records of the 27th Infantry division.*

> "In the Somme fighting in 1916, we lost our best men. The men who joined up after had not the temper, the hardness or the spirit of the men who had fallen."

WORK

1 Look at **Source A**. What impression does this source give you of Haig?

2 Look at **Sources B** and **D**. What do these sources tell us about the tactics used by the British to try and win the battle?

3 Look at **Source C**. In your answer to Question 1, you wrote down your impression of Field Marshall Haig. Does your impression of him change after reading **Source C**?

4 Look at **Sources F** and **H**. Is there any evidence in these sources that Haig's tactics to win the battle were successful?

a The Battle of the Somme was a complete disaster for the British. Explain whether you agree or disagree with this statement.

b And what is your opinion of Haig? Was he a 'butcher' and a 'donkey' for allowing thousands of men to needlessly die – or was he just trying his best to win the war?

The Home Front

AIMS

• to remember at least three ways that war had a direct impact on civilians at home.

The Great War had a greater impact on ordinary Brits – or civilians – than any previous war. When it started, Britain was the only fighting country that relied on volunteers for its army – but more and more men were soon needed. In 1916, the government passed the Military Service Act. First, all unmarried men between the ages of 18 and 41 were called up to join the army, navy or air force. Married men were conscripted later. By 1918, over six million men had gone to fight … and about one in ten was dead!

Women and war

With so many men fighting, women were needed to do their jobs. Before the war, no one would have dreamed of having female bus drivers, chimney sweeps or steel makers; now Britain needed them! Others found work in shipyards, drove ambulances and mended roads. Some became policewomen. In 1917, the Women's Land Army was formed to replace male farm workers who had gone to fight. For thousands of women, the war at last provided them with a chance to earn their own money, begin a new career and achieve some degree of independence. Later, in 1917, women could serve in the women's version of the army, navy and air force too. About 100 000 joined these organisations and some got really close to the fighting by working as nurses, cooks and driver mechanics.

By the end of the war, many men (including some politicians) were very impressed with the work women had done and were forced to change their views about the place of women in Britain. Many felt they had earned the right to vote! After the war, Parliament changed the voting laws and gave women over 30 the right to vote (but men could vote at 21).

FACT *Change for the better?*

In 1919, single women who married could carry on working as doctors and solicitors, instead of having to give up their jobs as they did before the war. But it was 1944 before female teachers who got married could keep their jobs! And women didn't get the same voting rights as men until 1928.

Source A ▼ *A female munitions factory worker.*

Source B ▾ *Munitions factories had employed women before the war but now their work was appreciated more than ever. This poem makes reference to the fact that the dangerous chemicals in bomb making turned their skin yellow, gave some cancer and sometimes left women sterile.*

```
The guns out there are roaring
    fast,
the bullets fly like rain,
the aeroplanes are cavetting,
They go and come again,
the bombs talk loud,
the mines crash out,
No trench their might
    withstands,
Who helped them all to do their
    job.
The girls with yellow hands.
```

Source C ▾ *Prime Minister Herbert Asquith, speaking in August 1916. What do you think he means by women's 'special claim'?*

```
"It is true that women cannot fight
with rifles, but they have aided in
the most effective way in the war.
What is more, when the war comes to
an end, don't women have a special
claim to be heard on the many
questions which affect their
interests? I cannot deny that claim."
```

Source D ▾ *A comparison of the quality and output in factories of men and women in 1918. It is little wonder that Herbert Asquith said, 'How could we carry on the war without women? There is hardly a service in which women have not been at least as active as men.'*

Quality

Metal – women's work better than men's

Aircraft woodwork – women equal to men

Bullet making – women equal to men

Shell making – women's work poorer than men's

Quantity

Metal – women's production equal to men's

Aircraft woodwork – women's production equal to men's

Bullet making – women's production equal to men's; in some cases, women produced 20% more than men

Shell making – women's production behind men's

Defence of the Realm Act (DORA)

This new law gave the government great power while Britain was at war. They could take over mines and railways and force workers to stay in jobs they thought were vital to winning the war. DORA gave the government control over the newspapers and radio too – all news had to be approved by the government before it was printed, so newspapers were filled with stories of heroic deeds and great victories … while defeats hardly got a mention! Also, it came to the government's attention that drunkenness was a huge problem – so a law was passed that limited the times that pubs opened (a law that only changed in 2005). It also allowed beer to be watered down.

Rationing

Much of Britain's food came from abroad by sea so the German navy tried to sink as many ships as it possibly could. By 1917, there was only six weeks' supply of food left in Britain! So the government started food **rationing** to make sure that food was shared out. Each person was allowed a set amount of meat, butter, sugar, bacon, ham and so on.

Attack from above

The invention of aircraft and **zeppelin** airships meant that people suffered as Britain was bombed for the first time. About 1400 people were killed during air attacks, mostly on the east coast in towns such as Great Yarmouth and King's Lynn. In June 1917, German bomber planes reached London and killed 162 people, including 16 children who died when their school was hit. This made the British very angry, especially with Germans living in Britain at the time (see **Source H**).

Source G ▾ *Zeppelins were about 200 metres long (two football pitches) and could carry 27 tons of bombs. In total, they made 57 raids on British towns, killing 564 people and injuring over 1300.*

Source E ▾ *Weekly rations in 1918.*

WEEKLY RATIONS IN 1918

SUGAR 8 OUNCES (226 GRAMS)

BACON 8 OUNCES (226 GRAMS)

LARD 2 OUNCES (56 GRAMS)

BUTTER 5 OUNCES (141 GRAMS)

MEAT 20 OUNCES (567 GRAMS)

Source F ▸ *This note was dropped on British towns from German airships. Why do you think they dropped these notes?*

"You English, we have come and will come again soon, kill or cure, Germany."

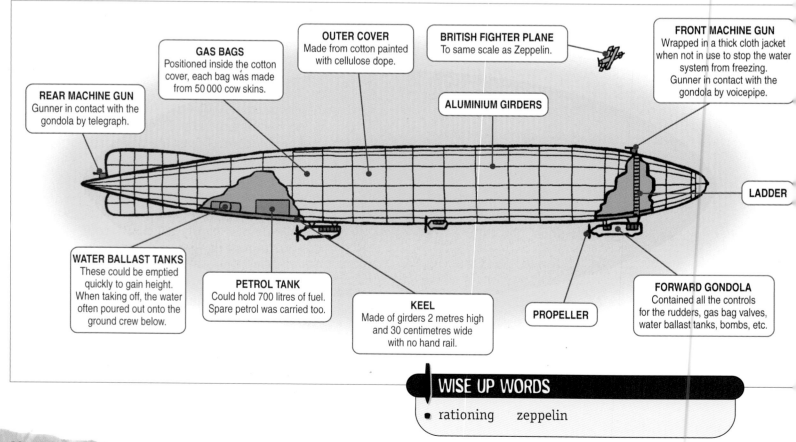

GAS BAGS
Positioned inside the cotton cover, each bag was made from 50 000 cow skins.

OUTER COVER
Made from cotton painted with cellulose dope.

BRITISH FIGHTER PLANE
To same scale as Zeppelin.

FRONT MACHINE GUN
Wrapped in a thick cloth jacket when not in use to stop the water system from freezing. Gunner in contact with the gondola by voicepipe.

REAR MACHINE GUN
Gunner in contact with the gondola by telegraph.

ALUMINIUM GIRDERS

LADDER

WATER BALLAST TANKS
These could be emptied quickly to gain height. When taking off, the water often poured out onto the ground crew below.

PETROL TANK
Could hold 700 litres of fuel. Spare petrol was carried too.

KEEL
Made of girders 2 metres high and 30 centimetres wide with no hand rail.

PROPELLER

FORWARD GONDOLA
Contained all the controls for the rudders, gas bag valves, water ballast tanks, bombs, etc.

WISE UP WORDS

- rationing   zeppelin

<u>Source **H**</u> ▼ *There were dozens of attacks like this all over Britain. In Keighley, Yorkshire, for example, an Irishman accused a German butcher (who had lived in Britain for 15 years) of poisoning his meat pie. The butcher responded by punching the Irishman in the face. Later that night, the Irishman returned with an angry mob and set the German's shop on fire! In fact, the government itself was so worried about Germans living in Britain that it had 30 000 of them arrested and sent them to holding camps. The Trading with the Enemy Act even confiscated German-owned business totalling £58 million. Some worried immigrants changed their names to blend in more; the writer Ford Hermann Hueffer became Ford Maddox Ford, for example. Most famously of all, King George (who had German ancestors) changed his surname from Saxe-Coburg-Gotha to … Windsor!*

WORK

1 **a** List at least four ways in which women helped the war effort.

   b Describe at least two ways in which women might have changed by doing this.

   c Why do you think many men were forced to change their views about women after the Great War? Try to use some of the sources (**A**–**D**) as evidence in your answer.

2 **a** What did DORA stand for?

   b Explain why the government introduced the measures it took under the Defence of the Realm Act.

3 Look at **Source E**.

   a Explain what is meant by the term 'rationing'.

   b Why did Britain have to ration during the war?

4 Look at **Sources F** and **G**.

   a What was a Zeppelin?

   b Why do you think that Zepplins created so much fear among ordinary British citizens. Give at least two reasons.

5 Look at **Source H**.

   a Describe what is happening in the photograph

   b Why do you think this attack, and many like it, too place?

Was it really a WORLD war?

AIMS ....
- to be able to remember:
  - five areas where fighting took place;
  - two reasons why the Great War can be called a WORLD War.

The Great War of 1914–18 has two other names. It is often called the First World War or World War I. You will hear all three of these names all the time. But was it really a WORLD war? Where exactly did the fighting take place? And which countries were involved?

The North Sea The war's one major sea battle — The Battle of Jutland — between the British and German navies — took place here in May 1916.

The Atlantic German submarines attacked British ships here. They sank several American ships too, most famously one called *Lousitania*, which was bringing ordinary citizens and supplies to Britain. The sinking of American ships was one of the factors that led to America joining the war.

Canada Canadian troops fought on the Western Front. Canada supplied tons of vital supplies too. Number of deaths: 56 119.

The Balkans Britain and France sent thousands of troops to help Serbia fight Austria–Hungary.

Turkey Turkey fought on Germany's side. British, France, ANZAC (Australian and New Zealand Army Corps) and Indian troops attacked Gallipoli in April 1915. It was a huge failure due to poor planning and fierce resistance from the Turks. Number of deaths: 325 000 (Turkish empire).

The Pacific Japanese, Australian and New Zealand troops captured German colonies.

Africa British troops atta[ck] colonies here. Most of th[e] each side were Africans. [Number of] deaths: 6926 (mainly Sou[th] although other African na[tions] sent soldiers to fight).

Falkland Islands British ships sank four German battleships here.

WORK

1 **a** List the three names most commonly given to the war you have been studying.

   b Why do you think it was known as the Great War at the time, and not one of the other two names?

2 So was it really a WORLD war?

   a Make four lists of the following:

     • All the places where there was fighting.

     • All the main countries that supplied troops.

     • All the areas that were affected in some way.

     • Key areas or major nations that weren't involved or affected in any way.

   b Write a paragraph which answers the question: 'Was the Great War really a WORLD war?'

The Western Front The main area of conflict. This area, mainly in France and Belgium, is where most deaths occurred.

Italy The Italians entered the war on the side of Britain and France in 1915. They mainly fought against Austrian troops and hoped to take territory from Austria after the war. Number of deaths: 650 000.

The Eastern Front Here, Russia fought against Germany and Austria–Hungary. The Germans massacred the Russians at Tannenberg (August 1914) but the battle stopped Germany conquering France because they had to split their forces to stop the Russian invasion. In 1916, the Russians badly damaged the Austrian army too. However, Russia suffered heavy casualities throughout the war — which helped lead to the Russian Revolution in November 1917 when ordinary Russians rebelled against the Tsar (Emperor). Russia then left the war and made peace with Germany.

India Over 850 000 Indian soldiers fought in all the major campaigns. They were lured into fighting by deceptive posters in Hindu and Urdu, which read: " Easy life! Lots of respect! Very little danger! Good pay!" India supplied tons of vital raw materials. Number of deaths: 47 746. In fact, nearly one-third of all men fighting for Britain were in the colonies of her empire. Indian solders fought especially well — 12 were awarded the Victoria Cross for 'exceptional bravery'.

The Middle East British military advisors worked with local Arab tribes to attack the Turkish army in Mesopotamia (now called Iraq) and Palestine.

Australia and **New Zealand** These two countries supplied thousands of troops to fight on the Western Front, the Middle East and most notably, at Gallipoli. Number of deaths: 58 460 (Australia) and 16 32 (New Zealand).

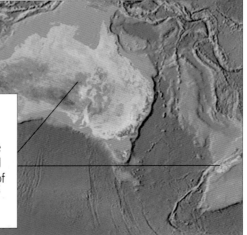

erman
s on
of
ans
so

Counting the cost

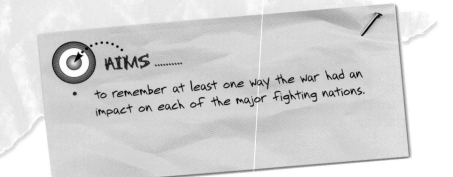
People at the time believed that the Great War was worse than any previous war in history. It was common to hear people say that it must be 'the war to end all wars'. So why did they think it was so bad? In what ways did nations suffer? And which nations suffered most?

France

The worst of the fighting took place in France – and the damage was staggering. Over two million people were made homeless because 750 000 houses had been destroyed. Over 20 000 factories, 1000 bridges, 30 000 miles of road, 2000 breweries and 1000 miles of railway line had been wrecked too. An area the size of Wales had been totally ruined as high explosive shells ripped up the rich soil into useless mud. Even today, some of the soil can't be used because of the dangers of unexploded shells just below the surface. Over a million animals – cows, sheep and donkeys – had disappeared too! Worst of all though, one and a half million young French men had died – and another 2 500 000 were wounded in the fighting.

Source A ▶
A painting by Christopher Nevison called The Road from Arras to Bapaume.

Britain

Unlike France (and Belgium), Britain had not been invaded by enemy forces. There had been some air raids by planes and airships that had killed over 1000 civilians, but Britain itself had not suffered the same damage as some other nations. About 750 000 British soldiers had been killed and another 1 500 000 wounded in the fighting. And Britain was deeply in debt too, having spent around £9 billion on the war, borrowing over £1 billion of it from America!

USA

The USA suffered a great deal less than the main European nations. American soldiers didn't join up with British and French forces until 1917 and they lost fewer soldiers (116 000) than many of the other fighting countries. America was not invaded either.

Belgium

The German army marched through Belgium when they attacked France and thousands of German soldiers stayed in Belgium for the next four years. The Germans took over Belgian factories, mines and farms too, using their goods and raw materials to make weapons and feed the army. Over 50 000 Belgium soldiers were killed too and a large area of the country, Flanders, was ruined by fighting.

Italy

Italy joined the war in 1915, on Britain and France's side. Their entry was mainly due to the fact that their allies promised them Austrian land when the fighting was over. Enemy forces had invaded the northeast of Italy and 600 000 soldiers had been killed.

> **FACT** *The Russians*
>
> Exhausted by war, hunger and bad government, the Russian people rebelled against their king in 1917. Later that year, a new government withdrew the Russian army from the war and asked for a peace deal with Germany. This deal was known as the Treaty of Brest-Litovsk. They paid a heavy price for their surrender – Germany took away lots of land in Western Russia, which included 80% of Russia's coal mines, 75% of their steel factories, 265 miles of their railway lines, 27% of their farmland and 30% of their population.

Germany

Two million German soldiers had been killed in the war and, by November 1918, Germany was on its knees. The country had not been invaded but all of its factories, farms and mines were exhausted because they had been dedicated to keeping the armed forces supplied. German civilians suffered too when the British navy blockaded German ports to stop food supplies getting in. They were soon starving and there were riots in the streets. Some soldiers and sailors refused to follow orders.

Other nations

There were heavy casualties in all of the main fighting countries. Germany's main ally, Austria–Hungary, lost 1 200 000 men while Turkey lost 325 000 and Bulgaria lost over 100 000. Russia lost 1 700 000 soldiers too.

Source B ▼ *German children queuing for soup from a charity kitchen in 1918.*

As you can see, every major nation that fought in the Great War suffered greatly. When countries fight wars, they usually expect to win. They also expect to get something for winning – land perhaps, or money, or a share of the losing countries' navy or air force.

So when the leaders of the winning countries met to discuss what to do with the losers, there was intense pressure on the politicians. On the one hand, some of the victorious politicians wanted to gain something from the defeated countries. On the other hand, there was pressure on them to make sure that any peace deal guaranteed that such a war could never happen again.

> **WORK**
>
> 1 Which country do you think suffered most in the Great War? Write a paragraph to answer which country you think suffered the most.
>
> 2 Look at **Source A**. What does this painting show? Do you think paintings are a useful source for historians? Explain your answer carefully.
>
> 3 Look at **Source B**. Why do you think the children are queuing for food?

Who were the 'Big Three'?

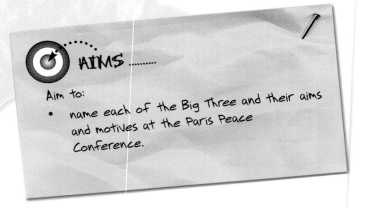

The Great War ended at 11:00am on 11 November 1918. Later that day, David Lloyd George (the British Prime Minister) said the following words in Parliament:

'At eleven o'clock this morning, the cruellest and most terrible war that has ever cursed mankind came to an end. I hope we can say that all wars came to an end this morning.'

Lloyd George was right to call it a cruel and terrible war. By 1918, much of Europe was in a mess – land devastated, farms destroyed, railways blown up and mines flooded. Millions had died – and millions more were weak and starving.

Most people in Europe looked to their leaders and politicians to sort out the mess. They hoped a peace deal might be sorted out that would end all future wars. So when a peace conference was arranged for January 1919, the attention of the world focused on the politicians attending the meeting.

The Paris Peace Conference

Representatives from all the countries who had declared war on Germany and her allies (over 30 in all) met up at the Palace of Versailles, near Paris, to decide what to do with their beaten enemy. It was the biggest peace conference ever held in the world's history. The Germans, who were top of most people's 'hit list', were not allowed to send anyone to put their viewpoint across. Nor were any of the losing countries! There was no invitation for Russia either – they had dropped out of the war in 1917 and most of Europe's leading politicians didn't trust the new Communist Russian government!

The Big Three

The three most important men at the peace talks were the leaders of the three most powerful winning countries. They were David Lloyd George, Prime Minister of Britain, George Clemenceau, Prime Minister of France and Woodrow Wilson, President of the USA. These men would make the most important decisions, so were known as the Big Three … and they each had their own views on what to do with the losing nations!

DAVID LLOYD GEORGE (Britain)

Background: Welsh lawyer with a gift for public speaking.

Aims:

• Lloyd George had been re-elected as Prime Minister in 1916 mainly because he made promises to treat Germany harshly. He realised he had to keep the people at home happy.
• He personally wanted a peace that would last – this would then allow Britain to rebuild its trade with other nations.
• He wanted to preserve the British empire – if he got a chance to take any German colonies, he would!

The British public: Newspapers were full of headlines such as 'Make Germany Pay' and 'They Must All Suffer'. Lloyd George was under pressure to be tough on Germany.

Relationship with the other two: Lloyd George and Clemenceau didn't really get on. However, he agreed with Wilson on lots of his ideas, but got annoyed when Wilson suggested that Britain should let some of the countries in her empire be independent.

WOODROW WILSON (USA)

Background: History professor at one of America's top universities, President since 1912.

Aims:

- Wanted Germany to be treated fairly so they didn't seek revenge in the future.
- Had a 14-point plan, which he hoped would guarantee world peace in the future. The most important of his ideas were:
  - Countries should stop making secret deals with each other — this, Wilson said, only leads to suspicion and misunderstanding between nations.
  - Countries should reduce their weapons and armed forces. This is called **disarmament**.
  - People living under the rules of foreign powers — for example, the Czechs living in the Austrian–Hungarian Empire — should be able to rule themselves. Wilson called this idea **self-determination**.
  - There should be a new organisation for keeping peace. Wilson hoped a '**League of Nations**' could be formed in which countries would all meet on a regular basis to sort out their arguments.

The American public: Americans were shocked by the casualties they suffered during the war (over 100 000 killed). There was public pressure on Wilson to keep America out of European problems.

Relationship with the other two: Wilson believed that Germany should be punished but not humiliated — so this made him clash with Clemenceau, who was determined to crush Germany. He clashed with Lloyd George too, who he thought cared more about the British empire than about future world peace.

GEORGE CLEMENCEAU (France)

Background: Journalist, politician since 1870s. At 78 years of age, old enough to remember France being invaded by Germany twice — in the 1870s AND in 1914!

Aims:

- Wanted Germany to pay for damage done to France in the war. The cost (according to Clemenceau): 200 000 000 000 gold Francs.
- Wanted to make Germany so weak that she could never attack France again — would mean taking away most of Germany's factories, armed forces and even land. And even suggested splitting Germany up into separate, small states, so it would cease to exist as a country!

The French public: Most French people supported Clemenceau's quest to cripple Germany and make her pay. He was affectionately known as 'The Tiger'.

Relationship with the other two: Didn't think either of them cared too much about France. There were rumours that he tried to hit Lloyd George during the talks.

Source A

A poster issued in 1918 urging people not to buy goods from German businessmen or German companies after the war.

Source B ▾ *Winston Churchill, November 1918.*

"Practically the whole German nation was guilty of the crime of aggressive war conducted by brutal means ... they must all suffer for it."

Source C ▾ *Sir Eric Geddes, a British MP, December 1918.*

"The Germans should pay every penny; they are going to be squeezed, as a lemon is squeezed, until the pips squeak."

The Big Three clearly had different ideas about what should be done ... so they argued about it! They all agreed with Wilson's idea for a 'League of Nations' to be set up – but disagreed vastly on the extent to which Germany should be punished. And all the time, they were under big pressure from people back home *and* from the hundreds gathered outside the negotiating rooms. At one point Lloyd George writes that 'stones were clattering on the roof and crashing through windows and sometimes wild men screamed through the keyholes at us'.

WISE UP WORDS

- self-determination   disarmament
  League of Nations

WORK

1 **a** Using the information on pages 66 and 67, draw and complete a 'Big Three' chart like the one below.

LEADER	COUNTRY	ATTITUDE TOWARDS GERMANY	MAIN AIMS

b Why do you think it was so difficult to work out a peace deal that would please everyone?

c What were the main differences in the aims of the 'Big Three'?

d Why do you think that Clemenceau wanted to be tougher on Germany than the other leaders?

2 Look at **Source A**:

a Choose three scenes from the poster and describe what the German is doing in each of them.

b What impression of the Germans do you think the artist is trying to give?

c What do you think the poster was trying to persuade British people to do?

3 Look at **Source C**:

a What does Geddes mean when he says 'they are going to be squeezed, as a lemon is squeezed, until the pips squeak'?

b Are his views similar or different to the aims of Lloyd George?

Was the peace settlement fair on Germany?

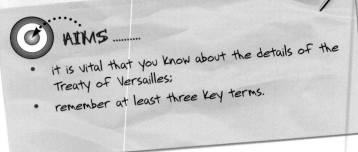

AIMS ....
- it is vital that you know about the details of the Treaty of Versailles;
- remember at least three key terms.

On 7 March 1919, the winning countries of the Great War announced what was going to happen to Germany for its part in the fighting.

Germany was to lose 10% of its land (containing about six million people), 12.5% of its population, 16% of its coalmines and nearly 50% of its iron industry. All of Germany's overseas colonies were to be taken away and given to the winners – and it was to lose most of its armed forces too! It was even going to be forced to accept the blame for starting the war and pay for all the damage done in the fighting.

The Germans were horrified … they just didn't expect their punishment to be this tough!

So did the German nation have to accept this punishment or was there another choice? How did ordinary Germans react to the news? And was the peace settlement unfair on Germany … or could it be justified at the time?

So what exactly did the peace deal say?

The peace deal with Germany is known as the 'Treaty of Versailles' because the agreement (or treaty) was signed at the famous royal Palace of Versailles, ten miles outside of Paris. It is a very long document (over 200 pages long) and contains over 400 sections or **clauses**, as they were known.

Source A ▶ *The main points of the Treaty of Versailles.*

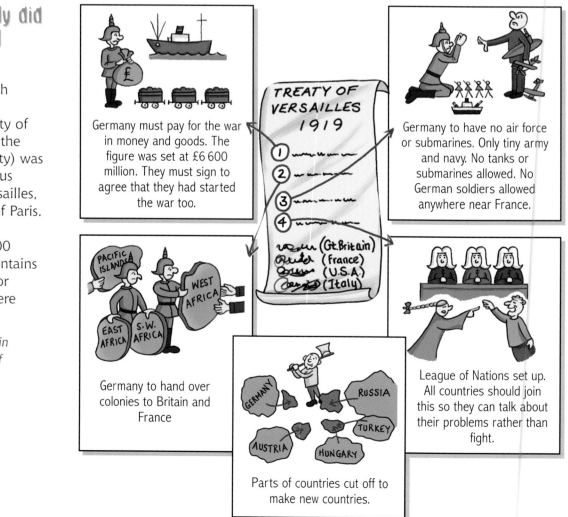

Germany must pay for the war in money and goods. The figure was set at £6 600 million. They must sign to agree that they had started the war too.

Germany to have no air force or submarines. Only tiny army and navy. No tanks or submarines allowed. No German soldiers allowed anywhere near France.

Germany to hand over colonies to Britain and France

League of Nations set up. All countries should join this so they can talk about their problems rather than fight.

Parts of countries cut off to make new countries.

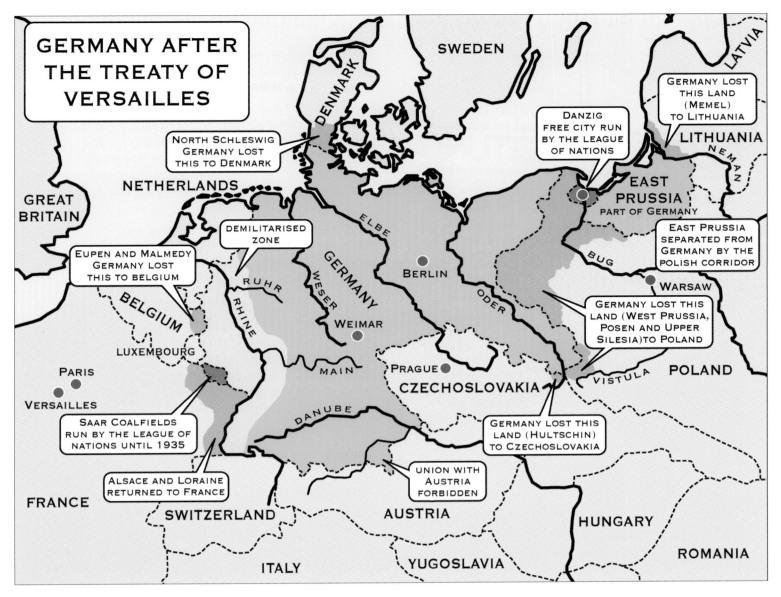

GERMANY AFTER THE TREATY OF VERSAILLES

SWEDEN

DENMARK

NORTH SCHLESWIG
GERMANY LOST
THIS TO DENMARK

LATVIA

GERMANY LOST
THIS LAND
(MEMEL)
TO LITHUANIA

DANZIG
FREE CITY RUN
BY THE LEAGUE
OF NATIONS

LITHUANIA

NEMAN

NETHERLANDS

GREAT
BRITAIN

DEMILITARISED
ZONE

ELBE

EAST
PRUSSIA
PART OF GERMANY

EUPEN AND MALMEDY
GERMANY LOST
THIS TO BELGIUM

RUHR

WESER

GERMANY

BERLIN

BUG

ODER

EAST PRUSSIA
SEPARATED FROM
GERMANY BY THE
POLISH CORRIDOR

BELGIUM

RHINE

WARSAW

LUXEMBOURG

WEIMAR

GERMANY LOST THIS
LAND (WEST PRUSSIA,
POSEN AND UPPER
SILESIA) TO POLAND

PARIS

MAIN

PRAGUE

VISTULA

POLAND

VERSAILLES

DANUBE

CZECHOSLOVAKIA

SAAR COALFIELDS
RUN BY THE LEAGUE OF
NATIONS UNTIL 1935

GERMANY LOST THIS
LAND (HULTSCHIN)
TO CZECHOSLOVAKIA

ALSACE AND LORAINE
RETURNED TO FRANCE

UNION WITH
AUSTRIA
FORBIDDEN

FRANCE

SWITZERLAND

AUSTRIA

HUNGARY

ITALY

YUGOSLAVIA

ROMANIA

Source B ▲ *A map showing the land lost by Germany in the Treaty of Versailles.*

So why did Germany sign?

The new German government was not invited to the peace discussions, which took place in the Palace of Versailles near Paris, France. Instead, they were told they had to accept their punishment or face invasion from Britain, France and the USA. Although many Germans would have preferred to fight again rather than accept such a harsh punishment, the new German government decided to sign the peace treaty rather than put the country through another war. With only an hour to go

before the deadline for signing the treaty ran out, the German government sent a message to Paris saying they agreed to sign. Two German politicians travelled to France and signed the treaty on 28 June 1919.

As you can see, the Treaty of Versailles was designed to cripple Germany by taking away land, money and weapons. The winning countries, especially France and Britain, had worked hard to make sure that Germany would never be a threat to them again. The American President, who didn't want to punish Germany so severely, worried that Germany may seek revenge in the future. He was right to worry!

Source C ▾ *From the front page of one of Germany's leading newspapers on the day the Treaty of Versailles was signed. The Hall of Mirrors is a huge mirrored room inside the Palace of Versailles.*

7 MARCH 1919

DEUTSCHE ZEITUNG

VENGEANCE GERMAN NATION!

TODAY, IN THE HALL OF MIRRORS, THE DISGRACEFUL TREATY IS BEING SIGNED. DO NOT FORGET IT. THE GERMAN PEOPLE WILL REGAIN THEIR PLACE AMONGST THE NATIONS, TO WHICH THEY ARE ENTITLED. THEN WILL COME VENGEANCE [REVENGE] FOR THE SHAME OF 1919.

Source D ▾ *Karl Nagerl, a schoolboy in 1919, remembers how he felt at the end of the Great War.*

"It was a relief when the war was over. Now we had to see what the consequences of defeat were ... when the terms of the Treaty of Versailles were announced, the German people were shocked at everything that was expected of us and dismayed at the payments we would have to make. They were sure to lead the German nation to ruin."

Reactions to the Treaty

Reactions to the peace deal were mixed. The Big Three themselves had conflicting ideas about what to do with Germany … and by the time the treaty was finished, none of them was particularly pleased with it. Clemenceau wanted the treaty to be much tougher on Germany, perhaps splitting it into smaller states – but Wilson stopped this from happening. Wilson himself thought the treaty was far too harsh and even said that, if he were a German, he wouldn't sign it! British Prime Minister, Lloyd George, despite coming home from France to a hero's welcome, wrote that if Germany 'feels unfairly treated she will find a way of getting revenge on her conquerors'.

Ordinary Germans hated the treaty and the people responsible for it. They called it **diktat** – a dictated peace – because the Germans were ordered to sign the treaty without having a chance to discuss it. Some Germans even hated the German government for signing it. They said it showed how weak they were and accused them of 'stabbing their own country in the back'.

Source E ▾ *Woodrow Wilson, speaking to his wife in June 1919.*

"Well it's finished, and, as no one is satisfied, it makes me feel we have a just peace, but it is all in the lap of the gods."

Source F ▾ *Marshall Foch, the French commander in charge of the allied armies in 1918, commenting on the Treaty of Versailles.*

"This isn't peace; it's just a fifteen year ceasefire."

WISE UP WORDS

- diktat clauses

Source G ▼ *This cartoon was published in Britain in 1919 and comments on the Treaty of Versailles.*

DER TAG!

Source H ▶

A German cartoon commenting on the peace treaty.

Source I ▼ *Lloyd George, 1919*

" These are terrible terms to force upon a country. We shall have to fight another war all over again in 25 years, at three times the cost. "

Source J ▼ *N. De Marco, The World This Century, 1987.*

" Wilson tried hard to make sure the people of the Austro—Hungarian empire were given self-determination. The Serbs, Croats and Slovenes had their own state — Yugoslasvia. Czechs and Slovaks had their own nation too. "

Source K ▼ *J. Traynor & I. Dawson, The Struggle for Peace, 1997*

" The treaties were a reasonable attempt to solve an impossible problem. It was impossible because the atmosphere of 1919 meant the allies could not be lenient towards the defeated countries. It would have been difficult to do better! "

WORK

1 Explain in your own words, what Germany had to accept in terms of:
i loss of land
ii reduction in armed forces
iii war guilt.

2 Look at **Source B**:
   a What was the effect on Germany of giving land to Poland?
   b Why do you think the Big Three did this?
   c Why do you think the area around the River Rhine was made into a demilitarised zone?
   d Why do you think the Treaty banned Germany from ever joining with Austria to become a single German-speaking country?

3 Look back at the aims of the Big Three on pages 66 and 67:
   a Who in your opinion was most pleased with the Treaty of Versailles? Give reasons for your answer.
   b Who do you think was least pleased with the Treaty?

4 Look at **Sources C** and **K**:

   For each source, make a note of whether you think it supports the Treaty of Versailles, or opposes it. For each judgement you make, you should also write a quote on a piece of evidence from the source that helped you make your decision.

5 Imagine you are a journalist for a neutral country reporting on German reactions to the Treaty of Versailles and deciding whether it was fair. Using the information over these four pages, write a short 250 word article which includes:
   • a headline on German reactions
   • reasons why Germany disliked the Treaty
   • your opinion on whether it was fair or not.

A new Europe

AIMS ....
- to be able to identify at least two ways each of the losing countries was punished at the end of the war.

The politicians at the Paris Peace Conference didn't just deal with Germany. They had her defeated partners – Austria–Hungary, Bulgaria and Turkey – to deal with too. So what happened to the other defeated nations?

One of the main ideas to come out of the peace talks at the end of the Great War was the idea of 'self-determination'. This was the belief that races who had lived under foreign rule for a long time – such as Czechs living under Austrian rule or Poles living in Russian territory – should be able to form their own nations and vote for their own leaders. The Paris Peace Conference, then, didn't just hand out punishments to defeated countries; it set up new nations by taking land from the losers and granting 'self-determination' to millions of Czechs, Poles, Slovaks, Serbs and many more! So how did they do it … and how did this affect the shape of Europe?

Turkey

- Turkey also had to pay money for war damages and cuts in its armed forces were imposed.
- Turkey lost most of its European land (to Greece and Italy).
- Other parts of the Turkish Empire – Syria, Palestine, Jordan and Iraq, for example – became British or French **mandates**. This means they were controlled by Britain and France until they were ready to rule themselves.
- Arabia became an independent nation.

NOTE: Turkey's punishment was known as the Treaty of Sèvres. In fact, the Turks hated the punishments so much they rebelled against its terms. Rather than get involved in a long fight with the rebels, the allies agreed to change it. In 1923, a new deal (called the Treaty of Lausanne) gave some land back to Turkey (from Greece), cancelled its reparations and said that Turkey could have as big an army as they wanted!

Austria–Hungary

- Austria and Hungary became separate, small independent countries.
- Both countries had to pay reparations for war damage and reduce their weapons and armed forces.
- Small areas of land were given to Italy.
- Croatia, Bosnia and Herzegovina were given to Serbia. This new larger nation was called Yugoslavia.
- Land was given to create the new state of Czechoslovakia.
- Land was given to the new state of Poland (which also received land from Russia and Germany).

NOTE: Austria's punishments were called the Treaty of St Germain and Hungary's as the Treaty of Trianon.

Bulgaria

- Bulgaria had to pay money for war damage and reduce its weapons and armed forces.
- Land was given to the new state of Yugoslavia.
- Bulgaria also lost some land to Greece.

NOTE: Bulgaria's punishments were known as the Treaty of Neuilly.

FACT *Russia*

The Russians weren't at the peace talks – but the peace deals still affected their country. As you know, Russia surrendered to Germany in 1917 – and Germany took a lot of Russian land. The peace deals at the end of the war gave Russia back most of the land – but not all of it. Finland, Estonia, Latvia and Lithuania (formally part of Russia) became independent states, part of southern Russia was given to Romania and some territory was given to form the new state of Poland.

Source A ▾ *Europe in 1914. Note the great empires of Austria–Hungary and Turkey (also known as the Ottoman Empire). Also, see that countries such as Czechoslovakia and Poland simply didn't exist.*

Source B ▾ *Europe after the Treaties of Versailles, St Germain, Trianon, Neuilly and Sèvres.*

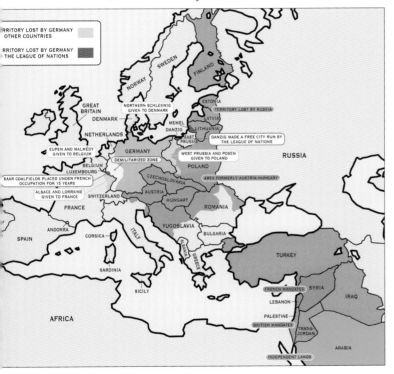

Source C ▾ *From the diary of Jules Cambon, a French diplomat at the peace talks in 1919.*

"In those parts of Eastern Europe where nationalities are mixed, finding a frontier that doesn't offend some feeling or interest is like trying to square a circle. What seeds of hatred are we solving on devastated soil?"

Source D ▾ *A modern historian commenting on the consequences of the peace deals (Peter Moss, History Alive, 1967, Hart-Davis Educational).*

"Poland was created from the Polish-speaking parts of Russia and Germany, and by other treaties Czechoslovakia and Yugoslavia were formed from land formerly belonging to Austria and Hungary. The vast majority of the inhabitants of these 'new' countries were Poles or Czechs or Slovaks or Serbs as the case might be, but as for the sake of convenience and defence, the frontiers of the states had to follow a river or a number of mountains, so sometimes a small number of German-speaking people had to be included. It was impossible, for example, to make sure that every person living in Czechoslovakia was a Czech or a Slovak, and these 'minority' groups of Germans disliked being under the rule of another government which spoke a different language and had different customs … a few years later, the Nazis accused the Polish and Czech governments of ill-treating the German inhabitants, and this made an excuse for taking back part of the land they had lost. This was one of the main causes of World War II."

WISE UP WORD

- mandates

WORK

1   **a**   In your own words, summarise what happened to Austria–Hungary, Turkey and Bulgaria after the Great War?

    b   What do you think would be the reaction of people in these countries to the terms of the Treaties?

2   **a**   What was meant by the term 'self determination'?

    b   Give three examples of 'self-determination' in the Paris Peace Treaties.

    c   What, according to **Sources C** and **D**, were some of the problems associated with giving people 'self-determination'?

Democracy and dictatorship

AIMS

- to understand the difference between a democracy and a dictatorship;
- try to remember the main features of each.

No two countries are run in the same way. The United States of America is run differently from France, which, in turn, is run differently from Britain. Laws are different (so are punishments, for example the death penalty); education, health care and political parties vary – even the side of the road upon which a car can be driven can change from one nation to the next. These differences have been in place for many years; they evolve over time leaving a situation where, today, we have hundreds of countries run in hundreds of different ways.

Despite these differences, it is possible to put most countries into one of two categories – **democracies** or **dictatorships**.

It was possible to do this in the 1920s and 1930s too. In fact, the disagreements and arguments about how governments should be organised spilled over into war – another one!

In order to clearly understand your studies on the build-up to another world war – World War II – it is important to know the main features of both a democracy and a dictatorship.

Type of government
DEMOCRACY

Origins Originally started in Ancient Greece. Developed gradually over hundreds of years, mainly in Europe and America.

Beliefs Ordinary people have a say in how their country is governed. They vote in regular elections in which there are several political parties to choose from. The people are represented by the organisations they elect – for example Parliament or councils.

Comments The people have a number of 'freedoms' or rights:

Freedom of speech (the right to say what you think)

Freedom of information (the right to read, listen to and watch what you want)

Freedom of belief (the right to follow any religion)

Freedom in law (the right to a fair trial – if arrested, 'you have a right to remain silent' too!)

Freedom of association (the right to join or form a political party, join a trade union or any other organisation – even the Boy Scouts!)

Examples from the 1920s and 1930s Britain, France and the USA

At the end of the Great War, many people hoped that democracy would spread to most countries of the world. In fact, many countries *did* introduce a democratic system when the war ended. Sadly, though, some countries were in such a mess after the war (and remained that way), that their newly elected politicians didn't seem to have any solutions to their problems. More and more countries listened to people who promised to make their lives better and their nations great again … at a cost – DICTATORSHIP. Amazingly, over 30 countries became dictatorships between 1919 and 1939. Unfortunately, some of these dictators would bring about another world war.

Two types of dictatorship

Powerful nations such as the USA, France and Britain were democratic countries in the 1920s and 1930s (they still are!). However, people in some other nations rejected democracy and turned to dictatorship instead. Some countries, such as Italy, had Fascist dictatorships, while the USSR (previously Russia) had a Communist dictatorship.

These next two pages aim to examine the ideas behind **Fascism** and **Communism** and show examples of each in action. You should look for similarities between these two types of dictatorship ... and the major differences too.

Type of government

DICTATORSHIP

Origins For thousands of years, some men have tried to totally control others. The controllers are usually backed up by large numbers of supporters and lots of weapons.

Beliefs Ordinary people have no say in how their country is run. There are no regular elections because the country is run by one political party or one man – the dictator (usually helped by his 'friends' and his army).

Comments People have very few 'freedoms' or rights:
There is no free speech. If they criticise their leaders, they are likely to be arrested.
There is no freedom of information – the dictator controls the newspapers, books, magazines, films and so on.
Not all religions are allowed – if any!
There is no legal freedom – the police can arrest whom they want, when they want and keep them in jail without trial.
People can only join groups or associations allowed by the dictatorship.

Examples from the 1920s and 1930s Italy, Spain, USSR (Russia) and Nazi Germany

NO ELECTIONS (this year or any other)

Signed: *The Dictator*

> **WISE UP WORDS**
> - democracies
>   dictatorships   dictator
>   Fascism   Communism

A COMMUNIST DICTATORSHIP

CASE STUDY 1: THE USSR

Communism is a theory. It is a set of ideas about a particular way to run a country. It was dreamed up by Karl Marx, a German living in London, in the 1840s. He wrote a book about his theory (*The Communist Manifesto*) ... and it turned into a best-seller.

Marx wrote that, in a Communist country, everyone would be equal (men *and* women) and everything would be shared. There would be no different classes and no great differences of wealth. There would be no private property and the government would run farms, factories and businesses for the benefit of all people. There wouldn't be any need for money or laws because everyone would live a simple life, sharing all they had with everyone else. One day, Marx hoped the whole world would be Communist. Not surprisingly, many poor, ordinary workers were attracted to this theory.

Then in Russia, in 1917, a group of Communists, led by a man named Lenin, managed to take over the country after a revolution. But the Communists in Russia ran the country as a dictatorship – they *forced* people to be equal and to share.

No other political parties were allowed to exist, only the Communist Party. Newspapers, books, films and radio broadcasts were all controlled by the Communists. Any person who spoke out against this was an 'enemy of the state' and sent to prison (or executed). Millions of people 'disappeared' in Communist Russia.

Nobody was allowed to have any open religious beliefs. Only the Communist way of life was to be worshipped. All work, housing, health care and education was controlled by the Communists. Jobs, houses, hospitals and schools were provided for all Russians. The state owned everything ... and provided for everyone.

As the years passed, fear of Communism in most other countries grew and grew, and Russia became more and more isolated.

Source A ▶
The Communist flag. The hammer and sickle (a tool used on a farm) was part of the new Communist flag to symbolise the unity between factory workers and farmers. Red is the traditional communist colour. In the 1920s, Russia officially changed its name to the USSR – the Union of Soviet (councils of workers) Socialist (Communist) Republic (country with no king).

Source B ▶ *Mussolini, Italy's Fascist leader, mounted huge displays, with uniforms and special salutes. Here he is pictured after a speech that encouraged university students to join the army. The words mean 'believe', 'obey' and 'fight'. Mussolini once said, 'A minute of the battlefield is worth a life time of peace ... better to live one day like a lion than a hundred years like a sheep'.*

CREDERE   OBBEDIRE COMBATTERE

A FASCIST DICTATORSHIP

CASE STUDY 2: ITALY

By 1919, Italy was in a bit of a mess – one in ten Italians was unemployed, food prices were high and riots were common.

Increasingly, Italians turned to a young politician called Benito Mussolini, an ex-soldier and teacher! Mussolini promised to bring discipline back to Italy ... at a price! He called his theory 'Fascism' and formed the Fascist Party in 1919.

The basic idea of Fascism was that the government should control the whole of a person's life (that's right, it's another type of dictatorship!). The government controls education, newspapers, films and radio, even sport. People are still free to run their own businesses and make money, but there are tight controls on the workers – they can't go on strike, for example. In return, Mussolini and his Fascist Party would 'look after' Italy. They would build roads and railways, which would give people jobs. Poor people would be given money to help them find work and the army would be increased in size in order to protect Italy's borders. The Fascists would aim to make Italy great again and among the elite nations of the world. To a Fascist, the theory of Communism was wrong: all people were *not* equal. Some were better than others. According to the Fascists, men were better than women; some races and nations better than others.

By 1922, Mussolini announced he was marching to Rome to take over. His supporters, all dressed in black uniforms, marched with him. The King of Italy gave in and made Mussolini Italy's new Prime Minister. Italy was now a dictatorship – Mussolini made all the laws; opposition to him was forbidden and opponents were beaten up or murdered.

By 1923, Mussolini's efforts to restore Italy had attracted the attention of a 34 year old up-and-coming politician who was living in Germany. His name was Adolf Hitler. Perhaps Mussolini's ideas could work in Germany too!

Source C ▶

Italy's Fascist flag. The symbol in the centre is called a 'fasces'. The bundle of sticks represented strength in number, unity and law – the axe symbolised power!

WORK

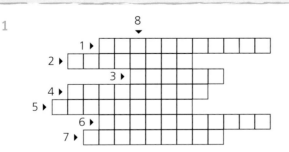

CLUES:

1 The freedom to read, listen and watch what you want.

2 In complete control of the country.

3 The freedom to say what you want.

4 Ordinary people have a say how their country is run.

5 Where votes are counted for several political parties.

6 The freedom to join or form a political party.

7 A type of dictatorship.

Now read down the puzzle (clue 8). Write a sentence or two to explain this word.

2 Work with a partner. One must choose to describe a dictatorship, the other a democracy. Using only ten words each, explain to your partner the political system you have chosen.
  • Use drawings to help you.
  • Perhaps you could mime some of the features of your system.

What was the League of Nations?

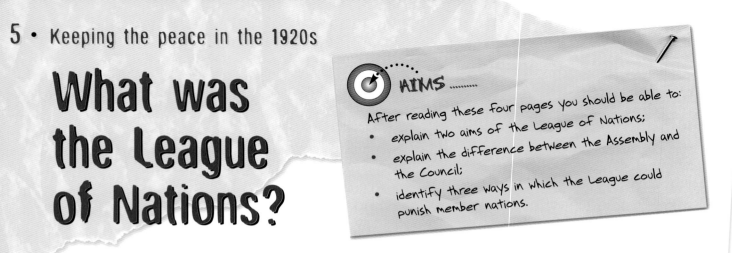

AIMS

After reading these four pages you should be able to:
- explain two aims of the League of Nations;
- explain the difference between the Assembly and the Council;
- identify three ways in which the League could punish member nations.

After the horrors of the Great War, the world's leaders realised they needed a peace that would last. The losing countries had been punished, but how were arguments going to be settled in the future?

One very good idea to come from the peace talks at the end of the Great War was something called the 'League of Nations'. It was USA President Woodrow Wilson's idea – and if he were around today to take part in an interview, he might answer questions about it like this ...

Q: So what exactly is this 'League of Nations'?

WW: The League of Nations is a kind of international club with its headquarters in Geneva, Switzerland. About 40 countries have joined up straight away, each agreeing that if one member country has a quarrel with another, they will send representatives to the League to try to settle the quarrel by discussion instead of going to war.

Q: You say that each country has agreed to talk instead of fight. Have they actually signed something to agree to this?

WW: Absolutely. The opening page of our 'rule book' – known as our **covenant** – states that all members of the League:
- promise not to go to war;
- agree to open and honest discussions;
- agree to act by international law;
- agree to respect all treaties and peace deals signed after the war;
- must sign this covenant!

Q: So is solving international disputes your only aim?

WW: Not at all. Although the main aim is to keep the peace, the League will also try to help out in other ways. The International Court sorts out shipping, fishing and border disputes, while the special commissions try to do good work such as freeing slaves, stopping the drug trade in opium and improving working conditions in less advanced countries. Our health programmes are already working on ways to wipe out killer diseases such as typhus and leprosy. The League aims to help out refugees made homeless by the war too and encourages countries to get rid of their weapons (disarm).

Q: It sounds like quite a complicated structure.

WW: I wouldn't say it is complicated – there's just a lot to do. This diagram might simplify things for you [see **Source A**].

Q: So what if a country breaks your rules?

WW: We have three main powers to make countries do what we want them to do. I like to call them the 'Three Ss'.

- Shame – the League would publicly criticise the aggressive country attacking the other nation. Hopefully, the shame of being openly criticised by the League will make them stop.
- Sanctions – if 'shame' doesn't work, we can impose sanctions. This means that all member countries would be urged to stop trading with the aggressive country until a lack of supplies brought the fighting to an end.
- Soldiers – our final punishment would be to send in troops to stop the aggressive country by force. The

League hasn't got its own army so would use soldiers from a selection of member countries. The theory behind all this is what we call **collective security**. This means that if we stick together, the nations of the world will be safer – the idea of 'safety in numbers' really!

Q: So which nations belong to the League?

WW: The first meeting was held in a Swiss hotel and 42 nations were represented. A big, new, permanent meeting place, specially designed for peacemaking, will be built soon in Geneva, Switzerland. Some of the most powerful countries in the world attended that first meeting – Britain, France, Italy and Japan – as well as some of the smaller nations such as Belgium and Holland. The losing nations in the Great War – Germany, Austria and so on – weren't allowed to join and neither was Russia because we don't recognise their new Communist government yet.

Source A ▼ *The structure of the League of Nations.*

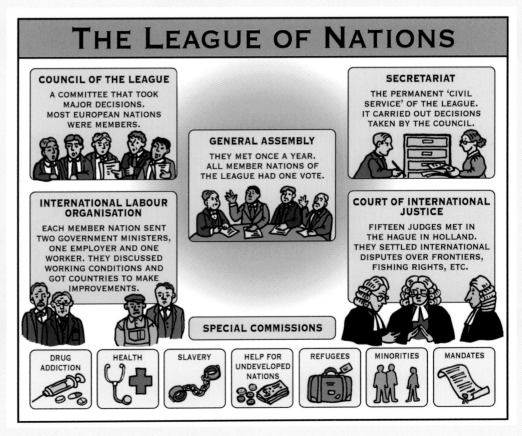

- The League doesn't have its own army – so can't force countries to stop fighting.
- Not all countries are members. The fact that three important nations – the USA, Russia and Germany – either didn't join or were not allowed to join straight away makes it look like a 'League of Some Nations' rather than a 'League of Nations'! And will France and Britain be *really* interested in the problems of the world – or just problems that affect them?
- The way the League actually works has a bit of a weakness too. The Assembly only meets once a year and every decision taken has to be agreed by all nations – this means that making decisions could be a very slow process!

Q: So the League of Nations then – what are your hopes … and fears?

WW: Silly question really! I obviously hope it changes things, that it helps preserve world peace and stops another horror conflict such as the Great War. I hope too that it can be a force for making the world a safer, healthier, more democratic place. My fears are obvious too. I hope that the League doesn't just become an organisation where a lot of talking takes place – and not a lot of action!

Q: I didn't hear the USA in that list of founder countries. Has your country joined?

WW: We aren't going to join! My idea – and my nation isn't part of it. I just couldn't get the rest of America to share in my enthusiasm for the League. The US Congress, our Parliament, voted against us joining – we just didn't want to get involved in sorting out problems for other countries. We call this **isolationism** – a policy that means we isolate ourselves from the world and look after ourselves.

Q: But after Europe has battered itself to bits fighting a war, the USA has emerged as the world's most powerful country. This is a real setback!

WW: I totally agree. The League needs America's money, troops and raw materials so that it can work properly and be a *real* threat to aggressive nations.

Q: So how powerful is the League … really?

WW: This is a difficult question to answer. There is a real will among the people of the world for this to work – but there are certainly some weaknesses right from the start.

Source B ▶ *A cartoon commenting on America's refusal to join the League of Nations. What is the message of the cartoon?*

Source C ▼ *Quote from the French Ambassador to London between 1920 and 1924.*

> "A cloud of tiny states does not equal in value one great power absent from the League."

Source D ▼ *A cartoon commenting on the fact that the League had no army to enforce its decision.*

WISE UP WORDS

• collective security   covenant   isolationism

FACT *Who joined?*

At first, none of the losing nations in the Great War were allowed to join – and neither was Russia. There were 42 founder members – rising to 54 by 1923, including Austria, Hungary and Bulgaria. Germany was allowed to join in 1926 and Russia joined in 1934.

WORK

1 What was the covenant of the League of Nations?

2 What were the League's aims?

3 Why do you think there are so many different organisations within the League?

4 You are a publicist for the League of Nations in 1920. Draw up a poster or a leaflet that could be sent out to ordinary citizens. Your work should include:
   • an explanation of how the League worked
   • the advantages of joining the League.

5 Why was it a weakness of the League that the USA, Russia and Germany were not part of the League when it started?

6 Look at **Source B**:
   a Which country is not a member of the League, according to the cartoonist?
   b Why do you think the cartoonist calls this country the 'keystone'?

7 Look at **Source D**: do you think this cartoon is supportive or critical of the League of Nations? Explain your answer.

How successful was the League of Nations in the 1920s?

⊙ AIMS ....

Your aims should be to:
- describe one success of the League and explain why it was successful;
- describe one failure and explain why it was a failure.

The main aim of the League of Nations when it was set up in 1920 was to keep the peace between nations by getting them to work together on solving international problems. During the 1920s, the League of Nations became involved in trying to settle a number of international disputes. Several of these quarrels are detailed in **Source A**.

Source A ▶ Some of the disputes the League of Nations tried to settle.

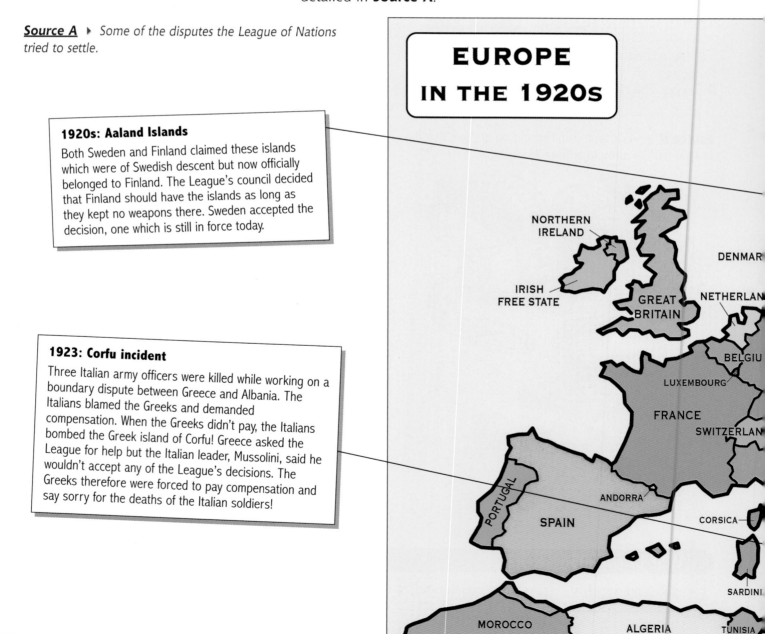

1920s: Aaland Islands

Both Sweden and Finland claimed these islands which were of Swedish descent but now officially belonged to Finland. The League's council decided that Finland should have the islands as long as they kept no weapons there. Sweden accepted the decision, one which is still in force today.

1923: Corfu incident

Three Italian army officers were killed while working on a boundary dispute between Greece and Albania. The Italians blamed the Greeks and demanded compensation. When the Greeks didn't pay, the Italians bombed the Greek island of Corfu! Greece asked the League for help but the Italian leader, Mussolini, said he wouldn't accept any of the League's decisions. The Greeks therefore were forced to pay compensation and say sorry for the deaths of the Italian soldiers!

EUROPE IN THE 1920s

1923: Memel

Memel, on the coast of Lithuania, was under control of the League of Nations. Most people who lived in and around the port were Lithuanian and the Lithuanian army invaded the area in 1923. The League agreed to give the port over to Lithuanian control as long it became an 'international zone' where ships of all nations were free to come and go.

1920–23: Vilna

Both Poland and Lithuania wanted control of the town of Vilna. The city itself was in the new country of Lithuania but most of its population was Polish. In 1920, the Polish army seized Vilna so Lithuania asked the League for help. The League was not keen to get involved because the two most powerful nations in the League, Britain and France, wanted to stay friendly with Poland as they saw Poland to be a strong barrier between Russia and Germany. The League did nothing in the end and Poland kept control of Vilna.

1921: Upper Silesia

Both Germany and the new country of Poland wanted control of this rich, industrial area full of mines and factories. Over one million people lived there — 700 000 had voted to be part of Germany and 500 000 voted to be part of Poland! The League decided to split the area between the two nations. Germany received over half the land and population, but the Poles had most of the factories. The Germans weren't happy with the decision but had no choice to accept the decision.

1925: Greece–Bulgarian dispute

Following a Greek invasion of Bulgaria, the League ordered both armies to stop fighting. An investigation blamed Greece for starting the war and it accepted the League's decision. This was seen as a great success for the league.

As you can see, the League dealt with several important disputes in the 1920s. In some cases, the League achieved great success – but, in others, it was made to look weak and powerless. The League's special agencies or commissions worked hard too. For example, the Commission for Refugees found homes for half a million former prisoners of war between 1920 and 1922 while the League's Health Organisation worked effectively to prevent the spread of disease.

As well as joining the League of Nations, a number of countries signed open peace pacts and deals with each other. Remember, though, that the League played no part in helping countries reach these agreements.

International relations with Germany began to ease when they signed the Dawes Plan in 1924. This deal said that Germany had longer to pay their war damage payments to the winning nations. Germany also borrowed money from the USA to help with the payments. In 1929, the Young Plan reduced the total amount Germany had to pay altogether. Germany was allowed to join the League of Nations in 1926. Progress was also made in relation to disarmament: 60 countries agreed to meet in Geneva in 1932 for a Disarmament Conference.

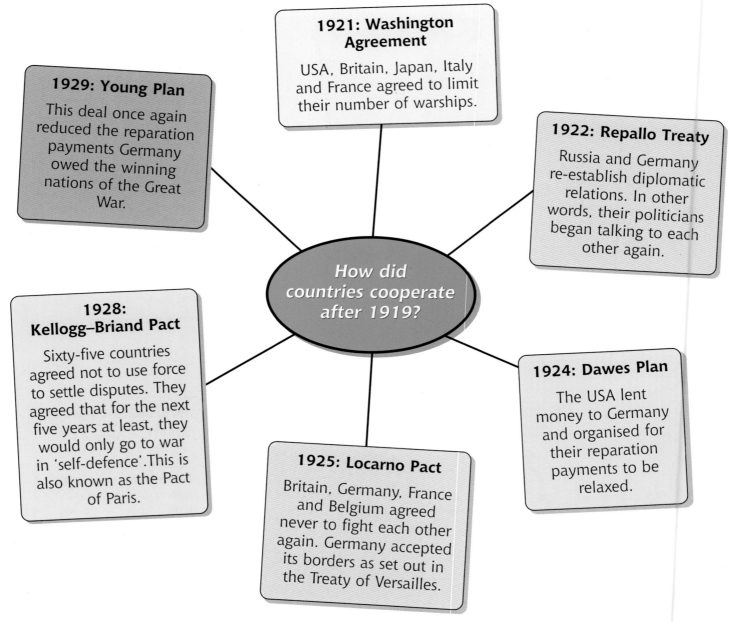

1921: Washington Agreement

USA, Britain, Japan, Italy and France agreed to limit their number of warships.

1929: Young Plan

This deal once again reduced the reparation payments Germany owed the winning nations of the Great War.

1922: Repallo Treaty

Russia and Germany re-establish diplomatic relations. In other words, their politicians began talking to each other again.

How did countries cooperate after 1919?

1928: Kellogg–Briand Pact

Sixty-five countries agreed not to use force to settle disputes. They agreed that for the next five years at least, they would only go to war in 'self-defence'. This is also known as the Pact of Paris.

1924: Dawes Plan

The USA lent money to Germany and organised for their reparation payments to be relaxed.

1925: Locarno Pact

Britain, Germany, France and Belgium agreed never to fight each other again. Germany accepted its borders as set out in the Treaty of Versailles.

Source B ▸

A cartoon about the Greece–Bulgarian dispute, 1925.

BALKANDUM AND BALKANDEE.

"JUST THEN CAME DOWN A MONSTROUS DOVE
WHOSE FORCE WAS PURELY MORAL,
WHICH TURNED THE HEROES' HEARTS TO LOVE
AND MADE THEM DROP THEIR QUARREL."—*Lewis Carroll (adapted).*

WORK

1 Read the following statements about the success of the League of Nations in the 1920s:

"The League's record as a peace-keeping body in the 1920s wasn't very impressive."

"The League could solve small issues, but in any major crisis involving powerful countries, it found itself ignored."

Which of these interpretations do you think is the most accurate? Give at least three reasons for your choice.

2 Choose one of the disputes that the League failed to settle. Try to suggest ways in which the League could have done better.

3 Look at **Source B**.

a About what dispute is the cartoon commenting on?

b What impression of the League does this cartoon give you?

Think carefully what was important about:

i the Washington Agreement of 1921

ii the Locarno Pact of 1925

iii the Kellogg–Briand Pact of 1928.

Why did the League of Nations fail in the 1930s?

The League of Nations, set up after the Great War as a way for countries to settle their quarrels peacefully, had some serious weaknesses right from the start. To begin with, fewer than half the nations of the world belonged to the League – so it hardly represented the *whole* world. And secondly, the League had no army to enforce its decisions – so any nation wishing to defy it could do so without fear! One historian even described the League of Nations as a 'toothless dog' – it could make a lot of noise, but didn't have any bite!

Despite these weaknesses, the League had some major successes in its first ten years. But it had some failures too. Even today, historians still argue about how successful the League was in the 1920s. However, they all agree that, in the 1930s, the League of Nations was a total failure (it must have been – World War II started in 1939!).

So what factors led to the failure of the world's first international peacekeeping organisation?

There is no single reason why the League of Nations failed in the 1930s. Like most major events, a number of factors combined to cause its downfall. Some factors were *more important* than others; some factors *led* to others or were *causes* or *consequences* of each event. A good historian is able to spot the links between factors and understand how they work together.

The three key factors that led to the failure of the League in the 1930s were:

- the effects of the Great Depression;
- the aggressive actions of some of the great powers;
- the failure of disarmament.

Study each factor carefully.

FACTOR 1: THE EFFECTS OF THE GREAT DEPRESSION

In the 1920s, world trade was dominated by the USA (it still is today really!). It was the richest country in the world and lent money to lots of countries to help them after the Great War. America lent millions and millions of dollars, to Germany in particular. America's massive population brought millions of goods from all over the world too. They brought expensive silk shirts from Japan, beautiful clothing and cars from Italy and all the latest electrical goods from Germany. These goods travelled around in British- and German-made cargo ships and most politicians agreed that world trade was good for world peace. After all, countries were less likely to fight if they traded with each other!

But, by 1929, America found itself in serious financial trouble:

- Thousands of banks and businesses went bust.
- Millions of American workers lost their jobs.

Now Americans couldn't afford to buy as many foreign goods as before. Soon factories all over Europe – in Italy, Japan, Britain and France, for example – had to close down. Unemployment shot up in all these countries too, as factory after factory closed when countries stopped trading with each other. This sudden slump in world trade is known as the Great Depression. In Britain, three million workers lost their jobs – in Germany, unemployment reached six million!

Source A ▾ *The effects of the Great Depression.*

Germany was one of the worst hit nations in the Depression. There was mass unemployment and poverty — and German politicians seemed unable to help. This changed the way Germans thought and behaved. They started supporting political parties that promised jobs if they were elected. In 1933, Germans elected Adolf Hitler and the Nazis as their leader. He had promised to restore Germany both at home and abroad. This was bad news for the League of Nations. Hitler openly talked about how much he hated it and promised to invade countries to get back all the land Germany lost after the Great War!

Great Britain was one of the great powers within the League of Nations. But with unemployment so high, the British government was unwilling to get involved in international problems while Britain itself was in trouble. They didn't want to spend money and use valuable resources sending troops to far away places when people in Britain were suffering!

The **French** government, worried about the situation in Germany with Hitler and the Nazis, began building a series of border defences against Germany. They began to build up their armed forces too — hardly the spirit of 'international cooperation', was it?

The **USA** wasn't in the League but could help out by not selling goods to aggressive countries if they invaded others. But the US government was unwilling to stop trading with nations — aggressive or not — while their own economy was in such a mess.

In **Italy**, another leading League of Nations power, their leader (Mussolini) hoped to invade other countries and build an overseas empire in order to take people's minds off the economic difficulties in Italy. Mussolini hoped that if Italy looked like a powerful and expanding nation, then ordinary Italians might be distracted from the problems their government faced!

Japan, a leading power in the League, was in trouble too. Unemployment was high and factories closed. No one was buying one of their main exports — silk — anymore. Japan's leaders, who were all army generals, decided to take over countries and steal their raw materials to use and sell. Clearly, Japan wouldn't be allowed to stay in the League long if they did this!

To make matters worse, American banks demanded all the money back they had lent to foreign countries. Thousands more businesses collapsed because they had no money to keep them going. Soon, people were living on the streets – cold, hungry … and angry!

So what has the Great Depression got to do with the failure of the League of Nations?

To put it simply, the Great Depression altered the way countries felt about themselves … and each other. The spirit of goodwill and optimism of the 1920s disappeared as countries began to 'look after themselves' in the 'hungry thirties'. The League was based on the idea of international cooperation – but, as a result of the slump, relations between countries worsened as trade dropped – and important political change took place within certain nations that threatened world peace. **Source A** demonstrates the effects of the Great Depression on six key countries – and shows how this slump in world trade harmed the work of the League.

Source B ▾ *A modern historian.*

"Voters blamed their government for unemployment and supported parties which promised jobs. As a result, new governments came to power in more than twenty countries. In many of the countries, the new leaders who took control became dictators … the spread of dictatorship was a threat to world peace because some of these dictators started acting aggressively towards other countries. They did so in an attempt to improve the situation in their own countries."

Source C ▾ *A cartoon by David Low, 1933. What is the message of this famous cartoon?*

THE DOORMAT.

FACTOR 2: THE AGGRESSIVE ACTION OF SOME OF THE GREAT POWERS

The countries that acted most aggressively during the Great Depression were Japan, Italy and Germany. So what motivated the politicians in these nations to attack others – and what did the League of Nations do to stop them?

Japan invades China

Source D ▾ *B. Catchpole,* A Map History of the Modern World, *1982.*

"The Manchurian affair showed that the League of Nations could not keep world peace."

Japan was badly hit by the Great Depression. No one was buying one of its main exports – silk – because people around the world just couldn't afford this luxury fabric. As a result, hundreds of factories shut down and millions were close to starvation. The Japanese government seemed unable to do anything about these problems, so the army generals came up with an extreme solution – they would invade foreign lands, take their raw materials and sell them! They could also force the people in the newly conquered land to buy Japanese-made goods!

In 1931, the Japanese army invaded the Chinese province of Manchuria. The army hadn't told the Japanese government about this but it soon realised that Manchuria's coal and iron ore were a rich prize.

China asked the League of Nations to do something about Japan's aggression … so they sent an enquiry team to investigate. A year later, the team presented its report (known as the Lytton Report). They concluded that Japan was in the wrong and asked them to leave Manchuria. The Japanese ignored the request and resigned from the League. Japan then continued with its invasion of China.

The message of this failure was clear – the League was powerless to control aggressive countries!

Italy invades Ethiopia

The Italian leader, Mussolini, wanted Italy to have a big empire, just like the ancient Romans. This, he believed, would bring him personal glory. He was also keen to take people's minds off the Great Depression hitting Italy.

Mussolini's biggest target was Ethiopia (then called Abyssinia), a country wedged between two Italian colonies in East Africa … and an area with fertile land and some rich raw materials. In 1935, the Italians attacked with the full force of the Italian air force and army. There was little the Ethiopian tribesmen could do in defence of a modern European invasion force armed with tanks, machine guns, flamethrowers and poison gas.

Haile Selassie, the Ethiopian Emperor, asked the League for help. The League immediately asked all its members to stop trading with Italy; the aim was to stop the Italian army by starving them of oil, food and weapons. But the economic sanctions didn't work. The USA, then the world's largest oil producer, didn't belong to the League, so carried on selling oil to Italy.

The British Foreign Secretary even worked out a deal with the French for dividing up Ethiopia (the Hoare–Laval Pact) which gave two-thirds of Ethiopia to the Italians, leaving the remainder for Haile Selassie. When news got out of this 'deal', there was a massive outcry and the two politicians were forced to resign. The Pact was dropped but the damage was done – two major powers, Britain and France, had been prepared to act outside of the League if it suited their own interests. Indeed, Britain and France had clearly demonstrated that they were keen to stay friendly with Mussolini – perhaps seeing him as a future ally against the threat of Hitler's Germany.

Italy resigned from the League and continued with its Ethiopian invasion. They had conquered the whole country by the end of 1936. Again, the message to other countries of the League's failure was clear – it was weak and didn't have the power or support to stop countries attacking others.

Source E ▾ *From* Punch *magazine.*

THE AWFUL WARNING.

FRANCE AND ENGLAND
(together ?).

"WE DON'T WANT YOU TO FIGHT,
BUT, BY JINGO, IF YOU DO,
WE SHALL PROBABLY ISSUE A JOINT MEMORANDUM
SUGGESTING A MILD DISAPPROVAL OF YOU."

Source F ▾ *A speech by Haile Selassie to the League of Nations, 1936.*

"I, Haile Selassie, Emperor, am here today to claim that justice which is due to my people and the assistance promised eight months ago when 50 nations asserted that aggression had been committed. I assert that the problem submitted to the assembly is a much wider one than the removal of sanctions. It is the very existence of the League of Nations. It is the value of promises made to small states that their integrity and Independence will be respected and ensured. God and History will remember your judgements."

Source G ▾ *Written by historian A. J. P. Taylor, 1966.*

"The real death of the League was in 1935. One day it was a powerful body imposing sanctions; the next day, it was an empty sham with everyone running from it as quickly as possible. Hitler watched."

Germany rearms

One of Hitler's first moves when he became German leader was to resign from the League of Nations. He hated the Treaty of Versailles (obviously – because it punished Germany so severely) and felt the League was tied to it. After all, one of the League's aims was to make sure Germany stuck to all the punishments made in the Treaty of Versailles!

Between 1933 and 1935, Hitler began to rearm Germany on a massive scale. He built over 2000 fighter planes, constructed dozens of new battleships and recruited over half a million soldiers. And all this was forbidden by the Treaty of Versailles.

So what did the League of Nations do about Germany's blatant disregard for the Treaty of Versailles? Absolutely nothing!

Source H ▾ *A German postcard produced in 1935. The aim of this postcard was to persuade people that it was unfair that Germany was not allowed to build up its armed forces but all other countries around them were. Do you think Hitler had a point? The orange area around the River Rhine was the part where no German troops were allowed at all.*

Germany's Disarmament and the Armament of her Neighbours

FACTOR 3: THE FAILURE OF DISARMAMENT

One of the main aims of the League of Nations was to encourage countries to get rid of their weapons. They failed to do this in the 1920s.

It seemed that no country wanted to even think about being the first to disarm – as this would leave them open for invasion!

The League (after five years of planning) eventually held a Disarmament Conference in Geneva in 1932. It was a disaster!

Countries just couldn't agree with each other on lots of key issues. For example, the bombing of civilians was banned but the planes capable of carrying out the bombings were still permitted. Also, the proposal to ban the making of chemical weapons was defeated. That's right, the Disarmament Conference couldn't get chemical weapons banned!

But bigger arguments surrounded what to do about Germany. For years, the Germans had said it was unfair that they had been the only major power forced to disarm after the Great War. The Germans wanted 'equality' – either let them build up their weapons to match other countries, or reduce other nation's armies to their size! When no clear agreement was reached, Adolf Hitler (Germany's new leader) walked out of the Conference. The next year, in 1933, Hitler withdrew Germany from the League itself … and back home in Germany, Hitler secretly began building up a massive army, navy and air force!

Source I ▾ *Poland's former Prime Minister, Padorevski, on his way to the Disarmament Conference in 1933.*

> "The problem with disarmament is that it is a very good idea – but everyone expects the other fellow to disarm first, but is not prepared to do it himself."

Source J ▾ *A cartoon from May 1934. What do you think it is supposed to mean?*

"MY FRIENDS, WE HAVE FAILED. WE JUST COULDN'T CONTROL YOUR WARLIKE PASSIONS."

DISARMAMENT CONFERENCE

COMMON PEOPLE OF THE WORLD

THE CONFERENCE EXCUSES ITSELF.

WORK

1 **a** What was the Great Depression?
   b In your own words, explain how the Great Depression made the work of the League of Nations more difficult.

2 Look at **Source C**.
   a What criticisms is the cartoonist making of: i) Japan; ii) the League?
   b Do you think that the cartoon would be equally appropriate if the figure of Mussolini was chosen instead of a figure representing Japan? Explain your answer.

3 Mussolini, Italy's leader in the 1920s and 1930s, once said, "The League is alright when sparrows quarrel: it fails when eagles fall out." What do you think that meant?

4 Look at **Source E**. What point is the cartoonist making about the powers of the League?

5 Why do you think the League imposed sanctions against Italy in 1935 but not against Japan in 1935?

6 Look at **Source H**.
   a In your own words, explain the point being made by the postcard.
   b Judging by what you have studied so far, do you think the point was a fair one?

7 The following were all **equally important** reasons for the failure of the League of Nations as a peace-keeping organisation:
   i   the USA's refusal to join
   ii the consequences of the Great Depression
   iii the aggressive actions of Germany, Italy and Japan.

   Do you agree with this statement? Explain your answer referring to i), ii) and iii).

Germany and the Great War

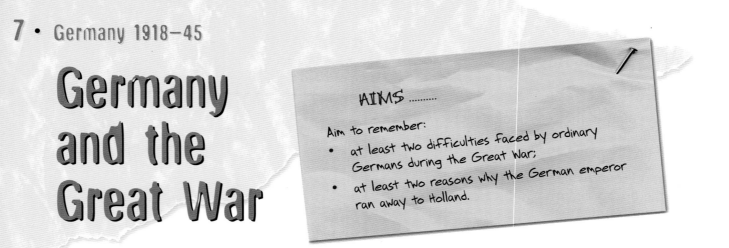

AIMS ....

Aim to remember:
- at least two difficulties faced by ordinary Germans during the Great War;
- at least two reasons why the German emperor ran away to Holland.

What were conditions really like in Germany during the war? How did these problems lead to revolution? And why exactly did the Great War end at 11:00am on 11 November 1918?

It did not take long for people in Germany to start suffering during the war. The British had a huge navy and decided to use it to stop supply ships getting to Germany throughout the war. If a ship taking food into Germany was spotted by a British ship, it would be asked to turn around … or be blown up! As a result, there were terrible food shortages in Germany from as early as 1915 (see **Source A**).

Source A ▼ *A description of conditions in Germany.*

" … the average adult German was living on 1000 calories a day — half the amount needed for a normal healthy diet. Coal was running short and, because gas and electricity were made from coal, there were power cuts as well. In many cities, all public buildings, cinemas and theatres were closed down. Lights in apartment blocks were put out early."

FACT *'flu*

During 1918, a killer virus called Spanish Influenza (or 'flu) swept across Europe. It killed an estimated 30 million people in total. In Germany, the years of hunger and dirt (there were shortages of soap and washing powder too) took their toll – nearly half a million German civilians and 200 000 German soldiers died in the summer of 1918.

As the war continued, there were demands in Germany for peace. In 1915, 500 women collected in front of the Reichstag (Parliament) buildings and said that they wanted their men back from the trenches. A year later, 10 000 workers assembled in Berlin's city centre to shout 'Down with war, down with the government'. The police quickly moved in to make arrests!

By the beginning of 1918, Germany was close to collapse. Early protests against food shortages by some had turned into a complete refusal to support the war at all by many. Even some soldiers had refused to fight! In August 1918, as Germany entered its fourth year of war, it seemed as if most German citizens were desperate for the war to end.

In October 1918, General Ludendorff, a leading army general, told a shocked Reichstag that they could never win the war. He thought Germany should 'abandon the war as hopeless' and advised that the British, French and Americans would perhaps treat Germany more fairly if they stopped fighting soon. However, ending the war wasn't a decision the Reichstag could make – it was Kaiser Wilhelm II's choice. He was Germany's all powerful emperor who made all the major decisions. Did he want to continue fighting or take advice from one of his best soldiers and ask for a ceasefire? The Kaiser decided to fight on!

On 28 October, the German navy, based in Kiel, was ordered out to sea to attack British ships. Sailors on the ships refused to follow orders – they just didn't want to fight any more. News of their **mutiny** began to spread. In ports nearby, other sailors refused to follow orders. Along with workers and soldiers, they began to take over towns and set up special councils to run them. In just six days, workers' and soldiers' councils were governing cities, such as Hamburg and Munich, all over Germany. The country was in chaos and there was little the Kaiser could do – he had lost control and his army generals refused to help him. On 9 November 1918, he **abdicated** and secretly left Germany by tram. He went to live in Holland, never to return.

Friedrich Ebert, the leader of Germany's largest political party, took the Kaiser's place as leader of Germany and promised to hold elections. If ordinary German people wanted him as their leader, they would get the chance to vote for him if they wished. Meanwhile, he gave the people what they really wanted – an end to the war. On 11 November, at 11:00am, Germany surrendered. The Great War was over.

FACT *Germany stands alone*

By 1918, Germany's only allies were Bulgaria, Austria–Hungary and Turkey. On 4 November, they had all surrendered, leaving Germany to fight on her own.

Source B ▾ *A photograph taken during the revolution in Berlin in the first week of November 1918. It shows soldiers and workers riding around the streets on a stolen lorry. Note the machine gun attached to the lorry's roof.*

Source C ▾ *Adapted from a list of demands from a workers' council in 1918. It gives you an idea of how Kaiser Wilhelm had limited the freedom of ordinary German citizens over the years.*

We want:

i)   peace;

ii) increased supplies of food;

iii) the right to free speech;

iv) the right to hold public meetings;

v)   the right to form trade unions;

vi) the release of all political prisoners;

vii) the introduction of general, equal and secret voting for all men and women over 20 years of age.

WISE UP WORDS

- mutiny   abdicate

WORK

1 **a** Make a list of the ways in which conditions in Germany got worse during the Great War.

   b Why did the war cause such bad conditions for ordinary Germans?

2 Look at **Source B.** What different clues are there in the photograph that Germany's emperor had lost control of Germany by November 1918?

3 **a** What is meant by the word 'abdicated'?

   b Why did Germany's emperor abdicate in November 1918?

4 Look at **Source C.** In your own words, summarise what many Germans

   a wanted in 1918

   b did not want in 1918.

What was the Weimar Republic?

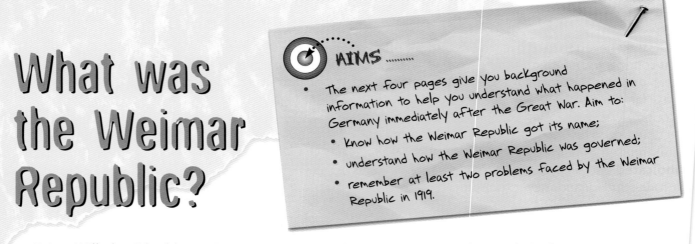

AIMS

- The next four pages give you background information to help you understand what happened in Germany immediately after the Great War. Aim to:
- know how the Weimar Republic got its name;
- understand how the Weimar Republic was governed;
- remember at least two problems faced by the Weimar Republic in 1919.

Kaiser Wilhelm II had been Germany's emperor since 1888. Despite having help from a Parliament, or Reichstag, which was elected by the people, it was the Kaiser who introduced laws, selected the men for important government jobs, declared war and made peace. He only allowed his Reichstag to change laws occasionally. There was a number of different political parties in the Reichstag but the Kaiser took none of them very seriously. In fact, he once called the politicians in the Reichstag 'a troop of monkeys, blockheads and sleepwalkers'. In short, Kaiser Wilhelm was a dictator with complete power.

So how would Germany cope now the Kaiser had run off to Holland? Who would lead the country and how would it be ruled? And would all Germans be happy with their new leaders?

The Kaiser left Germany on 9 November 1918. He had taken the country into a war of which many Germans were now thoroughly sick and tired. There were riots and rebellions all over Germany as millions of people grew close to starvation. Friedrich Ebert, the leader of the largest political party in the country, took the Kaiser's place as leader of Germany. On 11 November, Germany surrendered, bringing an end to a much-hated war. Next, Ebert ordered improvements to living conditions – a shorter working day, help for the unemployed, better housing and more food supplies. He guaranteed freedom of speech, freedom of religion and arranged elections for a new German Parliament. He declared that Germany would be a **democratic republic** from now on – there would be no Kaiser or emperor: instead, ordinary Germans could choose their leaders by democracy.

To many, it sounded like Ebert was the sort of leader who might do a good job. His actions so far seemed to show he cared about the citizens of Germany. But not everyone was pleased. A group of Communists (see Information box 1), known as the **Spartacus League**, wanted Germany to be run by soldiers' and workers' councils, not by a Parliament. They wanted Germany to be a Communist country,

like Russia, and tried to start another revolution in January 1919. Thousands of Spartacists (as they were known) roamed around the streets of Berlin firing guns and taking over important buildings. Ebert responded with a violent solution – he sent in a group of 2000 tough ex-soldiers known as the **Free Corps** to attack the Spartacists (see Information box 2). After three days of brutal street fighting, the Free Corps recaptured buildings and arrested Rosa Luxemburg and Karl Liebknecht, the leaders of the Spartacus League. After beating them savagely, the Free Corps shot them and dumped their dead bodies in the street. The Spartacus League's revolt was over.

FACT *Names, names, names*

Historians like to give names to different periods of time in a country's history, for example Tudor England, Victorian Britain or Nazi Germany. Between 1919 and 1933, Germany was known as the **Weimar Republic** or Weimar Germany. *Weimar* was the town where the newly elected politicians first met after the end of the Great War. A *republic* is a country run by a Parliament with no king, queen, Kaiser or emperor.

Information box 1: Communists

Communists believe in Communism. This is a political idea about how best to run a country.

- In a Communist country, everyone is equal (men and women) and everything is shared.

- There are no different classes and no great differences in wealth. As you might expect, this attracts poorer workers – Communist life sounds better than the one they've got!

- There is no private property and the government (or council) runs farms, factories and businesses for the benefit of all people.

- There is little need for money or laws because everyone lives a simple life, sharing all they have with others. Eventually, Communists believe that there will be no need for any governments or councils at all because people would live in harmony, only taking what they need and working as hard as they can.

- A belief in Communism or similar is sometimes known as **left wing**. For example, the Spartacus League was a left-wing political party.

Red is the traditional colour of Communism and Russia became the world's first Communist country in 1917 ... with their famous red flag.

WISE UP WORDS

- Free Corps   Spartacus League
  Weimar Republic   democratic republic
  left wing

Information box 2: The Free Corps

The Free Corps was a group of bloodthirsty ex-soldiers who had recently come home from the Great War. They hated the Spartacus League (and Communists in general) because they blamed them for stirring up trouble in Germany towards the end of the war. The Free Corps argued that this trouble was a major reason for Germany's defeat. There were other Communist uprisings in Germany (in Bavaria in May 1919 and a 'red rising' in the Ruhr in March 1920), which the Free Corps ended with savage brutality.

Source A  *The Free Corps in action, 1919.*

Now Ebert held the election that he had promised. His own political party, the Social Democrats, won most votes and Ebert became the new German President. Because of all the recent violence in Berlin, the newly elected politicians, with Ebert as President, met up on 11 February 1919 in a town in southern Germany called Weimar. They met to discuss how best to run Germany. This was the start of the Weimar Republic.

So how was the Weimar Republic governed?

In 1919, Germany's politicians drew up a set of rules for how Germany would be governed. This was called the Weimar **Constitution**. As you can see below, it was a very different system from the way Germany used to be run when the Kaiser controlled everything. In fact, the Weimar Republic was one of the most democratic countries anywhere in the world.

The President (Head of State)
- elected every seven years
- controlled army, navy and air force
- stayed out of day-to-day running of the country. In a crisis, he could rule on his own — without getting the support of the Reichstag — using special 'emergency powers'

The Chancellor (Prime Minister)
- chosen by the President (usually from the political party with most votes at an election)
- responsible for day-to-day running of the country — law and order, taxation, schooling, health care and so on
- must have the support of at least half the politicians in the Reichstag to introduce new laws

The Reichstag
- introduced laws
- members of the Reichstag (MPs/politicians) were elected every four years
- the voting system used was called **Proportional Representation** (PR). This meant that the number of politicians each political party had in the Reichstag was based on the number of voters they had. For example, if a party won 10% of the votes, it was given 10% of the seats

The German people (the electorate)

- all men and women over the age of 20 could vote
- they elected the President and the politicians in the Reichstag
- the Constitution guaranteed them basic freedoms, such as free speech

The structure of the Weimar Constitution

The new Constitution was incredibly fair. All Germans had equal rights, including the right to vote. The fact that all women over the age of 20 could vote shows that Germany was more forward-looking than many other countries. In Britain, for example, only women over the age of 28 could vote! However, the new system of government had several in-built weaknesses.

- Proportional Representation meant that lots of different political parties were able to win seats in the Reichstag. Sometimes there were over 20 different political parties all arguing over a single issue! This made it difficult to make decisions and introduce laws. In fact, between 1919 and 1933, no political party ever won more than half the votes in any election — and, as a result, they didn't get more than half the seats. With no **majority**, the leading party had to do deals with smaller groups in order to get anything done. Again, this made decision-making a very slow process.

- Also, many groups didn't like this new system of democracy, elections and Parliament at all. In fact, they didn't like any sort of change. Some of the older army generals, judges, upper-class families, rich owners of big factories and university professors longed for the 'good old days' when the Kaiser ruled Germany. The new system of government was linked to the surrender at the end of the Great War. They wanted one strong leader like they had before the war. It was argued that Germany was never this weak and defenceless when the Kaiser ruled (see **Source B**).

Source B ▼ *From the BBC series* History File: Nazi Germany, *Episode One.*

"Politicians! What is this democracy? We never used to have democracy. We had strong leaders like the Kaiser. We never voted for him and was Germany ever so weak under the Kaiser? I spit on freedom — it's the patriotic thing to do!"

Source C ▾ *A selection of political parties in Germany in the early 1920s. Their names are written in English but they have been given their German initials. Like political parties in Britain today, their beliefs and policies differed but the Social Democrats, the Democratic Party and the Centre Party tended to attract most votes in elections during the early and mid-1920s.*

WISE UP WORDS

- majority   Proportional Representation   Constitution

LEFT WING POLITICAL PARTY	COMMUNIST PARTY (KPD)	SOCIAL DEMOCRATIC PARTY (SPD)	GERMAN DEMOCRATIC PARTY (DDP)	CENTRE PARTY (ZENTRUM)	PEOPLE'S PARTY (DVP)	NATIONAL PEOPLE'S PARTY (DNVP)	RIGHT WING NATIONAL SOCIALIST GERMAN WORKERS' PARTY (NSDAP OR NAZIS)
SUPPORTERS	Working class	Mostly working class	Middle class, for example lawyers, writers and so on	Catholics from all classes (Germany was largely a Catholic country)	Middle class, mainly businessmen	Middle and upper classes, some ex-soldiers	Unemployed, mainly ex-soldiers. Some support from middle and upper classes who feared the Communists
ATTITUDE TO WEIMAR REPUBLIC Anti = against Pro = for	Anti-republic	Pro-republic Ebert Weimar, Germany's first President, was a Social Democrat	Pro-republic	Pro-republic	Pro-republic, but would like a return to having a Kaiser at some time in the future	Anti-republic	Anti-republic
POLICIES	Thought Germany should be a Communist country and run by workers' councils, not by Parliament	Believed everyone was equal. Wanted democracy and reforms to help ordinary working-class Germans	Believed in individual freedom – rights to hold peaceful meetings, form societies, freedom of speech and so on	Supported the interests and beliefs of the Catholic Church	Supporters of any policies that promoted trade and industry (and made them some money)	Wanted strong government, perhaps led by one strong politician or the Kaiser again	Wanted Germany to be a great nation again. Hated democracy and wanted strong government led by one man. Hated Communism because it states that all people are equal. Nazis believed that some races and nations were better than others. Wanted Germany to be a great military power once more

WORK

1 **a** Test your understanding of these pages by explaining the following terms:
- democratic republic
- Spartacus League
- Free Corps.

   b In your own words, explain why these groups fought against each other?

2 **a** Why do you think Ebert won the February 1919 election to become Germany's first president?

   b How did the 'Weimar Republic' get its name?

3 **a** Explain what is meant by the terms:
- Weimar Constitution
- proportional representation.

   b What is your opinion of Germany's new Weimar Constitution? TOP TIP: Don't just write 'it looks OK'! Try to have an opinion. Is it fair or unfair? Who benefits? What are its strengths and weaknesses? It is important in history to have your own opinion, after all, how often do you get asked in other lessons about your views? Remember, a good history student will always back up their opinions with evidence!

4 Look at **Source C**.

   a Which three major political parties did not support the new, democratic way Germany was governed?

   b Why did each of these parties dislike the Weimar Republic?

Germany and the Treaty of Versailles

AIM

• to be able to list at least three ways in which Germany was affected by the Treaty of Versailles.

On 7 March 1919, France, Great Britain and America – the main winning countries of the Great War – announced what was going to happen to Germany – a losing country – for their part in the fighting.

Germany was to lose about 10% of its land, 12.5% of its population, 16% of its coal mines and nearly 50% of its iron industry. They were to lose all overseas colonies and most of their armed forces. They were even going to be forced to accept the blame for starting the war and pay for all the damage done in the fighting. The Germans were horrified … they just didn't expect their punishment to be this tough!

So what could the German politicians do about the punishment? Did they *have* to accept it or was there an alternative? And how did ordinary people react to the news?

Source A ▼ *The main points of the Treaty of Versailles. All other losing countries – Austria, Hungary, Turkey and Bulgaria – lost land, had their armed forces reduced and had to pay for war damage too. Only Germany took the blame for starting the war.*

Germany was to be banned from having an air force, tanks or submarines. They could only have a navy of six battleships and a tiny army of 100 000 men. German soldiers were not allowed into the Rhineland, a **demilitarised** zone near France.

Land was to be taken away from Germany and given to her neighbours. This resulted in the country being cut in two. Germany was also forbidden from joining with Austria again and all of Germany's overseas colonies were taken away.

Germany must accept blame for starting the war and pay reparations for the damage. A special group would meet to decide how much Germany must pay for their 'war guilt'.

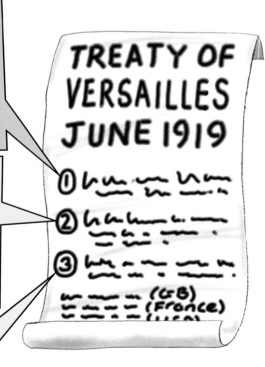

TREATY OF VERSAILLES JUNE 1919

The new German government was not invited to the peace discussions, which took place in the Palace of Versailles near Paris, France. Instead, they were told they had to accept their punishment or face invasion from Britain, France and the USA. Although many Germans would have preferred to fight again rather than accept such a harsh punishment, the new German government decided to sign the peace treaty – known as the **Treaty of Versailles** – rather than put the country through another war. With only an hour to go before the deadline for signing the treaty ran out, the German government sent a message to Paris saying they agreed to sign. Two German politicians travelled to France and signed the treaty on 28 June 1919.

Source B ▾ *From the front page of one of Germany's leading newspapers on the day the Treaty of Versailles was signed. The Hall of Mirrors is a huge mirrored room inside the Palace of Versailles.*

29 JUNE 1919

DEUTSCHE ZEITUNG

VENGEANCE GERMAN NATION!

TODAY, IN THE HALL OF MIRRORS, THE DISGRACEFUL TREATY IS BEING SIGNED. DO NOT FORGET IT. THE GERMAN PEOPLE WILL REGAIN THEIR PLACE AMONGST THE NATIONS, TO WHICH THEY ARE ENTITLED. THEN WILL COME VENGEANCE [REVENGE] FOR THE SHAME OF 1919.

As you can see, the Treaty of Versailles was designed to cripple Germany by taking away land, money and weapons. The winning countries, especially France and Britain, had worked hard to make sure that Germany would never be a threat to them again. The American President, who didn't want to punish Germany so severely, worried that Germany may seek revenge in the future. He was right to worry (see **Source B**)!

Ordinary Germans hated the treaty and the people responsible for it. They called it a **diktat** – a dictated peace – because the Germans were ordered to sign the treaty without having a chance to discuss it. Some Germans even hated the German government for signing it. They said it showed how weak they were and accused them of 'stabbing their own country in the back'.

WISE UP WORDS

- reparations   Treaty of Versailles
  Kapp Putsch   demilitarised   diktat

FACT *The Kapp Putsch*

A man called Wolfgang Kapp hated the government for signing the treaty. In Berlin, in March 1920, he gathered a group of 5000 men – police, some of the army and most of the Free Corps (ex-soldiers) – and took over the city. President Ebert and the government ran off! However, Kapp didn't have the support of the workers and they all went on strike. There was no gas, water, electricity, buses or trains. After only 100 hours as Germany's new leader, Kapp gave in and fled abroad. Ebert and his government returned.

Source C ▾ *Karl Nagerl, a schoolboy in 1919, remembers how he felt at the end of the Great War.*

"It was a relief when the war was over. Now we had to see what the consequences of defeat were … when the terms of the Treaty of Versailles were announced, the German people were shocked at everything that was expected of us and dismayed at the payments we would have to make. They were sure to lead the German nation to ruin."

WORK

1 a Why do you think many Germans hated the Treaty of Versailles?

  b How did some of them react to it in March 1920?

2 a Imagine that you run a German newspaper in 1919 that does not support the German government. Design a front page news story reporting on the Treaty of Versailles. It should include:
  - a powerful headline that captures the mood of ordinary Germans
  - a strong opening paragraph that sums up the treaty
  - a summary of the main points of the treaty
  - an explanation of why so many Germans are shocked, angry and humiliated. You might even include a few interviews here
  - a comment on the current leaders of Germany – why not draw your own political cartoon?

  b If you ran a German newspaper that supported the German government, in what ways would your new story be different?

1923: a year of crisis

AIMS ....

- After studying the next four pages, make sure you can:
  - explain what 'hyperinflation' means;
  - explain the link between the French invasion of the Ruhr and hyperinflation.

In December 1921, a loaf of bread in Berlin, Germany, would cost about four marks. This was an acceptable price for an ordinary food item that most Germans would eat on a regular basis. By September 1923, a loaf of bread cost about 1 500 000 marks. That's right … one and a half *million* marks! Unbelievably, by November 1923, a loaf cost 201 000 000 000 marks!

So what caused a loaf of bread – and everything else that Germans could buy – to shoot up in price so much? How did **hyperinflation**, as these price rises were known, affect different groups in German society? And how did ordinary Germans feel about their government during this period?

In the peace treaty at the end of the Great War, Germany was ordered to pay for all the damage done by the fighting. In 1921, it was announced that they had to pay 132 billion gold marks – or £6 600 000 000 – in equal yearly instalments for the next 66 years! Later that year, the German government scraped together their first instalment of two billion gold marks and handed it over to France and Belgium. These were the two countries that had been most damaged by the fighting. Some of it was gold but most of it was in goods such as coal, iron and wood.

In January 1923, Germany announced that they couldn't afford to pay any more. The French and Belgians didn't believe them and vowed to force Germany to pay. A few days later, 60 000 French and Belgian soldiers marched into the Ruhr, a rich, industrial area of Germany, full of coal mines and factories. They had decided to take what was owed to them by force. The consequences of this invasion were remarkable. They led to the amazing hyperinflation of 1923 and a 200-billion-mark loaf of bread! To understand how this happened, study the following cartoons very carefully.

1. French and Belgian soldiers began to take what was owed to them from Germany back to France.

to all German workers in the Ruhr **GO ON STRIKE** Signed German government.

2. The German government ordered its workers in the Ruhr to go on strike and not help the soldiers remove goods from the country. This was called **passive resistance**.

3. French and Belgian soldiers were tough with the strikers. Over 100 of them were killed and 150 000 people were thrown out of their homes as a punishment.

4. The German government met to discuss the crisis. They promised to continue paying the workers on strike. To make matters worse, the government was running short of money because the Ruhr wasn't producing coal, iron and steel to sell to other nations.

5. To pay their striking workers, the government printed large amounts of money – but this caused lots of problems.

6. The striking workers began to spend their money – quickly. They were being paid well – and wanted to spend, spend, spend – even though they weren't working! In response, shopkeepers began to put up their prices.

7. As shops raised their prices all over Germany, the government responded by printing even more money. The more money the government printed, the faster prices went up.

8. The faster prices went up, the faster people spent their wages. Soon workers were being paid twice a day. They carried their wages around in wheelbarrows. The price of goods could rise between joining the back of a queue and reaching the front!

9. As you might expect, the German government and the Weimar politicians lost a lot of support in 1923 as people looked for someone to blame.

German money was worthless by November 1923. The government had printed so much that it lost all its value. People started to use it to light their fire or make paper aeroplanes or kites to fly (see **Source A**). Not surprisingly, many Germans blamed their government for the mess because it was their decision to call a strike in the Ruhr and then to print so much money. For most, 1923 was the worst year since the end of the Great War and their democratically elected politicians seemed to have caused their problems.

Then, in the middle of the crisis, two politicians emerged on the scene. One was a 34 year old ex-soldier named Adolf Hitler; the other was a 45 year old financial genius called Gustav Stresemann.

In late 1923, disgusted with the chaos in Germany, Hitler and about 3000 followers of his Nazi Party tried to overthrow the government by starting a revolution in Munich. He failed and was thrown in prison for treason. Germany wasn't ready for Hitler yet!

Stresemann, meanwhile, was finalising his action plan to get Germany back on its feet again. He had just been elected Chancellor and when he took over at the end of 1923 Germany began to recover almost immediately.

Source A ▾ *A woman using worthless German banknotes to light her fire in 1923.*

Source B ▲ *A German banknote issued in 1923. Can you see how much it is worth?*

Source C ▾ *The memories of a German writer in 1923.*

"Two women were carrying a laundry basket filled to the top with banknotes. Seeing a crowd standing round a shop window, they put down the basket for a moment to see if there was anything they could buy. When they turned around a few moments later, they found the money was untouched, but the basket had been stolen."

Source D ▾ *Price for a loaf of bread (top) and one egg (bottom) in Germany, 1918–23.*

1918	0.6 marks
1921	4 marks
1922	163 marks
January 1923	250 marks
July 1923	3456 marks
September 1923	1 512 000 marks
November 1923	201 000 000 000 marks

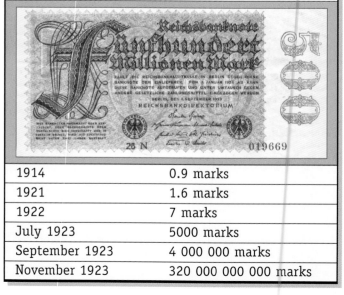

1914	0.9 marks
1921	1.6 marks
1922	7 marks
July 1923	5000 marks
September 1923	4 000 000 marks
November 1923	320 000 000 000 marks

Source E ▾ *Hyperinflation affected different people in different ways. However, there were far more losers than winners. How did hyperinflation affect different people?*

WINNERS	LOSERS
People who had borrowed money found it very easy to pay off their debts. If a person had borrowed 10 000 marks in 1920 (a lot of money then), they could now pay off their debt with one banknote!	People with savings in the bank were the biggest losers. Some people had saved all their lives to get 1000 marks in the bank – by 1923, it wouldn't even buy them a loaf of bread. Old people who lived on fixed pensions found their income wouldn't buy them what they needed any more. Many small (and big) businesses collapsed, as normal trade eventually became impossible because of the daily price changes.

WISE UP WORDS

• hyperinflation   passive resistance

Source F ▾ *A modern historian writing about the hyperinflation crisis of 1923.*

"Millions of people faced starvation as a result of the hyperinflation. People such as pensioners who were living on fixed incomes found that prices rose much faster than their earnings. So even if they could afford to buy food, they might not be able to pay for the gas to cook it. They lived in unheated houses because they couldn't afford coal and they froze because they couldn't afford to buy clothes.

The well-to-do [richer] suffered along with the poor, especially people with savings in the bank. People with thousands in the bank in 1918 now found their savings would not even buy a slice of bread or a piece of coal."

WORK

3 **a** What do you understand by the word 'hyperinflation'?

b In your own words, try to explain why hyperinflation occurred in Germany in 1923.

2 Look at **Source B**. The German banknote pictured here is worth 10 000 000 marks and was issued at the end of August 1923.

a Using **Source D** to help you, work out how many eggs you could have bought with this banknote in September 1923.

b How many eggs could you have bought in November 1923?

3 Look at **Source C**. In your own words, explain why the basket was stolen but not the money.

4 Explain how the following people would have been affected by hyperinflation:

i) an old woman, living alone on her fixed pension

ii) a school leaver who was looking for his or her first job

iii) a farmer who had borrowed money in 1919 and owed 5000 marks

iv) a married couple who had saved all their lives for retirement and had 20 000 marks in the bank.

5 Why do you think hyperinflation turned many ordinary Germans against their government?

Germany recovers

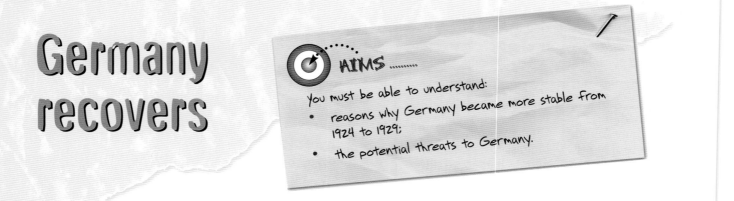

AIMS

You must be able to understand:
* reasons why Germany became more stable from 1924 to 1929;
* the potential threats to Germany.

1923 was a bad year in Germany. The French had invaded the Ruhr, one of Germany's richest industrial areas; hyperinflation had made money worthless and different political groups continued to cause trouble and think they could do a better job than the government. The Nazis had even tried to start a revolution and take over the country! But things didn't get any worse in Germany. In fact, after 1923, things started to get a lot better. Most historians put Germany's recovery down to the influence and hard work of one man – Gustav Stresemann. So how did he do it?

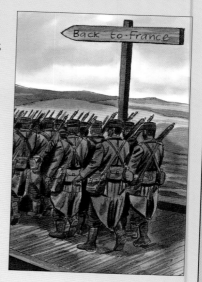

Source A ▶ *Gustav Stresemann. In 1923, he became Germany's Chancellor. Later he was Foreign Minister from 1924 to 1929. He was awarded the Nobel Peace Prize in 1926.*

Problem 1: Hyperinflation

Stresemann's solution: he stopped the printing of paper money and replaced all old money with a new currency called the Rentenmark. One Rentenmark replaced 1000 billion marks.

Success? Yes, Germans quickly accepted their new currency and hyperinflation ended.

Problem 2: The French troops in the Ruhr

Stresemann's solution: he knew that French troops had invaded the Ruhr because Germany had not kept up its reparation payments. In 1924, Stresemann attended a meeting with French, British and American leaders. The result was the **Dawes Plan**, which allowed the Germans to pay only what they could afford. They also had longer to pay.

Success? Yes, French troops left the Ruhr. However, some Germans thought Stresemann had 'given in' to the French by not demanding a complete end to all reparations – many thought Germany shouldn't be paying anything at all! In 1929, the **Young Plan** reduced the amount Germany had to pay even more ... but they still had to pay up to 1988!

Problem 3: No one trusted the Germans

The League of Nations Welcomes **GERMANY**

Stresemann's solution: he tried to improve Germany's relationship with other countries.

• In 1925, Germany signed the **Locarno Pact** with Britain, France, Belgium and Italy. They promised not to invade each other.

• In 1926, Germany was allowed to join the League of Nations.

• In 1928, Germany, along with 64 other countries, signed the **Kellogg–Briand Pact**. They all agreed not to go to war unless in self-defence.

Success? Germany definitely became a major European power again under Stresemann. The League of Nations even gave Germany 'great power status', which meant they took part in major decisions. However, some Germans criticised Stresemann for not demanding some of the land back from countries that had taken it from Germany at the end of the Great War!

Problem 4: German industry was in trouble after the Great War – factories were run down, there were few jobs, and poor schools, housing and hospitals.

Stresemann's solution: He organised big loans from America (this was part of the Dawes Plan). The Germans built new factories, housing, hospitals, schools and roads. This meant more jobs with Germans earning more money. Even some American companies (such as Ford and Gillette) set up factories in Germany.

Success? Slowly, Germany became more prosperous. Some called it a 'golden age'. A night out in Berlin in the late 1920s – cinemas, music halls, night clubs, beer halls, galleries – was meant to be one of the greatest forms of entertainment in the world! However, some feared that Germany relied on American loans too much – what if Americans suddenly wanted their money back?

Stresemann, one of Germany's most able and hard-working politicians, died of a heart attack in 1929. His time as Chancellor and later Foreign Minister had seen Germany enter a new era of peace and prosperity. Indeed, there were no attempts to overthrow the government between 1924 and 1929. Hitler and his Nazis, meanwhile, had become a bit of a national joke after their failed attempt to take over Germany in 1923. Hitler found difficulty trying to persuade Germans they needed him as their saviour when the country was doing so well. In 1924, about 5% of Germans voted for the Nazis. By 1928, their support had dropped – only 2% of Germans were voting for them … but their time would come!

Source B ▾ *From a speech by Gustav Stresemann in 1928.*

> "Germany is dancing on a volcano. If America calls in their loans, a large section of our economy would collapse."

WISE UP WORDS

• Dawes Plan Young Plan Locarno Pact Kellogg–Briand Pact

WORK

1 Copy and complete the table below. In the last column, you must give Stresemann a star rating to show how successful you think he was.

Problem	Stresemann's policy	Was it a success, failure or a bit of both? Explain fully	Rating ***** fantastic * poor
1 Hyperinflation			
2 French occupation of the Ruhr			
3 Germany's poor relationship with other countries			
4 German industry short of investment			

2 Suggest why the Nazis only got 2% of votes in the 1928 elections, even though they were a highly organised party with over 100 000 members.

3 Look at **Source B**. Why do you think Stresemann was so worried about the USA 'calling in their loans'? What would be the impact on Germany?

What was Adolf Hitler's early life like?

AIMS

Aim to remember:
- Five facts about Hitler's life up to 1920.

Adolf Hitler is one of the most **infamous** men ever to have lived. His time as leader of Germany only covered 12 years but what about his early life? What was he like as a young man? How and why did he get involved in politics? And why was this Austrian (yes, he wasn't German at all) chosen to be Germany's leader in 1933?

Adolf Hitler was born on 20 April 1889 in Braunau, a small town in Austria. His dad was a hard-drinking bully who worked as a postman. He died when Hitler was 14. His mum spoiled Hitler and insisted he went to a respectable school in order to get good grades and a well-paid job. But he failed his examinations and left school at 16. For the next two years, he read books, listened to music and painted pictures. His mum died when he was 17. After her death, he left his home town and travelled to Vienna, the capital city of Austria, looking for work.

Source A ▼ *One of Hitler's teachers said this about him after he left school.*

> "He always wanted his own way. He was boastful, bad-tempered and lazy … He ignored advice and got angry if he was told off."

In 1907, Hitler arrived in Vienna hoping to 'make it big' as an artist. He tried to get into the Vienna Art Academy, one of Europe's best art colleges, but failed to pass the entrance exam. Without any qualifications, he ended up living in a hostel for tramps.

For the next five years, Hitler earned money any way he could – cleaning windows, painting houses, drawing and selling postcards in the street. He grew to hate people of foreign races, particularly rich Jewish people. He felt that foreigners were ruining Austria by taking over all the jobs and introducing their way of life.

Hitler left Austria in 1913 to avoid being called into the army, and he went to live in Munich, Germany. When the Great War started in 1914, he decided to be a soldier after all, and volunteered to join the German army.

Hitler was in hospital when the war ended, temporarily blinded in a gas attack. He wrote that he buried his head in his pillow and cried when he heard the news. He blamed Germany's surrender on weak politicians … and of course, the Jews!

Source B ▼ *Hitler (on the left) in the trenches in 1916. He worked all through the war as a messenger in the trenches. It was a dangerous job – he was wounded badly several times. Once, when a piece of metal sliced through his cheek, he nearly died.*

Source C ▼ *A report of Hitler by his commanding officer during the Great War. Hitler worked all through the war, doing the dangerous job of taking messages between the trenches. The Iron Cross was the highest medal awarded in the German army.*

"REPORT ON LANCE CORPORAL HITLER.

THIRD COMPANY (VOLUNTEERS)

Hitler has been with the regiment since 1914 and has fought splendidly in all the battles in which he has taken part.

As a messenger he was always ready to carry messages in the most difficult positions at great risk to his own life.

He received the Iron Cross (Second Class) on 2 December 1914 and I now feel he is worthy of receiving the Iron Cross (First Class)."

Hitler stayed in the army after the war, spying on new political groups to see if they were dangerous. One group he investigated in May 1919 wasn't dangerous at all – they had few members and funds of only 7.5 marks – about £4. They were called the German Workers' Party (or 'Deutsche Arbeiterpartei' in German) and were one of many small political parties in and around Munich at this time. The German Workers' Party met in beer halls and Hitler soon began attending regularly in his own time because he liked what was being said. People made speeches about how the Treaty of Versailles made

Germany weak and how the country could become a great nation once more. It wasn't long before Hitler was making speeches himself and soon joined, becoming their 55th member.

By 1921, Hitler was running the party. He advertised for more members in newspapers, stuck up posters and gave passionate speeches. He also extended the party's name to the Nationalsozialistische Deutsche Arbeiterpartei (NDSAP) or the National Socialist German Workers' Party. They were known as the Nazi Party for short.

Source D ▼ *Letter from Hitler, 1921*

"In June 1919 I joined the German Workers' Party, then with seven members, and in which I believed that I had found a political movement in keeping with my ideals. Today it has grown to 4,500 and I take personal credit for this."

WISE UP WORD

- infamous

WORK

1 Here is a list of interesting dates in Hitler's life up to 1921:

   1914 1889 1919 1905 1903 1913 1907 1921

   a Write each date on a separate line in the correct chronological order. Beside each date, write what happened in that year.

   b Choose two events in Hitler's life that you would regard as important turning points. Explain why each event you have chosen was so important.

2 Look at **Source D**.

   a Hitler always said he was the seventh member of the German Workers' Party, even though he wasn't. Even his membership card showed he wasn't one of the earliest members! So why do you think Hitler always claimed he was such an early member?

   b What do you think Hitler means when he writes "I had found a political movement in keeping with my ideals"?

   c Why do you think Hitler took 'personal growth of the party'?

Why were the Nazis so popular?

AIMS

Aim to understand:
- how Hitler changed the Nazi Party;
- Why Hitler's ideas were so popular.

Under Hitler's influence, the Nazi Party grew and grew. There were 3000 members in 1920 and 5000 in 1921. Although based in Munich, there were soon members all over Germany.

So what made Hitler so popular? How did he rise so quickly from the leader of a small political party to the leader of a nation?

Hitler and the Treaty of Versailles

Germany was a mess when Hitler took over the Nazi Party. Harvests were poor and unemployment was high. Added to this was the fact that millions of Germans felt humiliated by the Treaty of Versailles. The winning countries had taken away land and money from Germany, and blamed Germany for starting the war. Germans also felt vulnerable to attack because they were forced to reduce their army and have no air force, submarines or tanks at all – and only a tiny navy. As soon as he took over the Nazi Party, Hitler started to criticise the Treaty of Versailles. He said it was unfair and any land taken away from Germany must be returned. He said the French, who many Germans thought were responsible for the Treaty being so tough, must be destroyed.

Prison and the book

These views made Hitler very popular and by 1923 the Nazi Party had over 50 000 members. Hitler even had his own private army of thugs called **storm troopers**, who went around beating up people who criticised him. In 1923, Hitler felt confident enough to try to take over Germany. He tried to start a revolution in Munich, one of Germany's major cities, hoping it would spread to other places. It failed and Hitler was put in prison for treason. While in prison, he wrote a book about his life and ideas called **Mein Kampf** – *My Struggle*. When Hitler was released in 1924 (for good behaviour), his book started to get him a reputation as a man whose ideas might be able to put

Germany 'on the right track' again. While many ordinary Germans didn't quite understand all his views, many certainly liked what they read and heard about his plans for a new Germany!

Hitler and publicity

The Nazis bought eight newspapers and printed millions of posters and leaflets to send out their message. Hitler took part in fabulous parades where he made passionate speeches. He held mass rallies to tell people of his ideas for a better Germany. Hitler even chose an old religious symbol to become the emblem of the Nazi Party (the **swastika**). By the end of 1928, over 100 000 Germans belonged to the Nazi Party.

A copy of Hitler's book, *Mein Kampf*, was owned by thousands of Germans. In it he criticises the Treaty of Versailles, argues that Jews and Communists are the cause of all Germany's problems and claims that true Germans are part of a master-race of humans, called Aryans, who should all be united under one leader. He writes that Germany could be reborn under his leadership.

Source A ▶ *The Nazi flag. The symbol in the centre is known as the 'crooked cross' or the swastika. It became Germany's official symbol in 1935.*

Source B ▼ *A Nazi parade in 1927. The Nazis had their own salute (the raised arm) to acknowledge each other.*

Source C ▼ *A Nazi election poster of 1932. The writing means 'Our last hope: Hitler'. Who do you think the poster was aimed at?*

Hitler and the Great Depression

By 1928, Hitler and the Nazis were very well known, but they were still only the eighth largest political party in Germany. Then, in 1929, world trade began to slow down. This means that countries stopped buying and selling to each other. German factories closed and people started to lose their jobs. Hitler took advantage of this and started to promise solutions to all Germany's problems. 'Vote for me' was Hitler's message, 'and I'll provide you with work and bread.' As more and more people lost their jobs, the Nazis got more and more votes. By 1932, the Nazis were the largest political party – and Hitler became Chancellor (Prime Minister) of Germany in January 1933.

WISE UP WORDS

Mein Kampf swastika storm troopers

WORK

It is 1933 and you are a journalist working for a British newspaper. Your editor has sent you out to Germany to write an article about the astonishing rise of Adolf Hitler, the new Chancellor, and his Nazi party.

Your opening sentences could be:

A new force has arrived in German politics. With their smart uniforms, interesting ideas and eye catching symbols, Adolf Hitler and the Nazi's are now the men in charge. So how do they do it?

In your article explain:

- Who Hitler is – a bit about his background perhaps (you might need to look back through a few pages in this book).
- The origins of the Nazi Party – what do they stand for, who do they appeal to, for example?
- How the Nazi party has grown – what tactics has Hitler used to get publicity?

What was it like to live in Nazi Germany?

AIMS

Make sure you can:
- explain how life was different for people in Germany depending on their circumstances, gender, age and race.

Adolf Hitler was asked to become Chancellor by the President of Germany, Paul von Hindenburg. At this time, the President was the most powerful man in Germany and the Chancellor was his chief minister. If the President thought Hitler wasn't doing a good enough job, he could sack him! Also, Germany was a democracy so Hitler could only make changes if the majority of the Reichstag (Parliament) agreed to them. Hitler knew that if he wanted to take control he needed to come up with some radical new plans – and he didn't take long to think of some!

In February 1933, the Reichstag building burned down – some say the Nazis started the fire themselves! A Communist was arrested (how convenient!) and Hitler managed to convince a worried President to pass an emergency 'Protection' law, banning the Communist Party. In the elections of March, the Nazis got more seats in the Reichstag than ever before – but not the majority that Hitler wanted. However, Hitler had managed to stir up enough fear to persuade the politicians in the Reichstag to agree to an **Enabling law** which allowed Hitler to make laws without asking them for approval. Soon, all trade unions and opposition political parties were banned; their leaders were arrested and, by July 1933, Germany was a 'one-party state'. When President Hindenburg died in August 1934, Hitler made himself Chancellor AND President. He started to call himself **Führer** (supreme leader) and immediately got all members of the army to swear an oath (promise) of loyalty to him.

State control

Hitler started to quickly change things. Having worked so hard to get into power, he was determined to stay there. His secret police force, the dreaded **Gestapo**, hunted out anyone who might be against Hitler. They had the power to arrest and imprison people without trial and set up a web of informers who would report any 'moaners' to them. Children were encouraged to report their parents or teachers if they spoke out against the Führer and, by 1935, every block of flats or housing estate had a 'local ruler' who listened for negative comments. By 1939, there were well over 100 000 people in prison for 'anti-Hitler crimes' … they were known as Enemies of the State.

Source A ▶ Part of a Nazi press release from 1934. 'Culling' means to kill or remove any unwanted people.

Hitler's 'hate-list'

Hitler was determined to crush anyone who didn't fully support him. He also believed that some races (such as the German!) were superior to others. He believed inferior races to be the Jews, Gypsies, Slavs (such as the Russians) and black people. From 1933 onwards, Jews in particular were targeted with a series of laws to make life more and more uncomfortable for them. They were sacked from jobs, banned from voting, forbidden from marrying non-Jews, barred from schools and even evicted

"The Nazi government must have total control over every aspect of life. Government will be in the hands of one person, a genius, a hero, with total responsibility for culling on behalf of a pure race in the national interest."

from their homes. When World War II began, the persecution grew even worse, culminating in the Nazis' masterplan to exterminate all of Europe's Jews in death camps! People who were disabled were also targets for Hitler because he thought these people should be eliminated so their illnesses and disabilities could not pass on to their children. Three hundred thousand men and women were compulsorily **sterilised** in families with **hereditary** illnesses; 720 000 mentally ill people were gassed, and 5000 mentally impaired babies killed.

Source B ▼ *This photo, taken in 1933, shows an **Aryan** woman and a Jewish man being bullied by Nazis. The woman's sign reads 'I live with a pig and only go with Jews'. Her husband's sign reads 'Instead of Jews, I only take young German girls to my room'.*

The young

Hitler took great trouble to make sure that young people were loyal to him and the Nazi Party. He realised that in future he may have to call on these people to put up with hardships, to fight and perhaps die for him. It was important therefore that young people thought that Hitler and the Nazis were the best thing that ever happened to Germany. He needed young men who were 'as fast as a greyhound, as tough as leather and as hard as steel'. He wanted tough, young girls too … but for an entirely different reason – they were to be the wives and mothers of a future generation of soldier.

Youngsters were **indoctrinated** to think like Nazis. Textbooks were rewritten to get across the Nazi message. Even teachers had to belong to the German Nazi Teachers' League and were made to put across Nazi ideas in their lessons – or face the sack. **Eugenics** was introduced to the school timetable, so students could study how to improve races!

Source C ▼ *A picture from a German school textbook in 1935. Children were taught to recognise Jews at a glance. Look for: i) the way the Jewish children and adult (on the left) have been drawn. Why have they been drawn this way?; ii) the reaction of the other children to the Jews' departure; iii) the Jewish boy on the right pulling another child's hair – why has this been included?*

Source D ▾ *This series of tests is what a Hitler Youth boy, aged 10 to 14, would have been expected to do to get an 'Achievement Award'. Girls would do a similar series but would be taught extra duties such as learning to make a bed!*

To gain your Hitler Youth Achievement award:

Complete the following lessons:

Life of Hitler
Germans abroad
Germany's rightful place in the world
National holidays of the German people
Five flag oaths
Six Hitler Youth songs

Complete the following athletic tests:

Run 60 metres in 10 seconds
Long jump 3.25 metres
Throw a small leather ball 35 metres
Pull up on a bar twice
Somersault backwards twice
Swim 100 metres

Hiking and camping tests:

A day's hike of 15 kilometres
Camp in a tent for three days
Put up a two-man tent and take part in putting up a twelve-man tent
Make a cooking pit and find water for cooking
Know the names of the most important trees
Use the stars to find your place on a map

Target practice:

Hit a bull's eye on a target at a distance of eight metres with an air gun

Outside school, young people had to belong to the Hitler Youth Organisation. From the ages of 6 to 18, boys and girls spent a few evenings a week and several weekends a year learning new skills and being taught how to show their loyalty to Hitler. Boys tended to learn military skills (model making, shooting practice and hiking) while girls learned about cookery, housework and motherhood.

Source E ▴ *In this photograph, Hitler is smiling at a six year old member of the Hitler Youth Organisation in full uniform. Why do you think this was a valuable photograph to the Nazis and was shown all over Germany?*

Women

Women were encouraged to stay at home and be good wives and mothers. Loans were given to newly married couples – the equivalent of a year's wages – to encourage them to have children. On the birth of the first child, they could keep a quarter of the money. On the birth of the second child, they could keep the second quarter, until on the birth of the fourth child, they could keep the lot! Medals were awarded to women who had most babies and Hitler himself said that the ideal woman should stick to the 'three Ks' – Kinder, Kirche and Kuche (children, church and cooking)!

Source F ▾ *A Nazi law written in 1943. It never came into effect.*

"All single and married women up to the age of 35 who do not already have four children should produce four children by racially pure German men. Whether or not these men are married is not important. Every family that already has four children must set the husband free for this action!"

The German people

The vast majority of Germans did well out of Hitler's rule between 1933 and 1939. Right from the start, he said he would provide work and bread, and restore national pride. He said he would make sure that Germany regained its rightful place in the world.

In 1933 there were six million people out of work, but this figure had reduced to 200 000 by 1938. The Nazis provided work by building roads, schools, hospitals, railways … and by making the army bigger and building tanks, fighter planes and battleships. Hitler started to get back land Germany had lost after its defeat in the Great War and many Germans felt a sense of pride in this. If the German people were prepared to ignore some of the crueller things happening to a minority of people, and not complain too loudly, it seemed that life was better under Hitler's leadership.

Source G ▾ *The feelings of a man who attended a Nazi rally in 1937.*

"I don't know how to describe the emotions that swept over me as I heard Adolf Hitler … when he spoke of the disgrace of Germany I was ready to spring on the enemy … I forgot everything but Hitler. Then, glancing around, I saw that the thousands around me were drawn to him like a magnet as well."

FACT *Mastermind*

Hitler was determined to control the way people thought. The Nazis controlled all newspapers, films, radios, plays, cinemas and books – and made sure they put across Nazi ideas. One of Hitler's most trusted friends, Doctor Joseph Goebbels, was put in charge of propaganda and **censorship**. He became a master of mind control. He had loudspeakers placed on all city streets so that people could hear Hitler's speeches when they were doing their shopping and ordered all books written by Jews or Communists to be destroyed. He banned jazz music because it was played mainly by black American musicians and even had a war film destroyed because it showed a drunk German soldier. He also introduced the death penalty for telling an anti-Hitler joke!

WISE UP WORDS

- Führer Gestapo sterilised eugenics hereditary indoctrinated censorship Aryan Enabling law

WORK

1 How did the Enabling law help Hitler become Führer?

2 Who do you think were 'Enemies of the state' in Hitler's Germany?

3 **a** Write down what is meant by the terms 'sterilised' and 'hereditary'.

   b Why do you think certain people were sterilised in Hitler's Germany?

4 **a** Why were boys and girls taught different things in schools?

   b What was the Hitler Youth Organisation?

   c Why do you think that Hitler and the Nazis put so much effort into organising the lives of young people?

5 Look at **Source F**. In your own words, explain how this law tried to encourage Germans to have more children.

6 When Hitler was campaigning for election, one of his slogans was 'work and bread'. How was Hitler successful in providing ordinary Germans with work and bread?

How did the Nazis control Germany?

AIMS

Make sure you can remember:
- two examples of Nazi terror methods;
- two ways in which the Nazis controlled the media.

The vast majority of Germans supported Hitler and the Nazis throughout the 1930s (or at least they said they did!) and the Nazis faced little opposition. So what did they do to make sure of this? Why were ordinary Germans so keen to let the Nazis continue to run their country? In short, how did the Nazis keep control?

The Nazis used a range of techniques to control Germany, best summed up in the following two information boxes.

METHOD 1: Terror

Heinrich Himmler was in charge of terror groups: special organisations that existed to terrorise people into accepting Nazi rule.

Gestapo

The secret police were known as the Gestapo. They spied on people they thought were a threat, tapped telephone lines and opened mail. They had the power to arrest, imprison without trial and torture anyone. They set up a huge network of informers who would report any 'grumblers' to them.

The police and law courts

The ordinary police continued their regular work but ignored most crimes committed by high-ranking Nazis. The law courts were under Nazi control too.

The SS

SS stands for 'Schutzstaffel', which means 'protection squad'. Set up in 1925, the SS was originally Hitler's private bodyguard. Gradually, it was built up to be the most important armed group in Germany. Mainly, the SS had three sections: one section looked after security – they could arrest anybody without trial and search houses. Another section was the Waffen SS – providing elite units in the army. The final section was the Death's Head Units – they ran the concentration camps and, later, the death camps.

Concentration camps

Large prisons were set up where any 'enemies of the German state' could be held for any length of time. Anyone the Nazis didn't like or anyone who had criticised Hitler was sent there. Inmates were forced to work hard and listen to Nazi ideas all day long. Some were even tortured or worked to death.

METHOD 2: Propaganda

To make sure as many people as possible realised how great the Nazis were, Hitler put someone in charge of what is known as **propaganda**. This means 'to spread information and ideas of a certain viewpoint in order to influence people's opinion'. Hitler employed a loyal leading Nazi named Joseph Goebbels to persuade large numbers of Germans to think what Hitler wanted them to think and believe. Goebbels was brilliant at his job.

Newspapers

- Only stories that showed the Nazis doing good things were printed. Newspapers that printed new stories that Goebbels hadn't seen were closed down.

Radio

- The Nazis controlled all radio stations – which were used to put across Nazi ideas.
- Cheap radios were produced – more Germans owned radios in the 1930s than Americans. The Nazis only made radios that couldn't pick up foreign broadcasts.

- Loudspeakers were placed in the streets, factories and cafes.

Films

- All film plots were shown to Goebbels before films were made. They had to show Nazis in a good way – and their 'enemies' in a bad way.

Books, theatre and music

- Writers were forced to write books and plays that praised Hitler and the Nazis.
- Books written by Jews, Communists or anti-Nazi journalists were banned.
- Jazz music was banned throughout Germany because it originated among the black people of America.

Mass rallies

- **Mass rallies** were held every year to celebrate Hitler's greatness – special arenas were built that could hold half a million people. They listened to choirs, bands and speeches, and watched firework displays and air shows. All were designed to show how impressive and well organised the Nazis were.

Source A ▾ *Adapted from Hitler's book, Mein Kampf, written in 1924.*

"The powers of ordinary people to understand are weak. And they quickly forget. So good propaganda has to be limited to a very few points. These must be as simple as possible and the slogans must be repeated until everybody has come to grasp the idea."

Source B ▾ *An instruction, given by Goebbels, to all newspapers in 1934.*

"In the next issue of your newspaper there will be a main article about a decision made by Hitler. No matter what his decision is, you will write that it is the only correct one for Germany."

WISE UP WORD

- mass rallies

WORK

1 a Describe two ways in which the Nazis controlled the public by terror.
   b Describe two ways in which the Nazis controlled people by propaganda.
   c Do *you* think one method of control was more important than the other? Or do you think terror and propaganda go 'hand in hand': neither could work without the other? Explain your answer carefully.

2 Write your own definition of propaganda in no more than 15 words.

3 Why do you think the Nazis only produced radios that couldn't pick up foreign broadcasts?

4 Look at **Source B**. What does this instruction tell you about the way the Nazis controlled Germany?

Did all Germans support the Nazis?

AIMS

After studying this spread, make sure you can explain:
- two reasons why Hitler remained popular;
- two methods of showing resistance to Hitler and the Nazis.

Many Germans admired Hitler and liked what the Nazis were doing. They supported them because of what they were achieving in Germany. Look at the four opinions in **Source A**, based on quotes from people living in Germany in the 1930s. They demonstrate why Hitler and the Nazis remained popular for many.

Source A ▼ *What people thought about Hitler and the Nazis.*

Factory worker

"I was one of six million people out of work in 1933. Hitler said he would provide 'work and bread' and he kept his promise. We worked long hours but have good working conditions. The Nazis even provide exciting leisure activities for us too!"

Businessman

"Hitler restored order to Germany, reducing crime and violence. He built up Germany's armed forces so businesses and factories made lots of money supplying goods to the army, navy and air force. He banned trade unions so people couldn't strike and he forced lazy people to work, which saved the country millions in dole money."

Schoolboy

"We were expected to join the Hitler Youth, which involved marching, singing, throwing hand grenades and firing guns. Most of us loved all this and I know Hitler will restore Germany to its rightful place in the world."

Farmer

"The government bought produce and gave farmers a guaranteed price for it. They also stopped the banks from taking land if farmers were in debt."

However, not everyone supported what Hitler and the Nazis were doing. Hitler had very clear ideas about the kind of Germany he wanted – and some groups just didn't fit in. Women, for example, found their career opportunities very limited because Hitler felt women should concentrate on having babies and looking after their husbands! Many minorities too, such as Jews and Gypsies, obviously opposed Hitler because they were so viciously persecuted. But thousands of ordinary Germans didn't fully support Hitler either. Some were uncomfortable with the new concentration camps and the dreaded Gestapo. Others were shocked at the treatment of the Jews … or the Gypsies … or the physically and mentally disabled. So how could ordinary Germans show their opposition to Hitler and the Nazis?

1. Grumbling

'Grumbling', or moaning as it is also known, was the lowest type of opposition to the Nazis. Often in the privacy of their own homes, people might tell an anti-Hitler joke or complain about the way their Jewish friend was being treated.

2. Passive resistance

This was when Germans publicly showed they didn't support the Nazis by refusing to do exactly as they were told. They may have refused to give the 'Heil Hitler' salute or refused to give money to the Hitler Youth member as he went from house to house collecting funds.

3. Open opposition

Some Germans openly declared their dislike of Nazi ideas and policies. Some groups such as the **White Rose** urged Germans to get rid of Hitler. They handed out anti-Nazi leaflets, put up posters and wrote graffiti on walls. Other groups blew up factories producing weapons or acted as spies and passed on military secrets to other countries. The leaders of Germany's two main religious faiths – Protestants (40 million members) and Catholics (22 million) – made some criticism of the Nazis too. For example, in 1941, the Catholic Church spoke out against Hitler's abuse of human rights, particularly the killing of physically and mentally disabled people.

4. Kill Hitler

Hitler and the Nazis could not be voted out, so one of the only ways to get rid of Hitler was to kill him. There *were* attempts on Hitler's life but not many. A Jewish plot to kill him in 1935 failed. The closest any Germans got to assassination was in July 1944 when the war was going very badly. A group of army officers detonated a bomb under a table where Hitler was meeting other Nazi leaders. Despite killing four men, burning Hitler's hair, bursting his eardrums and blowing some of his clothes off – the Führer survived!

Source C ▾ *This poem was written in prison by a German religious leader named Martin Niemoller. Even when Hitler started his National Reich Church (see Fact box), few spoke out against him.*

"First they came for the Jews — but I didn't speak out because I wasn't a Jew.

Then they came for the Communists — but I didn't speak out because I wasn't a Communist.

Then they came for the trade unionists — but I didn't speak out because I wasn't a trade unionist.

Then they came for me — and there was no one left to speak up for me."

WISE UP WORDS

- Reich Church   White Rose

Source B ▴ *Look carefully at this fantastic photograph. Can you find the worker, at the launch of this new battleship in 1936, who is refusing to give the 'Heil Hitler' salute?*

FACT *A new religion?*

Hitler hated Christianity (he wanted people to worship him ... and no one else!) but he didn't dare shut down all the churches because so many Germans were committed Christians. Instead, he said he'd leave them alone. But he didn't! He imprisoned any churchmen who made even a slight criticism of the Nazis and closed all church youth groups and church schools. He even set up a new Nazi church – the **Reich Church** – in an attempt to pull worshippers away from their traditional place of worship. In these new churches, only Nazis were allowed to preach, the Bible was banned (it was replaced by copies of *Mein Kampf*) and all crosses and religious objects were removed.

WORK

1 Look at **Source A**.
   a In your own words and by using just one sentence for each person, write down why they supported Hitler and the Nazis.
   b Choose another member of German society – a woman or a Jew perhaps – and write down what they might *honestly* say about Hitler if they had been allowed.
2 How could a person show their opposition to the Nazi regime without getting into trouble for it?
3 Look at **Source C**. What is the message of this famous poem?
4 How well did Hitler get on with the church in Nazi Germany?

Hitler goes to war

One of Hitler's main aims was to make Germany a powerful nation once more. He had fought as a losing soldier in the Great War of 1914–18 and, like millions of Germans, was humiliated by the punishment Germany received at the end of the fighting.

Hitler identified three things that he felt he must do in order to make Germany a world power once more:

1. Reclaim the land that Germany lost after the Great War. He felt he had to build up his army, navy and air force to do this.

2. Join together all German-speaking people into one big country.

3. Make Germany even bigger because he believed that true Germans were such a great and powerful race that they needed the extra living space (he called it **Lebensraum**) to reach their full potential.

Hitler knew that it would mean breaking the Treaty of Versailles if he were to achieve his three main objectives … but he didn't care! Hitler, like millions of Germans, hated the Treaty and would carry on with his master plan regardless (see **Source A**).

Source A ▼ *A speech by Adolf Hitler.*

> "The Treaty of Versailles is engraved on the minds and hearts of the German people. It is burned into them. Sixty million people find their souls aflame with a feeling of rage and shame. The people are joined in a common cry: 'We will have weapons again'."

Three days after becoming leader of Germany, Hitler ordered his military chiefs to start secretly building new tanks, submarines, battleships and fighter planes. This was known as rearmament. He ordered that every young man had to have army training in the new, bigger, German army. This was known as conscription. Then he took Germany out of the League of Nations, the international peacekeeping organisation set up after the Great War. The chances of a peaceful future didn't look good!

In late 1935, Hitler told the world about his increased army, navy and air force … but no one did anything!

In March 1936, Hitler got more daring. He sent German soldiers into the Rhineland, an area of Germany next to France where German soldiers were forbidden to go. But, once again, no countries stopped him – after all, he wasn't invading another nation, just moving soldiers around *within* his own, they thought! The same year, Hitler signed agreements with Italy and Japan – they agreed to stick up for each other if they were attacked.

In 1938, German troops marched into Austria, the country of Hitler's birth. Hitler had been threatening to invade Austria for years but the Austrian leader, a man named Kurt Schuschnigg, had worked hard to prevent it. Eventually, after Hitler moved his army close to Austria's border – and no other countries offered to help Austria – Schuschnigg resigned. The man who took his place as leader of Austria was a supporter of Hitler … and invited him to take over!

Hitler next turned his attention to the Sudetenland, a small area of Czechoslovakia that contained areas of people who spoke German as their first language.

Hitler told the world he wanted this region. Czechoslovakia wanted to keep it!

Chamberlain (the British Prime Minister) and other leaders made an agreement in Munich in September 1938, which said that Hitler could have *all* of the Sudetenland. Benes (the Czech leader) went along with this, thinking that Hitler would now leave his country alone. Hitler even said that he had no further territorial claims in Europe!

But Hitler lied. When he invaded the rest of Czechoslovakia, in March 1939, it seemed he wasn't satisfied with just the Sudetenland area – he wanted the whole country for living space! Suddenly, at last, the countries of Europe realised that Hitler could never be trusted and began preparing for war. They wondered if they would be next! Britain and France had each had enough of letting Hitler get away with things and agreed to help Poland if Germany invaded.

Sure enough, Poland was next. He threatened to invade in August 1939 but only after making a clever alliance with the USSR. Hitler thought that the Russians might feel threatened if he continued to push his soldiers in their direction (see **Source B**) so he made a deal with Stalin, the Russian leader. The **Nazi–Soviet Pact**, as the deal was known, said they wouldn't fight each other. A secret part of the deal said the Russians could have part of Poland, Hitler's next likely target, if they let the Germans invade.

WISE UP WORDS

- Nazi-Soviet Pact Lebensraum

On 1 September 1939, German troops invaded Poland. Britain and France decided enough was enough. Two days later, on 3 September, Britain and France declared war on Germany. World War II had started.

Source B ▼ *A map of Europe in the 1930s showing Hitler's gradual takeover.*

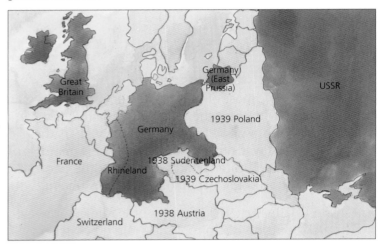

Source C ▼ *Part of Chamberlain's radio speech to the nation when he announced that Britain was at war with Germany, 3 September 1939.*

"This country is at war with Germany … may God bless you all. It is evil things that we are fighting against — brute force, bad faith, injustice, oppression and persecution; and against that, I am certain that right will prevail."

WORK

1 Draw this puzzle into your books and fill in answers to the clues.

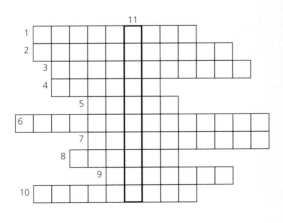

CLUES:

1 Taken back in March 1936
2 A small border area of Czechoslovakia
3 British PM in late 1930s
4 Nazi-_____ Pact
5 Czech leader
6 Invaded in March 1939
7 Germany's hated treaty
8 Invaded on 1 September 1939
9 United in 1939
10 A month of agreement and invasion
2 Now read down the puzzle (clue 11). Write a sentence or two about this word.

The 'Final Solution'

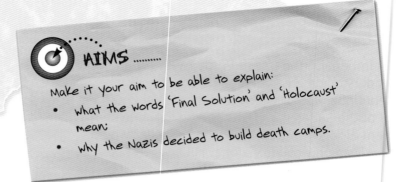

AIMS ....

Make it your aim to be able to explain:

• What the words 'Final Solution' and 'Holocaust' mean;

• Why the Nazis decided to build death camps.

By 1942, most of Europe was under Nazi rule and Hitler saw his chance to get rid of all the people he hated – tramps, the mentally impaired, the chronically sick, Gypsies, homosexuals, political opponents … and especially Jews. For many years these people had been treated very badly in Germany but, when war broke out in 1939, their treatment got worse … a lot worse! As Hitler's armies invaded more and more countries, more of the people he hated became trapped under Nazi rule. So the Nazis looked for a solution to their 'problem' – they looked for what they called a '**Final Solution**'.

On 20 January 1942, a group of leading Nazis met up just outside Berlin to discuss the quickest and cheapest way to destroy all the people on Hitler's hate list. The planning mainly focused on how to rid Europe of Hitler's sworn enemy – the Jews.

Six major extermination or death camps were built within Nazi-occupied Europe, specially equipped to murder thousands and thousands of people in huge poison gas chambers. Massive ovens were built to burn the bodies. The first death camp was opened by March 1942. Special squads of soldiers rounded up Jews in towns all over Europe and cattle trains brought them to the camps. German train companies even charged the Nazi government for one-way tickets.

Once inside the camps, 'prisoners' were sorted into two groups: those who looked over 15 years old, who were strong and healthy, were sent to the left; the sick, old, pregnant women and mothers with very young children were sent to the right. Those on the left, usually about 10–20%, were then put to work, helping the camp's guards murder the ones on the right. Any refusals to help resulted in an immediate death sentence. Those selected to die would then be marched off to what they thought were showers. They were even given soap and a towel! The 'showers' were poison gas chambers (see **Source C**).

Source A ▸ *A Jewish boy looking terrified as he is cleared out of his home before being forced onto a train to a death camp. This family had been living in what was known as a* **ghetto**. *These walled-off areas of large towns, where Jews had been forced to live in squalor for years, were dotted all over Nazi occupied Europe.*

Source B ▶ *A rare colour photograph taken inside a death camp. Here, just as the war ended, American soldiers, who have just found the camp, are forcing local Germans to walk around and view the bodies.*

Source C ▾ *From the memoirs of Rudolf Höss, the commandant of Auschwitz.*

"The 'final solution' meant the complete destruction of all Jews in Europe. I was ordered to establish extermination facilities at Auschwitz in June 1941. At that time there were already in Poland three other extermination camps — Belze, Treblinka and Wolzek …

I visited Treblinka to find out how they carried out their extermination. The camp commandant at Treblinka told me he had liquidated 80 000 in the course of half a year …

He used monoxide gas and I did not think his methods were very efficient. So when I set up Auschwitz, I used Zyklon B acid which we dropped into the death chamber, depending on climatic conditions. We knew when the people were dead because their screaming stopped. We usually waited half an hour before we opened the doors and removed the bodies. After the bodies were removed our special commandos took off the rings and extracted the gold from the teeth of the corpses.

Another improvement we made over Treblinka was that we built our gas chambers to accommodate 2000 people at one time, whereas at Treblinka their ten gas chambers only accommodated 200 people each."

By the end of the war, over six million people, mainly Jews, had been murdered in huge extermination camps. Some called this the '**Holocaust**', meaning 'sacrifice'. Others object to that term, preferring to use the word 'churban', which means 'destruction'. It has been estimated that, on average, 4000 people were murdered every day for four years, in these camps.

WISE UP WORDS

- Holocaust   Final Solution   ghetto

WORK

1 What was the final solution?
2 Rudolf Höss was in charge of Auschwitz death camp. After the war he was captured and put on trial for 'crimes against humanity' (he was later executed). At his trial in 1946 he said:

"let the public continue to regard me as a blood thirsty beast, a cruel sadist and a mass murderer – for ordinary people will never see the commandment of Auschwitz in any other light. They could never understand that he, too, had a heart and that he wasn't evil."

a Judging by Höss's own evidence in **Source C**, explain in detail why Höss can be considered evil. For your answer you might want to consider his attitude to the experiment – is he sorry about his actions or proud?
b Suggest why he thought he wasn't evil, despite the things he did at Auschwitz.

Germany at war

AIMS

Make sure you can explain:
- how World War II affected the home front in Germany;
- why some Germans began to turn against Hitler and the Nazis.

The German people certainly felt the impact of the war at an early stage – food and clothing had been rationed by November 1939 – but the news from the war zones was always good. In fact, the things Germany gained from victory – raw materials such as coal, oil and iron, and captured land with huge factories and slave workers – made many Germans feel that Hitler was right when he said that war would make Germany very rich and powerful. Then things began to go wrong!

Defeat

In 1941, Hitler's armies attacked the USSR (Soviet Russia). At first, German forces did well and got to within 60 miles of Russia's capital, Moscow. But a freezing Russian winter forced the Germans to stop. Their tanks wouldn't start, their guns wouldn't fire and their clothing wasn't warm enough. Soon, the huge Russian army began to push them back towards Germany. In one battle, at Stalingrad, over 80 000 Germans died and 90 000 surrendered. Only 5000 of them ever returned to Germany at the end of the war.

Hardship

There were severe food shortages. The Nazis responded by asking the German people to commit themselves totally to winning the war (a policy named **total war** by Goebbels). Everything was focused on making weapons, growing food and caring for wounded soldiers. Anything that didn't contribute to the war was stopped – beer houses, dance halls and even sweet shops were closed. Letter boxes were boarded up and magazines shut down. Cigarettes were hard to find – as was dairy produce such as milk and eggs. And toilet paper was impossible to get hold of! Factories were forced to stay open longer and even women were drafted in to work in them.

Bombing

From 1942, Britain and America began bombing German cities. Hitler had promised this would never happen. Night after night, major German cities were pounded by bomber planes and, not surprisingly, support for the Nazis began to weaken.

Source A ▾ *Approximately 150 000 civilians died when Dresden was bombed in February 1945. Most of them burned to death in a huge firestorm that raged for two days after the bombing.*

Source B ▼ *Based on an eyewitness account in Hamburg on the morning after a heavy bombing raid.*

"Wednesday Morning

28 July 1943

There's no gas, no electricity, no water, no telephone and the lift doesn't work. It's hard to imagine the panic and chaos. There were no trams, no underground subway and no railway trains. Most people loaded some belongings on carts, bicycles, prams or carried things on their backs and walked just to get away, to escape. People who were wearing Nazi Party badges had them torn off their coats and there were screams of 'Let's get that murderer'. The police did nothing."

Source C ▼ *From a secret Nazi report, 1943.*

"A large section of the nation cannot imagine how the war will end and the telling of rude jokes against the government, even about the Führer himself, has increased."

Source D ▼ *Written by Ruth Andreas-Friedrich, an anti-Nazi.*

"The English have made a shattering raid on Berlin … the city and all the western and southern suburbs are on fire. The air is smoky, sulphur-yellow. Terrified people are stumbling through the streets with bundles, bags, household goods, tripping over fragments and ruins."

FACT *An invasion of Britain?*

Britain was on Hitler's hit list in 1940. His plan was to destroy all Britain's airports and fighter planes before launching an all-out invasion of troops across the English Channel from France. So a fierce air battle raged over England in the summer of 1940 – the Battle of Britain. By September, Britain had just managed to keep the German planes from destroying all their planes … so Hitler gave up his plan to invade Britain and decided to bomb British cities and factories instead (known as the Blitz). He hoped to frighten Britain into surrender … but he didn't!

WISE UP WORD

- total war

WORK

1 **a** What was 'total war'?
   b In what ways did ordinary German citizens feel the effects of total war?

2 By early 1945 it was common to find hammer and sickle badges and six-pointed stars of David armbands for sale on the streets in major cities. Why might ordinary Germans want to buy these?

3 Look at **Source C**. Why do you think the amount of anti-Hitler jokes increased as the war stretched on?

4 Imagine you lived in a large German city during the war and wrote down one or two sentences every week about your life there. Write three entries:
   a The first entry should be written during the first few years of war.
   b The second entry should be made in the year after defeat at Stalingrad and the introduction of total war.
   c The final entry should be made late in the war when conditions in Germany are bad and bombing raids are common.

Have you been learning?

Read the following 1910 newspaper report very carefully. It appeared the day after a 'Votes for Women' march in London had turned to violence.

120 ARRESTED

Suffragettes attack House of Commons
Disgraceful scenes
Reckless women charge at police

True to their word, about 300 Suffragettes marched on the House of Commons yesterday and the scenes of violence were worse than any other of which they had been guilty. It was a picture of shameful recklessness. Never before have otherwise sensible women gone so far in forgetting their womanhood. One woman campaigner fell in the mud, to the disgust of decent men but to the delight of others. One obese Suffragette threw her untidy self against smiling policemen until she ran out of breath. A few more of the desperate pushed at the heroic police in rugby style until they were swung back by a powerful neck or waist grip. Arrests were only made in extreme cases and many women were sadly disappointed not to be taken into custody. Even so, 120 people were arrested, including some men.

a Who were the suffragettes?

b Is this newspaper report biased for or against the suffragettes? Quote any words or phrases that support your view.

c Rewrite the news article in an unbiased way, using the facts in the article.

d In what ways is your news report different from the original?

Task 2 Murder in Sarajevo, 28 June 1914

Look at the following eight statements about the events in Sarajevo on 28 June 1914. You may notice that the order of events is all mixed up *and* each statement contains two spelling mistakes.

- The Archduke is unhurt and his car speeds of to his meeting with the mayor at the town haul. He is furious.
- Franz Ferdinand and his wive arrive at Sarajevo raleway station at 9:28am.
- Immediately, Austria–Hungary blames Serba four killing the Archduke and plans an attack.
- The driver takes a rong turn and has to reverse back. At this moment, a Serbian terorist called Gavrilo Princip shoots and kills the Archduke and his wife.
- On there way to the town hall, a bomb is throne at the Archdukes's car and the explosion injures several people.
- Princip is arressted and beeten up in jail.
- The Archduck and his wife get into a dark-grean, open-topped car.
- After his meating, the Archduke desides to visit the injured people in hospital.

a With a partner, work out the correct chronological order of events.

b In your book, copy out each statement (in the correct chronological order) *and* correct each spelling mistake as you write.

c The events of 28 June 1914 started a chain reaction that drew most of Europe into a terrible war. Design a flow diagram that charts how each country was dragged into war in the few weeks after 28 June.

Task 3 Word Puzzle

a Draw this puzzle into your book and fill in the answers to the clues.

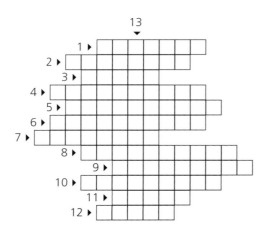

b Now read down the puzzle (clue 13). Write a sentence or two about this word.

1 _____ gun, weapon responsible for about 40% of all wounds inflicted on British troops.

2 The _____ Cross, Britain's highest bravery medal.

3 The area where fighting takes place.

4 The wasteland between the trenches.

5 A foot disease.

6 A blistering, burning, poisonous gas.

7 An ally of Germany, Austria–Hungary and Italy.

8 False or misleading information given out to spread certain points of view.

9 Deadlock.

10 The Treaty which punished Germany.

11 Famous Great War battle.

12 First used in 1916.

Task 4 Cartoon Time

Study this cartoon carefully. It was published in Britain in 1919 and comments on the Treaty of Versailles.

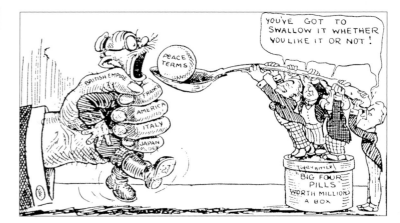

a Which country is represented by the man on the left being strangled by a large hand?

b Who do you think the four men holding the spoon are?

c What are the four men attempting to feed the man on the left?

d What point do you think the cartoonist was trying to make about the Treaty of Versailles?

Task 5 Question Time

Look at these genuine GCSE questions carefully. Why not try to complete one, two or even all of them as a revision exercise?

- What was the Schlieffen Plan?
- Explain how new weapons were supposed to end stalemate on the Western Front.
- "The Battle of the Somme was a complete disaster for the British." Do you agree with this statement? Explain you answer.
- Explain why the British government introduced the Defence of the Realm Act.
- How did the reforms of the Liberal government (1906–14) help the poor?
- What were the main differences between the suffragist and suffragette campaigns?
- What was the Great Depression?
- What is meant by the term 'Welfare State'?
- What did Woodrow Wilson hope to achieve from the Treaty of Versailles?
- What land did Germany lose in the Treaty of Versailles?
- How satisfied were the Allied leaders with the Treaty of Versailles? Explain your answer.
- Explain why Germany was made to pay reparations.

The melting pot

AIMS

The next two pages aim to show you what life was like for some of the new immigrants that chose to move to America in the early 1900s.

Remember:

- two reasons why immigrants moved to America;
- three facts about immigrant workers and/or the jobs they had;
- four groups that made up American society in the early 1900s.

Between 1850 and 1919, about 10% of the population of Europe left for a new life in America. It remains the biggest movement of people in recorded history. For some, like motor millionaire Henry Ford (son of an Irish immigrant and his Dutch wife), their experience of the new world would be a good one. For others, their new life would become a living nightmare, but why did over 40 million **immigrants** start a new life in America between 1850 and 1919?

America's newest citizens came from all over the world but particularly from Europe. Many fled a life of poverty, famine and persecution; others were attracted by the promise of a better life.

Source A ▾ *A recently arrived Russian immigrant, 1909.*

"There is freedom — freedom of speech, freedom of religion and a free press. And democracy too — we will get the chance to vote. And then schooling, we have the chance to learn. No application forms, no questions asked, no entry exams, no fees. Hopefully, education will help me make pots of money, have polish on my boots, eat white bread, soup and meat. America will be my dreamland."

Source B ▾ *Tony, a Greek-born restaurant owner, interviewed in 1939.*

"When I came here I knew nothing, couldn't even speak English. I had a terrible job as a cleaner but one day a customer asked me if I wanted to help him in his restaurant. I worked my way up, learning all the time, married an American woman and now I own my own restaurant. I'm a success — in fact, I believe any hard worker with common sense can make it here."

Source C ▾ *A Polish immigrant, 1919.*

"There is always trouble in my factory. Some don't like us new immigrants. Some say we take jobs from the Americans and we bring down wages because we are prepared to work for less. I've had my fingers broken and my food thrown over the floor."

FACT *The American Dream?*

Of the 2000 people on board the *Titanic* in 1912, nearly half were migrants looking for a new life in America.

FACT *Dublin the numbers*

In 1920, there were twice as many Irish people in New York as there were in Dublin, Ireland's largest city. New York City contained districts known by the names of the immigrants that dominated the area – Little Italy and Chinatown for example.

By 1920, American society was made up of more religions, more colours, more cultures and more languages than any other country in the world. But in the early 1920s, the government began cutting down on the number of immigrants by introducing new laws, which limited the number of new arrivals. A 1921 law allowed only 350 000 immigrants to enter America each year – this was cut to 150 000 by 1929. It seemed as if America's 'open door' for immigrants was beginning to shut!

So who exactly were the Americans?

Old immigrants

Large groups of white settlers began to arrive from Europe in the 1600s, particularly from Britain, Holland and Germany. Soon, the largest group of white settlers, the British, began to regard America as part of the British Empire. After about 150 years, the descendants of the early settlers started to hate being ruled from Britain. They fought, and won, a war of independence against the British and America became an independent country. By the 1900s, white, English speakers had become the most powerful and richest group in American society.

The first Americans

Sometimes known as Native Americans or 'Red Indians', the first Americans lived in tribes across America for thousands of years before white men arrived to live there. Gradually, white settlers from Europe took their land and forced them to live in special areas called reservations.

Black Americans

Millions of African men, women and children were taken to work as slaves on huge cotton and tobacco farms in America between 1600 and 1800. Slavery ended in 1865 and the slaves were set free but many remained near the farms to work.

New immigrants

A wave of new immigrants flooded into America from about 1850 onwards. They came mainly from eastern and southern Europe – Russia, Poland, Italy, Hungary, Czechoslovakia and Greece, for example. Over one million people left Ireland for America after major famines between 1845 and 1848. There was also a growing number of Chinese and Japanese immigrants.

WISE UP WORD

• immigrants

WORK

1 What is meant by the term 'immigrant'?

2 Look at **Source A**.
   a Why was the writer of this source so keen to go to school?
   b What does the source tell us about the conditions in Russia at that time?

3 Look at **Source C**. Why do you think this new immigrant faced such hostility?

4 **a** Write a sentence or two about each of these different groups that make up American society in the 1920s:
   • first Americans
   • old immigrants
   • black Americans
   • new immigrants.
   b Why was American society known as 'the melting pot' in the 1920s?

How is the USA governed?

AIMS

These two pages look at the way America is governed.

Aim to:
- Know the difference between state and central government;
- understand what the Bill of Rights and the US Constitution are;
- know the difference between America's two main political parties.

When British settlers first went to live in America, they established 13 different regions or living areas along America's east coast. The settlers were mostly farmers and grew crops such as tobacco and cotton. Gradually, over many years, the British settlers began to see themselves as Americans and got fed up with British control and taxation. On 4 July 1777, the 13 colonies decided they no longer wanted to be part of the British empire and declared their independence. The British sent soldiers over the Atlantic Ocean to sort out the American rebels and force them to stay loyal to Britain. They met fierce resistance and, after a long war, the Americans won their independence and the right to run their own country. The Americans joined their 13 colonies (or 'states' as they are now called) together to form the United States of America. George Washington was their first President and their capital city was named after him. The first ever flag of the USA was made up of 13 stars and 13 stripes. Today, the number of stripes remains the same but there are now 50 stars representing the 50 states.

Source A ▼ The 50 states of the USA.

After winning their independence, the Americans drew up a set of rules – a constitution – describing how the country should be governed.

It was decided that there should be two types of government. The *central* (sometimes called 'federal') government, based in Washington, DC, would control things that affected the *whole* country (such as foreign affairs, the army and the postal service). A *state* government would also operate in each individual state and would make laws that applied to their own state only.

Central government was to be made up of a president (elected every four years), a cabinet of advisors and **Congress** (like a parliament) made up of elected people from the different states.

The American people could also vote for their state government, with each state having its own laws, its own police and court system, and its own governor in charge. Gambling, for example, may be against the law in one state but quite legal in another. Convicted murderers may receive the death penalty in some states but be sentenced to life imprisonment in others.

Further, the police of one state could not chase a criminal across 'state-lines' into another state. Only the FBI (Federal Bureau of Investigation) could cross state borders while attempting to solve very serious 'federal crimes' or catch criminals who had committed crimes in more than one state.

> **FACT** *Vote for me!*
>
> Voters had two main political parties to choose from:
>
> - The **Republican Party** liked to preserve traditions and stay out of people's lives wherever possible (a policy called **laissez faire**, a French phrase roughly meaning 'leave alone'). They didn't believe in high taxes – which pleased rich people and businessmen! Republicans left these people alone to create jobs and spend their money.
> - The **Democratic Party** was more of an ordinary people's party, preferring to intervene in everyday life if it was needed. They favoured helping those in need – the poor or elderly for example.

WISE UP WORDS

- Democratic Party   Republican Party
  laissez faire   Congress

The Democrats had more support in the southern states (where there were more poor people), while the Republicans had more support in the north (where there were more industries, more jobs and more wealth). Democrats were seen by many as more liberal (prepared to change things); Republicans were seen as more conservative (traditional).

Source B ▾ *The first part of the American Constitution was the Bill of Rights. However, some states found ways to get around offering these rights to everyone and, by 1919, many states refused to recognise the right to vote of women, blacks and Native Americans.*

BILL OF RIGHTS

The American government has guaranteed that its people have the right to vote. There are also other rights and freedoms. They include:

- Freedom of speech (people can say what they want – within reason!)
- Freedom of belief (people can worship who they want)
- Freedom of information (the right to read and listen to what they want)
- Freedom in law (the right to a fair trial, freedom from unfair arrest)
- Freedom of assembly (the right to meet in groups)
- Freedom of protection (the right to carry a weapon to protect yourself – which is why licensed guns are still legal in America)

WORK

1 a Why do American's today celebrate 'Independence day' on 4 July each year?
  b Explain why today's American flag has 50 stars and 13 stripes.
2 a What is the difference between 'central' and 'state' government?
  b How does the American system of government try to protect the freedom of the people?
  c Which groups in particular were not given the same rights as most white English-speaking Americans?

How far did the US economy 'boom' in the 1920s?

AIMS

After completing the work on the next four pages, you should be able to:

- explain how different factors helped America become the richest country in the world;

- identify different groups that didn't make lots of money in the 1920s.

In 1926, the American government announced that American workers were earning, on average, nearly twice as much money as workers in any other country in the world. It said that the standard of living in the USA was the highest it had ever been in the country's history – Americans were officially the richest people in the world! So why had people started to earn more than ever before? What sort of things were Americans making and buying in such huge numbers? And did all Americans benefit during this 'golden age'?

World War I

America didn't join in World War I when it started. Instead, it sold food, weapons and other goods to Britain and her allies. This created many jobs in America and made lots of businesspeople very rich. America eventually joined the war in 1917, on Britain's side, after the German navy had sunk lots of American ships – and they found out that the Germans were secretly scheming to help Mexico invade America once a suitable plan could be drawn up. Over 100 000 American soldiers died fighting, but the impact was much greater in countries such as France, Germany, Russia and Britain, which had all been exhausted by the war. In these countries, millions of men had been killed and they had lost valuable farmland, railway lines, factories, cattle and so on. Now the USA, not touched by any of the fighting, produced a high percentage of the world's basic goods (see **Source B**). Skilled inventors and businessmen were now able to exploit these resources and make fortunes from them.

Source A ▶ An illustrator's copy of a famous American recruitment poster.

Source B ▼ *By 1920, America was now one of the world's leading producers and suppliers of raw materials. This chart shows the percentage of the world's resources made in the USA. Indeed, America was fortunate that it had important raw materials, such as coal, iron ore and oil. It didn't have to pay other countries for them!*

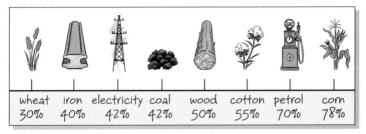

| wheat | iron | electricity | coal | wood | cotton | petrol | corn |
| 30% | 40% | 42% | 42% | 50% | 55% | 70% | 78% |

New things to buy

In 1916, only 15% of American homes had electricity – but nearly 70% of homes had it by 1927. This meant that workers could spend their hard-earned money on any number of ultra-modern 'gadgets' which had recently been invented – vacuum cleaners, gramophones (ask your teacher!), toasters, washing machines, radios, telephones, refrigerators, watches, irons, ovens and much more. Huge demand for these goods created jobs in the factories that made them.

Source C ▼ *An advert for an electric water heater, 1921.*

New ways to make things

American businesspeople, such as Henry Ford, were very quick to see the advantages of using the very latest technology to produce goods. He made huge numbers of cars, built bit by bit, pulled along on an assembly line, in a massive high-tech factory in Detroit. Glass, steel, rubber and leather went in one end of his factory – cars came out of the other: one every *ten* seconds! Many **consumer goods** – radios, telephones and ovens – were produced like this. And all the time, as companies got better and quicker at making them, the cheaper the goods became. The more products that people bought, the more jobs were created.

Source D ▼ *The growth in sales of consumer goods during the 1920s. Amazingly, by 1929, America made nearly 50% of all the world's consumer goods.*

Cars
1919 – 9 million
1929 – 26 million

Telephones
1919 – 10 million
1929 – 20 million

Radios
1919 – 60 000
1929 – 10 million

Refrigerators
For every refrigerator in 1921, there were 167 by 1929.

New ways to buy and sell

The desire to own these new consumer goods was increased by fantastic advertising campaigns. Colourful **billboards**, newspapers and magazines urged people to buy the latest gadget and keep up with their neighbours. Department stores sold the goods on every high street and, for those who didn't live near a large enough town, there was the latest catalogue, full of goods to choose from that could be delivered to your door. In one famous catalogue, you could buy anything from a tractor to a coffee cup, to a pair of pants! Cinemas and radios carried advertisements too, even encouraging people to take advantage of new 'buy now, pay later' schemes, which meant buyers could pay for goods in small instalments over a fixed period of time. Six out of ten cars were bought this way.

Source E ▼ *Companies such as Coca-Cola made millions because they spent money on advertising slogans, like 'The pause that refreshes', which became known over the whole of America. However, some slogans would be illegal today – one cigarette maker claimed their product 'protected the voice and stopped you coughing'!*

Source F ▼ *From an American news article, 1927. Have you ever bought something solely as a result of an advertisement?*

"Advertising makes people want things they didn't even know they wanted. It changes our habits and our way of life, affects what we wear, what we eat and how we pay."

FACT *Buy, buy, buy*

A selection of consumer goods available to buy in 1925, which are still familiar today.

Help from the government

To help American businesses, the government put high taxes (**import duties** or **tariffs**) on foreign goods entering the country, making foreign-produced goods more expensive. So when faced with the choice of an expensive foreign car or handbag – or a cheaper American-made one – customers would usually choose the one produced in their own country. The government also cut taxes paid by rich people and companies – they wanted rich people to have as much money as possible so they could start more companies and create more jobs!

FACT *'You've got hala, halla, hely ... bad breath!'*

In 1921, the company that made Listerine Mouthwash used the rather serious-sounding medical word *halitosis* in an advertisement for their product, instead of the more commonly used phrase *bad breath*. This was clearly designed to make people worry that they had a serious medical condition ... it worked! Within five years, sales rose from 100 000 bottles to four million bottles a year.

A good time for all?

Not everyone enjoyed the high wages and fantastic job opportunities of the 1920s. In fact, by 1928, half the population was living below the poverty line. They included:

- Farmers – new high-tech machinery such as combine harvesters meant they produced more food than ever before. Unfortunately, there was more food available than the population could eat so it remained unsold ... and Canada was producing lots of cheap food too! Farmers who couldn't sell food made little money and were either evicted from their land or forced to sell up. Cotton and wool farmers suffered too. New artificial fibres, such as rayon, were being used to make clothing. Cotton and wool factory workers also suffered because there was less demand for their products. Six hundred thousand farmers lost their farms in 1924 alone!

- Coal miners – coal mines began to close as oil, gas and electricity were increasingly used as alternatives to heat homes and cook food.

- Black workers – thousands of black Americans worked on farms in the south. As farms closed, they lost their jobs. Many made their way to the cities but could only find low paid jobs – and some factories operated an all-white policy!

WISE UP WORDS

- consumer goods   billboards   import duties   tariffs

Source G ▼ *A poor family of farm workers. What signs are there in the photograph that this family is poor?*

WORK

1 **a** The 1920s are often called the 'boom times' by historians. What do you think the phrase 'boom time' means?

   b Here are seven reasons why there was a 'boom time'. Explain how each one could cause an economic boom:
   - World War I
   - new consumer goods
   - the assembly line
   - advertising
   - 'buy now pay later' schemes
   - import duties
   - low taxes.

   c Show how some of the factors are related to each other, for example the goods produced quickly and cheaply on an assembly line would not sell without a good advertising campaign.

2 What changes to the American way of life were brought about by the boom?

3 Did all Americans enjoy the boom times? Give examples in your answer.

What were the 'Roaring Twenties'?

For many, the 1920s was a period in American history when people were having lots of fun, enjoying loud music, wild parties and new forms of entertainment. Millions of people had more money and more leisure time than ever before. It became known as the 'Roaring Twenties'.

Having fun

It was a time of **crazes** – marathon dancing and flagpole sitting became popular. People would see how long they could dance without stopping or how long they could sit on top of a flagpole without falling off. Alvin 'Shipwreck' Kelly set the record when he remained on top of a flagpole for 23 days and seven hours!

Source A ▲ Two flappers being arrested.

Look at **Source A**. The young women in the photograph are **flappers**. They have just been arrested on a beach in Chicago for being 'indecently dressed'. To put it simply, their swimming costumes are just too revealing for the 1920s – they have shown too much flesh and have shocked an onlooker into calling the police!

Flappers, the fashionable, independent young women of the 1920s, rebelled against the way women had been treated for many years. They hated the fact that men had the best jobs and earned the most money. They rebelled against the sort of clothes that women were traditionally expected to wear (see **Source B**) and detested the role that many men assumed that women should take – the role of wife and mother.

Source B ▼ A woman of 1900.

- long hair, tied up under a hat
- pale skin, little make-up
- tight corset that pulled in the waist
- long sleeves, covering the arms
- long dress, covering legs

Source C ▼ *Flappers were mainly middle- and upper-class women from the northern states of America. They earned their own money and rebelled against their restricted lives. For many poorer women, and those in the more traditional southern states, life went on as it had done for many years.*

- short hair
- cocktail
- Chanel No. 5 perfume
- suntan and make-up
- bangles and long beads
- low waist
- high hemline
- cigarette
- flesh-coloured stockings

Source D ▼ *The president of Florida University, 1923. Many older people saw flappers as an example of the evils of modern life. These people felt that family life, religion and traditional values were threatened by their new freedom.*

"The low-cut dresses, the stockings and short skirts are born of the devil and are carrying the present and future generations of this country to destruction."

Source E ▶ *Two flappers bravely dancing the Charleston on the roof of a Chicago hotel in 1926. The Charleston, the One Step, the Black Bottom and the Tango, were favourite dances in the 1920s. As **jazz** music swept the nation on radios and in nightclubs, these high-energy dances were a welcome relief to the old ballroom dancing and waltzes of America before the war.*

Source F ▼ *A marathon dancing competition, 1928. Helen Jarm was American champion. Using many different partners, she managed to dance for 1120 hours in 1932.*

Sport

It was a golden age for American sport. For the first time, sportspeople became sports *stars* with celebrity status. Radio broadcasts, newspapers and magazines helped bring major sports events to a mass audience. The 1920s was the decade when baseball, boxing, golf and horseracing became massive sports. Around 60 million radio listeners heard the 1927 World Heavyweight Boxing title fight between Jack Dempsey and Gene Tunney.

New music

Jazz was the most popular music of the 1920s. For the first time, whites were exposed to black music – and they loved it! This new sound, originating in the black neighbourhood of Harlem, New York, provided great opportunities for black musicians such as Louis Armstrong and Bessie Smith. They made big money from nightclub and radio performances and record sales.

Source G ▼ *A popular jazz musician talking about the 1920s. Even today, the 1920s are known as the Jazz Age.*

"Music is entering more and more into the daily lives of people. The Negro musicians of America are playing a great part in this change. They are not held back by traditions. They have new ideas and constantly experiment. They are causing new blood to flow into the veins of music. The jazz players make their instruments do entirely new things, things trained musicians are taught to avoid … Jazz has come to stay because it is an expression of the times — the breathless, energetic, super active times in which we are living."

FACT *Lucky Lindy*

In May 1927, Charles A. Lindbergh became the first man to fly non-stop across the Atlantic Ocean from New York to Paris in his plane *Spirit of St Louis*. He had taken five sandwiches, two pints of water and an inflatable boat. He took no map and no parachute!

After a 33.5-hour flight, he touched down in Paris and immediately became a superstar. At one point, he was so famous that he couldn't send his clothes to the dry-cleaners because the staff kept them as souvenirs!

Source H ▼ *A poster advertising a performance by Louis Armstrong and his band. Ironically, many of the clubs in which the country's most famous jazz performers worked had an 'all-white' policy – the only blacks allowed in were the musicians! Even Harlem's legendary Cotton Club was run and owned by whites.*

SAINT LOUIS BLUES

Featured by LOUIS ARMSTRONG *and his* ALL STARS *in the* COLUMBIA RECORD ALBUM No. CL 591

The movies

One of the biggest success stories of the 1920s was the movie industry. Hollywood, just outside the Californian city of Los Angeles, enjoyed year-round sunshine and many of the big movie companies – MGM, Warner Brothers and Paramount – had their studios there. Movies were already big business before the 1920s, with weekly audiences of 35 million in 1919 but, during the next decade, audiences nearly trebled to a high of 100 million people a WEEK going to the movies to watch films in 1930. That's as many as go to visit the cinema in a year in Britain today. Part of the success of the movie industry was something called the **star system** – a term used to describe the way movie studios promoted their stars, not just the films they were in. The film companies made sure that the media had full access to the stars, making them do magazine interviews, photo shoots and public appearances. They knew that people were attracted to their lifestyles, copying the way their favourite stars ate their dinner, wore their clothes and styled their hair. Film-makers even realised that the star of a film was often more important than its plot – people would pay to see the film even if it was terrible! By 1929, Hollywood film studios were making over 500 films a year, giving employment to thousands and entertainment to millions who flocked to see comedies, romances, adventure stories and historical epics.

Until 1927, all movies were silent. Words appeared on screen at regular intervals and a piano player provided background music. Then *The Jazz Singer* was released, the first 'talking film', or 'talkie' as they were known. This boosted cinema audience figures to an all-time high because moviegoers were desperate to see how their favourite movie star spoke. In fact, 'talkies' ruined the careers of many actors and actresses who looked great … but had strange voices or funny accents!

WISE UP WORDS

- star system   crazes   jazz   flappers

Source I ▼ *Charlie Chaplin who, along with Rudolf Valentino, Clara Bow and Laurel and Hardy, was one of the most famous stars of the 1920s.*

WORK

1 What were flappers and why do you think they shocked some sections of American society?

2 What entertainment was available to Americans in the 1920s?

3 Who was Charles A. Lindbergh and why do you think he was known as 'the flying fool'?

4 What was the 'star system'?

5 Draw a diagram or create a poster or leaflet that summarises the main features of entertainment and popular culture in the Roaring Twenties. You are limited to using 100 words.

How widespread was intolerance in the 1920s?

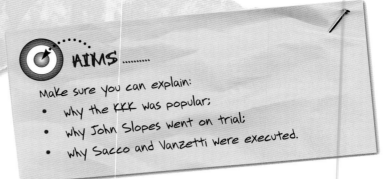

AIMS

Make sure you can explain:
- Why the KKK was popular;
- Why John Slopes went on trial;
- Why Sacco and Vanzetti were executed.

Despite boasts that America was the 'land of the free', there are a great many examples of persecution and intolerance in the 1920s. For example, many white, Anglo-Saxon Protestants (WASPs as they were known) thought that letting more and more people into the country was 'diluting' America's 'pure' race! And WASPs made up the majority of US citizens. So the idea that the US was a land of opportunity for all was losing popularity. Indeed, the intolerance to different races, new ideas and new immigrants can be summed up by the following three studies: the KKK, the Monkey Trial, and the Sacco and Vanzetti case.

The Ku Klux Klan

One of America's most racist terror groups was a secret society known as the Ku Klux Klan or KKK. Dressed in white sheets, white hoods and carrying American flags, their methods of violence and intimidation included whipping, branding with acid, kidnapping, castration and lynching. They stripped some of their victims and put burning hot tar and feathers on their bodies.

Most of the members were poor whites who were afraid of blacks and immigrant workers because they were prepared to work for low wages. But the KKK also had members who were policemen, judges, teachers and politicians. Fortunately, the mass appeal of the KKK did not last long.

Source A ▼ *A new member swears an oath of loyalty to the KKK while a young black man is tarred and feathered. This picture is based on an event that took place in Texas in 1923.*

Source B ▾ *KKK secret codes. Why did they need, or want, a secret language?*

Klonversations Kode-book

WORD	MEANING
Ayak	**A**re **y**ou **a K**lansman?
Akia	**A K**lansman **I a**m.
Kigy	**K**lansmen **I g**reet **y**ou.
Sanbog	**S**trangers **a**re **n**ear, **b**e **o**n **g**uard.

The Monkey Trial

In July 1925, a 24 year old biology teacher named John Scopes went on trial in Tennessee for teaching biology in a biology lesson! Even today, millions of Americans know this as the 'Monkey Trial'.

The origins of the trial lay in an idea that had swept across America in the late 1800s and early 1900s called Charles Darwin's **theory of evolution**. He argued that human beings gradually evolved from apes over millions of years. For many people all over the world, not just in America, this was too much. Darwin was suggesting that there did not need to be a God to explain human existence!

Many Americans were very religious people who went to church regularly and believed that everything in the Bible was true. Darwin's theory opposes this view totally, claiming that life on earth, including humans, evolved slowly – man *wasn't* created in one day. In 1924, six states in the 'Bible Belt' – a very religious area of America in the south and mid-west – decided to put a stop to this new theory being taught and passed laws making it illegal for teachers to teach the theory of evolution.

John Scopes decided to put the law to the test in Tennessee, one of the states that had banned Darwin's theory. He taught it to a class of 14 year olds and agreed to let his friend sue him for breaking the law.

There was little doubt that Scopes was guilty, so the defence team instead focused on the arguments for and against evolution. As a result, it became known as the 'Monkey Trial'.

After a ferocious trial, the jury returned their verdict – Scopes was guilty and fined $100. However, Scopes and his supporters always claimed they had won a moral victory because they had demonstrated that some laws were worth breaking when they pose a threat to a person's freedom of speech and thought.

Source C ▾ *John Scopes (front row, light suit) surrounded by his legal team, in the Monkey Trial. His main lawyer, Clarence Darrow, is pictured on the left holding his famous white hat.*

Sacco and Vanzetti

In April 1920, a robbery took place at a shoe factory in South Braintree, Massachusetts. The robbers stole $15 000 and shot two of the staff dead. A month later, two Italian-born immigrants – Nick Sacco and Bart Vanzetti – were arrested and charged with their murders. Their trial began in May 1921 and lasted 45 days. In July, the jury found them guilty and the judge sentenced them to 'death by electric chair'. But were Sacco and Vanzetti really guilty? Or were they just innocent victims who suffered because many Americans were becoming tired – and scared – of the millions of immigrants pouring into the country?

By 1920, the American government had started to reduce the number of immigrants they were letting into America. One reason for limiting immigration was fear of Communists and **anarchists**. Anarchists believe that countries should not be ruled by organised governments with set laws and rules, but by a system where everyone rules themselves through voluntary cooperation.

Against this background of fear, the armed robbery and murder took place in the shoe factory in Massachusetts. The two men arrested had two decisive factors against them from the start – Nick Sacco and Bart Vanzetti were not only Italian immigrants who spoke very little English … they were both anarchists too!

Study the evidence for and against them at their trial. Were Sasco and Venzetti really guilty or just innocent scapegoats of a public who hated immigrants – and especially anarchists?

Source D ► *The judge, Webster Thayer, said this just after the trial. He also called them 'dagos', 'wops' (two derogatory words used to describe Italians) and 'sons of bitches'.*

> "Did you see what I did to those anarchist bastards?"

Source E ► *A top American lawyer said this about the judge in charge of the trial. 'Reds' was a word used to describe Communists and anarchists. In fact, this period of political intolerance at the start of the 1920s is known as **the Red Scare**.*

> "I have known Judge Thayer all my life. He is narrow minded, half educated, unintelligent and full of prejudice. He is carried away by fears of Reds which has captured about 90% of the American people."

Source F ► *Sacco and Vanzetti in prison, 1921. The trial was reported all over the world and there were demonstrations in major cities against the verdict – the American Embassy in Paris was even bombed.*

Source G ▼ *Based on Bart Vanzetti's last statement, made just before he was executed.*

"I am not guilty of these crimes. I have never commit a crime in my life. I have never steal, never kill, never spilt blood. I do not wish any misfortune, even to a dog or snake. I am suffering because of my beliefs. I am suffering because I am an Italian. If you executed me two times more and I was born again, I would still live my life the same."

Source H ▼ *The case for and against Sacco and Vanzetti.*

EVIDENCE AGAINST SACCO AND VANZETTI

- 61 eyewitnesses identified them as the killers.
- Both men were carrying loaded guns when arrested. The bullets were the same size as those that killed the two men.
- Both men 'acted guilty' when arrested and told some lies to the police.
- Vanzetti had a previous conviction for armed robbery in December 1919.

EVIDENCE FOR THE DEFENCE

- 107 people confirmed that Sacco and Vanzetti were somewhere else on the night of the robbery/murders.
- Witnesses nearly all disagreed over what the two men were wearing on the night in question.
- Several other men confessed to the murders.
- It is no crime in America to carry a loaded gun. Sacco and Vanzetti said they carried one because they were worried about being attacked because of their political beliefs.
- Sacco and Vanzetti spoke poor English. Their lawyers argued they got confused under police questioning and lied as they thought they were being victimised because they were foreigners and anarchists.

Despite years of public demonstrations, protests, legal arguments and appeals, the two men were executed by electric chair on 23 August 1927. In 1977, 50 years after their execution, the Governor of Massachusetts granted Sacco and Vanzetti a formal pardon and accepted that an unfair trial had taken place.

WISE UP WORDS

- anarchists   the Red Scare   supremacy theory of evolution

WORK

1   a   What was the Ku Klux Klan?
   b   Why do you think some whites formed the Ku Klux Klan?
   c   Why were Klan members not always punished when they broke the law?

2   Look at **Source A**.
   a   In your own words, explain what is going on in the picture?
   b   Suggest two reasons why Klan members wore white hoods.

3   a   Why did John Scopes face trial in July 1925?
   b   Why do you think the trial became known as the Monkey Trial?
   c   In what way did the trial show how some Americans were intolerant?

4   Look at **Sources D** and **E**.
   a   What impression do you get of Judge Thayer by reading these sources?
   b   Do you think he would have given Sacco and Vanzetti a fair trial?

5   Look at **Source G**.
   a   Why, according to Vanzetti, were he and Sacco found guilty?
   b   Is this statement a useful piece of evidence that helps us to decide whether the two men were guilty or not? Explain your answer carefully.

6   Look at **Source H**.
   a   What were Sacco and Vanzetti accused of?
   b   What were the main differences between the evidence for the prosecution and evidence for the defence?

What was Prohibition and why did it fail?

AIMS ....

After these two pages, you should be able to:

* write at least one sentence about each of the Wise Up Words on the facing page;
* list the reasons why Prohibition was introduced ... and why it failed.

At midnight on 16 January 1920, America introduced a new law. Seconds later, millions of people were breaking it. They would continue to break it until the law was repealed (ended) in 1933. Most of the lawbreakers would never get punished.

Some historians say that America's newest law was one of the country's biggest ever mistakes. So what law were people so keen to break? How did they break it? And why was it introduced in the first place?

Prohibition, as the new law was known, prohibited (banned) any American from selling, making or carrying around any drink containing more than 0.5% alcohol (most beers, for example, contain 5% alcohol). The ban on booze wasn't a sudden thing. For many years there had been a strong campaign against alcohol, led by pressure groups such as the **Anti-Saloon League**. Many Americans supported a ban, claiming that the 'demon drink' damaged family life and caused idleness, sickness and debt.

Source A ▼ _From an American school textbook, written, not surprisingly, by a person in favour of Prohibition._

"A cat or dog can be killed if it drinks a small glass of beer. A boy once drank whiskey from a flask he had found and died the next day."

FACT _The law_

Prohibition is actually a nickname. Officially, the ban on alcohol is the 18th Amendment [change] to the United States Constitution. The Amendment states that '... the manufacture, sale or transportation of intoxicating liquors ... within the United States ... for beverage purposes is hereby prohibited.' Interestingly, it was never illegal to buy or drink it! The **Volstead Act** later set down penalties for breaking the new law.

Prohibition never worked. The reason for this was quite simple – people still wanted to drink. They were prepared to break a law they never wanted ... and criminal gangs were only too willing to get the alcohol for them. These gangs ran illegal bars called **speakeasies**, which sold **bootleg** alcohol smuggled in from abroad by **bootleggers**. They also sold **moonshine** – a home-made spirit that was sometimes so strong it caused serious illness. In fact, deaths from alcohol poisoning went up from 98 in 1920 to nearly 800 in 1926! Speakeasies were hidden away in cellars or private hotel rooms and drinkers had to give passwords or knock on the door in code to gain entry.

Source B ▶

Advertising an illegal speakeasy in a newspaper or magazine was against the law. Instead, signs and directions were chalked onto the pavement to show the way.

A few years after the introduction of Prohibition, criminal gangs were making millions from bootlegging and speakeasies. They made so much money that they could bribe many police, lawyers and judges to cooperate with them and not prosecute. They also made money through fixing horse and dog racing, brothels and **racketeering**. This was when businessmen and shopkeepers paid money to the gangs to stop them smashing up their premises. One gang leader, the famous Al Capone, made $10 million a year from racketeering. Indeed, it was estimated that at one point in his career his illegal activities were generating nearly $6 million dollars a day. Other gang leaders, or **gangsters**, as they were known, included Dutch Schultz, 'Bugs' Moran, 'Lucky' Luciano, 'Machine Gun' Kelly and Vito 'Chicken Head' Gurino! These men settled their business rivalries in gunfights and bomb attacks and led to a new phrase being used in America – **organised crime**.

By the 1930s, it was clear that Prohibition was just not working – there were now approximately 200 000 speakeasies in America! In New York alone, there were 32 000 speakeasies, yet there were only 15 000 bars before Prohibition – it seemed that the law to ban booze was making it more popular than ever!

By 1933, many realised that the Prohibition experiment had failed. The attempt to make America a less violent, more honest and moral country had resulted in the rise of gangsters and organised crime and police corruption! In early 1933, one of new American President Roosevelt's first steps was to **repeal** Prohibition. Americans could (legally) drink again.

Source C ▾ *US police catch a group of bootleggers with crates of illegal alcohol hidden in their car.*

Source D ▾ *Based on an interview with Elmer Gertz, a Chicago lawyer in the 1920s.*

"You'd go into what seemed like an ordinary restaurant that served fried chicken and spaghetti. The wine would be served in coffee cups so that if the place was raided, you'd appear to be drinking coffee not wine … Prohibition taught Americans to disrespect the law … it taught them that crime *could* pay."

WISE UP WORDS

- Prohibition   Anti-Saloon League   Volstead Act   speakeasies   bootleg   bootleggers   moonshine   racketeering   organised crime   gangsters   repeal

WORK

1 **a** Copy and complete the puzzle below using clues 1–8.

   1 Illegal bar
   2 Alcohol smuggled in from abroad
   3 A gangster's favourite weapon
   4 American word for a bar
   5 To officially bring a law to an end
   6 Nickname of the law to ban alcohol
   7 Home-made booze
   8 Act that set down the penalties for breaking the law

   b Now read down the puzzle (clue 9). Write a sentence or two about this person.

2 Look at **Source D**.

   a How did diners conceal their alcoholic drinks?

   b What does this source tell us about the public's attitude toward prohibition?

   c According to this source, what was one of the worst consequences of Prohibition?

   d Why do you think Prohibition failed?

Why did Wall Street 'crash'?

AIMS ....

After studying these four pages, you should be able to explain these words:
- shareholder • investor • dividend • stock market.

In 1928, Herbert Hoover became President of America. He won the election easily. His political party, the Republicans, had been in power for over seven years and during that time, the boom times had swept across much of America.

So why, just six months later, did it all go wrong?

On average, wages of American workers had risen by 11% between 1921 and 1928. During the same period, the average working week dropped from 47.4 to 44.2 hours per week. So people, on average, worked less and earned more. Also, throughout the 1920s, ordinary Americans had all sorts of new inventions (the motor car, radio and so on), new forms of entertainment (jazz clubs, cinemas and so on) and new fashions to choose from. Hoover, President at the time, believed that with a lot of hard work and a bit of good fortune, anyone could make money – and he pointed to the **stock market** as one of his examples.

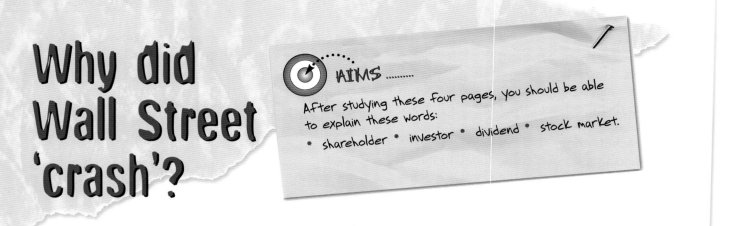

Source A ➤ *An investor makes money on the stock market.*

So how does the stock market work?

- To set up a company you need money – for wages, equipment, land and so on.

- Most companies get this from **investors**. In return, investors own a share of the company. They become **shareholders**.

- Shareholders make money by:
  i) receiving a share of the company profits – a **dividend** – each year.

ii) selling their shares for a higher price than they paid. Shareholders will get more money than they paid for their shares if the company does well and makes good profits. However, shareholders might not be able to sell their shares if the company is doing badly – a shareholder could be stuck with a share that no one wants to buy and that pays no dividends!

- Shares are bought and sold on the stock market ('stock' is another word for a share). In America, the country's stock market is in New York, on Wall Street.

During the 1920s, 'playing the stock market', as it was known, became a national craze. Several million people, not just the rich, but ordinary Americans, bought shares in all sorts of companies … and made money by selling them – only to buy more shares to try to make more money. Perhaps it seemed that Hoover's prediction of an end to poverty would soon come true.

Millions of Americans agreed with Hoover when he said that the end of poverty was in sight – none more so than the millions who had made money from the stock market. In 1920, there had been only four million people who owned shares – by 1929, there were five times as many! For a while, it seemed that every investor – the housewife, the car worker, the shopkeeper, the chauffeur and the factory owner – won when playing the stock market!

Source B ▼ *The price of shares in ten US companies. From which company would you have liked to have bought $100 worth of shares in 1928? How much would your shares be worth if you sold them in September 1929?*

Source C ▼ *Wall Street after the Crash. Worried crowds gathered outside the Stock Exchange on 29 October 1929, trying to find out what had happened to the values of their shares. At one point, the police arrived to keep order.*

WORK

1 In 1928 President Hoover confidently predicted 'the poor man is vanishing from among us'. What do you think made him say this?

2 What is a stock market?

3 Why did Americans invest money in shares in the 1920s? Give a full explanation, in your own words, of how someone might make a profit from 'playing the stock market'.

COMPANY	2 March 1928 COST OF ONE SHARE (CENTS)	3 September 1929 COST OF ONE SHARE (CENTS)
American Can	77	182
Anaconda Copper	54	162
Electric Bond and Share	90	204
General Electric Company	129	396
General Motors	140	182
New York Central	160	256
Radio	94	505
US Steel	138	279
Westinghouse E&M	92	313
Woolworth	181	251

Source D ▾ *Author Geoffrey Pensett talking on the TV series* America's Century.

"There was a janitor called George Gallies who had $1000 in the Bank of the United States. It had taken Gallies 40 years to save $1000. After spending two nights and two days in the pouring rain outside this shuttered, locked bank, beating on the walls with his hands in frustration, he realized he was never going to see ten cents of his money. So he went back to the basement where he lived and he hanged himself in despair. That's what bank failures did — they crushed hundreds of thousands of ordinary people like George Gallies."

The crash

During the 1920s, it seemed as if the stock market was an easy way to get rich. Anyone could buy shares, watch their value rise and then sell the shares later at a higher price. Banks were more than willing to lend money to these share speculators (another word for an investor) knowing that they would get their money back soon — with interest!

However, disaster was just around the corner. Not all Americans had the wealth to buy the goods made by companies and there was a limit to the number of cars, radios, telephones and refrigerators the more wealthy people could buy. After all, a family home is highly unlikely to have more than one oven, vacuum cleaner or refrigerator. American factories were **overproducing** – making goods faster than they could sell them – and profits were beginning to fall!

To begin with, in September 1929, one or two cautious people began to sell their shares. They were worried that they wouldn't get their share of company profits at the end of the year. As word spread about the falling profits of leading American companies, more and more people began to sell their shares. The result was astonishing. Shareholders realised that their shares (which were only pieces of paper entitling them to a share of company profits) were only worth something if someone was willing to buy them. As they tried to turn their shares into cash, they dropped their share price to attract a buyer. On 24 October 1929, 13 million shares were sold on the Wall Street Stock Exchange (five times as many as on a normal day) and share prices in nearly all companies began to drop. The price of a share in the General Electric Company fell from $3.15 to $2.83 and shares in radio fell by 24 cents. Some investors called this **Black Thursday**; others called it the 'Crash'.

Once the rush to sell began, the situation got worse and worse. People just didn't want their shares – they wanted their cash instead – so they dropped their prices more and more to attract a buyer. On Tuesday 29 October, there was another mad panic to sell shares – at any price. Sixteen million shares were sold during the day and the average price of shares dropped 40 cents. Shareholders lost a total of $8000 million!

As the year went on, things got even worse. Many Americans had borrowed money from banks to buy shares, hoping to pay back their loans when the shares rose in price. But when share prices fell, investors couldn't sell their shares for a high enough price to be able to pay their bank back in full. If enough customers couldn't pay back their loans, the banks went bankrupt. When this happened, ordinary people who had savings in the bank lost all their money (see **Source C**). In 1929 alone, 659 banks went bust!

FACT *How does a bank work?*

American banks in the 1920s, which were often small, one-town operations, had two parts:

- Savings – people put their savings into the bank; the bank rewarded them each year with an interest payment, for example 5% of what you saved. If you saved $1000, the bank would give you a $50 interest bonus.

- Loans – people could borrow money from the bank, but would have to pay the bank an interest payment each year, for example 10% of the loan. If you borrowed $1000, you would have to pay back $1100.

In 1929, the problems started when people couldn't pay back their loans because they'd swapped their money for new worthless shares. The bank had loaned out all the 'savings' money to those who wanted loans. The money had gone ... and banks went bankrupt.

▼ **Source E** *The cost of one share in ten American companies. Imagine if you had borrowed money from a bank to buy 100 Radio shares in September 1929 ... and then tried to sell them in November when the bank asked for its money back!*

COMPANY	3 September 1929 COST OF ONE SHARE (CENTS)	13 November 1929 COST OF ONE SHARE (CENTS)
American Can	182	86
Anaconda Copper	162	70
Electric Bond and Share	204	50
General Electric Company	396	168
General Motors	182	36
New York Central	256	160
Radio	505	28
US Steel	279	150
Westinghouse E & M	313	102
Woolworth	251	57

WISE UP WORDS

- overproducing   investors   shareholders   dividend   stock market   Black Thursday

WORK

1 a Why did some people begin to sell their shares in September 1929?

   b What happens to a share price as more and more people begin to sell?

   c What happened on 'Black Thursday'?

2 Look at **Source D**.

   Why do many banks, like the one used by George Gallies, go 'bankrupt' as a result of the crash?

3 Look at **Source E**.

   a Imagine you had bought 100 shares in 'Radio' in September 1929. How much would you have paid for them?

   b How much would you be able to get if you sold your 100 shares after the crash in November 1929?

   c How much money would you have lost?

The impact of the Wall Street Crash

AIMS ....

After studying these four pages, you should be able to:

- explain how the Wall Street Crash affected different sections of American Society;
- produce a flow diagram showing how the Wall Street Crash led to the Great Depression.

The shock waves of the Wall Street Crash were soon felt throughout America. By 1930, most Americans were starting to use the word **depression** to describe America's problems. A depression is a time in a country's history when things are bad – factories close, banks fail and unemployment reaches record levels – and there seems no end to the problems. America's depression was so bad that people even started calling it the Great Depression – they said that they had never known it so bad.

Who was affected?

It wasn't just investors – ordinary citizens lost money in the crash. Banks were hit hard when customers who had borrowed money to buy shares couldn't afford to pay it back. By 1933, nearly 5000 banks had gone bankrupt, including one of America's largest banks: the Bank of the United States, based in New York. Four hundred thousand people had savings accounts with the Bank of the United States, almost one-third of New Yorkers … all lost their money.

American industry was also badly affected by the crash. Factory owners couldn't sell their goods at home or abroad (foreign countries taxed US goods heavily), so factories shut down. Hardest hit were car factories. Four and a half million cars were sold by US car manufacturers in 1927. By 1932, only a quarter of that figure was sold.

Factory closures led to record levels of unemployment. In many areas over 25% of the workforce was without a job, and in some places it was as high as 70%. High unemployment meant that more people had less to spend – leading to even more companies going out of business. By 1933, over 100 000 companies had gone bankrupt and over 12 000 people were losing their jobs every day. Many citizens couldn't pay their rent or their mortgages, so became homeless. Makeshift shanty towns made of scrap metal and old cardboard boxes began to appear on the outskirts of major towns. They were called 'Hoovervilles', a sarcastic reference to the President.

Farmers too were badly hit by the Great Depression. As people had less money to spend on food, farmers found it harder to get people to buy their produce. As a result, farmers found it hard to pay their mortgages and equipment loans. By 1933, over 200 000 farmers had been evicted from their farms. To make matters worse, the farmers who had managed to keep their farms found that a severe drought in the mid-west turned millions of acres into an unfarmable **dust bowl**, which saw the top layer of soil blow away.

Source A ▼ _A typical Hooverville town._

Source B ▾ *Unemployed workers sit outside a closed-down cafe in New York, 1930. Note the young girl on the right sitting next to her dad. Some of these men were architects but, during the Depression, building construction and design fell by 92%*

Source C ▾ *Marty Glickman, a famous sports writer remembering his childhood. When families had nothing to eat, they would usually join a huge queue – a* **breadline** *– in order to get some free bread and soup from a charity organisation.*

"On one occasion, my father came home and asked what was for dinner and my mother said, 'There's nothing'. How could that be? How could there be nothing? It was one of the few times in my life that I was scared."

Source D ▾ *From* The Grapes of Wrath, *a novel written by John Steinbeck in 1939. It tells the story of a poor farming family from Oklahoma who travel to California during the Great Depression in search of a new life.*

"There was a Hooverville on the edge of every town … the houses were tents, weed-thatched enclosures, paper houses, a great junk pile. The man drove his family in and became a citizen of Hooverville – always they were called Hooverville … if he had no tent, he went to the city dump and brought back cartons and built a house made of corrugated paper. When the rains came, the house melted and washed away."

Source E ▾ *From* The Grapes of Wrath *by John Steinbeck. Thousands of farms were destroyed by high winds and drought, especially in the states of Oklahoma and Arkansas. In total, 350 000 'Okies' and 'Arkies' made their way towards the rich farming states of California and Oregon, hoping to work on fruit farms. However, most were disappointed – some towns banned the migrants, putting up signs saying 'Okies go home' – and the fruit farmers themselves were suffering too – people simply couldn't afford as much fruit!*

"They streamed over the mountains, hungry and restless as ants, scurrying to find work to do – to lift, to push, to pull, to pick, to cut – anything for food. 'The kids are hungry. We've got no place to live.' Like ants scurrying for work and most of all for land … They were hungry and they were fierce. And they hoped to find a home and they found only hatred."

Source F ▾ *A letter written to the President by a white woman during the Depression. The poverty of many whites increased their racist opinions and led them to turn against Black Americans even more.*

"dear sur,
… it looks like you could do something to help out the poor white people the negroes can get work where the poor white man cannot … there is a negroe working in the post office and white men can't get a job to feed his family … and negroes being worked ever where instead of white men it don't look that it is rite and is not rite …"

So what did President Hoover do? Hoover remained convinced that America would recover soon. In January 1930, he said, 'We have now passed the worst'.

He eventually set up the Reconstruction Finance Corporation, which lent money to businesses in trouble and made some small loans to farmers. He also set up a huge road and dam building programme which created jobs in the construction industry. However, his policies came too late. In November 1932, there was a presidential election and Hoover hoped for re-election. But Hoover stood no chance – his time as President was about to end!

The Bonus Army

After two years of Depression, many ordinary Americans didn't think the President was doing enough to help them. Some people joined together to organise protests, hoping to improve their conditions.

The biggest protest took place in Washington, during the boiling hot summer of 1932. In fact, the protest got so heated that the President feared for his life. He even barricaded himself inside a cupboard in his home, the White House … and then sent in the army!

The men who caused such concern for President Hoover were ex-soldiers from World War I. There were 25 000 of them in total and they were very hungry … and very angry! They had gone to Washington to ask the government to help them to survive the Depression by paying their war pensions – a $500 bonus – early. They had built a **Hooverville** on a park just in front of the White House.

Hoover and the government refused to pay, so the Bonus Army – as the ex-soldiers now called themselves – decided to stay. Hoover publicly called them 'criminals', which annoyed the ex-soldiers even more – despite the fact that Hoover himself knew that 95% were indeed veteran soldiers!

After a few tense days, Hoover called in the troops. Led by an army general called Douglas MacArthur, four companies of infantry, four mounted cavalry troops, a machine gun squad and six tanks attacked the protesters.

Two protesters and a baby (some ex-soldiers brought their families) were killed in the battle that followed. Pictures appeared in newspapers all over the country.

To many Americans, Hoover had had his last chance – there was a presidential election soon. To others, as the smoke from the burning Hooverville dripped over the nation's capital, it seemed as if America was near to a revolution.

Source G ▾ *General Douglas MacArthur, featured in* The Memoirs of Herbert Hoover, *written by Hoover in 1953.*

"That mob was a bad-looking mob … beyond a shadow of a doubt, they were about to take over in some way. Had he [President Hoover] let it go on another week, I believe … our Government would have been very severely threatened."

Source H ▾ *An eyewitness' account of the attack on the Bonus Army.*

"They came with their gas bombs and their bayonets. The troops fired the shacks on the edge of the camp. Tanks and soldiers guarded the bridge back into the city so that no protesters could get into Washington. They might disturb the sleep of a few of the Government's officials!"

Source I ▲ *The Bonus Army demonstrate against the Depression.*

WISE UP WORDS

- Hooverville   breadline   dust bowl
  depression

WORK

1 Look at **Source B**. Imagine you were one of the unemployed workers, sitting outside the New York cafe in 1930. Imagine that the person who took the photograph has also asked you to talk about your experiences of the Great Depression. You have agreed to do it, but have told the photographer that you will send him the answers to his questions by post.

Write down the way the Great Depression has affected you and America itself. You might include:

- How investors, banks, American industry, workers, farmers – and even foreign countries have been affected.
- Details about breadlines and Hoovervilles.
- Your thoughts on the work of Herbert Hoover.
- Your response to the Bonus March of 1932.

Why did FDR win the 1932 election?

AIMS ....

These two pages will help you to identify reasons:
- Why FDR won the 1932 election;
- Why HH lost the 1932 election.

Every four years, in November, an election is held for the post of President of the USA. The two main candidates for the 1932 election were Herbert Hoover (hoping to be re-elected) and Franklin Delano Roosevelt, also known as FDR. The election was taking place in the depths of the Depression – so what were their ideas for dealing with it? What was each candidate really like? What sort of lives had they led? And, of course, who won?

HOOVER

Hoover belonged to the Republican Party, traditionally favoured by businessmen and wealthier people. Republicans believed it wasn't the government's role to interfere too much in the everyday lives of its citizens (a policy called 'laissez faire', meaning leave alone). You may wish to go back to the section 'How is the USA governed?' to refresh your memory on the Republican Party.

POLITICAL CAREER: Orphaned at the age of eight, he worked in an office when he left school. By the time he was 40 he was a multi-millionaire, after working all over the world as a gold-mine engineer. He then returned to the USA to take up politics; an excellent early career in politics, doing a great job helping to feed starving people in Europe after World War I. He became President in 1928 at a time when many Americans were making lots of money and could afford luxuries such as cars, radios and telephones. He said that soon all Americans would have 'two cars in every garage and a chicken in every pot'.

IDEAS FOR DEALING WITH THE DEPRESSION: Didn't do much to begin with. Hoover thought of Americans as **rugged individuals**, people who could overcome any problem without help and achieve success through their own hard work (like he had!). As a result, he decided to leave America to recover on its own. Only after a few years of depression did he lend money to businesses and farms in trouble and make cash available to states to help their unemployed.

WISE UP WORDS

- rugged individuals   New Deal

FDR

FDR belonged to the Democratic Party. Turn to page 132 to refresh your memory on the Democratic Party.

POLITICAL CAREER: He had an important job organising the navy during World War I. Nearly killed by polio, a spinal disease, in 1921. He spent the next five years fighting to recover but never fully regained the use of his legs. He used a wheelchair for the rest of his life. Went back into politics in 1928, becoming Governor of New York, a very important job.

IDEAS FOR DEALING WITH THE DEPRESSION:

As Governor of New York, he spent $20 million in tax money helping the unemployed – the first Governor of any state to do this. This, he told people, was how he intended to deal with the Depression if he became President. He promised America the three Rs:

- **R**elief – help for the old, sick, unemployed and homeless;
- **R**ecovery – government schemes to provide jobs;
- **R**eform – make America a better place for ordinary people and ensure a depression like this could not happen again.

He called his new ideas 'a **New Deal** for the American people' and without giving away too much detail, convinced people that it would lead to a better life. He took his message around the country, sometimes making 15 speeches a day, and his official campaign tune – the famous song 'Happy Days Are Here Again' – could be heard everywhere he went. The phrase 'New Deal' caught the imagination of the public and would lead him to one of the biggest election victories in American history. In FDR, people saw hope for the future – a man with a plan. His words made them feel that at last, someone was on their side!

Source A ▾ *This is a copy of a famous poster. Published by the Democratic Party, it makes fun of Republican candidate Herbert Hoover's 'do nothing' reputation. In many people's eyes, Hoover didn't act quickly enough to help people during the Depression – instead, he decided to 'leave alone' and tell people to 'keep smiling' because things would get better soon!*

Smile away the Depression

Smile us into Prosperity
wear a
SMILETTE!
This wonderful little gadget will solve the problems of the Nation!

APPLY NOW AT YOUR CHAMBER OF COMMERCE OR YOUR REPUBLICAN NATIONAL COMMITTEE

WARNING – Do not risk Federal arrest by looking glum!

FACT *'And the winner is ...'*

FDR won a staggering victory. In 1932, there were 48 states in America – and 42 of them chose FDR. This was the biggest ever victory recorded in an American election!

WORK

1 **a** What was a 'rugged individual'?
   b Can you think of anything in Hoover's life that might have led him to believe in 'rugged individualism'?

2 What is meant by the term 'New Deal'?

3 In 1932, Hoover famously said that the election was 'a contest between two styles of government'. What did Hoover mean when he said this?

4 Look at **Source A**. Explain how this poster attacked Hoover's policies?

5 Why did Roosevelt beat Hoover in the 1932 election?

The New Deal

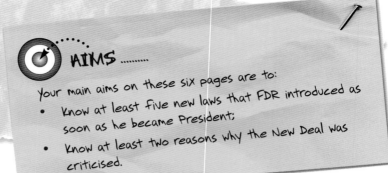

AIMS

Your main aims on these six pages are to:

• Know at least five new laws that FDR introduced as soon as he became President;

• Know at least two reasons why the New Deal was criticised.

Franklin Delano Roosevelt had promised Americans a New Deal. He knew he had to devise ways to help millions of people hit hard by years of the Depression … quickly! In a famous speech made on the day he was sworn in as President, he promised 'action and action now'. He didn't disappoint people. In the first 100 days of FDR's time as President, Americans saw more action being taken to end the Depression than they had seen since it began. And in his first week in charge, FDR made three changes that instantly made Americans realise he meant business!

Change No. 1 Banks

Over 5000 banks had closed down since 1930. People didn't trust banks any more; they kept their cash at home (and tried not to spend too much of it). FDR's **Emergency Banking Act** closed all banks for a four-day 'bank holiday'. Every bank was inspected – only honest, well-run banks with enough cash were allowed to reopen. Government lent some money to banks to help them. Decent banks could now lend money to well-run businesses – creating jobs as they expanded.

<u>Source A</u> ▼ *Part of one of FDR's famous **fireside chats**.*

> *"I can assure you that it is safer to keep your money in a reopened bank than under the mattress."*

Change No. 2 The economy

FDR's next move saved money. The **Economy Act** cut the pay of everyone working for the government, army, navy and air force by 15% and saved nearly a billion dollars.

Change No. 3 Beer

The **Beer Act** made it legal to make and sell alcohol again. People were fed up with all the problems Prohibition had caused – gangsters, corrupt cops, dodgy deals – and now alcohol was legal the government could raise money by taxing it!

FACT *Radio*

FDR used the radio to explain his ideas. He was the first President to do this. His fireside chats, as they were called, were a great novelty for the American people – he even spoke about his family and his pet dog, Fala.

What were the 'alphabet agencies'?

FDR didn't have a fixed plan about how to deal with the Depression when he became President. He surrounded himself with clever men and women with fresh ideas and gave them encouragement. He called them his **Brain Trust**. Sometimes their new ideas worked, sometimes they didn't. On occasions, some ideas clashed with others, but, on the whole, the American public was pleased to see their new President trying to help them to overcome their problems.

FDR's new ideas, measures and laws soon picked up a nickname – they were called **alphabet agencies** because the various organisations that provided a service were known by their initials.

HELP FOR THOSE IN NEED

FERA (Federal Emergency Relief Agency)

$500 million given to states to help homeless, starving people. Money spent on soup kitchens, blankets,  clothes and nursery schools (so parents could go out and find a job in the day).

HOLC (Home Owners' Loan Corporation)

Government loaned money at very low rates of interest to people who couldn't keep up with their mortgage payments.  300 000 homeowners helped in the first year.

HELP FOR FARMERS

FCA (Farm Credit Administration)

Loans to farmers who were unable to meet their mortgage payments. $100 million loaned out in 18 months.

AAA (Agricultural Adjustment Agency)

By the end of the 1920s, farmers had been producing too much food. As a result, prices for wheat, oats, barley, tobacco and cotton had fallen (if there is a lot of something, a farmer can't ask a high price). The AAA paid farmers to produce less and destroy some of the food they had already produced! They hoped that food prices would rise because it was in short supply (if there is less of something, a farmer can ask for more money). The idea worked – between 1933 and 1939, farmers' incomes doubled. However, the government was heavily criticised for this idea – the government was destroying food and forcing up prices to help farmers at a time when millions in the cities were hungry.

HELP FOR INDUSTRY AND WORKERS

NRA (National Recovery Act)

The NRA encouraged workers and employers to get together to work out a code of fair conditions. Any business or factory that guaranteed a decent wage, improved working conditions and set a limit on hours of work per week was allowed to use the symbol of the NRA – a blue eagle – to help advertise its products.

Buyers of a 'blue eagle product' could tell it had been made to a good standard under decent conditions. It also stated that workers should have the right to join a trade union, something that had been banned in some industries.

HELP FOR THE UNEMPLOYED

CCC (Civilian Conservation Corps)

Unemployed 18 to 25 year olds were given food and shelter in the countryside. For one dollar a day, they did conservation work – planted trees, dug canals, stocked rivers with fish, cleared footpaths and strengthened river banks against flooding. They started a programme to control mosquitoes – and ended malaria in America. Some money was sent home to their families too. CCC created jobs for 2.5 million men.

PWA (Public Works Administration)

The PWA was given funds of $3300 million. Money was spent buying materials and employing millions of skilled workers to build schools, housing, hospitals, bridges, courtrooms and dams. The PWA also built ten ships and 50 airports.

CWA (Civil Works Administration)

The CWA provided temporary work for four million men, building schools, airports, roads and even 150 000 public toilets! The CWA changed its name to WPA (Workers' Progress Administration) in 1935. When the man in charge of the schemes, Harry Hopkins, was criticised for wasting taxpayers' money by giving work to unemployed researchers to write a book on the history of the safety pin, he said, 'Hell, they've got to eat just like the rest of us!' By 1941, the CWA and WPA had spent $11 000 million and provided work for eight million people.

FDR's theory behind many of his alphabet agencies was simple – the government creates jobs by spending money; once the workers earn wages, they start buying goods. Firms and businesses then start hiring new workers; these new workers spend money and so on. Some people used the phrase 'priming the pump' to describe this idea.

How successful was the TVA?

In January 1933, FDR visited an area of America called the Tennessee Valley. He was so shocked by what he saw that he called the area 'our nation's number one problem'. Within weeks, he set up a special alphabet agency – the Tennessee Valley Authority (TVA) – to help those who lived there.

- The Tennessee River flooded every spring, washing away millions of tons of soil and destroying many farms. The river dried out in the summer and high winds blew away even more soil.
- Only three out of every hundred farms had electricity.
- Half of the three million people living in the valley relied on charity donations.
- There were hardly any factory jobs.
- Levels of vitamin deficiency and disease were amongst the highest in the country.

Source B ▼ *A map showing parts of the USA covered by the TVA (80 000 square miles).*

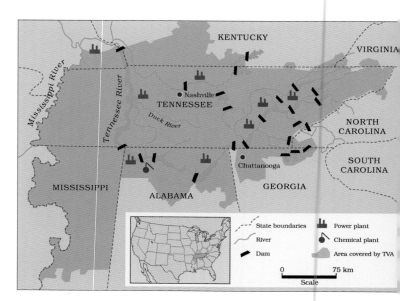

It didn't take the man in charge of the TVA long to realise that most of the area's problems were directly linked to the Tennessee River. To control it, they built over 30 dams. At the touch of a button, dam managers could close huge gates whenever the river threatened to flood. These dams had many benefits:

- They provided cheap electricity, created when powerful turbines built into the walls of each new dam were spun around by jets of water released from the lakes behind them. By 1940, the TVA was America's biggest producer of electricity, attracting jobs and factories to the area.
- They made the river much calmer, ideal for water transport.
- They controlled flooding, which meant that farms could perform better and grow more crops.
- The lakes created behind them produced a new holiday area. New housing and water sports facilities were built alongside the lakes.

The TVA was one of the most impressive alphabet agencies. The Tennessee River was tamed, thousands of jobs were created, the land was conserved and the health and well-being of an entire region improved. To many, the TVA was the pride of FDR's New Deal.

The New Deal under attack

Not everyone liked FDR's New Deal. Some thought it interfered too much in the lives of ordinary Americans, while others believed it didn't help people enough.

The rich

To help pay for the New Deal, FDR made rich people pay more tax. Not surprisingly, they didn't like this! They resented some of the ways FDR's alphabet agencies paid people to plant trees, paint pictures and stock rivers with fish – they said this was a waste of money.

Businessmen

Many businessmen, especially wealthy ones, didn't like the way the New Deal 'interfered' with business and gave more rights to workers. The NRA codes, for example, were criticised by company bosses

because they allowed workers to join trade unions and forced employers to pay minimum wages, improve working conditions and set limits on hours of work. While workers benefited from the NRA codes, some businessmen didn't like them because they had to pay for the changes!

Republicans

Millions of people still supported the Republican Party. Republicans, if you recall, believed in 'laissez faire' – the idea that the government should not interfere in the running of the economy. Many were 'rugged individuals' too, believing that people should be left to live their own lives and sort out their own problems. As you can imagine, many Republicans were horrified by the way this huge government-run scheme – the New Deal – was dominating people's lives. Some said that Roosevelt was behaving like a dictator and making the government too powerful. Others claimed that all this government help would make Americans 'soft' and 'unable to stand on their own two feet'. Some even worried that alphabet agencies such as the TVA would become so common that the whole of America – not just the Tennessee Valley – would soon be controlled by the government … and this was the type of system that Communist Russia had!

Supreme Court

The Supreme Court is America's highest court. Consisting of nine top judges, its job is to make sure that any new laws are legal and do not go against America's strict Constitution. There are many parts to America's Constitution but one of them outlines the role of the President. The rules state that he or she is only responsible for national affairs affecting *all* states. State governments are responsible for all other affairs. So, for example, the President – or *federal* government as it is known – makes decisions on issues that affect the whole country (such as wars and taxes), while the *state* governments deal with things that affect their own state, such as whether to have the death penalty or not. In 1935, the Supreme Court ruled that one of FDR's alphabet agencies, the AAA, was illegal. They said that giving help to farmers was a matter for *state* governments, not the *federal* government. As a result, all the help that the AAA gave to farmers stopped!

The Supreme Court also declared many of the NRA codes illegal. They ruled that the federal government had no right to improve rules on business – it was up to state governments to do it.

FDR, furious at the decisions of the Supreme Court, decided to take action – he came up with his Second New Deal.

Source C ▾ *A British cartoon from* Punch *magazine on the quarrel between FDR and the Supreme Court. The cartoon is called* The Illegal Act. *What point do you think the cartoonist is trying to make?*

THE ILLEGAL ACT.

PRESIDENT ROOSEVELT. "I'M SORRY, BUT THE SUPREME COURT SAYS I MUST CHUCK YOU BACK AGAIN."

What was the Second New Deal?

By 1935, both FDR and the New Deal were being criticised. FDR's next phase of plans was often called the 'Second New Deal'. This time FDR made sure his plans and schemes applied to Americans in all states.

SSA (Social Security Act)

Government pensions were provided for old people, widows and disabled people. The SSA also established a system of payments for the sick and unemployed.

NLRA (National Labour Relations Act)

Workers were allowed to join trade unions so they could campaign for better pay and conditions. In the past, some employers, such as Henry Ford, had sacked workers who had formed groups or unions. Now it was hoped that bosses would have to listen if their workforce was unhappy. The NRLA was seen as a replacement for the NRA.

FSA (Farm Security Administration)

Government loans were given to tenant farmers (people who rented land from a large landowner) so they could buy their own land. The FSA also set up clean, healthy camps to help poor farming families who had lost their own farms or left them to find work around the country.

SCA (Soil Conservation Agency)

Money was given to farmers who conserved and improved the soil on their farms. The SCA was seen as a replacement for the AAA.

FACT *Fair for everyone?*

The New Deal did little to correct some of the prejudices in US society. For example, in 1937 the average pay for a woman was still 50% less than men – and no New Deal law specifically attempted to assist black Americans – and the racial problems continued to simmer.

In November 1936, FDR faced his second election. Voters had the chance to show whether they supported his New Deal or not. FDR won easily, receiving more votes than any other president in American history. In a speech soon after his victory, FDR joked, 'It seems everyone is against the New Deal … except the voters!'

Source D ▼ *FDR's idea of **priming the pump** was influenced by an Englishman, J. M. Keynes, who said that governments should spend money in times of depression to get the economy going again.*

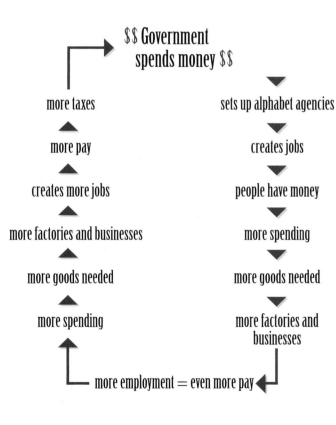

$$ Government spends money $$

more taxes

more pay

creates more jobs

more factories and businesses

more goods needed

more spending

sets up alphabet agencies

creates jobs

people have money

more spending

more goods needed

more factories and businesses

more employment = even more pay

Source E ▼ *From the hit 2003 film* Seabiscuit, *a true story about a famous American racehorse from the 1930s.*

"They call it 'relief' but it was a lot more than that. It had dozens of names — NRA, WPA, the CCC — but it really came down to just one thing. For the first time in a long time, someone cared. For the first time in a long time, you were no longer alone."

WISE UP WORDS

- Brain Trust   alphabet agencies   FERA
AAA   PWA   HOLC   NRA   CWA   FCA
CCC   WPA   'priming the pump'
Emergency Banking Act   Economy Act
Beer Act   fireside chats

WORK

1 **a** What were 'fireside chats'?

   b With so many problems to deal with in the USA, why did FDR bother to tell people about his dog?

2 Give at least one example where FDRs New Deal helped:
   i) the homeless
   ii) homeowners
   iii) farmers
   iv) workers
   v) the unemployed.

3 What did FDR mean when he said he was 'priming the pump' of America's economy?

4 Why was the work carried out by the Tennessee Valley Authority so important?

5 **a** What problems did Roosevelt experience with the Supreme Court?

   b How did FDR address these problems?

6 Look at **Source C**.

   a What is the message of the cartoon?

   b In your opinion, does the cartoonist support the work of FDR or not?

America and World War II

AIMS ....

Over the next two pages, aim to understand:
- why unemployment levels began to increase after 1937;
- how America became involved in World War II;
- what effect the war had on the American economy.

When FDR was re-elected as President in November 1936, he still believed he had lots of work to do. But he was getting more and more worried by the amount of money being spent on his job creation schemes and projects, such as the WPA and TVA. In response, he decided to cut down the amount spent on his New Deal programmes – but this created a problem. Unemployment jumped by three million because the government was no longer providing people with many jobs. At the same time, thousands of workers in the car and steel industries went on strike as part of the campaign for better wages and conditions.

By 1938, some people were commenting that America was 'sliding downhill' towards depression again. Unemployment had reached 10.5 million and car and steel production were falling month after month. Even FDR himself acknowledged that the New Deal had come to an end by January 1939. But events in Europe were about to provide a dramatic solution to some of America's problems.

America and World War II

America had kept out of the affairs of other countries for several years. They called it isolationism. But when World War II began in September 1939, America supported Britain and France against Hitler's Germany and their allies. FDR feared that if Germany defeated Britain and France, then America may come under attack soon after. The President didn't send American soldiers to actually fight against the Nazis – instead he was to sell top-quality, American-made weapons to Britain and France. Both nations were eager to buy!

- **Cash and Carry:** In November 1939, Britain and France began buying weapons, warships and planes from America. This created valuable jobs at a time when unemployment was rising. However, in June 1940, Germany attacked and defeated France. Britain stood alone as Hitler's armies began invading most major European countries. When the British government ran short of money, FDR gave them 50 warships … and began thinking of another way to support the British.

- **Lend–lease:** In March 1941, when Britain was desperately short of money, FDR agreed to a 'lend–lease' deal. Instead of selling, America would 'lend' Britain up to $7000 million worth of weapons. Most people knew that America would never get, or want, them back! They struck a similar deal with Russia when Germany attacked them in June 1941.

Despite their official position of **neutrality**, it was clear that America supported Britain's war against Hitler's Germany. However, not all Americans were pleased with events. Organisations such as 'The Mothers' Crusade' and the 'America First Committee' had big, public anti-war demonstrations because they feared America might get dragged into a European war. But others soon began to see the benefits of an end to isolationism. As America began to rearm in case they were forced to enter the war, millions found jobs building fighter planes, battleships and tanks. Unemployed men became trainee soldiers, sailors and pilots. When the American people voted FDR in as President AGAIN in 1940, unemployment was starting to drop. In 1941, there were just 5.5 million unemployed compared to over ten million only four years before. To some, it seemed as if World War II, and not FDR's New Deal, was beginning to get Americans back to work.

Source A ▼ *Chrysler, the car manufacturers, began making tanks in the late 1930s. This photograph shows tanks on an assembly line. In total, America produced 297 000 fighter and bomber planes, 86 000 tanks and 12 000 ships between 1939 and 1945.*

Source B ▼ *Raymond Moley, a member of FDR's government, who was sacked in 1936.*

"After 1936, our economy began to slide downhill and our unemployment increased … it was the war that saved the economy and saved Roosevelt."

Pearl Harbor

America officially entered World War II in December 1941. After several years of supporting Britain and her allies by selling and loaning them weapons, FDR and Congress finally made the decision to send men to fight. So why did America join in? What happened on 7 December to make America suddenly end many years of neutrality?

The roots of America's entry into World War II lie in their relationship with Japan. During the 1930s, Japan began to invade many of the countries surrounding them, including China. Japan, a relatively small country with a large population, wanted to get its hands on the food and raw materials that these nations produced – rice, coal, tin, rubber and oil. In protest at Japan's aggression, FDR vowed not to sell any oil or steel to Japan. The Japanese weren't happy; their industries used millions of tons of US steel and oil every year!

As the relationship grew worse and worse, Japan's military leaders planned a secret and surprise attack on US ships at a naval base in the Hawaiian Islands called Pearl Harbor. It was from here that American battleships would attack Japan if ever war broke out.

The Japanese thought that if they destroyed enough ships, the Americans would be unable to stop them from taking the territory they wanted. By the time the Americans rebuilt their navy, the Japanese would be too strong and have enough food and raw materials to ever be removed from any of the countries they had invaded.

At 7:55am on Sunday 7 December 1941, 183 Japanese bomber planes attacked the American navy at its base at Pearl Harbor. The Americans were caught completely by surprise. In just under two hours, 21 US warships were sunk or damaged, 177 US planes were destroyed and over 2000 men were killed. The Japanese lost just 29 planes.

The next day, America and Britain declared war on Japan. Three days later, Germany and Italy, Japan's official allies, declared war on America. Now the world's richest, most powerful country was involved in what was to become the world's most expensive, most destructive and most famous war.

WISE UP WORD

- neutrality

WORK

1 Why did unemployment start to rise after 1937?
2 Write a sentence or two about each of the following
  a isolationism
  b neutrality
  c cash and carry plan
  d lend–lease.
3 Look at **Source B.**
  a Raymond Moley was sacked by FDR in 1936. Explain how this might have affected his attitude towards FDR.
  b Does the bias in this source mean it is of no value to historians?
  c Did Raymond Moley have a point? In what way could it be argued that 'the war saved the economy'?

Russia at the beginning of the 20th century

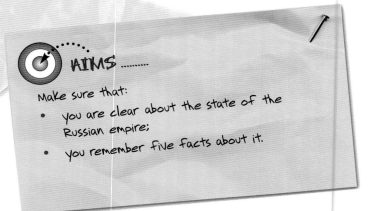

🎯 AIMS ....

Make sure that:

• you are clear about the state of the Russian empire;

• you remember five facts about it.

Russia is a huge country. It is twice the size of the USA and Canada put together ... and when a railway was completed in 1917 that linked Moscow (in the west of Russia) to Vladivostok (in the east), it took 13 days to complete the journey!

So how was this vast country ruled? What sort of people lived there? And how did Russia compare with other leading European nations?

The people

Russia, after centuries of war and conquest, had become a land of 22 different nationalities. In 1900, the population was approximately 125 million. Only 40% of these people actually spoke Russian as their first language, which made running the country a very difficult job.

Source A ▼ *The Russian empire in 1900. Of a population of 125 million, only 55 million regarded themselves as Russians – the others were made up of 22 different nationalities.*

Eight out of ten people in the Russian Empire were peasants who could neither read nor write. These peasants were becoming more and more unhappy because they did not own the land they worked on and most lived a miserable life growing just enough food to feed their families. If a peasant managed to make any additional money, it was usually taken from them in taxes by greedy landowners who lived in luxury.

THE RUSSIAN EMPIRE IN 1900

① ESTONIA
② LATVIA
③ LITHUANIA

EUROPE

ST PETERSBURG

MOSCOW

ODESSA

CRIMEA

GEORGIA

RUSSIAN EMPIRE

TRANS-SIBERIAN RAILWAY

WESTERN SIBERIA

EASTERN SIBERIA

VLADIVOSTOK

ASIA

THE PEOPLE OF THE RUSSIAN EMPIRE

A RUSSIANS   G ARMENIANS
B FINNS   H UZBEKS
C POLES   I KIRGHIZ
D UKRAINIANS   J KAZAKHS
E COSSACKS   K MONGOLS
F GEORGIANS   L TARTARS
     M YAKUTS

Source B ▶
Russian peasants (sometimes known as serfs) in 1900.

Power

Russia was ruled by one man – the **Tsar** (a Russian word for Emperor). At the turn of the century, the Tsar was a man called Nicholas II of the Romanov family. He was a weak man who believed, like all Tsars, that he had been chosen by God to rule Russia. All power rested with the Tsar – and he was backed by a small group of advisors and army leaders who came from some of Russia's wealthiest families. He even had a secret police force – the Okhrana – to spy on people who didn't fully support him. The Tsar's word, quite literally, was law.

Towns and cities

The two most important cities in Russia at this time were Moscow and St Petersburg. These, and many other towns and cities, had grown rapidly by 1900 as Russia began to **industrialise**. Thousands of peasants flooded into the towns to work in a whole range of industries – mining, iron and steel, textiles, oil, food production and railways. Foreign countries invested heavily in these factories.

But the pace of development created many problems. Living and working conditions in the fast-growing cities were terrible – and the new breed of factory-owners, businessmen and entrepreneurs did little to protect their workforce. Unrest and discontent increased. Indeed, the cities became a breeding ground for revolutionary ideas.

Source C ▶ *Tsar Nicholas II with his family.*

Source D ▼ *A chart to show the growth of industry in Russia at the beginning of the 20th century.*

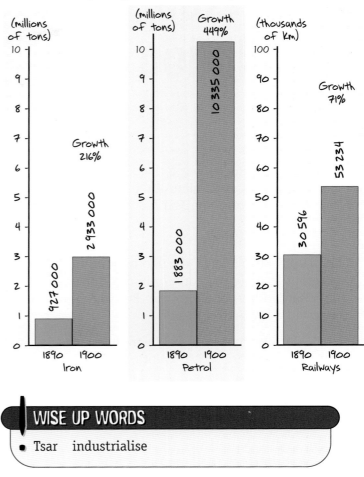

WISE UP WORDS

- Tsar   industrialise

WORK

1 Look at **Source A**. Why did the size of Russia make it difficult to rule?

2 Look at **Source B**. How can you tell that the people in this photograph are poor?

3 In what ways was Russia changing at the beginning of the 20th century?

4 **a** What does the word 'Tsar' mean?

  b Write down two facts about Russia's Tsars.

  c Imagine you are a minister in the Tsar's government. You are concerned about the problems in Russia and wish to inform him about the situation. Write a report for him, making sure you mention:
  i the conditions of the peasants
  ii the contrast between rich and poor
  iii conditions for workers in the towns
  iv the 'revolutionary ideas' you are hearing about.

The 1905 revolution

AIMS

You must know:
- Why the 1905 Revolution began;
- how the Revolution led to the establishment of the Duma.

In 1905, Russia was a divided nation. Out of a population of 125 million, only 55 million regarded themselves as Russians – the rest were made up of 22 different languages. In an attempt to unite the country, the Tsar led his people to war. But war with Japan sparked a revolution. How?

War with Japan

By 1905, Russia was a divided nation. In an attempt to unite the country in a common cause, the Tsar led his people to war. But war with Japan sparked a revolution. How?

In 1904, war broke out between Russia and Japan. The Russo–Japanese War went badly for Russia. Once the Russian navy opened fire on British boats in the North Sea after mistaking them for Japanese warships! When they finally faced the Japanese fleet in the Battle of Tsushima in May 1905, the Russians were decisively defeated. Humiliatingly, the Tsar was forced to ask the Japanese for peace.

Bloody Sunday

At the same time, a peaceful demonstration of about 200 000 workers was held in St Petersburg. Some protesters even held portraits of the Tsar to show their support for him. The workers had all signed a petition asking for better wages, shorter hours and better conditions. The Tsar wasn't in St Petersburg at the time but his elite guards shot at the protesters and killed 200 people. This was called Bloody Sunday. Suddenly, the Tsar's reputation as 'The Little Father of Russia' was in tatters.

Revolution

Within days, a revolution had started as properties were looted and buildings were set on fire. 2.5 million people went on strike; several rich landowners were murdered and some sailors in the navy refused to follow orders. Workers in major cities set up their own councils (called soviets) and set up law courts, established police forces, organised food supplies and even created their own newspapers – all without permission of the Tsar!

The Duma

Eventually, the Tsar realised he had to face up to the situation. In a document called the **October Manifesto**, he promised the Russian people a **Duma** (an elected parliament) and civil rights such as freedom of speech. Reassured by this, the people halted all their revolutionary action and went back to work. However, the Tsar's loyal police force and army quickly moved in to arrest any strike leaders and 'trouble-makers'. And, although elections took place and the Duma could ask the Tsar to make changes, he could ignore and over-rule any decision it made. Even today, historians still disagree about the impact of the Duma (see **Sources A** and **C**).

Source A ▼ *From Peter Moss' History Alive.*

"There had been a minor revolution in 1905, and as a result the Czar had been forced to allow a parliament of sorts, called the Duma, to be elected. It had little power, however, and the Czar could over-rule any measures it passed. Having at last a parliament, only to find it completely useless, made the people more bitter than ever in their hatred of the ruling class."

Source B ▾ *A painting showing the first day of the 1905 Revolution on 9 January 1905 by Vladimir Egorovic Makovskij.*

Source C ▾ From Nigel Kelly and Greg Lacey's Modern World History.

"It would be easy to conclude that Russia's experiment with parliamentary democracy was a sham. However, the existence of the Duma was evidence that the Tsar's position had changed. For the first time people could share in Russia's political life. The Duma could debate important issues, people could read about them in the newspapers, the Tsar's ministers went to the Duma to answer questions — in short, there was more freedom and openness than before. Russia had begun to evolve towards a more modern, democratic system of government. Who knows where this might have led had it not been for the interruption of the First World War?"

WISE UP WORDS

• October Manifesto   Duma

WORK

1 What was the importance of:
   a the Russo–Japanese War; and
   b 'Bloody Sunday'
   in triggering the 1905 revolution?

2 How did the Tsar manage finally to defeat the 1905 revolution?

3 Look at **Sources A** and **C**.
   a What was the Duma?
   b How have these two historians interpreted the 1905 Revolution differently and why do you think this is?

4 In your opinion, who won the 1905 Revolution? Explain your answer carefully.

'From each according to his ability; to each according to his needs'

AIMS

- to be able to explain the idea of 'Communism';
- to understand the difference between a Bolshevik and a Menshevik.

This rather confusing phrase sums up a new political theory that was taking hold in some areas of Europe in the late 1800s and early 1900s. The theory has a variety of names, but the most common title is 'Communism'.

Revolutionary ideas

Unhappiness with the system of government in Russia had been brewing for many years – and Russia was very backward compared to other European nations. Different groups had different ideas about how to improve things … and, among the crowded slums of Russia's expanding towns and cities, revolutionary ideas spread quickly.

Some groups decided to use violence. In 1881, revolutionaries had killed Tsar Alexander II when a bomb exploded next to his horse-drawn carriage (see **Source B**). In 1911, the Tsar's chief advisor, Stolypin, was assassinated despite the fact that he was trying to introduce reforms!

The Tsar's government reacted to the threats by using secret police to hunt down and imprison people who were working against them. Sometimes people were sent to Siberia – a freezing cold wasteland in northern Russia – for years. Those who escaped went to other countries, where they wrote revolutionary newspapers that were smuggled into Russia.

Revolutionary groups

The most important of Russia's revolutionary groups in the early 1900s were the followers of a German political thinker (who lived in Britain) called Karl Marx. Marx wrote books (with his friend Friedrich Engels) that described how unhappy workers (who he called 'proletarians') would rise up together and destroy the governments of their countries. This 'community' of workers would then unite throughout the world to create 'worldwide Communism'. Marx wrote, 'Let the ruling classes tremble at a Communist revolution. The proletarians have nothing to lose but their chains. They have a world to win.'

The followers of Karl Marx were known as 'Marxists'– and they believed in his political theory called 'Communism'. **Source A** explains this theory.

Source A ▼ _From Derek Heater's_ Our World this Century.

THE THEORY OF COMMUNISM

1 CLASS CONFLICT is the most important of all happenings throughout history.

2 THE FINAL QUARREL between social classes is between the middle class (bourgeois-capitalist) and the working class (proletariat).

This will break out as a **REVOLUTION** – this happens in industrialised countries where there is a large number of working-class people in the towns to rise up in revolt.

3 AFTER THE REVOLUTION the party rules the country for a while on behalf of the working class.

The government is called the Dictatorship of the Proletariat.

4 When all opposition to the new government has been crushed, no government is needed because all people are treated fairly and are contented.

THE STATE WILL WITHER AWAY.

5 Then the **COMMUNIST SOCIETY** comes into being. There are no different classes. All people are treated in the following way:

FROM EACH ACCORDING TO HIS ABILITY;
TO EACH ACCORDING TO HIS NEEDS.

Source B ▸ *Tsar Alexander II is assassinated at St Petersburg.*

Communism describes a type of society where there would be no social classes and no great differences in wealth. Each person would work as hard as they could at what they were good at – and only take what they needed. This idea was particularly well received in Russia – a society where over 80% of the population lived in desperate poverty and did all the work while the rest owned most of the land and lived in luxury.

In Russia, a political party started up that believed in the ideas of Karl Marx. They were called the Social Democrats … but they argued among themselves a lot. In 1903, they split into two groups – the **Bolsheviks**, who believed in seizing power at the first opportunity; and the **Mensheviks**, who believed in cooperating with other political groups to improve the lives of ordinary Russians. By far the most powerful group was the Bolsheviks. Their leader was a man who used a secret name, Lenin, to escape the attention of the Tsar's secret police. His real name was Vladimir Ilyich Ulyanov … and his revolutionary ideas meant he wasn't really safe from the Tsar's secret police – so he left Russia and lived in exile in various European countries from 1900 to 1917.

Source C ▸
A portrait of Vladimir Lenin.

FACT *Political parties*

The Social Democrats were not Russia's only political party. Other parties elected by the Duma included the Kadets – middle-class professionals who wanted to keep the Tsar but have a better decision-making parliament, and the Social Revolutionaries (SRs) who were mainly supported by peasants. The SRs wanted to get rid of the Tsar and divide the land up among the peasants.

WISE UP WORDS

- Bolsheviks   Mensheviks

WORK

1 One historian has described Russia in the early part of the 20th century as 'ripe for revolution'.
   a What do you think this phrase means?
   b Do you think Russia was 'ripe for revolution'? Explain your answer carefully.

2 Make a copy of the grid below and fill in the answers to the clues.

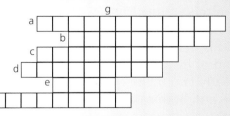

a Workers
b A follower of Marx who believed in cooperation
c Middle-class capitalists
d A follower of Marx who behaved in seizing power quickly
e _____ Marx
f A common name for Marxist theory

Now read down the puzzle (word g) and write a sentence or two about this word.

How did the Great War affect Russia?

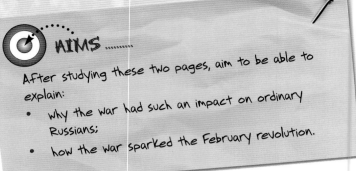

AIMS

After studying these two pages, aim to be able to explain:

- why the war had such an impact on ordinary Russians;
- how the war sparked the February revolution.

When the Great War broke out in August 1914, the people of Russia cheered the Tsar and gave him their support. Like people all over Europe, Russians felt very patriotic and supported the war. However, it went very badly for the Russians – culminating in a revolution that led to the Tsar giving up his throne.

So why did the war go so badly? What effect did it have on Russia? And what, exactly, made the Tsar abdicate?

Fighting the war

Russian soldiers fought very bravely during the war and they won some important early battles against the Germans. But a shortage of decent equipment and the poor way in which they were led meant they suffered two major defeats in the battles of Tannenberg and the Masurian Lakes (see **Source A**).

While the ordinary men at the front were often half-frozen and half-fed, the majority of rich army generals were enjoying themselves far away from the fighting, making pots of money in lots of illegal ways!

The Tsar himself made things worse by going to the front to lead the army … which he wasn't very good at! This made him responsible for the defeats, in many people's eyes. It also left the government back in Petrograd (the Russian capital's name was changed from St Petersburg during the war) in the hands of his German wife, the Tsarina, and a rather odd friend of hers – a monk called Rasputin! By 1917, nearly two million Russians had been killed fighting – and both soldiers and civilians had completely lost their enthusiasm for the war.

Source A ▼ A Russian General, 1914.

"In recent battles, a third of the men had no rifles. The poor devils had to wait until their comrades fell before their eyes and they could pick up weapons."

Conditions back home in Russia

The war caused severe food and fuel shortages in Russia. There were so many men fighting in the army that there weren't enough people to take in the harvest. And the war clogged up the railways with military transport too, so food couldn't get into the towns either. All the railway engines and weapons factories needed fuel as well, so ordinary Russians had to do without it.

And all the time, injured soldiers were coming home from the fighting telling stories of defeat, bad generals, poor equipment and next to no medical supplies.

After a particularly cold winter in 1916, the Russian people could stand it no longer.

Revolution

Source B ▼ Rioting in Petrograd, March 1917.

By February 1917, people all over Russia were starving and freezing. The revolution was actually started by women when, on 8 March, they went on a march through Petrograd demanding bread … which turned into a riot.

Factory workers soon joined the rioters on strike. When the Tsarina called in the troops to fire at the rioters, they refused and started to help the protesters. Workers and soldiers even set up their own council – the Petrograd Soviet – to coordinate what was now a revolution.

Source C ▾ *While the Tsar was at the front taking control of*

the army, Russia was left in the hands of his wife, Alexandra. But she was heavily influenced by a drunken monk called Gregori Rasputin who had strange hypnotic powers that seemed to be able to cure her son's illness. There were even rumours that the Tsarina and Rasputin were lovers. Eventually, a group of rich young noblemen, worried about Rasputin's influence, poisoned, shot and then drowned him in December 1916.

On 13 March, the Tsar got back from the fighting and saw the chaos in Petrograd – but it was too late for him to do anything about it. None of the soldiers was loyal to him any more and he abdicated on 15 March. Immediately, the Tsar and his family were seized and imprisoned.

A new leader

Alexander Kerensky, a member of Russia's Parliament (the Duma), set up a provisional or temporary government and promised to hold elections and divide up the land among the peasants. At the same time, soldiers and workers were electing their own councils – or soviets – in the big cities and issuing their own orders. For this reason, the time between March and November 1917 is sometimes called the **Dual Government** because the Provisional Government (run by Kerensky) AND the 'city Soviets' (run by soldiers and workers) were making decisions in Russia.

But Kerensky's Provisional Government made one major mistake – they confirmed Russia's involvement in the Great War … so the food and fuel shortages continued.

It would not be long before there was a second revolution!

Source D ▾ *Written by Philip E. Mosley, late Professor of International Relations, Columbia University.*

"The immediate cause of the March Revolution of 1917 was the collapse of the Tsarist regime under the gigantic strain of World War I. The underlying cause was the background economic condition of the country, which made it unable to sustain the war effort against powerful, industrialised Germany."

WISE UP WORD

- Dual Government

WORK

1 **a** Why were Russia's armies unsuccessful in the Great War?
   b How did the war affect Russia?

2 Look at **Source C**.
   a What point is the cartoonist trying to make?
   b Why did Rasputin have so much influence over the Tsar and his wife?
   c What effect would Rasputin's power have on people's feelings about the Tsar?
   d Do you think this cartoon would be seen in Russia? Give reasons for your answer.

3 It is December 1916 and you are an opponent of Russia's involvement in the war. Design a poster or write a leaflet which will turn the Russian people against the war.

4 There were many reasons for the Tsar's abdication in 1917. Try to list the reasons under three headings: long term, short term and triggers. You will first need to establish what is meant by the three terms – and then look back through this chapter to remind yourself of some of them.

5 What is meant by the term 'Dual Government'?

'Peace, bread and land'

AIMS

Over the next four pages to try to learn why Russians had <u>another</u> Revolution in 1917.

By March 1917, Russia had a new type of government … well, two new types of government actually. The Tsar had gone and both a Provisional Government AND lots of workers' councils – or Soviets – in the major cities had taken control. At first, the Soviets supported the work of the Provisional Government – but it didn't stay like that for long.

Read the following story carefully. It shows how the failures of the new Provisional Government led to a second Revolution in 1917.

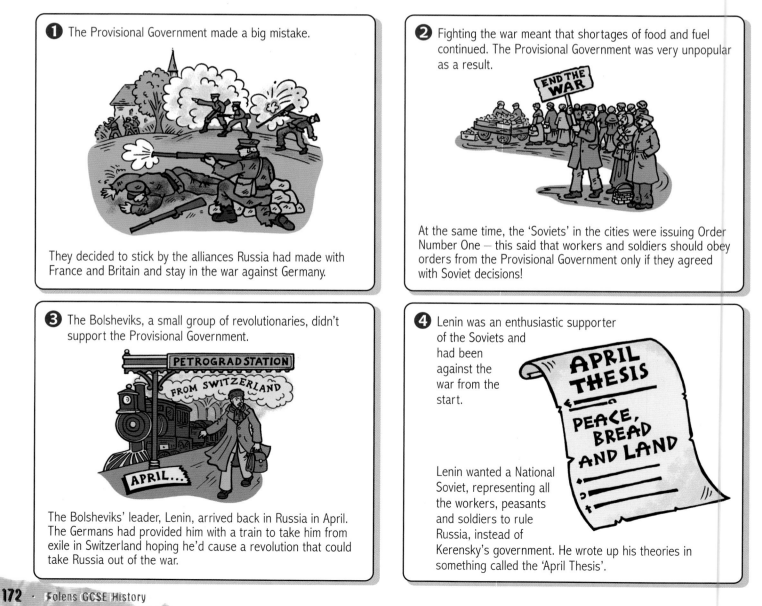

1 The Provisional Government made a big mistake.

They decided to stick by the alliances Russia had made with France and Britain and stay in the war against Germany.

2 Fighting the war meant that shortages of food and fuel continued. The Provisional Government was very unpopular as a result.

END THE WAR

At the same time, the 'Soviets' in the cities were issuing Order Number One — this said that workers and soldiers should obey orders from the Provisional Government only if they agreed with Soviet decisions!

3 The Bolsheviks, a small group of revolutionaries, didn't support the Provisional Government.

PETROGRAD STATION

FROM SWITZERLAND

APRIL...

The Bolsheviks' leader, Lenin, arrived back in Russia in April. The Germans had provided him with a train to take him from exile in Switzerland hoping he'd cause a revolution that could take Russia out of the war.

4 Lenin was an enthusiastic supporter of the Soviets and had been against the war from the start.

APRIL THESIS

PEACE, BREAD AND LAND

Lenin wanted a National Soviet, representing all the workers, peasants and soldiers to rule Russia, instead of Kerensky's government. He wrote up his theories in something called the 'April Thesis'.

5 The Bolshevik messages of 'Peace, bread and land' and 'All power to the Soviets' were popular.

In July, the Bolsheviks tried to get control of the government but were defeated. Lenin had to leave Russia for Finland. This is sometimes called the 'July Days'.

6 Lenin was a wanted man after the failed revolution in July. For now, the Bolsheviks were organised by Trotsky.

Trotsky began gathering weapons for another Bolshevik takeover. The Bolshevik army was called The Red Guard.

7 In August, a Russian army general called Kornilov, who supported the Tsar, turned his army against the Provisional Government. The Provisional Government asked the Bolsheviks for help in defeating him.

The Provisional Government gave weapons to the Bolsheviks (who had tried to overthrow them a month before!).

8 General Kornilov's attempt to get rid of the Provisional Government failed.

The Bolsheviks were more popular than ever … and now they had lots of weapons!

9 In October, Lenin arrived back in Petrograd. He felt the time was right for another revolution.

Brilliantly organised by Trotsky, the revolution was planned for 6 November.

10 Late at night on 6 November, Trotsky's Red Guards, helped by sailors from Kronstadt, took over Petrograd's bridges and telephone exchanges.

By morning, Petrograd was cut off from the rest of Russia.

11 The next day, the Bolsheviks took over government buildings, banks and the railway station.

At 9:40pm, the warship *Aurora* fired a few shells over the Winter Palace where the Provisional Government was meeting … and Red Guards stormed the building. There was no resistance. Similar uprisings were organised in other major towns.

12 The Provisional Government left Russia and all power passed to the all-Russian Congress of Soviets which had just been created. It had a Bolshevik majority.

This group elected a Sovnarkom (a government) with Lenin as Chairman (Prime Minister), Trotsky in charge of foreign affairs and the less-well known Stalin in charge of nationalities!

This Bolshevik seizure of power was called the November Revolution. Lenin, the leader, believed in the ideas of Karl Marx and Communism – where workers run the country for the benefit of all.

So what would Lenin's Russia be like?

Source A ▸ *A false passport and disguise enabled Lenin to escape into Finland after an order for his arrest was issued by the Russian Provisional Government in July 1917.*

Source B ▾ *Russian soldiers firing rifles outside the Winter Palace.*

WORK

1 Write a sentence or two to explain the following terms:
 • Order Number 1
 • April Thesis
 • the Red Guard.
2 The three nouns in the slogan 'Peace, land and bread' appealed to three different groups in Russian society. Which groups were they?
3 Why were the Bolsheviks:
 a weakened by the 'July Days'
 b strengthened by the Kornilov rebellion?
4 Put the following events in the correct chronological order:
 • Lenin arrives in Russia from exile in Finland
 • Kornilov rebels against the Provisional Government
 • Lenin becomes chairman of Russia's new government
 • Lenin arrives in Russia from exile in Switzerland
 • the Provisional Government leaves Russia
 • Red Guards storm the Winter Palace
 • Lenin issues the April Thesis
 • Red Guards take over Petrograd's bridges and telephone exchanges
 • Soviets begin issuing Order Number 1
 • the Provisional Government announces that Russia will continue fighting in the war.

Life in Lenin's Russia

Lenin and the Bolsheviks had forced themselves into power in October 1917 despite the fact that there were only 250 000 Bolsheviks in the whole of Russia (there was a population of 125 million remember!).

Lenin's challenge now was to remain in power long enough to ensure that his true Communist ideal – a state where everything belongs to the people and the country is run for the good of everyone – could come into being.

So how did life change in Lenin's Russia?

New ideas

Lenin set to work immediately and went about making five key changes to Russian life in order to ensure a Communist state:

1. **Peace** – Lenin was against the war from the start, saying that the real enemies of the Russian people were not the Germans but the greedy landowners and factory owners. Lenin at once signed a peace treaty with Germany, although it meant that Russia lost vast amounts of its best industrial and farmland in Poland and the Ukraine (see **Source A**).

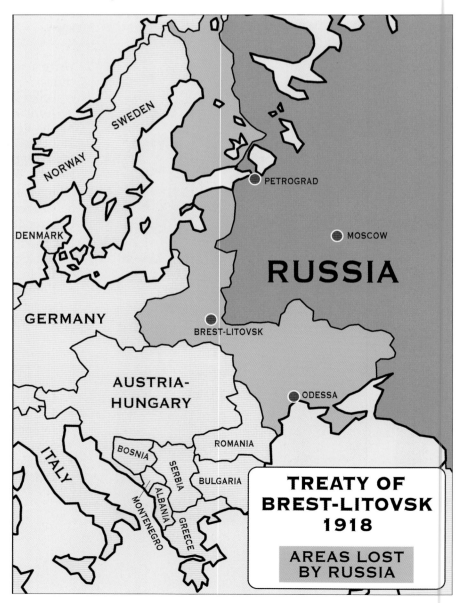

TREATY OF BREST-LITOVSK 1918

AREAS LOST BY RUSSIA

Source A ▸ *The Treaty of Brest-Litovsk took away 25% of Russia's population, 25% of the railway system, 35% of the grain-producing area and 70% of the industry.*

2. The economy – Lenin passed a law that said that all land previously owned by the nobles should be given to the peasants. They were told to work on the land by themselves or in groups. All factories, mines, workshops and railways were handed over to workers' committees.

3. New laws – Lenin brought in an eight-hour day for all workers, as well as unemployment pay and a pension scheme. Other laws gave women equal rights. Divorce was made easier and free education was planned. Religion was banned, and so was the teaching of history! The teaching of science was promoted.

4. Propaganda – a huge campaign was mounted to teach everyone to read. Special trains toured Russia showing films about how the new Communist government would benefit them.

5. Dictatorship – elections were held for a national Parliament in January 1918 … but Lenin's Bolsheviks only won 175 out of 707 seats. Most votes went to one of Lenin's rival political parties, the Social Revolutionaries (SRs). When the new National Parliament (known as the Assembly) met for its first meeting, Lenin's Red Guards surrounded the building – and sent the politicians home! It was never allowed to meet again. Lenin declared that Russia would be ruled by 'the dictatorship of the proletariat' – which was really the dictatorship of Lenin. And Lenin's secret police force, the **Cheka**, was ordered to arrest, torture and kill anybody who Lenin thought was trying to destroy his Communist state.

Source B ▼ *Trotsky's word to the new Russian Assembly shortly before Russia's first freely elected Parliament was closed for good.*

"You are a mere handful, miserable and bankrupt. You may go where you belong, to the rubbish-heap of history!"

Source C ▼ *Lenin addressing a meeting at the Putilov works in Petrograd, 1917.*

FACT *Leninism?*

Lenin believed in the ideas of Karl Marx. Marx's ideas were called Communism. Communists believe that the means of production (factories, farms and so on) should be owned by the whole community (hence 'Communism'), not as in Capitalism, where individuals (who might be very rich) own the means of production and leave the rest to be poor.

When Lenin took over power of Russia, he introduced partial Communism, and all factories and farms were run by councils. But Lenin himself still had control over all laws, banks, newspapers and police … which is more like dictatorship than Communism. Lenin himself thought that Russia needed to be controlled harshly at first before true Communism came into being. Indeed, some historians call Russia at this time a Leninist country rather than a Communist one!

Civil war

Not everyone was happy with the way Lenin and the Bolsheviks were doing things. Some groups within Russia still supported the Tsar, for example, while foreign powers such as the USA, Britain and France were worried because the Bolsheviks had declared they wanted to cause revolutions all over the world.

All the different groups who were against Lenin and the Bolsheviks were known as the **Whites** – and they were a very mixed bunch (see **Source F**).

For three years, the White armies fought against the Bolsheviks' Red Guard in a fierce and bloody Civil War. Many atrocities were committed by soldiers on both sides (see **Source D**). And, at first, it looked as if the Reds would lose – but they survived. This was mainly due to the fact that Trotsky, Lenin's right-hand man, organised and inspired his troops brilliantly. He began a **Red Terror** campaign that meant that anyone who opposed the Bolsheviks was shot. Trotsky even jailed the families of Red Army generals to keep them loyal! Lenin brought in something called **War Communism** too. This meant that the whole population had to provide supplies for the Red Army. Under War Communism, striking workers could be shot and anyone could be forced to work.

But while Lenin and the Bolsheviks were organising Russia for war, the Whites were arguing among themselves. They didn't coordinate their attacks properly and were never really united. By 1920, the Civil War was over and the White armies were defeated.

Source D ▶ *Red Army victims piled up by White soldiers.*

Source E ◄ *At the start of the Civil War, one of the aims of the Whites was to put the Tsar back on the throne. That became impossible after May 1918 when the Bolsheviks executed the Tsar, his wife, four daughters and young son. This photograph shows the room in which they were shot.*

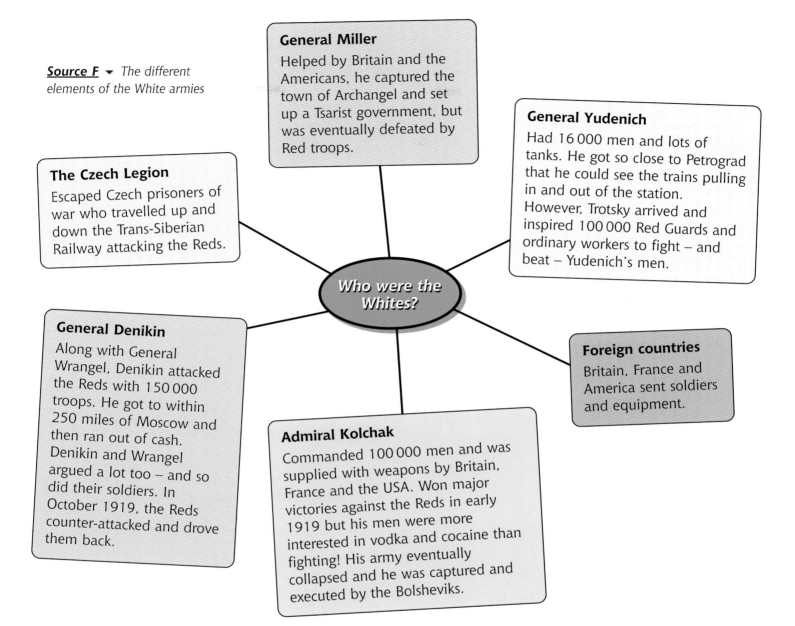

Source F ▼ *The different elements of the White armies*

General Miller
Helped by Britain and the Americans, he captured the town of Archangel and set up a Tsarist government, but was eventually defeated by Red troops.

General Yudenich
Had 16 000 men and lots of tanks. He got so close to Petrograd that he could see the trains pulling in and out of the station. However, Trotsky arrived and inspired 100 000 Red Guards and ordinary workers to fight – and beat – Yudenich's men.

The Czech Legion
Escaped Czech prisoners of war who travelled up and down the Trans-Siberian Railway attacking the Reds.

Who were the Whites?

General Denikin
Along with General Wrangel, Denikin attacked the Reds with 150 000 troops. He got to within 250 miles of Moscow and then ran out of cash. Denikin and Wrangel argued a lot too – and so did their soldiers. In October 1919, the Reds counter-attacked and drove them back.

Foreign countries
Britain, France and America sent soldiers and equipment.

Admiral Kolchak
Commanded 100 000 men and was supplied with weapons by Britain, France and the USA. Won major victories against the Reds in early 1919 but his men were more interested in vodka and cocaine than fighting! His army eventually collapsed and he was captured and executed by the Bolsheviks.

Famine and rebellion

By 1921, Russia had been at war for seven years – first the Great War, then Civil War. When the Bolsheviks introduced War Communism, which meant that Red Army soldiers went out into the countryside to seize food, the nation came close to a state of collapse. Many peasants saw no point in growing food only to have it taken away from them and food production dropped by 50%. Soon, towns were deserted as people went out into the countryside to look for food – and factory production dropped by 90%. When there was a terrible drought in 1921, a famine swept Russia which claimed as many as 25 million victims. In early 1921, there was a mutiny among sailors in Kronstadt, only 35 miles from Petrograd. The sailors had been some of Lenin's fiercest supporters but now they called for another revolution. They were disgusted by Lenin's War Communism and hated the sorry state of Russia. Trotsky and the Red Army brutally crushed the rebellion but the whole episode worried Lenin. He wondered how long it would be before others in Russia would rise up and throw out the Bolsheviks.

New Economic Policy (NEP)

The Kronstadt mutiny and the famine led Lenin to make some changes in Russia. He backed down on his tough Communist regime and decided to let some aspects of Capitalism return (see **Source G**). He brought in what he called the New Economic Policy, which meant that peasants who had been forced to hand over most of their produce to the war effort were allowed to keep some and sell it for profit. Gradually, despite it being against all the principles of Communism, a better class of peasants – the Kulaks – began to appear. Small traders, called NEPmen, were allowed to set up businesses. Salaries were paid to experts to run the factories and bonuses were paid to those who met production targets.

At the same time, local nationalities that had been forced to follow Communism and nothing else were allowed to bring back their own customs and language. Churches, mosques and market bazaars were re-opened.

Gradually, the economy picked up and the people were much happier. But Lenin was criticised a lot by some of the older Bolsheviks. They said he had 'sold out' to Capitalism. Some even left the Party.

Source G ▼ *Lenin, 1921.*

"We were forced to resort to War Communism because of the war – it was a temporary measure. Our poverty and ruin are so great that we can't hope to restore large-scale factory production at one stroke. Hence it is necessary to help restore small industry. The effect will be the revival of Capitalism on the basis of a certain amount of free trade."

Source H ▼ *NEP production figures.*

Year	1913	1921/22	1926
Factory production (million roubles)	10 251	2004	11 083
Pigs (millions)	20	12	22
Coal (millions of tons)	29	9	28
Grain (millions of tons)	80	38	77
Cattle (millions)	59	46	62
Steel (thousands of tons)	4231	183	3141

The Soviet Union

After winning the Civil War, Lenin captured other areas of the former Russian Empire (such as the Ukraine) and organised them into socialist republics governed by a Soviet. In 1922 these republics were organised into one united state – the Union of Soviet Socialist Republics (the USSR).

Stalin or Trotsky?

In 1918, a rival politician called Dora Kaplan tried to kill Lenin by shooting him. The doctors removed several bullets but were forced to leave two inside his body. Four years later, he suffered a stroke and never fully recovered. He died in January 1924.

Many thought that Lenin's successor would be Leon Trotsky – the brilliant organiser of the October Revolution and second in command of the Bolshevik Party. However, Joseph Stalin, the secretary of the Communist Party, got the job.

So why did Stalin become the USSR's new leader and not Trotsky?

The struggle for power between Stalin and Trotsky was really a struggle about what the Soviet Union would become in the future.

- Trotsky believed in encouraging 'world revolution' where all nations of the world would be run by workers' councils.
- Stalin believed in the idea of 'Communism in One Country', which meant that Russia had to develop as a strong industrial power first before there was any attempt to spread Communism around the world.

The struggle between the two men lasted four years – but gradually Stalin emerged as the leading figure. As a master of political trickery, he used his position as secretary to put his supporters in key positions. And he used propaganda brilliantly too. He stage-managed Lenin's funeral to make it appear that he had been very close to him. He even told Trotsky the wrong date for Lenin's funeral, so Trotsky turned up a day late.

Increasingly, Trotsky found himself isolated and, after Stalin became party leader, he was gradually removed from all his jobs. In 1928, he was sent to Siberia and was finally banned from the Soviet Union in 1929. Stalin was then able to remove other leading Bolsheviks from their posts so that he was in complete control. Trotsky himself was murdered in 1940, when a Stalinist agent drove the end of an ice-axe into his skull!

Source I ▾ *From Lenin's* Political Testament, *1922. Lenin wrote these words shortly before his death. Not surprisingly, Stalin stopped the publication of Lenin's* Political Testament.

"Comrade Stalin, having become General Secretary, has concentrated enormous power in his hands. I am not sure that he always knows how to use that power wisely. On the other hand, Comrade Trotsky … is probably the most able man in the Central Committee, but too self-confident, too much attracted by administration.

Stalin is too crude and this fault is very bad … in a General Secretary. Therefore I propose to comrades to find a way to remove Stalin and appoint a man more patient, more loyal, more polite, more attentive to comrades."

[Final paragraph added by Lenin in January 1923.]

Source J ▾ *The new flag of the USSR. Red is the traditional colour of Communism, while the gold star represents unity, the hammer represents industry and the scythe agriculture.*

WISE UP WORDS

Cheka   Whites   Red Terror   War Communism

WORK

1 **a** Why did the Bolsheviks win the Civil War?
   b Why do you think the Bolsheviks didn't want the Royal family to be captured by the Whites?

2 What were the differences between War Communism and the New Economic Policy?

3 Look at **Source H**.
   a Why do you think the figure was so low for pigs and cattle in 1921/22?
   b Why do you think the increased production of grain encouraged workers to return to the towns?
   c How might this have made an impact on factory production?
   d According to these figures, how successful was Lenin's New Economic Policy by 1926?

4 Lenin promised the Russian people 'Peace, bread and land'. By the time of his death in 1924, how successful had he been in carrying out his promise?

5 Look at **Source I**.
   a What does Lenin consider dangerous about Stalin?
   b Which of the two, Stalin or Trotsky, do you think Lenin prefers? Give reasons for your answer?

6 **a** What were the main differences between Stalin and Trotsky as potential leaders of Russia?
   b How did Stalin establish himself as leader of the USSR?

How did Stalin change the Soviet Union?

AIMS ....

Make sure you can explain the following key terms:
- collective farm;
- dekulakisation;
- the terror;
- cult of personality.

Joseph Stalin ruled the Soviet Union from around 1928 until his death in 1953. During his reign, he had complete control over one of the world's largest nations.

But when Stalin came to power, the Soviet Union was a second-rate, thoroughly unmodern state. Even Stalin himself said that Russia was '100 years behind some of the other more advanced countries'. Yet, by the 1940s, Russia was strong enough to stand up to Hitler's mighty Nazi army – and eventually defeat it. Indeed, the Soviet Union then went on to become one of the great two superpowers that dominated world affairs for the next 50 years.

So how did Stalin change the Soviet Union?

Stalin's character

Stalin was born in 1879 in Georgia in the far south of the Russian Empire. He was one of the few Bolshevik Party leaders who came from a working-class background (his drunken father made shoes for a living). Stalin's real name was Iosif Vissarionovich Dzhugashvili, but he used lots of false names when he was a young man because he was constantly being sought by the Tsar's secret police for his 'revolutionary activities'. He finally settled on 'Stalin' in 1913. It means 'man of steel'. By the time of the 1917 revolutions, Stalin was established as one of the Bolshevik leaders and Lenin had even given him the important job of running the Party's newspaper, *Pravda*.

Gradually, Stalin took on more and more responsibility in Lenin's Russia, carefully putting his supporters into key posts all over the country.

By the time of his death, Lenin thought Stalin had become too powerful … but it was already too late. When Lenin died in 1924, Stalin was in an ideal position to gradually sack, imprison – or even execute – his main political opponents until, by 1928, he had emerged as sole leader of the Soviet Union.

As ruler, Stalin was utterly ruthless in the way he governed. Millions were sent to prison or died because of him. He was a secretive, lonely man who worked long hours in the Kremlin (the headquarters of government in Moscow). He trusted no one – and terrified most who knew him – although he also managed to persuade the ordinary citizens of Russia that he was the kind, generous, all-knowing, almost god-like saviour of Russia.

Source A ▼ *A photo of young Stalin in 1900.*

Source B ▼ *A modern historian, 1999 (Nigel Kelly and Greg Lacey,* Modern World History, *Heinemann, 1999).*

"As a young man, Stalin trained as a priest but he was expelled because he became involved with local revolutionaries. In his late teens … he devoted himself to revolutionary activities, including bank raids to raise party funds … when not in prison, he was constantly sought after by the secret police. It was a hard and secretive way of life and it left Stalin with a taste for conspiracy and subterfuge [underhand tactics]."

Changes on the farms

From 1928 onwards, Stalin began his ambitious plans to modernise the country. He began with farming. First he announced that individual ownership of land would stop.

The small farms the peasants owned were taken away and put together to create large state or '**collective farms**'. Each farm was called a **kolkhoz**. The peasants could keep their own homes and a small plot of land (a big garden) but all carts, horses, tools and cattle had to be given over to the kolkhoz.

The peasants were paid a wage to work on these state farms. Ninety percent of the kolkhoz produce was sold to the state at a fixed price and the profits shared out. The kolkhoz kept the other 10%.

Any peasants, especially the better-off ones – called **kulaks** – weren't happy about losing their land … so Stalin decided to 'wipe them out as a class'. In 1929, he said, 'We must smash the kulaks'. Some were shot or sent to prison; others were forced to settle on poor-quality land. In total, this '**dekulakisation**' programme wiped out about five million kulaks. In addition, bad harvests and awful weather in 1932 and 1933 resulted in widespread famine – and millions more Russians died of starvation (see **Source C**).

Source C ▼ *Agricultural production 1928 and 1933.*

Product	1928	1933
Cattle (millions)	70.5	38.4
Pigs (millions)	26	12.1
Sheep and goats (millions)	146.7	50.2
Grain (million tons)	73.3	68.4

Source D ▼ *From Geoffrey Hosking's* A History of the Soviet Union, *1985. Here he is describing the job of Communist officials who went into the countryside to carry out the dekulakisation programme.*

"The Communist officials searched everything, breaking down doors, tearing up cushions, ripping up floorboards, and confiscated not only food but often furniture, clothes, tools. Many peasants, expecting this, sold their belongings, and slaughtered their cattle for meat. Viktor Kravchenko saw one woman who set fire to her own home. She shrieked at him, 'Murderers! We've worked all our lives for our home. You won't have it. The flames shall have it!'

When he entered a village, he was surprised by the complete silence. 'All the dogs have been eaten', he was told. 'We've eaten everything we could lay our hands on — cats, dogs, mice, birds … the trees have been stripped of their bark, for that too has been eaten.'

Special roadblocks were set up on roads leading into major cities to stop peasants from coming in and begging for bread. When an American worker in Samara saw an old woman and two children lying close to death in the street, a Red Army soldier warned him off, saying, 'These people do not want to work. They are kulaks. They are enemies of the Soviet Union.'"

Changes in the factories

Stalin's main method of modernising Russia was through a series of five-year plans for each of the country's main industries. Gosplan, the main government planning office, set high targets for industries such as coal, steel and oil – targets that had to be met every five years. Factory managers then had to calculate targets for every shift and every worker. Stalin even forced prisoners from his labour camps (Gulags) to work on large-scale building projects, such as roads and canals.

But Stalin was only ever concerned that his industry produced more and more basic raw materials – so he didn't bother increasing the output of consumer goods. As a result, workers were forced to live without many of the new luxury items that people all over Europe were using. Workers lived in poor-quality housing and worked long hours for low wages. Food was sometimes rationed too – and any worker who missed a shift or criticised the state could have their food rations taken away! But life did improve by the end of the 1930s. Life was certainly tough and wages still very low, but more people were working so most families had a bit more money to spend. The Communist state also provided free education and medicine – and bonuses if targets were met. And, as an industrial power, Russia was transformed by 1938, second only to the United States.

Source E ▾ *Targets and achievements of the five-year plans. As you can see, targets were rarely met – but the industrial growth is still an amazing feat.*

Product	Output in 1928	Output in first five-year plan 1928–33			Output in second five-year plan 1933–37		
		A	B	C	A	B	C
Coal (million tons)	36.0	76.2	65.3	64.0	155	130	128
Steel (million tons)	4.0	10.6	6.0	6.0	17.3	18	18
Oil (million tons)	1.7	22.4	21.1	21.0	47.5	29	26

Key

A = target; B = official Soviet figures; C = Western estimates

Source F ▸ *Massive publicity was given to a Ukrainian miner called Alexei Stakhanov. In 1935, with a team of two men, he mined 102 tons of coal in one six-hour shift – 14 times the average. Soon 'Stakhanovites' became the new term to describe workers who achieved near superhuman production targets. They received better wages, housing and health care than 'ordinary' workers.*

Stalin's Russia was not as equal as a Communist state should have been in theory. Women, for example, had equal rights with men – but traditional male attitudes at home meant that they still had to take on all the childcare and domestic chores. Interestingly, not one woman held a high position in government during Stalin's years in power.

In 1926, 51% of Russians over the age of ten could read. By 1939, the figure was up by 81%. Clearly, Stalin's compulsory literacy policy was making an impact.

'The terror'

For many Russians, Stalin provided stability and security. But his secret police (who had a variety of names – OGPU, NKVD and so on) arrested anyone who criticised his policies or his leadership. In fact, it has been estimated that the secret police arrested about eight and a half million people during the 1930s, of whom about a million were shot!

But Stalin seemed most paranoid about other leading Communists and from about 1935, he set out to **purge** (clean out) society by eliminating his political opponents. These purges – as they were called – began in December 1934 when the popular Communist Party boss of Leningrad, Sergey Kiro, was killed in a car crash. The crash was probably arranged by Stalin himself.

One by one, the old Bolsheviks were arrested. Some were shot, but others were forced to take part in great 'show trials' and confessed to ridiculous 'crimes' after torture in order to save themselves. And after purging the 'old guard', as they were called, Stalin turned on the army – 81 out of 103 top generals and admirals were killed.

Astonishingly, as many as three million 'opponents' were killed during the 'terror' as it was sometimes called. Another two million were sent to labour camps where many died of ill treatment.

Source G ▼ *How the purges affected the 'old guard' – well known members of the Bolshevik Party. This poster was published in 1938 by supporters of Trotsky.*

Source H ▼ *A sarcastic French 'travel poster' published in the 1930s. The man on the right (Stalin) is saying 'Visit the USSR's pyramids'.*

'The cult of the personality'

In Stalin's Russia, people were not allowed to think for themselves – they were told what to think by the government. In schools, children were taught Stalin's version of history; for example photographs were retouched and the names of rivals such as Trotsky were removed from official histories of the Revolution (see **Source I**). Stalin's picture appeared everywhere too – in schools, offices, factories, town squares and stations. Even places were named after him, such as Stalingrad, Stalinko and Stalino.

The mass media – radio, films and newspapers – were all controlled by the state too. As a result, the state's slogans and messages were everywhere. Even artists, poets and writers were brought under state control too (see **Source J**).

Indeed, Soviet citizens were taught to believe that Stalin was all-knowing and all-powerful. And no criticism was allowed so there was never any chance for ordinary Russians to hear another viewpoint. The result was a kind of hero worship known as 'the cult of the personality', which helps to explain why so many ordinary people looked upon Stalin as a god.

Source J ▾ *After 1932, all writers had to be members of the state-controlled Writers' Union in order to get their work published. This poem was published in* Pravda, *the government-controlled newspaper, in 1936. Songs, poems, pictures and stories about Stalin filled newspapers, cinemas, storyboards, radio and school textbooks. Children were taught to think of him as the 'Father of Russia' and were even taught to tell the police if their parents criticised him.*

> *O great Stalin, leader of the peoples,*
> *Thou who brought men to birth,*
> *Thou who makes fruitful the earth,*
> *Thou who restored the centuries,*
> *Thou who makes the spring bloom,*
> *Thou who makes musical chords vibrate,*
> *Thou splendour of my spring, oh thou*
> *Sun reflected by millions of hearts.*

Source I ▾ *Two versions of a famous photograph of Lenin, taken in 1920. Both show Lenin making a speech. The original (on the top) shows Trotsky and Kamenev standing on the right. But after the two men were expelled from the Communist Party by Stalin, the photo was re-touched by experts. Note how the two men have disappeared from the picture on the bottom. This photograph then appeared in history textbooks used in schools all over the Soviet Union.*

Source K ▸ *From a poem written in the 1930s about Stalin by Osip Mandelstam, who later died in one of Stalin's labour camps. An 'Ossetian' is someone from Ossetia, Georgia – the area where Stalin was born.*

His fingers are fat as grubs
And words, final as lead weights, fall from
  his lips,
His cockroach whiskers leer
And his boot tops gleam,
Around him a rabble of thin-necked leaders –
Fawning half-men for him to play with,
They whinny, purr or whine
As he chatters and points a finger,
One by one forging his laws, to be flung
Like horseshoes at the head, the eye or the
  groin,
And every killing is a treat
For the broad-chested Ossetian.

WISE UP WORDS

- purge   collective farms   kolkhoz   kulaks
  dekulakisation

WORK

1 Look at **Source D**.
   a Why did the government officials visit the area?
   b What evidence is there in the source that many in the countryside were starving?

2 What were the five-year plans and why were the introduced?

3 Look at **Source E**.
   a Of all the targets set by Stalin in both the first and the second five-year plans, which was the only target to be achieved?
   b Does the fact that the production targets were rarely met mean that the five-year plans were a failure? Explain your answer carefully.
   c Why do you think there are differences between output figures given by the Soviets and the figures compiled by the West?

4 Look at **Sources G** and **H**.
   a What is the purpose of each source?
   b Which, in your opinion, is the most effective?

5 Look at **Source I**.
   a How has the second photograph been changed?
   b Why do you think the change was made?
   c What do these photographs tell us about Stalin's methods of government?
   d What do these photographs tell us about the difficulties historians face when writing about the Soviet Union under Stalin?

6 Look at **Source K**. Why do you think Stalin didn't like this poem? Explain your answer using details of the poem.

Task 1 How strong was the League of Nations?

The League of Nations was an international peace-keeping organisation set up at the end of the Great War. From the start people could see that it had major strengths ... but major weaknesses too. Look back over your studies on the League of Nations, then copy and complete a chart like the one below.

Key element	Strength	Weakness
Membership of the League	Strong nations, such as Britain, France, Italy and Japan were members of the League	Decision-making
Powers of the League		
Attitude of Britain and France towards the League		

Task 2 Prejudice

The word 'bias' means one-sided. There is a lot of bias in history, where only one side of the picture is shown. Perhaps only the good points – or the bad points – of something are presented, but never both.

Bias exaggerates or distorts what has been said or done. An advertisement on the TV is an example of bias. It never tells you the bad points of the product ... or that you may be able to buy better, cheaper versions from somewhere else!

'Prejudice' is an extreme form of bias – where an artist or a writer, for example, reveals their dislike or hatred for a particular person, race, minority group, class of people or way of life. In Nazi Germany, prejudice was everywhere!

Study this picture carefully. It appeared in a German school textbook in the 1930s. Then answer the following questions.

a How have the Jewish people been drawn? Describe your feelings as you look at them.

b How is the non-Jewish child drawn?

c What do the geese appear to be doing in the picture?

d The Nazis controlled all pictures that appeared in school textbooks. What does this picture tell us about the Nazis?

e Why do you think the Nazis targeted children with their prejudice?

Task 3 Russian anagrams

In the anagram list below you will find:

- a murdered Tsar
- the first ever Russian parliament
- a drunken holy man
- the new name for the capital city
- the leader of the Provisional Government
- Lenin's political party
- the treaty between Russia and Germany
- Stalin's rival for leadership after Lenin's death
- the richer peasants
- the hero coal-miner
- the OGPU and NKVD
- the word for getting rid of political opponents

All the answers are given below, but the words and letters have been mixed up. Can you unravel them?

ROTTKYS   PANURSIT   TCEESR LOPCIE   HLOSAINC

NIGGUPR   UMAD   SRETB-OTILKSV   RKYNEEKS

KKALUS   ROTEPAGRD   AKATSVHON   HEKIVLOSB

Task 4 USA anagrams

In the anagram list below, you will find:

- A person who has bought shares
- The name of a share in a company's profits
- Another word for a share
- The street in which the New York stock exchange sits
- The month in which the Wall Street Crash took place
- Nickname for the day of the 'Crash'
- The US President at the time of the Wall Street Crash
- The official word for producing too many goods that people can't afford to buy
- The name given to the long period of high unemployment that followed the 'Crash'
- A queue of people wanting food
- A town made from rubbish
- A group of ex-soldiers who marched to Washington, DC

All the answers are given below, but the words and letters have been mixed up. Can you unravel them?

HHDRSOLEEAR   EDIINDDV   TOCKS   LALW RTETSE

BCRTOOE   KLCBA ASHDTRYU   RBRHTEE VOROHE

NUOPORVERCTIOD   RNDEALBIE   ONSBU RYMA

VOIOERHVLEL   ERATG ERPDSIEOSN

Task 5 Question time

Look at these genuine GCSE questions carefully. Why not try to complete one, two or even all of them as a revision exercise?

- Explain why the League of Nations was established.
- What was the structure of the League of Nations?
- How successful was the League of Nations at keeping peace in the 1920s? Explain your answer.
- What were Hitler's main beliefs?
- Explain why Hitler became Chancellor in 1933.
- Why were women and children such an important part of Hitler's plans for Germany?
- "The most important factor enabling the Nazis to control the German people was their use of propaganda." Do you agree with this statement? Explain your answer.
- Why was there an economic boom in the USA in the 1920s?
- What were the main features of the 'Roaring Twenties'?
- Explain why Wall Street crashed.
- What were the main features of the New Deal?
- What were the main weaknesses of the Provisional Government of 1917?
- Why did the Whites lose the Civil War?
- What was Collectivisation?
- Why did Stalin introduce the five-year plans?

Was it Hitler's war?

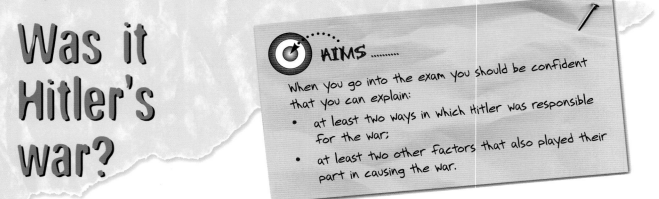

World War II began in 1939, just over 20 years after the end of the Great War. It was to involve more countries – and kill more people – than any other war before or since. Most people lay the blame for starting the war firmly at the feet of one man – Adolf Hitler, leader of Germany. In fact, shortly after World War II, a famous British historian wrote that 'World War II was Hitler's personal war – he intended it, prepared for it and chose the moment for launching it'.

So how true is this opinion? What evidence supports this view? Was Hitler totally to blame for the outbreak of war – or did other factors play their part?

So what did Hitler say?

One of Hitler's main aims was to make Germany a powerful nation once more. He had fought as a losing soldier in the Great War of 1914–18 and, like millions of Germans, was humiliated by the punishment Germany received at the end of the fighting (see **Source A**).

Source A ▶ *A summary of the Treaty of Versailles – the agreement reached at the end of the Great War. No German representatives were allowed to discuss the treaty – they just had to accept it or face invasion. Not surprisingly, the German people hated it. Hitler swore revenge!*

Hitler identified three things that he felt he must do in order to make Germany a world power once more:

1. He wanted to get all the land back that Germany lost after the Great War. He felt he had to build up his army, navy and air force to do this.
2. He wanted to join together all German-speaking people into one big country.
3. He wanted to make Germany even bigger because he believed that true Germans were such a great and powerful race that they needed the extra living space (he called it Lebensraum) to reach their full potential. He realised that he may have to take land from smaller, weaker countries in order to do this.

TREATY OF VERSAILLES

- THE GREAT WAR IS GERMANY'S FAULT SO THEY MUST PAY FOR IT. THE MONEY WILL GO TO THE WINNING COUNTRIES. THEY ARE TO PAY £6 600 000 000 (IN INSTALMENTS UP TO 1988!).
- GERMANY MUST BE MADE WEAK. THEY ARE ALLOWED ONLY A SMALL ARMY (100 000 MEN), A SMALL NAVY (SIX BATTLESHIPS) AND NO SUBMARINES, FIGHTER PLANES OR TANKS.
- GERMANY MUST HAND OVER SOME OF ITS LAND (ABOUT 10% IN TOTAL) TO THE WINNING COUNTRIES. THEY WILL LOSE 16% OF THEIR COALFIELDS AND HALF THEIR IRON AND STEEL INDUSTRIES. SOME OF THE LAND WILL BE USED TO MAKE NEW COUNTRIES SUCH AS CZECHOSLOVAKIA AND POLAND.
- GERMANY MUST NEVER UNITE WITH AUSTRIA EVER AGAIN.
- NO GERMAN SOLDIERS CAN GO NEAR FRANCE, TO AN AREA KNOWN AS THE RHINELAND.

SIGNED BRITAIN, FRANCE, USA, ITALY AND OTHER WINNING COUNTRIES

Hitler knew that it would mean breaking the Treaty of Versailles if he were to achieve his three main objectives ... but he didn't care! Hitler, like millions of Germans, hated the treaty and would carry on with his master plan regardless (see **Source B**).

Source B ▼ *A speech by Adolf Hitler.*

"The Treaty of Versailles is engraved on the minds and hearts of the German people. It is burned into them. Sixty million people find their souls aflame with a feeling of rage and shame. The people are joined in a common cry: 'We will have weapons again'."

Source C ▼ From Mein Kampf, *written by Hitler in 1924.*

" · The reunion of Germany and Austria is our life task

· Germany has an annual increase of nearly 900 000 people. New land must be secured for our population; we turn our gaze to land in the East. When we speak of new land we mean Russia and her border states."

Source D ▼ *A speech made by Adolf Hitler in the 1920s.*

"Instead of everlasting struggle, the world preaches everlasting peace — but there will never be a solution to the German problem until we return to the idea of struggle."

Source E ▼ *From a book, written in 1934 by A. Rausching, No Retreat.*

"Do you seriously intend to fight the West?" I asked.

Hitler stopped and looked at me. "What else do you think we're arming for?" he replied. "We must proceed step by step so that no one will impede our advance. How to do this I don't know yet. But that it will be done is guaranteed by Britain's lack of firmness and France's internal disunity."

Source F ▼ *An extract from Hitler's last will and testament, written just before he committed suicide in May 1945.*

"It is not true that I wanted a war in 1939. It was brought about by Jews. After my experience of the First World War, I never wished for a second war against England."

So what did Hitler do?

Germany builds weapons

Early in 1933, three days after becoming leader of Germany, Hitler ordered his military chiefs to start secretly building new tanks, submarines, battleships and fighter planes. This is known as rearmament. This was all banned by the Treaty of Versailles. He then took Germany out of the League of Nations, the international peacekeeping organisation set up after the Great War. The chances of a peaceful future didn't look good!

In 1935, Hitler told the world about his increased army, navy and air force in a speech at a massive rally in Berlin ... but no countries did anything about it! Some countries didn't want to stand up to Hitler because they were scared Germany might invade, while others (such as Britain) felt that Germany should be allowed to build up their armed forces if they wanted to. After all, they were only protecting themselves, weren't they?

Source G ▾ *Hitler checks out some of his new troops in 1936. The style of marching shown in the photograph is known as 'goose-stepping'.*

Source H ▾ *Frank Roberts, who worked for the British Foreign Office, 1930–68, speaking on a TV programme in 1999.*

"The general view in Britain was that the French and British had been too harsh on Germany in 1918 and that this should be rectified. There was a slight feeling that we ought to have done better, perhaps even a feeling of guilt."

Also, in 1935, Britain signed a deal with Germany (the **German–Anglo Naval Agreement**), allowing Germany to increase the size of its navy to 35% of the size of the British navy. It seemed that British attitudes to Germany had softened so much that Britain was now allowing Germany to break the terms of the Treaty of Versailles! A year later, Hitler ordered that every young man had to have army training in the new bigger German army. This was known as conscription. Three countries – Britain, Italy and France – openly criticised Hitler's plans to expand his army, but no country took military action.

For the time being, it seemed that Hitler was 'getting away' with everything he tried – so what would he do next?

FACT *Saar Plebiscite*

The first area of land that Germany 'got back' was a rich industrial region called the Saar. This German area was put under the League of Nation's control for 15 years after the Great War. In 1935, the people who lived there had a choice to join France or remain part of Germany. A massive majority chose to stay with Germany.

Source I ▾ *Millions of dollars spent on weapons.*

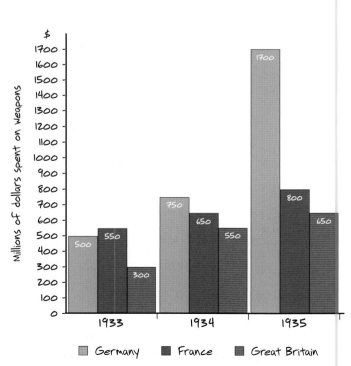

The Rhineland

In 1936, Hitler made his most daring move yet. In March, he sent German soldiers into the Rhineland, an area of France next to Germany where German soldiers were forbidden to go.

It was a massive gamble. Britain and France had agreed ten years earlier to use their armies to stop Germany entering the Rhineland – and Hitler only had 30 000 fully equipped troops.

But the gamble paid off. Not one country stood up to Hitler – after all, he wasn't invading another nation, just moving soldiers around *within* his own country, they thought. One British political advisor even said 'The Germans are only going into their own back garden'. The same year, Hitler signed agreements with Italy and Japan to stick up for each other if they were attacked.

By now, Hitler's actions were starting to make world news – many wondered what Hitler would do next!

Source J ▼ *This cartoon appeared in the* London Evening Standard *in 1936.*

Source K ▼ *Hitler, speaking to his advisors after the Rhineland invasion.*

> "The 48 hours after the march into the Rhineland in 1936 were the most nerve-wracking of my life. If the French had opposed us then we would have had to withdraw with our tails between our legs. Our forces were not strong enough, even to put up a moderate resistance."

FACT *The Spanish Civil War*

In 1936, a fierce civil war broke out in Spain between the government and part of the army, led by the Fascist General Franco. Germany and Italy helped Franco with men, money and weapons, mainly because he had similar political views to Hitler and Mussolini – and also because it was a good opportunity to try out all the new tanks, guns and planes that Germany and Italy had been developing. With their help, Franco won the war and, when World War II started, the Nazis had well-tested weapons, whereas British equipment often broke down and developed faults.

WORK

1 Look at **Sources B** and **C**. Make a list of Hitler's aims.

2 Look at **Sources E** and **F**.
   a In what way does Hitler criticise Britain and France in **Source E**?
   b Does Hitler contradict himself in **Sources E** and **F**?

3 It is 1936 and you work for the British Government. Write a briefing paper for the British Prime Minister which outlines Hitler's plans – and his actions – up to 1936. Make sure you include details on:
   • Hitler's aims – what has he said?
   • Hitler's actions – what has he done?

You should conclude your paper with your own assessment of whether the PM should be worried about Hitler. Points to think about:
   • Britain is a key member of the League of Nations, which is supposed to make sure Germany follows the Treaty of Versailles.
   • Many in Britain thought the Treaty of Versailles was too harsh (see **Source H**).
   • Some people in the British Government were more worried about Communist Russia than Germany. They felt that a strong Germany may stand up to Russia and stop the spread of Communism.

4 Look at **Source J**.
   a Who is the figure walking over the backs of the 'spineless leaders'?
   b What is meant by the person's hand gesture?
   c How, according to the cartoonist, could the 'spineless leaders' stop this person?

Anschluss with Austria

One of Hitler's main aims was to unite all German-speaking people in one country. He decided to start by joining Germany with Austria (they speak German in Austria you see). However, this union – or Anschluss – was banned by the Treaty of Versailles, so Hitler had to go about it very carefully.

Hitler began by telling his supporters in Austria to stir up trouble by starting riots and setting fire to important buildings. Hitler's plan was to make it look as if the Austrian leader, Kurt Schuschnigg, could not control his country. Then Hitler offered to send the German army into Austria to 'restore order'. When Hitler moved his troops close to the Austrian border, Schuschnigg asked Britain, France and Italy to help … but all three refused. Schuschnigg resigned. An Austrian Nazi, Seyss-Inquart, took his place and immediately asked Hitler to send in the German army to 'restore order'. In fact, you might say that Hitler invaded Austria by invitation. A few months later, Hitler held a public vote to see whether Austria supported the move – and 99.7% of Austrians voted 'yes'. However, many thought the vote was unfair because armed German soldiers stood next to many of the voting booths to put pressure on the voters. And while former leader Schuschnigg was forced to clean toilets, the world began to realise that Hitler might soon be unstoppable. He had broken the Treaty of Versailles again – and no one had stopped him!

> **FACT** *If at first you don't succeed …*
>
> Hitler had tried to unite with Austria once before – in 1934. He arranged for his supporters in Austria to kill the Austrian leader, Dollfuss, and then invite him to take over. But Italian leader, Mussolini, was suspicious of Hitler at the time and threatened to use force to stop him. Hitler abandoned his plans – but learned two valuable lessons. First, he needed to build up his armed forces so he was a match for anyone … and secondly, he needed to make friends with Italy. By 1938, he had done both of these!

Source L ▾ *Written by Austrian leader Kurt Schuschnigg in 1948. He is writing about what Hitler said to him during the months leading up to the Austrian invasion in 1938.*

"Listen. You don't really think you can move a single stone in Austria without me hearing about it the very next day, do you? You don't seriously think you can stop me, or even delay me for half an hour, do you?

Think it over, Herr Schuschnigg, think it over well. I can only wait until this afternoon … I don't believe in bluffing. All my past is proof of that."

Source M ▶ *An Austrian girl gives a flower to an 'invading' German soldier, March 1938. Many Austrians wanted to be part of Germany and rejoiced when the Germans invaded. Austrians and Germans share a similar culture, customs, religion and language … and Adolf Hitler was Austrian too! Note the swastika flags in the background – clearly the Austrians in this town were happy to see the Germans.*

Source N ▲ The darker side of Hitler's invasion of Austria. This photo, of Austrian Jews cleaning streets in 1938, was typical of the treatment they received. Within six months of the German invasion, a concentration camp had been built to deal with Austrian Jews.

WORK

1 In your own words, explain how and why Hitler invaded Austria.

2 Look at **Source L**.
   a What do you think Hitler meant when he said: 'I don't believe in bluffing. All my past is proof of that'?
   b Can you give any examples of Hitler's previous actions that support this claim?

3 Look at **Source M**.
   a What does this photograph tell us about the feelings of ordinary Austrians when Hitler invaded in 1938? Give reasons for your answer.
   b Do you believe all Austrians felt like this? Explain your answer.
   c What does this tell you about the use of photographs as evidence?

4 Look at **Source N**. What does this photograph tell you about the nature of the Nazi rule in Austria?

The Czech crisis

Look at **Source O**. By 1938, Hitler had already claimed back the Saar and the Rhineland, and united with Austria. Hitler next turned his attention to the Sudetenland, a border region of Czechoslovakia that contained areas of people who spoke German as their first language. Hitler told the world he wanted this region (he wanted to unite all German-speakers, remember!) – but the Czechs wanted to keep it.

Once again, Hitler tried to use his favourite 'bully-boy' tactic.

Source O ▾ *A map of Europe in the 1930s showing Hitler's gradual takeover.*

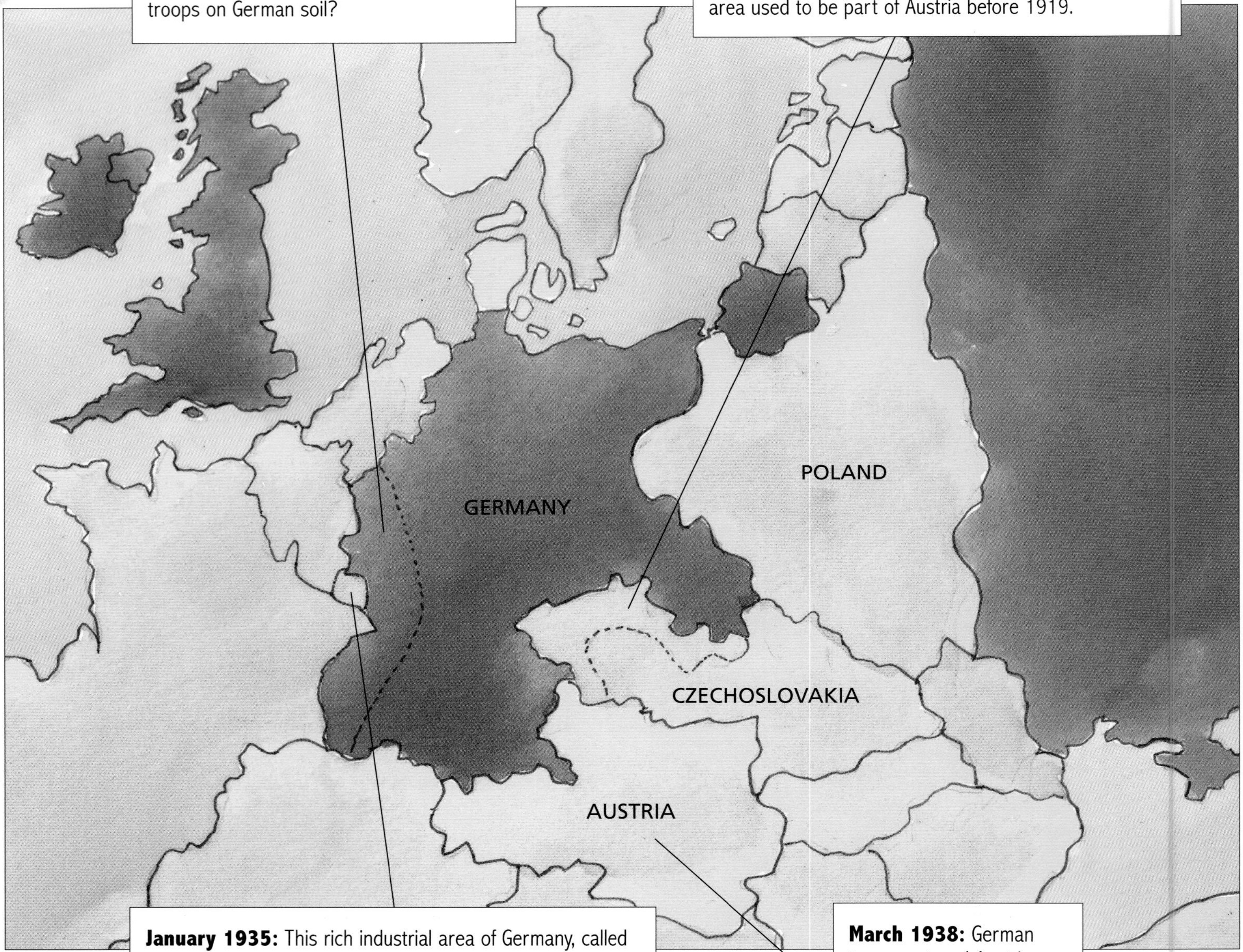

March 1936: German troops marched into the Rhineland, breaking the Treaty of Versailles. Britain and France did nothing. Why shouldn't Germany be allowed to have troops on German soil?

The Sudetenland was the richest part of Czechoslovakia, containing coalmines, power stations, good farmland and the famous Skoda weapons factory. Three million people here spoke German because the area used to be part of Austria before 1919.

POLAND

GERMANY

CZECHOSLOVAKIA

AUSTRIA

January 1935: This rich industrial area of Germany, called the Saar, had been under the control of the League of Nations for 15 years. The League allowed the French to run its valuable coalfields. After a vote, the Saar war returned to Germany. This was in accordance with the Treaty of Versailles and it had the full backing of the League of Nations.

March 1938: German troops entered Austria. Germany and Austria became one country. This 'Anschluss' broke the Treaty of Versailles.

He ordered his supporters in the Sudetenland to let off bombs and start riots, so it looked as if the Czechs couldn't control their own country or protect the German speakers living in the area. He then sent the German army to the border – and demanded that the Czechs give up the area. The Czechs refused.

In September 1938, Neville Chamberlain, the British Prime Minister, tried to sort the problem out. He first visited the Czechoslovakian leader, Benes, who said Hitler could only have the areas of the Sudetenland where most of the German speakers lived. Chamberlain, thinking this was quite fair, visited Hitler with the offer. But Hitler said he wanted *all* of the Sudetenland!

Source P ▾ *An adapted version of the 'piece of paper', signed by Chamberlain and Hitler in September 1938.*

We, Hitler and Chamberlain, have had a further meeting today and are in agreement that the question of British–German relations is very important.

We regard the agreement signed last night [allowing Germany to have the Sudetenland] and the Anglo–German Naval Agreement [a deal in 1935 where Britain allowed Germany to have a bigger navy] as symbolic of the desire of our countries never to go to war with one another again.

We are resolved that we shall use consultation to deal with any other questions that may concern our two countries and we are determined to continue our efforts to assure the peace of Europe.

Neville Chamberlain   **Adolf Hitler**

September 1938

On 28 September, Chamberlain and several other leaders met Hitler once more. Benes wasn't even invited. After several hours of discussion, an agreement was reached that said that Hitler could have all of the Sudetenland. Benes went along with it, hoping that Hitler would now leave his country alone. Hitler said he was happy with the outcome and the world breathed a sigh of relief. In Britain, Chamberlain was a hero – he had even got Hitler to sign a piece of paper saying he was satisfied with everything and didn't want anything else (see **Source P**).

FACT *Appeasement*

In the 1930s, many people were afraid of war. The horrors of the Great War were still fresh in people's memories. As a result, countries such as Britain and France decided to let aggressive leaders such as Hitler have their own way rather than stand up to them. It was hoped that this course of action would avoid a large-scale war. This was called **appeasement** – trying to keep the peace through negotiation.

WISE UP WORDS

- German–Anglo Naval Agreement appeasement

WORK

It is the day after the Munich Agreement has been signed in September 1938.

Write five different newspaper headlines for a variety of newspapers. You must think carefully about your headlines, trying to imagine whether the newspaper would see the Munich Agreement as a wise policy, perhaps a triumph – or a 'cowardly cop out'. Write headlines for:

- a British newspaper that generally supports the government
- a Czechoslovakian newspaper
- a German newspaper
- a British newspaper that often criticises the government
- an American newspaper (remember they are a neutral country at this time, trying to keep out of European affairs).

So why did Prime Minister Chamberlain 'appease' Hitler?

Neville Chamberlain's negotiations with Hitler in 1938 were known as appeasement. This means giving in to some of Hitler's demands in order to avoid war.

Some historians have since criticised the policy of appeasement, mainly due to the fact that Hitler kept on invading country after country, despite promising not to! But at the time, only a few people were against appeasement – why?

Reason No. 1

Many British people were anti-war and believed strongly in disarmament.

Reason No. 2

After the horrors of the Great War, many felt that war should be avoided at all costs.

Reason No. 3

Many British people agreed with Hitler when he said the Treaty of Versailles was unfair.

Reason No. 4

Many felt that Britain was too far away and too weak to help other European countries.

Reason No. 5

The British government wasn't sure they could get enough volunteers to fight another major war.

Reason No. 6

Some felt that events in Europe were not any of Britain's business.

Reason No. 7

There was a feeling that a strong Germany would stop the growth of Communism spreading from Russia to the rest of Europe.

Reason No. 8

Some British people were in favour of what Hitler was doing in Germany – and felt he needed Britain's support.

i) Evidence ▼ *Written by Harold Nicholson, a British advisor during the Paris peace talks, 1919.*

"The Treaty of Versailles is neither fair or wise. There isn't a single person amongst the younger generation who isn't unhappy with it."

ii) Evidence ▼ *Neville Chamberlain, writing in a letter to his sister in 1938.*

"You only have to look at a map of Europe to see we couldn't do anything to save Czechoslovakia from being overrun by German troops."

iii) **Evidence** ▾ *H. A. L. Fisher, History of Europe, 1936.*

Hitler is a guarantee that Russian Communism won't spread towards the West.

iv) **Evidence** ▾ *The British attitude to disarmament: the results of a survey carried out in 1937.*

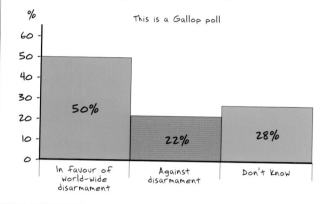

v) **Evidence** ▾ *Neville Chamberlain, speaking in 1937.*

"War wins nothing, cures nothing, ends nothing. When I think of the seven million young men cut off in their prime, the 13 million who were maimed or mutilated, the misery and suffering of the mothers and fathers … in war there are no winners, only losers."

vi) **Evidence** ▾ *L. C. B. Seasman's Post Victorian Britain, 1966.*

"Hitler attacked Communists, trade unions and pacifists [people who are against all war]. These were the same policies that some British political parties were following."

vii) **Evidence** ▾ *Results of a survey carried out in December 1937. The question asked was 'If a war broke out, would you volunteer to fight?'*

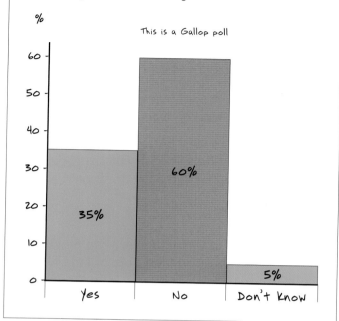

viii) **Evidence** ▾ *Neville Chamberlain, speaking in 1938.*

"How horrible, fantastic, incredible it is that we should be digging trenches and trying on gas masks here because of a quarrel in a faraway country between people of whom we know nothing."

WORK

Study the above reasons why the British government followed a policy of 'appeasement'. Try to match the reasons (1 to 8) with the correct evidence (i to viii).

1939: Europe's last year of peace

When British Prime Minister, Neville Chamberlain, returned from his meeting with Hitler in Munich in 1938, he was treated like a hero. To many, Chamberlain had stopped a war by giving Hitler the Sudetenland, the German-speaking area of Czechoslovakia he had wanted for so long. Chamberlain said 'It is peace for our time' and Hitler himself promised that the Sudetenland was the last piece of land he wanted.

But just 11 months later, Britain and Germany were at war as World War II began. So what happened during those months to push Europe into war once again?

Hitler lies

Hitler was lying to Chamberlain when he said that the Sudetenland was the last area of land he wanted. In March 1939, he met with the leader of Czechoslovakia and threatened to bomb Prague, the capital city, unless German troops were 'invited' into the country. Hitler was using his favourite 'bully-boy' tactic again!

The Czechs gave in to the threat and on 15 March German troops marched into Czechoslovakia and made the western half of it into part of Germany. Hungary and Poland grabbed the rest … and Czechoslovakia ceased to exist!

Source Q ▼ *From* The Nazis: A warning from History, *TV series, 1999.*

"Hitler eventually saw the Czech leader at 1:15am. He announced that in a few hours' time, German troops would invade his country. At 4 o'clock in the morning, the distraught Czech leader signed over his people into Hitler's 'care' … and when Hitler marched his troops from the Sudetenland into the rest of Czechoslovakia, he showed that his claim that he only wanted to unite German-speaking people was a sham. The country the troops now entered had never been German and had no German-speaking majority within it — this was an invasion!"

Source R ▼ *The German invasion of Czechoslovakia. Note how the cheering crowds that greeted German soldiers when they marched into German-speaking Austria and the Sudetenland are gone.*

New promises

Most of Europe now realised that Hitler could not be trusted – and it was easy to see where Hitler would strike next. He made no secret of the fact that he wanted an area of Poland known as the 'Polish Corridor', which had been taken from Germany in 1919. In fact, it was the only piece of land taken from Germany at the end of the Great War that Hitler hadn't taken back yet.

Now Britain and France had each had enough of letting Hitler get away with what he wanted. Enough was enough, they declared, and offered Poland their so-called **Polish guarantee**. Britain and France both promised to help defend Poland if it was invaded.

Two rival alliances

The Polish guarantee didn't bother Hitler at all. Four days after Britain and France announced their promise to Poland, Hitler gave secret orders to his armed forces to be ready to invade in September! Hitler made a **Pact of Steel** with Italy in which they agreed to help each other in any war.

By the summer of 1939, then, Europe was divided into two enemy camps – similar to the way Europe was divided into rival alliances before the start of the Great War in 1914. Was history repeating itself? Britain and France were in one camp, while Germany and Italy were in the other. The only country not pulled into one of these rival camps yet was Russia. But that was about to change!

The Nazi–Soviet Pact

Russia's leader, Joseph Stalin, had listened as Hitler said he wanted 'living space' from Russia for many years. He also knew Hitler hated Russia because it was a Communist country. Hitler and Stalin, then, were natural enemies and Stalin feared a German invasion of Poland would be followed by a German attack on Russia.

So Stalin looked for help and offered to join Britain and France in their deal to protect Poland. But the British and French didn't trust Stalin and the alliance never happened.

Instead, in a move that shocked the world, Hitler and Stalin made a peace deal with *each other*. The Nazi–Soviet Pact said that Germany and Russia would not fight each other. They also secretly agreed to attack Poland and divide it between them! This meant that Hitler could get his Polish Corridor and not have to worry about Russia joining Britain and France in trying to stop him.

Source S ▾ *The Egyptian cartoonist, Kem, comments on the Nazi–Soviet Pact, August 1939. He worked for the British government.*

Source T ▾ *Based on W. R. Keylor's* The Twentieth Century World, *1992.*

"With the Nazi-Soviet Pact, Hitler secured Russia's acceptance of Germany's invasion of Poland. He also gained relief from the threat of a war on two fronts, once he had turned his forces westwards towards Britain and France. Stalin, on the other hand, obtained postponement of a war with Germany that Russia wasn't prepared to fight. The Pact gave Russia time to build their armed forces."

It's war

A week after Hitler and Stalin signed their deal, German soldiers invaded Poland on 1 September 1939. Russian forces invaded soon after … and soon Poland ceased to exist.

To Hitler's surprise, Britain and France stuck up for Poland and declared war on Germany and Italy on 3 September. They didn't declare war on Russia though! And because Britain and France had such big empires – in Africa, Asia and the Far East – this European war would soon spread all over the world! And so World War II began!

Source U ▾ *Written by Russian historian, Kukushkin, in 1981.*

"Why did Britain and France help Hitler achieve his aims? By rejecting Russia's proposal of a united front against Germany, they played right into Hitler's hands. They tried to appease Hitler by giving him Czech land. They wanted to direct German aggression eastward against Russia and the disgraceful Munich deal achieved this.

As a result, Russia stood alone against the growing German threat. In this situation, Russia had to make a non-aggression deal with Germany. Some British historians tried to prove that this Treaty helped to start the Second World War. The truth is it gave Russia time to strengthen its defences."

Source V ▾ *Part of Chamberlain's radio speech to the nation when he announced that Britain was at war with Germany, 3 September 1939.*

"This country is at war with Germany … may God bless you all. It is evil things that we are fighting against – brute force, and faith, injustice, oppression and persecution; and against that, I am certain that right will prevail."

Source W ▶ *German expansion, 1933–39.*

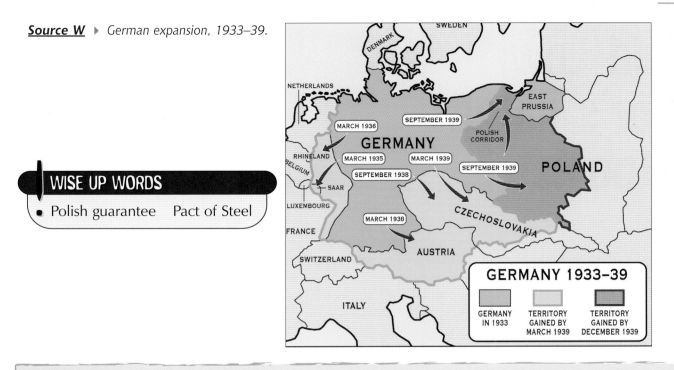

WISE UP WORDS

• Polish guarantee   Pact of Steel

WORK

1 Look at **Source R**.

  a Why hasn't the German army been greeted by cheering crowds as they were in the Rhineland, Austria and the Sudentenland?

  b What do you think the Germans hoped to achieve with this military parade through Prague?

2 Look at **Source S**.

  a Why do you think the cartoonist has drawn: i) Hitler and Stalin tied together; ii) each man with their hand on their gun?

  b Write a caption for this cartoon.

3 Look at **Sources T** and **U**.

  a What do the two sources agree about?

  b What does **Source U** reveal about Soviet attitudes towards Britain and France?

4 Look back over pages 190–203. Put the following events in the run up to the outbreak of World War II in the correct chronological order:

  • Munich Crisis
  • Nazi–Soviet Pact
  • German invasion of Poland
  • Hitler becomes leader of Germany
  • Re-occupation of the Rhineland
  • Germany and Austria unite
  • Germany leaves the League of Nations
  • outbreak of World War II
  • Pact of Steel
  • German army occupies Prague.

  Explain why these events must have happened in the order you have put them in.

5 **a** Long-term causes of an event are those that create situations where an event could occur. Short-term causes are events that trigger the event to happen at a particular time. Below is a list of some causes of World War II. Add any others to the list, then sort them into short- and long-term causes:

  • Treaty of Versailles
  • world economic depression
  • Munich Crisis
  • German invasion of Poland
  • failure of the League of Nations
  • Hitler's racist views
  • appeasement
  • Nazi–Soviet Pact.

  b Which do you think is the most important long-term cause of the war? Explain your answer carefully. Top tip: Try to work out what would happen if a particular cause had not occurred. If you find one that might have prevented another cause from happening, then this is the most important cause.

6 So was the war all Hitler's fault? Imagine Hitler survived the war and is on trial in 1945. He is charged with planning and starting World War II.

  a What evidence would the prosecution bring to the trial?

  b What evidence would you put forward in his defence?

David Low: Hitler's hated cartoonist

AIMS ....

Try to work out:
- the message from each of Low's political cartoons and look carefully at how the cartoonist tries to get his point across.

David Low was a cartoonist. He drew mainly political cartoons, which were often funny but made a serious point at the same time. You can see similar types of political cartoons in lots of newspapers today. Born in New Zealand in 1891, Low moved to Britain after the Great War. By the 1930s, he had drawn thousands of cartoons that had appeared in newspapers all over the world. To put it simply, by the 1930s he was the most famous cartoonist in the world … and Hitler hated him. Why?

David Low took his cartoons very seriously. He believed that cartoons should not just amuse people; they should try to educate them as well. Throughout the 1930s, Low had a clear point of view about the international issues of the time. He believed passionately in personal freedom and democracy – and hated dictators such as Hitler and Mussolini who limited the rights of people in their country and persecuted thousands. Low hoped that, by making fun of Hitler and Mussolini, he could encourage opposition to them.

Look carefully at the following three famous Low cartoons. Try to work out the message of each of them.

CARTOON 1 ▶ (Published on 10 May 1935, London Evening Standard.) *This cartoon appeared when Mussolini's Italian army was attacking Ethiopia (Abyssinia). As a result of this cartoon, Low's cartoons were banned in Italy.*

Josef Goebbels (Nazi Propaganda Minister)

Mussolini (Italian dictator), off to invade Ethiopia

Herman Goering (Nazi air force Minister)

*Hitler

The 'girls' are happy because Mussolini had gone off to invade Africa, leaving Europe to them.

Why do you think Low has drawn a skull and bones here?

Note how Low calls Mussolini's invasion a 'gamble'. Why do you think Mussolini didn't want ordinary Italians to see this cartoon?

What point is being made about Britain and France's response to the Anschluss between Germany and Austria?

Massive German army, represented by a large German soldier

Whose hand do you think is 'working' the Germany army?

" Why should we take a stand about someone pushing someone else when it's all so far away.. "

INCREASING PRESSURE.

What do you think is down here?

The eggs represent the British empire. It was very fragile at the time because countries in the empire, such as India, wanted their independence, but Britain wanted to hold onto it.

Other countries near to Austria

David Low's cartoons were banned in Germany from 1933 onwards, just after he had criticised Hitler and his attitude to the League of Nations. Italy banned his cartoons two years later. But the cartoons were still published all over the world. In 1937, they were discussed by Hitler on a visit to Germany by a leading British politician. Hitler was furious about Low's personal attacks and, when the politician returned to Britain, he talked to Low about how mad he made the German leader. Low decided to leave Hitler alone for a while, but when Hitler continued with his aggressive foreign policy, he felt his restraint had been pointless … and continued to criticise Hitler as much as before.

CARTOON 2 ▲ *This cartoon was published in 1938 and comments on the union between Germany and Austria.*

CARTOON 3 ◀ *Published in October 1938. It comments on the piece of paper signed by Hitler after the Munich Conference on which he promises not to fight Britain.*

Why do you think these British politicians have been drawn as sheep?

What is Low's message about Britain's defence against Hitler?

Evening Standard, Wednesday, October 5, 1938

I will be good
(SIGNED)
Adolf Hitler

OUR NEW DEFENCE   (Copyright in All Countries.)

Neville Chamberlain (British PM)

Why do you think Low has included a globe here?

WORK

1 What conclusions can you draw from his cartoons about David Low's political views?

2 Using the cartoons on this page, describe the skills a political cartoonist might need.

3 **a** Why do you think newspapers publish political cartoons?

   b Why do you think Low's cartoons were banned in Germany and Italy?

4 Imagine you have been asked to write a 100 word biography of David Low which is due to appear in a book called *The Who's Who of Great Cartoonists*. Write a suitable tribute.

An overview of World War II

🎯 AIMS ....
- try to remember key terms such as Blitzkrieg, Blitz and D-Day;
- identify at least two of the key turning points of World War II.

Blitzkrieg

Germany invaded Poland on 1 September 1939 using a new method of fighting called Blitzkrieg ('lightning war') – (see **Source A**). The Polish army was beaten in about a week. Blitzkrieg involved fast-moving columns of tanks, supported by infantry soldiers and dive-bomber attacks. Parachutists were dropped behind enemy lines the night before to destroy enemy strongholds and cut their wires.

Britain and France had promised to protect Poland, but were too far away to stop the invasion. As a result, after Poland had been defeated, there was very little fighting for about six months. Instead, the British army crossed over to help their allies, France and Belgium, to set up defensive positions along their borders.

Source A ▼ _The Blitzkrieg method of warfare._

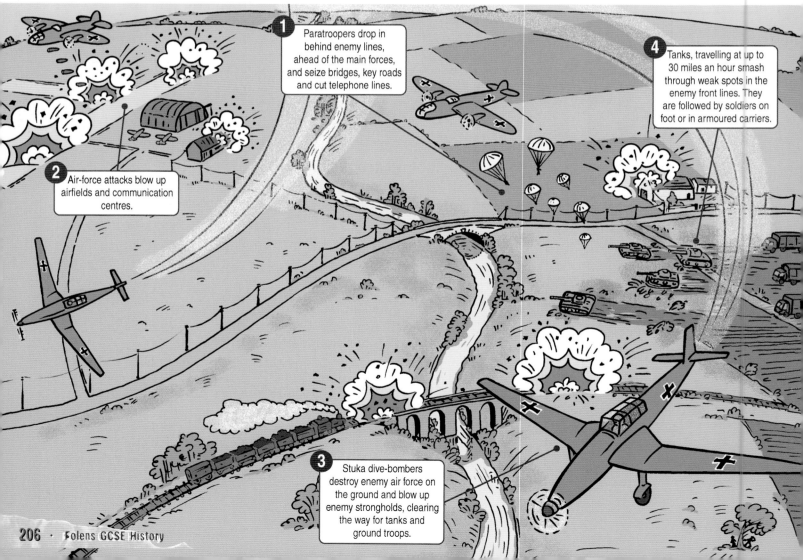

1 Paratroopers drop in behind enemy lines, ahead of the main forces, and seize bridges, key roads and cut telephone lines.

2 Air-force attacks blow up airfields and communication centres.

3 Stuka dive-bombers destroy enemy air force on the ground and blow up enemy strongholds, clearing the way for tanks and ground troops.

4 Tanks, travelling at up to 30 miles an hour smash through weak spots in the enemy front lines. They are followed by soldiers on foot or in armoured carriers.

Then, in April 1940, the German Blitzkrieg tactics were used to attack France, Denmark, Norway, Holland and Belgium. In just a few months, Hitler's armies occupied much of the centre of Europe and there was little the defending armies could do. Thousands of British, French and Belgian troops escaped to England in a fleet of yachts, paddle steamers, warships and even rowing boats from Dunkirk (see **Source B**).

Source B ▼ *An artist's impression of the evacuation of Dunkirk.*

The Battle of Britain and the Blitz

In 1940, then, Britain stood alone without a single ally except for countries in her empire (such as India), or former empire countries (such as Australia). Hitler, though, wanted to complete his domination of Europe by invading Britain. But before he could transport his troops across the English Channel, he had to destroy Britain's air force. He began by carrying out a series of massive air raids on military air bases in southern England in the summer of 1940. As you might expect, the British air force fought back and, in August and September, the skies over Kent, Surrey, Sussex and Essex were a smoking mass of fighting aeroplanes as British Spitfires and Hurricane fighters fought

against German Messerschmitt and Heinkels (see **Source C**).

But here, over the skies of southern England, Hitler was defeated for the first time. He lost the Battle of Britain and abandoned his plans for invasion for the time being. Instead, he launched massive night bombing raids on major British cities, hoping to bomb Britain into surrender (see **Source D**).

Source C ▼ Fight over Portland *by Richard Eurich, painted in 1940. Eurich went to watch the 'dogfights' in the air over southern England every day during the Battle of Britain.*

Source D ▼ *A photograph of the results of German bombing in London. On 14 October 1940, a bomb killed 64 people sheltering in an underground station in London. This period was known as the* **Blitz***.*

Source E ▼ Hitler's conquests up to 1940.

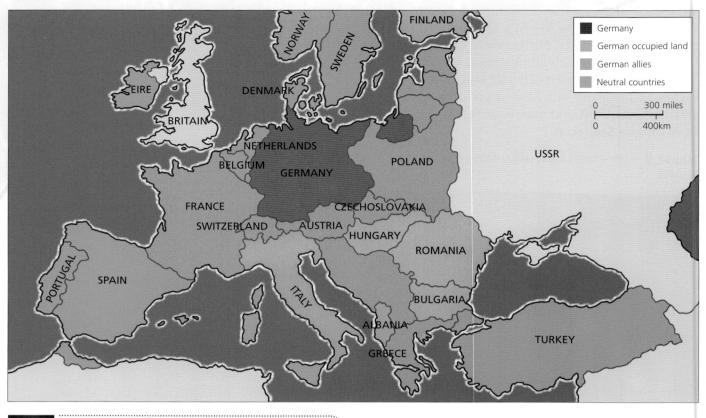

NORWAY · SWEDEN · FINLAND

Germany
German occupied land
German allies
Neutral countries

0   300 miles
0   400km

EIRE · DENMARK · USSR

BRITAIN · NETHERLANDS · POLAND

BELGIUM · GERMANY

FRANCE · CZECHOSLOVAKIA

SWITZERLAND · AUSTRIA · HUNGARY

PORTUGAL · SPAIN · ITALY · ROMANIA

BULGARIA · ALBANIA · TURKEY · GREECE

FACT *The Blitz*

During the Blitz, German bombers dropped 18 800 tons of bombs on London and 11 700 tons on other British cities such as Bristol, Plymouth, Coventry, Glasgow and Hull. They killed 61 000 civilians. Of every 26 houses in Britain in 1939, 17 were untouched, eight were damaged by air raids and one was destroyed.

More German victories

Despite the onslaught every night from German bombers, the British held on. And, by 1941, Hitler had turned his attention towards his old hated enemy – Russia.

In April 1941, the Germans helped their Italian allies invade Greece, Yugoslavia and Albania. They had invaded Egypt too and were driving the British out.

When Germany attacked Russia, in June 1941, the Russians were pushed back and back until, in October, Hitler was only 60 miles from the capital city Moscow. It seemed, as winter started to set in, the German army was unstoppable.

Japan enters the war

Then, at the end of 1941, the Japanese entered the war. In an attempt to knock out America's navy in one go (and give them control of the rich lands of the Far East), they launched a surprise attack on the great American naval base of Pearl Harbor in Hawaii. Thousands of American servicemen were killed and dozens of US fighter planes and warships were destroyed. The USA declared war on Japan and her allies (Italy and Germany), but for now Japan won victory after victory against America. Japan seized the British colonies of Hong Kong, Malaya and Burma too – as well as the French colony of Indo-China. By early 1942, the war seemed lost for Britain, Russia and America. The Germans were almost in Moscow and had nearly pushed the British out of Africa, and in the east, Japan was pushing back American forces and was close to invading India and Australia. Then, in the space of a few months, three major battles changed the whole course of the wars!

Source F ▼ *The attack on Pearl Harbor.*

Key turning points

- **The Battle of Midway (June 1942)**: In the Pacific Ocean, the Japanese were beaten by American forces in the great air and sea battle of Midway Island. The Japanese advance was stopped and gradually the Americans began to drive them back, island by island.

- **The Battle of Stalingrad (August 1942–January 1943)**: In Russia, after four months of very fierce hand-to-hand, house-to-house fighting in the city of Stalingrad, a significant proportion of the German army surrendered. Gradually, Russian forces began to push the German army out of Russia back towards Germany. This was the first time the Germans had retreated. At the same time, British and American bombers began night and day air raids on Germany itself.

- **El Alamein (October–November 1942)**: In Africa, at El Alamein, British troops defeated the Germans. With help from the Americans, the British drove the Germans out of North Africa and invaded Italy. British war leader, Winston Churchill, called El Alamein 'the turning point of the war'!

Source G ▼ *Through the windowless side of a ruined building, a photographer records the horrific street fighting that proceeded, literally, from one building to the next in Stalingrad.*

By the end of 1943, the invasion of Italy was in full swing. As Italian forces surrendered, their leader, Mussolini, was captured and shot (see **Source H**).

Source H ▾ *The bodies of Benito Mussolini and Clara Petacci, his mistress, hang from the roof of a gasoline station after they had been shot by anti-Fascist forces while attempting to escape to Switzerland.*

In Britain, an invasion of France was planned that aimed to push German forces in the west towards Germany. The invasion date was set for June 1944.

D-Day

On 6 June 1944, British, American and other allied troops landed on beaches in Normandy, France, and forced the Germans back, despite brutal fighting. In July, Hitler's opponents in Germany tried to blow him up and a German attempt to re-take some of the land they had lost failed in December.

Source I ▾ *American troops landing on Normandy beaches (north-west of France), arriving as reinforcements during the historic D-Day.*

Germany surrenders

By April 1945, British and American forces were moving fast towards Berlin (Germany's capital city). All along the way, they were freeing villages, towns and even countries from the German occupation. In the east, the Russian armies were advancing too. The German army was being beaten in battle after battle and food supplies in major German towns were running short.

Hitler and his closest followers retreated to a special underground bunker under Berlin's streets and, on 30 April, Hitler killed himself. Within days, Germany surrendered and the war was over … in Europe!

Nuclear bombs

Victory in Europe meant that more troops could be sent to fight the Japanese. However, before the invasion could take place, a decision was made to drop two nuclear bombs on the Japanese cities of Hiroshima and Nagasaki. The Japanese, rather than face the complete destruction of their islands, surrendered on 14 August. World War II was officially over.

Source J ▾ *This photograph was circulated by the Russian army shortly after Hitler's death. Many at the time thought it was Adolf Hitler. However, the photograph was soon exposed as a fake – it wasn't Hitler at all but an unfortunate body double.*

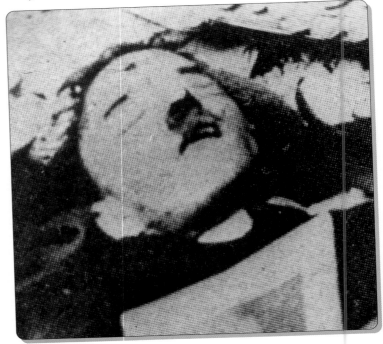

Source K ▲ *This is a photograph of a test explosion of a nuclear bomb on 25 July 1945. (You can see some of the old warships they used to test the blast.) The man who developed the bomb, Robert Oppenheimer, was so overawed by its power, he said, 'I am Death, the destroyer of worlds'. The bomb dropped on Hiroshima was the equivalent of 20 000 tons of dynamite. When US President Truman heard of the bombing, he said, 'This is the greatest thing in history'.*

Source L ▼ *When countries joined (and left) the war.*

1939	1940	1941	1942	1943	1944	1945

GERMANY

ITALY

JAPAN

BRITAIN

FRANCE

USSR

USA

The critical year: Britain alone against Germany & Italy

Source M ▼ *World War II deaths.*

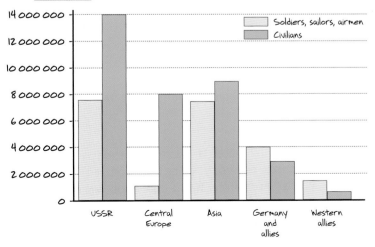

□ Soldiers, sailors, airmen
■ Civilians

Source N ▼ *The cost of the war.*

THESE ARE WHAT THE MONEY SPENT BY BRITAIN ON THE WAR WOULD HAVE BOUGHT (AT 1940 PRICES)

| 2 NEW HOUSES AND 2 NEW CARS FOR EVERY FAMILY IN BRITAIN | 100 000 NEW SCHOOLS AND 100 000 NEW HOSPITALS | A MOTORWAY TWICE AROUND THE WORLD | A DECENT STANDARD OF LIVING FOR EVERYONE IN THE WORLD. |

BRITAIN'S WAR BILL £ 40 000 000 000

INSTEAD IT WAS SPENT ON TANKS, SHIPS, PLANES, BOMBS, SOLDIERS, SAILORS AND AIRMEN

| GERMANY'S WAR BILL WAS MORE THAN TWICE THE SIZE OF BRITAIN'S | AMERICA'S WAR BILL WAS MORE THAN THREE TIMES THE SIZE OF BRITAIN'S | THE TOTAL COST OF THE WAR HAS BEEN ESTIMATED AT £ 390 000 000 000 |

WISE UP WORD

- Blitz

WORK

1 Draw a timeline from 1939 to 1945. Add at least ten key battles, events or interesting facts.

2 Look at these three headings:
   - 'Bad times for the Brits'
   - 'The tide turns'
   - 'Victory'.

   a Decide whereabouts on your timeline you would put these headings. Mark them on your work, remembering that it is okay for the headings to cover a number of months – even years.

   b Explain why you have put each heading in the place you have chosen.

Dunkirk: victory or disaster?

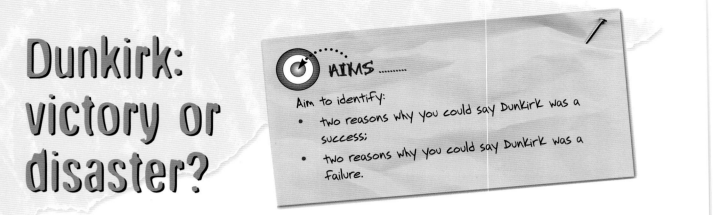

AIMS

Aim to identify:
- two reasons why you could say Dunkirk was a success;
- two reasons why you could say Dunkirk was a failure.

When war officially began in September 1939, British troops crossed the English Channel into France to help France to prepare for a German attack. When Germany finally invaded France in April 1940, they quickly beat the British and French back towards the English Channel. By the end of May, nearly half a million British and French soldiers had been pushed back so far that they were trapped between the sea and the advancing Germans. At that moment, it looked as if all was lost for Britain and France. Hitler was close to wiping out the entire British army (and thousands of French troops) before the war had really got under way!

At the last moment, the British government organised a huge rescue operation known as 'Operation Dynamo'. The plan was to evacuate the troops to Britain by warships. They were helped by dozens of ordinary citizens in hundreds of small boats, paddle steamers, fishing boats, yachts and even rowing boats.

Between 26 May and 4 June over 800 boats rescued 215 587 British soldiers and 127 031 French soldiers from the beaches of Dunkirk.

Read **Sources A** to **E** carefully. The sources show how the evacuation was reported at the time.

Source A ▾ From cinema newsreels, May 1940.

"More cheering evidence of the success of this amazing military exploit is the presence in Britain of large numbers of French soldiers. They are showered with hospitality and find the tea of old England almost as refreshing as their coffee …

Enjoying an unexpected seaside holiday, they lie in the sun, awaiting orders to return to France.

The story of that epic withdrawal will live in history as a glorious example of discipline [amongst the troops] … Every kind of small craft — destroyers, paddle steamers, yachts, motor boats, rowing boats — has sped here to the burning ruins of Dunkirk to bring off the gallant British and French troops."

Source B ▾ A headline from the Daily Mirror, June 1940.

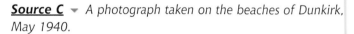

"Bloody Marvellous."

Source C ▾ A photograph taken on the beaches of Dunkirk, May 1940.

Source D ▾ Winston Churchill, British Prime Minister, 4 June 1940.

"Dunkirk has been a miracle escape. But we must be very careful not to call it a victory. Wars are not won by evacuations."

Source E ▼ *From BBC Radio's Six o'clock News, 31 May 1940.*

"All night and all day men of the undefeated British army have been coming home. From interviews with the men, it is clear they have come back in glory; that their morale is as high as ever, and that they are anxious to be back again 'to have a real crack at Jerry [the Germans]'."

Now look at **Sources F** to **J**, published some time after 1940. They give a slightly different version of the events of Dunkirk.

Source F ▼ *This French poster was published by French people who believed that the British had deliberately left 40 000 French soldiers behind at Dunkirk. In fact, the British did take out some of their troops before they told the French army, so the French held back the Germans while the British loaded onto ships. The poster says '1940 – Dunkirk. The English stop the last of the French who came to protect their retreat from getting on the boats.'*

Source G ▼ *A modern historian.*

"The British army left behind 2500 guns, 20 500 motorbikes, 64 000 other vehicles, 77 000 tons of ammunition, 416 000 tons of supplies and 165 000 tons of petrol. 68 000 soldiers were killed or taken prisoner."

Source H ▼ *A BBC reporter commenting in 2000.*

"Dunkirk was a military disaster — and took the British public by surprise … but almost at once, victory was being plucked from defeat and the newspapers began to manufacture the Dunkirk myth … The government encouraged it to flourish — and allowed nothing to be published which might damage morale. Dunkirk was a military defeat but a propaganda victory."

Source I ▼ *From Steven Waugh's Modern World History.*

"The British government hoped that at least 50 000 men could be rescued. In fact, around 340 000 men were rescued. The escape was referred to as a miracle but huge amounts had to be abandoned, including 475 tanks, 1000 heavy guns and 400 anti-tank guns. The BEF [British Expeditionary Force] had been forced to retreat, leaving the French to fight on alone. Churchill turned the evacuation into a national triumph playing up the role of the small boats and trying to build up morale and create 'The Dunkirk Spirit'."

Source J ▼ *The Second World War by Sean Lang.*

"The troops had to leave all their tanks and heavy guns behind, so although Operation Dynamo became known as the 'The Miracle of Dunkirk', really the allies had been soundly beaten."

WORK

1 Look at **Sources A** to **E**.
   a After studying these sources, which word best describes the events at Dunkirk – 'victory' or 'disaster'? Give reasons for your answer.
   b Why do you think that Dunkirk was mainly reported as if it was victory at the time?
   c Do you think that the British government was right to report Dunkirk as a 'victory'?

2 Look at **Sources F** to **J**.
   a What are the main differences between these sources and the pair of sources you have studied earlier (**A** to **E**).
   b Why do you think there are these differences?

Who were the 'Few'?

AIMS ....
- What was 'Operation Sealion'?
- Why was Britain not invaded on 15 September 1940?

Towards the end of 1940, posters such as the one in **Source A** began to appear all over Britain. They featured five smiling fighter pilots and a famous quotation from Britain's Prime Minister, Winston Churchill. So why was this poster published? Why were the pilots smiling? And why did 'so many' people have to be thankful to 'so few'?

Source A ▾ A copy of one of Britain's most famous World War II posters.

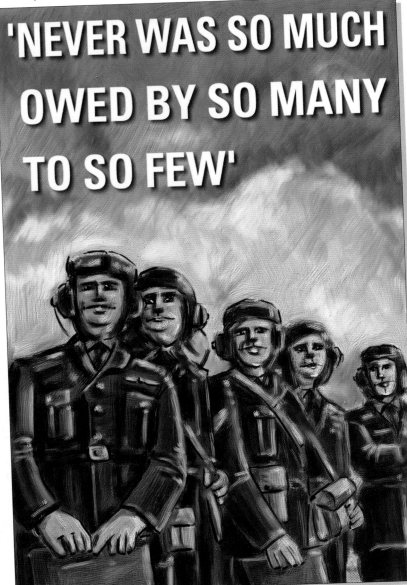

'NEVER WAS SO MUCH OWED BY SO MANY TO SO FEW'

By July 1940, Hitler was master of Europe. He was friendly with, or his armies had successfully invaded, most European countries. Now only Britain and the USSR stood in his way ... and Britain was to be first on his hit list.

On 1 August 1940, Hitler signed top secret plans to begin the invasion of Britain. Code-named 'Operation Sealion', the aim was to get German soldiers on to British soil by 15 September. After that, German troops would move towards London and other major British cities with the goal of controlling the whole country by Christmas.

The success of Operation Sealion hinged on the complete defeat of Britain's air force. Hitler believed that if the Luftwaffe (German air force) could win control of the skies, it would be far easier for German ships to transport soldiers over the English Channel to begin the land invasion of Britain. If the RAF was destroyed, British planes could not attack the ships bringing across his troops.

Source B ▾ *A summary of Operation Sealion. The RAF was the Royal Air Force, the official title of Britain's air force.*

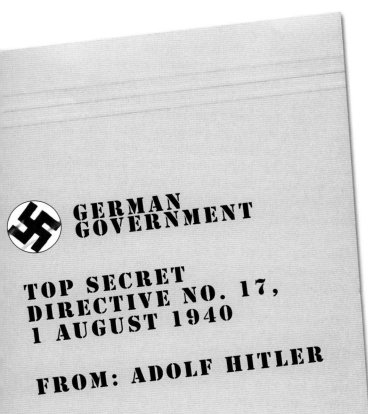

GERMAN GOVERNMENT

TOP SECRET DIRECTIVE NO. 17, 1 AUGUST 1940

FROM: ADOLF HITLER

In order to establish the conditions necessary for the final conquest of Britain, I intend to step up the air and naval war more intensively.

i) From 6 August, German bombers should attack British airfields and destroy all the RAF's aircraft. These bombers should be protected by fighter aircraft.

ii) If Britain does not surrender after all her aircraft are destroyed, the German army, escorted by the German navy, will land on beaches between Folkestone and Brighton on 15 September.

Throughout the summer of 1940, German and British pilots fought each other in the 'Battle of Britain', high above southern England. From the start, the odds were stacked against the British:

- The Germans had 824 fighter planes and 1017 bombers in service. Britain only had about 600 fighter planes.

- It took five minutes for German planes to cross the Channel from France. However, it took 15 minutes for British planes to take off and reach the invading planes after they were spotted.

- Many of the British pilots were part-timers and had not received the same level of training or experience as the Germans, who trained 800 new pilots a month. The British trained just 200.

Source C ▾ *A photograph of RAF pilots 'scrambling' to get to their planes to intercept approaching enemy aircraft. Over 3000 pilots fought against the Germans in the Battle of Britain. Over 2000 were from Britain but they were joined by New Zealanders (102), Poles (141), Canadians (90), Czechs (86), South Africans (21), Americans (7) and many more.*

Source D ▼ *The RAF used Spitfire and Hurricane fighter planes, while the Germans used the Messerschmitt ME-109. Although the Hurricane was the most commonly used British plane, it was the Spitfire that Germans feared the most.*

Aeroplane	Top speed	Manoeuvrability	Fire power
Spitfire	600kph	Could turn very sharply	8 machine-guns
Messerschmitt ME-109	570kph	Could turn quite sharply	2 machine-guns 2 cannons

Source E ▼ *A German pilot commenting on each of the main fighter planes. What do you think he means by the phrase, 'could not take as much punishment'?*

"The ME-109 was quicker than the Hurricane and about the same as the Spitfire. I think our guns were better too. On the other hand, the British fighters could turn tighter than we could. I also felt that the ME-109 could not take as much punishment as the British planes."

By the end of August, the RAF was only days away from defeat. Its airfields were badly damaged and it didn't have enough pilots. However, the Germans were encountering big problems too. Brand new radar technology meant that the British could detect enemy planes before they reached Britain. A system of 51 radar stations directed British fighters to the Germans in a matter of minutes, leaving them enough fuel to attack the German planes time and time again. In fact, it soon became clear that the Germans were losing more planes than the British. More importantly, the Germans were only making about 150 new planes a month while the British were producing over 550!

Source F ▼ *A Spitfire pilot who fought in the Battle of Britain.*

"Throughout it all the radio is never silent — shouts, oaths [swearing], encouragements and terse [short, sharp] commands. You single out an opponent. Jockey for position. All clear behind! The bullets from your eight guns go pumping into his belly. He begins to smoke … and you break into a tight turn. Now you have two enemies. The 109 on your tail and your remorseless, ever-present opponent 'G', the force of gravity. Over your shoulder you can still see the ugly, questing snout of the 109. You tighten the turn. The Spit protests and shudders and when the blood drains from your eyes you 'grey out'. But you keep turning, for life itself is at stake. And now your blood feels like molten lead and runs from head to legs. You black out! And you ease the turn to recover in a grey, unreal world of spinning horizons. Cautiously, you climb into the sun ... your opponent has gone — disappeared."

15 September 1940 was a turning point in the Battle of Britain. This was the day that Hitler had singled out as the beginning of the invasion of Britain. But the Luftwaffe had still not defeated the RAF. Hitler did not want to send German troops across the Channel while the British still had fighter planes in the air.

At 2:00pm, Prime Minister Winston Churchill asked his air force commander what British fighter planes were available other than the ones in the air. 'There are none', came the reply. However, 15 September saw the final major engagement of the Battle of Britain. On that very day, Germany lost 60 aircraft to Britain's 25! The next day, Hitler postponed Operation Sealion 'until further notice'. He had failed to defeat the RAF by his 15 September deadline and was forced to cancel his invasion plans. Instead, he started to target London in huge night-time bombing raids in an attempt to bomb the British into surrender.

The RAF pilots who fought in the Battle of Britain became known as the 'Few', after Winston Churchill honoured their victory with this speech: 'Never in the field of human conflict was so much owed by so many to so few.'

Source G ▼ *A German bomber, a casualty of the Battle of Britain. Note the British soldier guarding the aircraft from 'souvenir hunters'.*

Source H ▼ *Fighters and bombers lost by the Luftwaffe in the Battle of Britain. Which set of figures do you think is most accurate and why?*

Date	Official British figures	Official German figures	Figures agreed after the war
8–23 August	755	213	403
24 August– 6 September	643	243	378
7–30 September	846	243	435
TOTAL	2244	699	1216

WORK

1 Why did Hitler feel he had to destroy the RAF?

2 Look at the following list of reasons why Germany lost the Battle of Britain. Explain, in your own words, how each reason made a difference to the outcome of the battle:
   • the British had radar
   • Hitler lost patience and started bombing London
   • the Germans miscalculated how many British planes they shot down.

   Can you add any reasons of your own to explain why Germany lost the Battle of Britain?

3 Look at **Source H**.
   a What differences are there between the three sets of figures?
   b Why are they so different and which set of figures do you believe most?

4 a In your words, explain what Churchill meant when he said "Never in the field of human conflict was so much owed by so many to so few."
   b About one out of every six young men who fought in the Battle of Britain was killed – yet there was never any shortage of volunteers to fight. Why do you think this was? **Source F** might help you!

'Mr and Mrs Jones would like a nice little boy'

AIMS

- to know what 'evacuation' was and why it was necessary;
- to know what it was like to be evacuated.

People in most of the fighting countries expected their cities to be bombed during the war. As soon as war broke out thousands of children were moved away from the places most likely to be bombed (large industrial cities) and into the countryside where they would be safer. This was known as **evacuation**. The French moved thousands away from their border with Germany. The Germans did the same. In Britain, nearly 1.5 million people had been moved into 'safe zones' by the end of September 1939.

Source A ▼ *Numbers of people evacuated by the British government in September 1939.*

School-children	Mothers and children under five	Pregnant women	Blind and disabled people	Teachers
827 000	524 000	13 000	7000	103 000

The government took over Britain's entire transport system – all the buses and trains – for four days in order to get children out of the major cities.

Armed with suitcases full of clothes, a gas mask packed into a cardboard box and a name tag tied to their coats, thousands of children left the familiar surroundings of city life for a completely new experience in the countryside. Some would love their new life … but many others would hate every second of it!

Source B ▼ *An evacuated child, photographed in September 1939.*

None of the children knew where they were going and nothing prepared them for the ordeal they would go through when they reached their countryside reception areas. There were two main methods of finding a new home or 'foster family'.

Grab a child – the children were lined up and local people would choose the ones they wanted. Obviously, the smarter, cleaner girls would go first ... and the dirtier, scruffy little boys would be left until last.

Source C ▾ *The thoughts of one young girl remembering what happened to her and her brother when she was evacuated.*

> "Villagers stood around watching us as we got out of the bus and went into the school. What followed was like an auction. Villagers came in to choose children. 'Mr and Mrs Jones would like a nice little boy.' Nobody wanted the awkward combination of a girl of 11 and such a small boy, from whom I had promised my mother never to be separated. We were left until the very last. The room was almost empty. I sat on my rucksack and cried."

Hunt the home – evacuated children, or evacuees as they were called, were led around the town or village and taken door-to-door. Homeowners were asked if they would foster a child for a while.

Source D ▾ *An example of a family who had to hunt for a home.*

> "They unloaded us on the corner of the street; we thought it was all arranged, but it wasn't. The billeting officer [the man in charge of housing the children] walked along knocking on doors and asking if they'd take a family. We were the last to be picked. You couldn't blame them; they didn't have any coloured people there in those days."

Pause for thought

Suppose you were evacuated *now*. You can take just five of your things with you. Write a list of what you would take, giving reasons for each.

Evacuation wasn't easy for anyone – evacuees *or* hosts. Some children settled down happily and loved their new lives in their new homes and schools – others hated country life and were homesick. The country people had to put up with a lot too. Some of the children arrived badly clothed, very thin and covered in lice and nits. Some of the rougher evacuees shocked their foster families by swearing and being naughty. One young evacuee in Northallerton, Yorkshire, spent a whole day blocking up the local stream – later that night it was found that he'd flooded six houses and the local church!

Source E ▾ *A 13 year old boy remembers his evacuation to Buckinghamshire with his sister Rosie.*

> "Rosie whispered. She whispered for days. Everything was so clean. We were given face cloths and toothbrushes. We'd never cleaned our teeth up till then. And hot water came from the tap and there was an indoor toilet. And carpets. And clean sheets. This was all very odd and rather scary."

Source F ▾ *Unhappy times for an 11 year old girl evacuated to Cambridgeshire.*

> "My foster mum thought she was onto a good thing with me and the other 11 year old girl I was put with. We did her shopping for her, cleaned her house, cooked, washed up and even looked after her whining three year old when she went out."

Source G ▼ *An extract from the* Newcastle Evening Chronicle *in 1940. Some boys found country life hard to get used to!*

> "One evacuated child from the South of England who, on arrival at the billet [his new home], was asked by the hostess, 'Would you like some biscuits, dear?' 'Biscuits?' the boy replied. 'I want some beer and some bloody chips. That's what I get at home!"

Source H ▼ *One rich woman from Devon, commenting on the evacuees in her house.*

> "I love my six lads from London as if they were my own. They've made this dreary, lonely war quite enjoyable for me."

FACT *Picture this*

Many city children had never seen a farm animal before. They were shocked to see what cows, chickens and sheep looked like. In October 1939, BBC News broadcast this description of a farm animal written by a young evacuee. Can you guess what he's describing?

"It has six sides ... at the back it has a tail on which hangs a brush. With this it sends flies away so they don't fall into the milk. The head is for ... growing horns and so that the mouth can be somewhere ... the mouth is to moo with. Under the [animal] hangs the milk ... when people milk, the milk comes and there is never an end to the supply. How the [animal] does it I have not realised ... one can smell it far away. This is the reason for fresh air in the country."

In case you weren't sure, the boy is describing a cow!

After a few months of life in the British countryside, most children returned to their lives in the city. The enemy bombers hadn't arrived as expected and by March 1940, nearly one million children had gone home. However, later that year the mass bombing of British cities – 'the Blitz' as it was known – began and many, but not all, children returned to the country.

FACT *Unwanted or forgotten?*

When some of the evacuated children finally returned home after the war, they found their homes had been bombed and their parents were missing. Some parents had even abandoned their children on purpose. About 40 000 children remained 'unclaimed' after the war!

Source I ▼ *From T. Hewitt, J. McCabe and A. Mendum* Modern World History, *1999.*

> "The children had mixed experiences. Some were happy, helping on farms and eating better than they had ever done. Others had a miserable time. Some were seen as a burden by their foster families. They also missed their own families, far away in the cities. Many country families were in for a shock. They had to deal with children who wet their bed and who couldn't use a knife and fork."

Source J ▾ *The actor Michael Caine remembers his evacuation experience.*

"Clarence and I used to sleep together and poor Clarence use to wet the bed 'cos he was a nervous kid. She [the foster mother] could never tell who'd done it so she used to bash the daylights out of both of us. So, of course, the more Clarence got hit the more he'd wet the bed. It was then we started to get locked in the cupboard."

Source K ▾ *A government poster issued in 1940.*

WORK

1 Why were children evacuated?
2 Look at **Source B**. The little boy looks deep in thought. In no more than 100 words, write down what you think the boy is thinking. Attempt to describe his emotions and thoughts.
3 Look at **Sources C** and **D**.
   a Describe the two different methods used to find these two young families a home.
   b Write down the reasons why they each had problems finding a new home.
4 Look at **Source E**. What does this source tell us about the sort of life Rosie and her brother led before the war?
5 Who do you think enjoyed evacuation more: the evacuees or their host families? Try to give reasons for your answer.
6 **Source I** is from a modern school textbook. Is it more reliable than **Source J**, which is from someone who actually experienced evacuation? Explain your answer carefully.
7 Look at **Source K**. Does this poster prove that the government was successful in persuading people to evacuate their children? Explain your answer carefully.

Total war

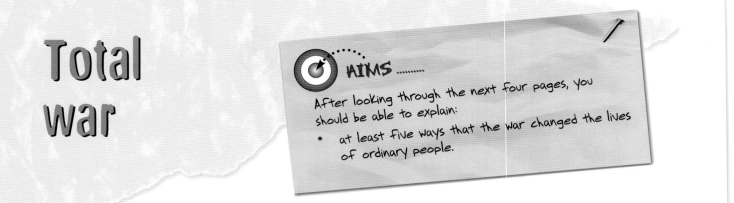

🎯 AIMS ....

After looking through the next four pages, you should be able to explain:
- at least five ways that the war changed the lives of ordinary people.

World War II is sometimes called a total war. This means that the whole country – civilians AND soldiers – were involved in the war in some way.

So what was it like to live through 'total war'?

Preparing for war

When the war began, everyone expected to be bombed from the air, so everyone prepared for it. Millions of people built their own bomb shelters in their back gardens and the government issued nearly 40 million gas masks as a precaution against gas bombs. 'Blackout' instructions were sent to every household telling people how important it was to keep lights out at night so that German bomber planes couldn't see city targets from the air (see **Sources A**, **B** and **C**).

Source A ▼ These shelters are called Anderson shelters and were sunk into the ground in people's back gardens.

Source B ▶ Gas masks were used to protect people from gas attacks.

Source C ▼ Blackout instructions issued by the government in 1939.

INSTRUCTIONS FOR 'BLACKOUT'

* All street lighting will be put out at night.
* Cars must be driven with masked headlights – but kerbs will be painted white for drivers and pedestrians to see in blackout conditions.
* Windows, skylights, glazed doors, or other openings that could show light, will have to be screened with dark blinds on the glass so that no light is visible from the outside.
* Air raid wardens will patrol streets looking for any sign of light.

The Blitz begins

In July 1940, the Luftwaffe (German air force) started to bomb Britain. Airfields and communication centres were targeted first in preparation for a German invasion – but when the Germans failed to defeat the planes of the Royal Air Force, they switched to bombing cities instead. London was first bombed on 7 September 1940, two weeks after the British had bombed Berlin. The bombing of London and other major cities was known as the Blitz … and the effects were devastating (see **Sources D** to **H**).

Source D ⏷ *A photograph taken after a bombing raid on London, 1941.*

Source E ⏷ *The ruins of Coventry Cathedral after a German night time air raid destroyed the centre of the city in 1940.*

Source F ⏷ *People using the platform of a tube station in London as an air raid shelter.*

Source G ⏷ *A milkman reading a notice, 'Called Up OHMS – Back As Soon As We Beat Hitler', painted on a boarded up shop front. OHMS means 'on his majesty's service', which means they are fighting for 'King and country'.*

Source H ⏷ *King George VI of Great Britain, Queen Elizabeth and Prime Minister Winston Churchill inspecting bomb damage at Buckingham Palace.*

Some bizarre preparations were made in case the Germans actually invaded. Signposts were taken down on major road junctions and names were removed from railway stations.

War work

Britain itself was organised during the war as never before. The government had power to move people from 'non-essential' to 'essential' jobs such as coal mining or steel making. Single women were recruited too, many of them into the **Women's Land Army** to help with food production (see **Sources I** to **K**). Women could also join versions of the army, navy and air force too, or work in industry.

Source I ▶ *In total, about 80 000 women joined the Land Army.*

Source J ▾ *During the war, women took over a lot of jobs that men normally carried out.*

'We could do with thousands more like you…'

JOIN THE WOMEN'S LAND ARMY

Source K ▾ *Proportion of workers in various jobs who were women, 1938 and 1944. Married women were not called up to work – but many decided to work despite looking after their families as well.*

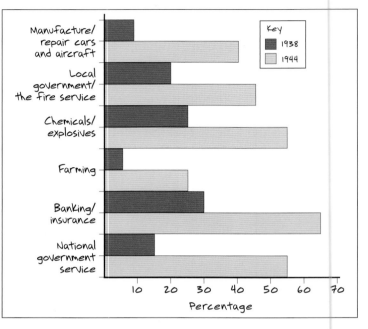

Key
1938
1944

Manufacture/repair cars and aircraft
Local government/the fire service
Chemicals/explosives
Farming
Banking/insurance
National government service

Percentage

Source L ▾ *An interview with a woman from Newham, south London, 1983.*

"I was sent to a farm in Essex. It was very hard work. Sometimes we biked eight miles or so before beginning and eight miles back home at night. The people in the country didn't make it easy for you; we weren't really welcome. All we had in the Land Army digs were sausages, every day for nine months. We used to cook them in water. They were horrible."

Dad's Army

Men who were too old to fight joined the LDV (Local Defence Volunteers). Their role was to work in their local area and prepare it for attack. They weren't paid and to begin with they didn't even have weapons – men even patrolled Blackpool Pier, armed with broomsticks painted black to look like guns! They were rather cruelly nicknamed the Look, Duck and Vanish Brigade, or 'Dad's Army' because so many of them were over 50!

Rationing

Today, much of Britain's food (and other goods such as petrol and clothing) comes from overseas. It was the same during the war. However, German U-boats (submarines) were sinking so many of the supply ships coming to Britain that the country was running out of food. So, in 1940, the government introduced rationing. This meant that every person was entitled to a fixed amount of certain sorts of food, fuel and clothing. Many felt this was a fair system because rich people could no longer buy up all the food, leaving poorer people with nothing! And the government encouraged people to grow their own food in their back gardens or in allotments. The slogan was Dig for Victory.

Source M ▾ *Ivy Green remembers rationing in an oral interview, 2007.*

> "Rationing generally meant you could always get a basic diet of bacon, cheese, eggs, milk and so on. Bread was never rationed nor were vegetables — mainly because people grew their own a lot, I think. But items that weren't rationed were hardest to find — make-up, razor blades, bananas, for example. And you couldn't get silk stockings either — I knew girls who would stain their legs and draw a line up the back of them to give the impression they were wearing them."

Source N ▾ *People were issued with a ration card and bought goods on a points system. The amounts varied from time to time, depending on their availability.*

WEEKLY RATIONS

Bacon or Ham (113 grams)
Sugar (227 grams)
Cooking Fat (227 grams)
Cheese (57 grams)
Tea (113 grams)
Meat – 6p worth (about 227 grams)
Dried Eggs (a packet each month)
Half an Egg (about one each fortnight)

PEOPLE BOUGHT THESE ON A POINTS SYSTEM

FACT *Let's go shopping*

Every person was given 66 clothing coupons a year to spend. To give you some idea of how far that would go – a pair of shoes was 5 coupons, a jumper 4, a jacket was 11 and a pair of gloves was 2.

WISE UP WORD

• Women's Land Army

WORK

1 Write a sentence or two explaining the following words or phrases:
   • Anderson shelter
   • blackout
   • Blitz
   • total war.

2 Look at **Sources D** to **H**. Imagine you work as a government censor and your job is to decide which of the photographs (D to H) you will allow newspapers to publish.
   a Choose at least two which you will permit newspapers to use. Give your reasons for your choice, writing a caption for each one.
   b Which ones will you ban? Explain why you don't want them appearing in Britain's newspapers.

3 In what ways did women's lives change during the war?

4 Look at **Sources M** and **N**.
   a What was rationing?
   b Why did the government have to start rationing?
   c Why did so many people see rationing as a fair system?
   d Compare the 'ration diet' with our own diet today. Make a list of the main differences. Then explain which diet you prefer and why. Remember that the amounts in **Source N** are weekly rations.

'The only thing that ever really frightened me'

AIMS

Make sure you know:
- two reasons why the allies won the Battle of the Atlantic;
- two reasons why winning the Battle of the Atlantic was important for the allies.

Soon after the war was over, Winston Churchill, Britain's war leader, said that the most important battle of the whole war was the one fought out in the Atlantic Ocean. He admitted that it was 'the only thing that ever really frightened me during the war'.

So why was Churchill so worried? Why did he think the Battle of the Atlantic was the key conflict of the war?

The Battle of the Atlantic was the term used to describe the fight between German U-boats (submarines) and the British and American ships that brought goods into Britain by sea. Germany had almost won the Great War in 1917 by cutting off Britain's supplies. By the time of World War II, Britain still depended on importing food and oil from abroad by sea. From the start of the war, Admiral Doenitz (in charge of the German U-boats) decided to sink any ships going in and out of Britain. The Germans decided that they might not need to invade Britain – they could win the war by starving the British into submission.

The impact on Britain of the 'U-boat peril' (as Churchill called it) was spectacular. By July 1940, the Germans had sunk 25% of Britain's supply ships. A year later, Britain was importing just 40% of the food they would normally import during peacetime.

Source A ▾ Winston Churchill.

"The Battle of the Atlantic was the key feature of the war. Never for one moment could we forget that everything happening elsewhere on land, sea or air depended on its outcome."

Source B ▾ Admiral Doenitz, German U-boat commander.

"Britain's ability to maintain her supply lines is the decisive factor for the outcome of the war."

Churchill worried that there was a very real danger of starvation in Britain! But then things began to get better for the British.

- The allies began to use a convoy system. This meant that the supply ships were protected by warships. The U-boats found it hard to sink the supply ships because they were guarded (see **Source D**).

- The convoy escorts used an underwater radar system called Asdic. This helped them find U-boats and sink them using depth charges (see **Source E**).

- Long-range bomber planes were developed that were very successful at spotting U-boats and sinking them.

- The British developed ULTRA, a system that could de-code secret German radio messages. This meant that the allies knew where the U-boats were.

Source C ▼ *A painting by H. R. Butler of a U-boat sinking a supply ship.*

Source D ▼ *The convoy organisation. Destroyers and Corvettes were types of battleships that could protect the merchant ships bringing goods into Britain.*

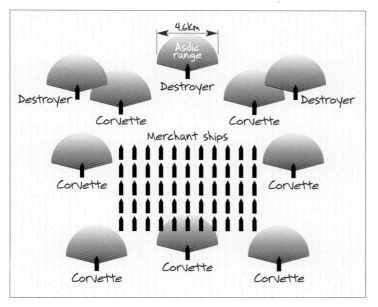

Source E ▼ *Asdic produces a sound echo that reveals a U-boat position. Large explosives, called depth charges, are dropped to the submarine's estimated depth and exploded next to it.*

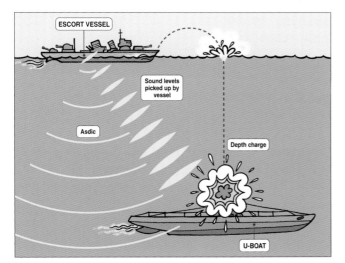

Source F ▼ *Allied shipping losses (in tons).*

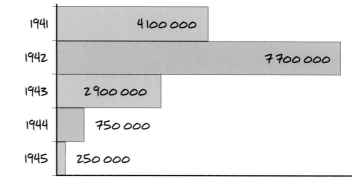

Source G ▼ *German U-boats sunk.*

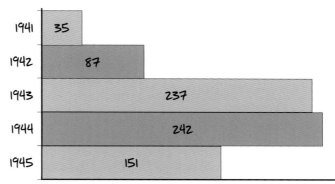

By the end of 1943, the allies were winning the Battle of the Atlantic. Indeed, by then, the German sailors were beginning to call their submarines 'steel coffins'. Out of 863 U-boats that sailed, 754 were sunk. And out of the 39 000 U-boat sailors, over 27 000 died and 5000 were captured.

WORK

1 Look at **Sources A** and **B**.
   a According to the sources, how important was the Battle of the Atlantic?
   b Why do you think both Churchill and Doenitz felt that the Battle of the Atlantic was so important?

2 a Explain the significance of each of the following in allowing allies to defeat Germany in the Battle of the Atlantic:
   • the convoy system • long-range bombers
   • Asdic • ULTRA.
   b Do you think one of the above is more important than the others?

3 Look at **Sources F** and **G**. In your opinion, when did the Battle of the Atlantic begin turning in favour of the Allies and against Germany? Use evidence to back up you opinion.

Should Dresden have been bombed?

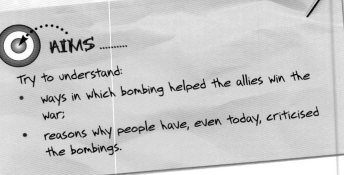

AIMS ....

Try to understand:
- ways in which bombing helped the allies win the war;
- reasons why people have, even today, criticised the bombings.

At about 9:00pm on 13 February 1945, 805 British bomber planes dropped 2690 tons of bombs on the German city of Dresden. Before long, an area of 11 square miles was burning so ferociously that temperatures reached 1000 degrees celsius. The city blazed for seven days, during which time an estimated 150 000 people were burned to death.

In 1992, a bronze statue of a man in RAF uniform was unveiled in London. The statue was of Sir Arthur 'Bomber' Harris, the Head of Bomber Command and the man whose idea it was to bomb Dresden. Immediately, protesters threw paint at the statue and demanded its removal.

So do you agree with the protesters – should the statue be removed? Was it wrong to bomb Dresden? Or, as Sir Arthur Harris thought, was the attack necessary to shorten the war and save British lives?

Your task over the next four pages is to formulate an opinion. You must establish:
- why the attack took place in the first place
- why the raid caused so many deaths
- what the bombing of Dresden achieved.

Your ideas and opinions will then be used to complete a final piece of work.

Why bomb Dresden?

American and British planes dropped nearly three million tons of bombs on 131 German cities. This killed nearly one million men, women and children, and made eight million people homeless. German planes dropped bombs on British cities too – 40 000 people died in air raids on London, Coventry, Glasgow, Hull and other cities.

When the war began, both sides had tried to use **precision bombing** to hit key targets, such as factories, ports, bridges, major roads and railway stations. The idea was to destroy the enemy's ability to fight by making it impossible to make weapons, build ships or move soldiers around. However, precision bombing didn't work – bombs didn't always hit their targets and damage was often easily repaired – so **area bombing** was introduced instead. This devastating new type of attack meant that whole towns and cities were bombed in order to make sure that *everything* was destroyed.

Source A ▾ *Advice given to the British government in 1942 by a senior scientific advisor.*

> "Investigations seem to show that having your house destroyed is most damaging to morale ... there seems no doubt that this will break the spirit of the [German] people."

Source B ▾ *Sir Arthur Harris, Head of RAF Bomber Command, 1942.*

> "Destroy a factory and they rebuild it. If I kill all their workers it takes 21 years to provide new ones."

In October 1944, a detailed report by the British on Dresden concluded that the city was an 'unattractive target'. In other words, there was no point in bombing the place! However, in January 1945, British spies reported that thousands of German soldiers were collecting in Dresden before being sent off to fight. All of a sudden, Dresden had turned into a key bombing target – and this may have influenced the decision to attack.

Source C ▾ *Sir Arthur Harris, 1945.*

> "Dresden has become the main centre of [the] defence of Germany. It has never been bombed before. And, as a large centre of war industry, it is very important."

Source D ▶

The statue of Sir Arthur Harris put up in London in 1992. Interestingly, he was the only war commander not to have a statue made immediately after the war!

Pause for thought

What is the difference between precision and area bombing?

What evidence is there so far that Dresden was a military target?

What evidence is there so far that Dresden was *not* a military target?

Source E ▾ *A British poster showing Lancaster bombers attacking a target in Germany. What was the purpose of this poster?*

The big raids on Germany continue. British war plants share with the R.A.F. credit for these giant operations.

THE ATTACK BEGINS IN THE FACTORY

Why did so many die?

The planes dropped a mixture of **incendiary** and high explosive bombs. Incendiary bombs are specifically designed to start fires. Dresden, being an ancient city with many wooden-framed buildings, started to burn very quickly. The fact that the city was packed with people running away from the Russian army meant that any large fire was sure to kill thousands of people.

The bombs soon created a **firestorm**. In a firestorm, the hot air that rises from burning buildings is replaced by cooler air rushing in from outside. Soon, hurricane-force winds of up to 120mph were 'superheating' the fire.

Source F ▾ *One survivor remembers the firestorm. She was interviewed in 1985.*

"I saw people clinging to the railings, burnt to cinders. I kicked what I thought was a big tree stump — but it was a person, burnt to death. There was a big heap of arms, legs, bodies, everything — I tried to piece together a leg, arm, fingers, body — to recognise one of my family — but I passed out."

Pause for thought

What are incendiary bombs?

Why did Dresden burn so fiercely?

Source G ▾ *Victims of the bombing of Dresden, February 1945. Some of the dead had been collected and laid out in a sports hall. Note the survivors arriving to identify bodies of relatives and the coffins stacked up at the back of the hall.*

What did the attack achieve?

Historians have argued for years about the bombing of Dresden – did the attack help Britain win the war? Some are sure it helped while others questioned whether it was necessary at all. Perhaps the following sources will help you form your opinion.

Source H ▾ *From an article written by historian, Dr Noble Frankland, in 1985.*

"Every day that the war went on cost the lives of countless more … so the numbers killed at Dresden, dreadful as they were, were nothing like so dreadful as the numbers of people Hitler was killing … A decisive blow was needed to end the war quickly."

Source I ▾ *From a letter written by Sir Arthur Harris to Prime Minister, Winston Churchill. Churchill had begun to doubt whether the raid on Dresden was justified.*

"Attacks on cities … tend to shorten the war and so preserve the lives of allied soldiers … I do not personally regard the whole of the remaining cities of Germany as worth the bones of one British soldier."

Source J ▾ *Adapted from the report of the British Bombing Survey Unit, set up at the end of the war to study the effects of area bombing on Germany.*

"Many German towns were severely devastated by bombing, but the effect on the amount of weapons, tanks and fighter planes the Germans produced was small … the bombings didn't make the German people lose the will to fight either. The German people proved calmer and more determined than anticipated."

Source K ▶ *A photograph of Dresden after the bombing. The main railway station and the headquarters of Air Command escaped total destruction.*

Source L ▼ *The view of an RAF pilot who took part in the attack.*

"It struck me at the time, the thought of women and children down there. We seemed to fly for hours over a sheet of fire — a terrific red glow. You can't justify it."

Pause for thought

Look at all the sources written by Sir Arthur Harris (**Sources B**, **C** and **I**). What is your opinion of Harris based on these sources? Try to use quotes from the sources to back up your statements about him.

What other evidence might a researcher need to collect before forming a fuller opinion of Harris?

Source M ▼ *German war production, 1940–44*

	1940	1942	1944
Fighter/bomber planes	10 200	14 200	39 500
Tanks	1600	6300	19 000
Heavy guns/ cannons	4400	5100	24 900

WISE UP WORDS

- precision bombing   area bombing incendiary   firestorm

WORK

"Sir Arthur Harris, you have been accused of a very serious crime. You are charged with ordering the bombing of the city of Dresden on 13 February 1945, using 2690 tons of bombs, killing over 150 000 people. It will be argued that this was unnecessary and therefore a criminal act of war."

As you know, there is a 12 foot statue of Arthur 'Bomber' Harris in central London. Imagine events took a very different turn. Imagine Germany won the war and Arthur Harris was put on trial for 'war crimes'.

You need to take on the role of either the prosecution or the defence. Once you have decided how you are going to act, you need to consider the following points in order to prepare your closing argument (the speech given to the jury before they make their final decisions):

- Was Dresden an acceptable target or not?
- The types of bombing that took place.
- The difference types of target.
- Was Harris acting in the best interests to try to win the war or was he guilty of killing innocent people?
- What do you think people felt about bombing of German cities?
- In a war, is everyone who helps build weapons a fair target?
- Did the bombings actually achieve anything?
- Was this an effective way of helping to win the war?

When you have considered these points and re-read the section 'Should Dresden have been bombed?', prepare a closing argument in defence or for the prosecution of Sir Arthur Harris.

The end of World War II: why were nuclear bombs used?

AIMS

Make sure you can:
* explain why America was pulled into World War II;
* offer your own opinion on whether you think nuclear bombs should have been dropped on Japan.

At 7:55am on Sunday 7 December 1941, 183 Japanese bomber planes launched a surprise attack on Pearl Harbor, an American naval base in the Hawaiian Islands. These islands are part of the USA, despite being thousands of miles away from the rest of the country! In just under two hours, 21 US warships were sunk or damaged, 177 US planes were destroyed and over 2000 men were killed. The Japanese lost just 29 planes.

The next day, the USA and her major ally, Britain, declared war on Japan. Three days later, Germany and Italy, Japan's official allies, declared war on the USA. Now two more major powers had joined the war – the USA fighting alongside Britain and Japan fighting on Germany and Italy's side.

The USA and Japan had been rivals for many years. Both countries wanted influence and control over the rich lands of the Far East, which contain coal, oil, timber, rubber, gold, gas, copper and so on. By attacking the ships in Pearl Harbor, the Japanese were attempting to make sure that the USA couldn't use its navy to stop them taking all the land they wanted. For a while, their plan seemed to work, as the powerful Japanese army, navy and air force took more and more of the Far East (see **Source A**).

Source A ▼ *The war in the Far East, 1941–42. By May 1942, the Japanese had gained control of Hong Kong, Guam, Wake, Malaya, Singapore, the Dutch East Indies, Burma, the Philippines and New Guinea. The loss of Singapore was a huge blow to the British and was Britain's biggest defeat in the war – 80 000 troops were taken prisoner.*

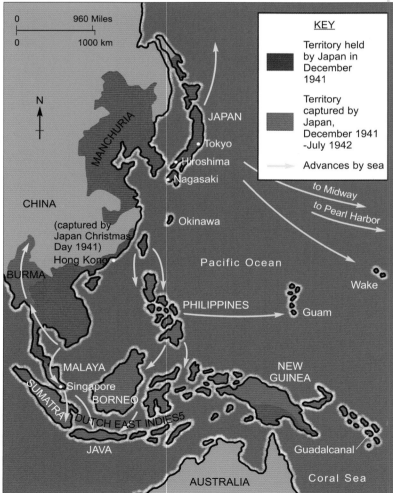

By the end of 1942, the USA was fighting back, winning important battles and taking back land in the Far East. By 1944, American soldiers were getting nearer and nearer to Japan, capturing one island at a time. The Japanese had fought fanatically, believing it was a great honour to die for their country. Suicide bombers called **kamikaze** pilots flew planes packed with explosives into American ships, both sides suffering huge losses.

By July 1945, the Japanese were in a desperate position. The war in Europe was over, as the Germans and Italians had been beaten. Hitler had shot and poisoned himself on 30 May 1945. Now Japan was fighting on alone and many thought it was close to surrender. The US President, Harry S. Truman, had an important decision to make – how was he going to end the war with Japan … quickly?

Final victory

The US President decided to use a deadly new weapon – a nuclear bomb successfully developed in the USA in 1945.

At 8:15am on 6 August 1945, a B29 bomber called *Enola Gay* dropped the world's first nuclear bomb on the Japanese town of Hiroshima. Eighty thousand people were killed instantly. Three days later, the Americans dropped another bomb on Nagasaki.

Over 40 000 were killed this time. The next day, Japan gave up and World War II was over.

But was it right to use nuclear bombs? And why did the USA decide to drop the bombs when many experts believed the Japanese were days away from surrender?

Source B ▾ *A description of some men found hiding in bushes after the bombings (from J. Hershey's account of the effects of the bomb).*

"Their faces were burned, their eye sockets hollow, the fluid from their melted eyes had run down their cheeks. Their mouths were mere swollen, pus-covered wounds, which they couldn't open wide enough to take a drink from a teapot."

Source C ▾ *A schoolboy remembering the bombings (from BBC Children at War, 1989).*

"My uniform was blasted to shreds. The skin at the back of my head, my back, both hands and both legs had peeled off and was hanging down like rags."

Source D ▾ *A photograph of the city of Hiroshima after the bomb. In total, 70 000 of the city's 78 000 buildings were totally destroyed.*

So why did the Americans drop the bombs?

Several reasons have been suggested.

> Some Americans believed that Japan would never surrender. Experts calculated that over half a million American soldiers would die if they had to invade Japan.

> The bombs cost a lot of money to develop (over $2000 million) so the Americans wanted to test it properly.

> The Japanese had been very cruel to any soldiers they had captured. Some Americans felt they needed to be taught a lesson.

> The USA wanted to show the world, in particular the USSR, how powerful and advanced it was.

FACT *Hot stuff!*

The temperature at the centre of the explosion reached 300 000 degrees centigrade, 50 times hotter than the surface of the sun. Some people were vaporised; others died days, weeks, months or years later from horrific burns or radiation sickness.

Source E ▼ *A British prisoner of war, 1945.*

"There is no doubt in my mind that these bombs saved many more lives than the tens of thousands they killed. They saved prisoners of war … allied servicemen and millions of Japanese — for, let there be no mistake, if the [Japanese] Emperor and his cabinet had decided to fight on, the Japanese would, literally, have fought to the last man."

Source F ▼ *From a 1965 interview with James Byrnes, US Secretary of State.*

"We were talking about the people who hadn't hesitated at Pearl Harbor to make a sneak attack, destroying not only ships but the lives of many American sailors."

Source G ▼ *This is what Kasai Yukiko, a high school pupil, was told to do by her teacher if the Americans invaded in 1945.*

"Even killing one American soldier will do. Use your awls [woodwork tools] for self defence. Aim for the enemy's belly. Understand? The belly? If you don't kill at least one, you don't deserve to live."

Source H ▼ *Admiral William Leahy, one of President Truman's advisors in 1945. He wrote this in 1950.*

"This barbarous weapon was of no real use in our war against Japan. They were already defeated and were ready to surrender … the scientists and others wanted to make this test because of the vast sums that had been spent."

Source I ▼ *From a booklet against nuclear weapons, published in 1985.*

"There were two slightly different types of bomb. Nagasaki was simply an experiment to try out the second type."

Source J ▶ *A British cartoon from 1945.*

JAPAN WAS SEEKING PEACE **BEFORE** THE FIRST ATOM BOMB WAS DROPPED ON HIROSHIMA, ACCORDING TO DOCUMENTS JUST LEAKED TO THE U.S. PRESS.

VICKY

*"DON'T YOU SEE, THEY **HAD** TO FIND OUT IF IT WORKED..."*

Source K ▾ *Some comments made in interviews by people who lived in Hiroshima in 1995. They are in answer to the question: 'Why do you think the bombs were dropped?'*

"Mainly to show the military strength of the USA at that time."

"To damage Japan and demonstrate the power of the allied countries."

"Because Hiroshima was a big city that was worth destroying. There was a military base there."

"Because they had them."

"This is not a simple issue; there are many reasons. They were: to stop the war, to save American soldiers and to show their power."

"To experiment with their new technology but couldn't they have dropped it on an uninhabited island nearby?"

WORK

1 Why were both Japan and the USA interested in the Far East in the years before World War II?

2 **a** Why do you think Japan attacked Pearl Harbor?
   b Do you think the attack was a surprise to the Americans? Give reasons for your answer.

3 **a** How did the USA achieve final victory in the war against Japan?
   b President Truman described the dropping of the bomb on Hiroshima as the 'greatest thing in history.' What do you think he meant?

4 **a** Read through the four reasons that have been suggested to explain why the USA dropped nuclear bombs on Japan in 1945.
   b Then read through the **Sources E** to **K**. All of these sources can be matched to one of the four reasons. Try to match each of the seven sources to a reason, making sure you write out the evidence from the source that made you match it to one of the reasons.

5 **a** Do you think the USA was right to use the bomb? Please note this is a difficult question as there are good arguments on both sides.
   b Do you think they needed to drop two bombs?

United Nations?

AIMS
- understand what the United Nations does;
- know who the members of the Security Council are;
- know what the UN Declaration of Human Rights is.

Towards the end of World War II, Britain, Russia and the USA realised that something must be done to prevent such a terrible war ever happening again. After a series of meetings, the leaders of the three countries decided to set up a club of nations and invited all other countries of the world to join (except Germany and Japan). A special skyscraper was planned in New York to house the representatives of each country where, it was hoped, problems between nations could be settled through discussion and not fighting. This new organisation had a name – the United Nations Organisation, or UN for short – and it held its first meeting in April 1945, a few weeks before World War II officially ended. Representatives from 51 countries were there.

Security Council

Five of the most powerful countries were members of the Security Council (Britain, France, USA, Russia and China). Six other countries (later ten) sent representatives to sit on the Council for two years at a time. They still meet whenever there is a dispute between any countries that looks like boiling over into war. They can stop one country attacking another by:

- asking them to stop
- asking all other members of the UN to stop trading with the quarrelling states until a shortage of supplies forces them to give up the war
- sending in soldiers – or peacekeepers – from several UN countries to stop the fighting or prevent it from spreading.

Any decisions need a 'yes' from all five permanent members.

The General Assembly

A sort of world Parliament, with each country having one vote.

Secretary-General

A key person who manages the whole operation and leads the UN.

World Health Organisation (WHO) (see **Source C**)

Mounts health campaigns, does research, runs clinics and vaccinates against infectious diseases.

Source A ▾ *The United Nations Building in New York. It was opened in 1952.*

Source B ▾ *The UN has a charter or collection of aims, which was first listed in September 1945. All countries must sign the UN Declaration of Human Rights before being allowed to join.*

UN DECLARATION OF HUMAN RIGHTS

- All human beings are born free and equal.
- Everyone has the right to life, liberty and freedom from fear and violence.
- Everyone has the right to protection of the law without discrimination.
- Everyone has the right to a fair trial and will not be arrested without good reason.
- No one shall be a slave.
- No one shall be tortured or punished in a cruel, inhumane or degrading way.
- Everyone has the right to seek **asylum** from persecution in other countries.
- Adult men and women have the right to marry, regardless of their race or religion.

International Labour Organisation (ILO)

Tries to protect workers all over the world by improving their conditions, pay, rights and insurance.

Children's Fund (UNICEF)

Helps underfed, poorly treated or neglected children throughout the world.

International Court of Justice

Based in Holland. Fifteen judges, each from a different nation, settle legal disputes between countries before they lead to war.

Educational, Scientific and Cultural Organisation (UNESCO)

Tries to get countries to share each other's films, books, music, sport and scientific discoveries so that they understand each other more and are less likely to fight.

Source C ▾ *One of the World Health Organisation's (WHO's) greatest successes was the elimination of smallpox, one of history's biggest killers, through a massive vaccination programme.*

Source D ▶ *The UN logo. What do you think it means? By 1960, 100 countries were members of the UN. This increased to 127 members by 1970, 154 by 1980 and 184 by 2000.*

WORK

1. Imagine you are representing your country at one of the first meetings of the UNO. You are holding a press conference. What would be your answers to these questions?
   - Why is this new organisation necessary?
   - What is the Security Council and how can it stop one country from attacking another?
   - Are all nations of the world in the UNO?
   - Why do all countries have to sign the Declaration of Human Rights before being allowed to join the UN?
   - People throughout the world are weak and vulnerable after war – how will the UNO help them?

2. Look at **Source B**. Do you think that some of the rights are more important than others? Explain your answer carefully.

3. Look at **Source D**.
   a Draw the logo of the UN.
   b Explain what you think the logo means.

What was the Cold War?

During World War II, the United States, the Soviet Union and Britain fought together to defeat Nazi Germany and Japan. As the war drew to a close, it was obvious that the USA and the USSR were going to be by far the most powerful countries in the post-war world. It was also clear that the huge differences between the two new '**superpowers**' were going to be a lot harder to ignore once their mutual enemy had been defeated. So just what were these differences? How could allies turn to enemies so quickly? And how did this '**Cold War**' shape the world after 1945.

Source A ▾ *American and Russian soldiers meet at the end of World War II. Russian troops had arrived from the east while the Americans arived from the west and met up around Berlin, Germany's capital.*

Source B ▾ *Capitalism versus Communism.*

Different ways to run a country

The common goal of defeating Hitler had papered over enormous cracks between the two superpowers. Both countries were organised according to completely different **ideologies** (see **Source B**).

Differences over the past

There was a history of bad feeling between the wartime allies that ran back to 1918. The Western Capitalists had been greatly worried by the Russian Revolution and believed that it threatened their way of life. The West sent troops to Russia in 1918 in an attempt to destroy the new Communist government. Churchill, Britain's secretary for war at the time, said the Soviet regime should have been 'strangled at birth'. Stalin had forgotten none of this.

Joseph Stalin, known as 'Uncle Joe' in the West during the war years, had been very unpopular in the 1930s. The brutal way in which Stalin ran the Soviet Union won him few friends in Europe and America. The Nazi–Soviet Pact that Stalin signed with Hitler in 1939, which caused the division of Poland – and Britain and France's entry to the war – had not been forgotten by the West.

To many in the Soviet Union, the way in which the West had taken and handed over large areas of their land to Poland in 1919 still caused anger. The Western allies' performance in World War II had not improved relations either. Stalin couldn't understand why, if the Americans had entered the war at the end of 1941, they did not invade until 1944. He was convinced that the West deliberately stalled so that the Soviets would have to do most of the fighting. Nine out of ten German soldiers killed in the war died fighting the Soviets. The combined deaths suffered by Britain, France and the US totalled less than a million. The Soviets lost 11 million soldiers and 12 million of its civilian population – more than one in ten people in the USSR died.

Differences over the future

What to do with Europe after the war, quickly became a source of disagreement between the superpowers. When they met in Yalta, in 1945, real divisions appeared. The West was eager that the countries that had been occupied by the Nazis should hold free elections so that they could choose the type of government that they wanted. They also wanted Germany to recover quickly so that they could buy and sell goods with them.

The USSR, on the other hand, had very different plans. Russia had been invaded through Germany in 1812, 1914 and 1941, and Stalin was keen to stop this from happening again. He thought Russia would be safer if he created a 'buffer' of friendly countries between Germany and the USSR. To make things safer still, he wanted to extend Poland east and severely weaken Germany.

The three leaders did agree that Germany would be divided into four zones, with the USA, USSR, Britain and France controlling a zone each. They agreed that free elections were to be held in Eastern Europe and that a United Nations Organisation was to be created when the war ended.

But there were major issues that the leaders could not agree on. Just where Poland's border with Germany was going to be was left undecided as Roosevelt and Churchill were unwilling to agree to give so much of Germany to the Poles. The Western leaders were also horrified by the amount of reparations that Stalin was intending to take from Germany.

Source C ▶ *Many historians have argued that the Cold War began at Yalta in February 1945. It was by then a question of time before Germany was defeated and the 'Big Three' – Roosevelt, Stalin and Churchill – met to decide the future of the world. It was at Yalta that World War II alliances weakened and the Cold War divisions appeared.*

Potsdam

By the time Britain, the USA and the USSR got together again at the Potsdam Conference in July 1945, Germany had been defeated, Roosevelt had died and Churchill had lost the British General Election. Harry S. Truman was now the American President and Clement Atlee was the British leader. Truman was far more suspicious of Stalin and took a more aggressive stance with him. He thought Stalin was behaving like a bully in Europe and was suspicious of his attempts to create a 'buffer' against Germany. Stalin had imprisoned many non-Communist leaders in Eastern Europe despite the promises he made of free elections. Truman grew ever more wary of Stalin and failed to tell him about the atomic bomb that America had developed and was intending to drop on Japan. The amount in reparations Germany was to pay was decided, as was the location of Poland's eastern border – but more tensions were created than resolved.

The atomic world

The dropping of atomic bombs on the Japanese cities of Hiroshima and Nagasaki illustrated that mankind now had the ability to destroy itself completely. For the next 50 years, a divided world lived under the shadow of the enormous atomic mushroom clouds. The US refusal to share the scientific secrets of the bomb convinced Stalin that the Americans would use its power to dominate the world. He ordered his own scientists to develop a Soviet bomb as quickly as possible. The terrible power that these bombs gave to the countries that possessed them further increased the mistrust between the East and West.

Source D ▼ *Castle Romeo Detonation in the Pacific Ocean.*

The Soviet Satellite States

Despite the Soviet promises of free elections made at Potsdam, the countries freed from the Nazis by the Red Army were destined to remain under Soviet control. These East European countries became known as '**Satellite States**' and were controlled by the Russians from Moscow (see **Source E**).

Source E ▼ *Post-war Europe.*

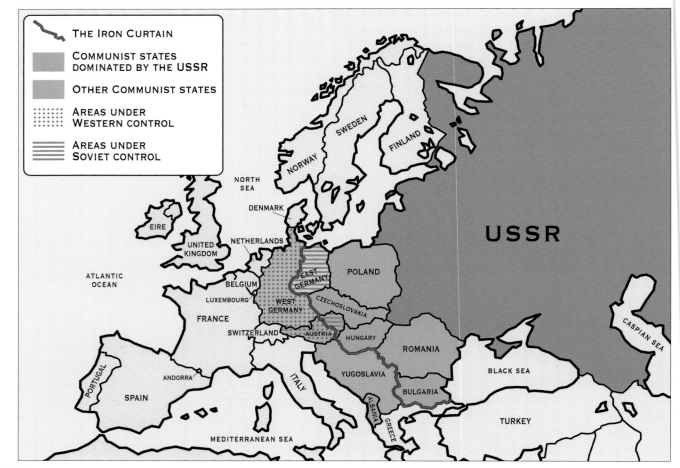

- THE IRON CURTAIN
- COMMUNIST STATES DOMINATED BY THE USSR
- OTHER COMMUNIST STATES
- AREAS UNDER WESTERN CONTROL
- AREAS UNDER SOVIET CONTROL

The Iron Curtain

Winston Churchill, despite no longer being the British leader, summed up the feelings and fears of many in the West when he made a very famous speech in March 1946. Churchill said: 'From Stettin in the Baltic to Trieste in the Adriatic, an Iron Curtain has descended across the continent.' President Truman agreed and decided to do something about it.

The Truman Doctrine

In March 1947, Truman made a speech in which he set out America's foreign policy for years to come. He said that America would come to the aid, with money and military help, of countries that were in danger of being taken over by Communism. That way, America would 'contain' Communism and stop it spreading from country to country 'like a row of dominoes falling down'. This attitude towards the worldwide spread of Communism became known as the Truman Doctrine.

Source F ▼ *An extract from Truman's speech. Here, Truman argued that the world was becoming divided into two camps – the Capitalist camp and the Communist camp. The Capitalist world, he claimed, was free while the Communist world was not. To protect the free world, the USA would use its economic and military strengths.*

"At the present moment in world history nearly every nation must choose between alternative ways of life – the choice is often not a free one. One way of life is based on the will of the majority, free elections and freedom of speech and religion. The second way of life is based upon the will of a minority forcing themselves upon the majority; it relies upon terror, a controlled press and radio, fixed elections and a lack of personal freedom. I believe the United States must support people who are trying to resist being enslaved by armed minorities or by outside pressures. I believe we must help people work out their own destiny in their own way."

WISE UP WORDS

- ideologies   Satellite States   superpowers

The Marshall Plan

It had been argued for many years that Communism gained support when economic conditions were bad. Truman's main concern was that Communism would appeal to the desperate people of Europe who had been battered by five years of war. So in order to help Europe recover (and obviously stop the spread of Communism), Truman offered money to all European nations. He even offered money to the Soviet Union – but they turned it down! Stalin saw American money as a bribe for European countries to follow the American way of life. In total, the Americans gave Europe $13.15 billion of 'Marshall Aid'. **Source G** shows how this total was divided between the various countries.

Source G ▼ *The Marshall Plan, or Marshall Aid, as the money became known, was actually a nickname. It was officially called the European Recovery Plan and was launched by General George Marshall, a US politician.*

COUNTRY	AMOUNT OF AID
UK	$3.2b
France	$2.7b
Italy	$1.5b
West Germany	$1.4b
Netherlands	$1.1b
Greece	$694m
Austria	$677m
Belgium/Luxembourg	$556m
Denmark	$271m
Norway	$254m
Turkey	$221m
Ireland	$146m
Sweden	$107m
Portugal	$50m
Trieste	$32m
Iceland	$29m

WORK

1 What were the main differences in ideology between the two superpowers?

2 a Give three reasons why the Soviet Union was suspicious of the Western allies?
  b Give three reasons why the Western allies were suspicious of the Soviet Union.

3 Why was it so difficult to reach a satisfactory agreement at the Yalta and Potsdam Conferences?

4 What was: a) the Iron Curtain; b) the Truman Doctrine; and c) the Marshall Plan?

The Berlin Crisis, 1948

AIMS

Aim to:
- know why the superpowers fell out over Germany;
- be aware of why the city of Berlin became the focus of the crisis;
- understand how and why full-scale war was avoided.

There was nothing the West could do about countries still occupied by the Red Army. Likewise, there wasn't much the Soviets could do about the countries liberated by the Western allies. The one country that was controlled by both East and West was Germany – and this was where the Cold War's first flashpoint occurred.

1948 was one of the worst years of the Cold War. In fact, the confrontation in Berlin was a time when the Cold War might have become a 'hot' war. So why did Berlin become such a flashpoint?

The German problem

After Hitler was defeated, the allies were uncertain about the future of Germany. After long negotiation, it was decided that Germany should be divided into four zones – controlled by one of the four allies (USA, Britain, France and the Soviet Union). Germany's capital city, Berlin, despite being deep inside the Soviet zone, was also divided into four (see **Source A**).

Source A ▼ *Divided Germany and divided Berlin.*

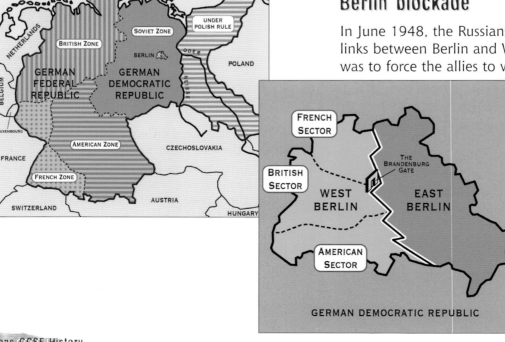

Tension increases

In March 1948, France, Britain and the USA decided to unite their three zones of Germany into a single state – later called West Germany. They did the same in Berlin. This angered the Soviets because the Western allies didn't tell the Soviets they were going to do it. Stalin was made even madder because he had been promised some reparations from Germany but hadn't received much yet. On the other hand, the Western powers were frustrated with the Soviets because they felt that all Stalin cared about was stripping Germany of everything valuable.

Berlin blockade

In June 1948, the Russians cut off all road and rail links between Berlin and West Germany. The plan was to force the allies to withdraw from their three zones of Berlin because they wouldn't be able to survive without food and fuel. Stalin hoped that this would result in West Berlin coming completely under his control.

Tough decision

The allies knew that they couldn't leave two million West Berliners to starve. Troops could deliver supplies over land but this would mean marching into the Soviet zone and directly confronting Soviet soldiers. That could have meant war. The solution they chose was to supply West Berlin by air and hope that the Russians would have the good sense not to shoot down any Western aircraft.

The Berlin Airlift

The Americans and British organised a round-the-clock airlift of essential supplies such as food, fuel and medicine. A cargo plane left an airfield in West Germany every 30 seconds and in 11 months a total of 275 000 flights delivered an average of 4000 tons of supplies every day. Stalin clearly expected the West to give up and hand over the city but, when he realised that this wouldn't happen, he ended the blockade and re-opened the roads in May 1949.

Results of the crises

The West saw this as a victory. They had survived and stood up to the Soviet Union. A week later, the Western allies announced that their zones would officially join together to form the Federal German Republic or West Germany. Stalin responded by turning the Soviet zone into the German Democratic Republic or East Germany. A permanent state of hostility now existed between them.

NATO and the Warsaw Pact

The division between the East and West was confirmed with the formation of two rival defence organisations. The North Atlantic Treaty Organisation (NATO) was a military alliance linking 11 major Western powers together. Its main members were the USA, Britain, France, Italy and Canada. West Germany joined in 1955. By then, the USSR had responded with its own military alliance of East European Communist states. The Warsaw Pact, as it was known, linked the USSR with East Germany, Poland, Czechoslovakia, Hungary, Romania, Albania and Bulgaria. The Cold War, it seemed, was here to stay.

Source B ▸ *A political cartoon that depicts Russia as a bear with a stranglehold over Berlin.*

Source C ▸ *For nearly a year, American and British transport planes flew around the clock to deliver essential supplies after Stalin closed all other routes to Berlin.*

Source D ▸ *The fate of over two million Berliners depended on the planes getting through.*

WORK

1 Give two reasons why Stalin had grown frustrated by the Western allies' actions in Germany.

2 Do you think the artist who drew **Source B** was from the Soviet Union or the West? Give reasons for your answer.

3 There was a number of options open to the Western allies.

 a Complete the following table:

OPTION	ADVANTAGES	DRAWBACKS
1 Ignore Russians and barge through blockade		
2 Pull out of Berlin		
3 Supply West Berlin by air		

 b Why did the Western allies choose to supply Berlin by air?

4 What were the long-term consequences of the Berlin Crisis?

Cold War madness

AIMS

Aim to:
- understand how nuclear weapons shaped the Cold War;
- understand why both sides built more and more bombs despite not wanting to use them;
- be aware of the reasons why the superpowers took steps to limit both the amount of bombs and who had them by the end of the 1960s.

At exactly 7:00am, on 29 August 1949, the Soviet Union detonated its first atomic bomb. America had lost the nuclear monopoly. The knowledge that the Soviets had 'the bomb' caused panic in the West and it immediately set about trying to re-establish its advantage.

The super bomb

American atomic scientists were already discussing the possibility of building a 'super bomb'. By using hydrogen atoms, they believed it would be possible to create a thermo-nuclear device roughly 1000 times more powerful than the bomb dropped on Hiroshima. But the scientists were split over whether they should create a weapon that could destroy all human life on the planet. When President Truman heard about the debate in 1950, he cut it short: 'What the hell are we waiting for? Let's get on with it.' The starter's pistol had been fired in the deadliest arms race in human history.

Both sides rushed to develop ever more powerful weapons in ever-greater numbers. On 30 October 1961, the Soviet leader Nikita Khrushchev announced that the Soviet Union had just detonated the largest bomb that the world had ever seen. The explosion at Novaya Zemlya was the equivalent of 50 million tons of TNT – more than *all* of the explosives used by *all* of the countries in World War II – in just one bomb. Khrushchev said he hoped that: 'We are never called upon to explode these bombs over anybody's territory. This is the greatest wish of our life.'

So why did both sides spend such huge amounts of money developing weapons that they hoped never to use? What was the thinking behind **stockpiling** such enormous numbers of these weapons? And what were the dangers of this strategy?

Source A ▾ *The explosion at Novaya Zemlya – the biggest explosion in the history of the world.*

Mutually Assured Destruction

Despite wishing never to use their nuclear weapons, both sides built more bombs in order to scare the other side from using theirs. That way, neither superpower would start a war because it would mean the certain destruction of their own country – and the world! Mutually Assured Destruction, better known by its apt acronym MAD, was the theory that put the world on a knife's edge. Every time the superpowers disagreed with each other, whether over Berlin, Cuba, Vietnam or Afghanistan, the very existence of every living thing was at risk. For 40 years, the total destruction of the human race and all other life on earth was a daily possibility.

Source B ▲ *President John F. Kennedy watching a missile launch from one of America's submarines.*

Constant alert

Both sides tried to make sure that they would be able to **retaliate** if they came under nuclear attack. From 1961 until the 1990s, America kept 12 giant B-52 bombers in the air, 24 hours a day, 365 days a year. Each B-52 carried four thermo-nuclear bombs, each with pre-designated targets in the Soviet Union. In addition to the B-52s, missile bases were hidden all over the USA, with ICBMs (Intercontinental Ballistic Missiles) on permanent standby. From the early 1960s, submarines lay on the bed of every ocean, completely invisible and untraceable, waiting for months on end for the command to fire their nuclear missiles. At any one moment, the USA could launch 144 Polaris missiles from its submarine fleet.

Source C ▶ *B52 bombers constantly circled the USSR waiting for the order to deliver their terrible weapons to their targets.*

Source D ▼ *Millions of American school children were trained to 'duck and cover' by Bert the Turtle in the event of a nuclear attack. Incredibly, they were told that crawling up into a ball would make them safer!*

Source E ▼ *One hundred thermo-nuclear weapons would have guaranteed the total destruction of the world and would have been enough to deter any attack. By the end of the Cold War, the superpowers had 40 000 between them. This photograph shows a test explosion of a nuclear bomb on 25 July 1945.*

FACT *The whole world in his hands*

The man in charge of America's fleet of B-52s had the authority to launch a 'retaliatory attack' without the permission of the President. In 1957, General Thomas Power, a man described as 'not stable' by his predecessor, was made Head of Strategic Air Command. When asked about his job, Power answered: 'The whole idea is to kill the bastards. At the end of the war, if there are two Americans and one Russian left alive, we win.' This man had the ability to launch a massive nuclear attack without the permission of anybody else.

The 'nuclear club' expands

On the 16 October 1964, Communist China joined the nuclear club. Their leader, Chairman Mao, seemed less terrified of nuclear disaster than the Soviet and American leaders. When the Russians told Mao of the terrible effects of an American nuclear attack, he said: 'We may lose more than 300 million people. So what? War is war. The years will pass and we'll get to work producing more babies than before.'

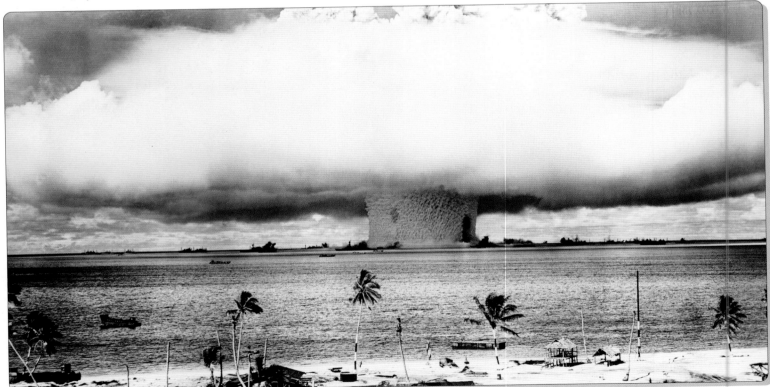

Source F ▲ *Children ducking and covering under desks.*

SALT

The more countries that had nuclear weapons, the more chance there was of them being used or being set off accidentally. In 1968, the Soviet Union, the United States and Britain signed the Nuclear Non-Proliferation Treaty, which stopped the transfer of nuclear secrets to other countries. France and China refused to sign.

In 1969, US and Soviet negotiators sat down in Helsinki to begin the Strategic Arms **Limitation** Talks (SALT). After more than three years of negotiations, both sides agreed on limits of the number of certain missiles they would build.
SALT 1, signed in 1972, may not have achieved much, but it was the first attempt to slow down the arms race and at least the superpowers were talking.

WISE UP WORDS

• retaliate   limitation   stockpiling

WORK

1 Why did the superpowers enter a 'nuclear arms race'?
2 Explain the thinking behind:
   a mutually assured destruction
   b what the political dangers of such a policy are.
3 **a** Give one reason why the world was a more dangerous place after nuclear weapons were invented.
   b Give one reason why the world was a safer place after nuclear weapons were invented.
4 Look at **Sources D** and **F**. Why do you think the US government taught children to 'duck and cover' in a nuclear attack?

Alternative battlefields: chess, sport and space

AIMS

Aim to know:
- reasons why and how the superpowers tried to prove their superiority without resorting to war.

The impossibility of winning a nuclear war prevented the superpowers from competing on the battlefield. Because of this, both countries invested a huge amount of money and resources trying to prove which way of life was superior in ways that didn't involve fighting. This turned normal sporting competitions into matters of national honour. It also meant that ordinary citizens of both countries found themselves transformed into superstars, carrying the hope and pride of entire civilizations.

Chess

Chess had been extremely popular in Russia since the 1800s and, under the Communist government, it had been turned into a national obsession. This widespread popularity and the inclusion of chess lessons in schools meant that the Soviet Union's Grand Masters dominated the chess world. In 1972, at the World Championships in Reykjavik, a 29 year old American called Bobby Fischer changed all that and made the front page of newspapers all over the world.

Fischer was the first Westerner to reach the final of a World Championship and he faced the reigning Number 1, a Russian named Boris Spassky. The press attention this attracted caused the shy and private Fischer to refuse to take part. Henry Kissinger, one of the most powerful men in America, telephoned the young chess star and tried to convince him to play. Eventually, Fischer agreed, but the pressure seemed to have got to him. He badly lost the first game and forfeited the second. Moscow prepared to celebrate the latest piece of evidence that proved Communism was superior.

However, Fischer won the third game and didn't look back. In a series of spectacular victories for America, Spassky was left stunned in his chair long after the game had finished, unable to believe that he had lost the world title.

An American becoming World Chess Champion caused a sensation and was a powerful propaganda victory for the West. Bobby Fischer himself saw the match as 'The free world against the lying, cheating, hypocritical Russian. It's given me great pleasure as a free person to have smashed this thing.'

The Soviets claimed that the Americans had used hypnosis and electronic devices to 'control' Spassky and make him play badly. They even insisted that the Icelandic Police 'sweep' the room for mind controlling 'bugs'.

Source A ▾ *A simple chess game between the American Fischer (on the right) and the Russian Spassky (on the left) came to symbolise the struggle for supremacy between the two superpowers.*

Sport

The famous British author, George Orwell, described sport as 'war without the shooting'. This was especially true during the Cold War as both sides tried to outdo each other in sport – and there is no bigger sporting stage than the Olympic Games.

The 1952 Olympics in Helsinki was the first time that the two superpowers went head-to-head in the sporting arena. America won this first battle, taking home 40 gold medals to the USSR's 22. The prestige that America gained from this victory ensured that both sides invested huge amounts of money developing both athletes and tactics.

The USSR eventually won the 'battle of the Olympics' – winning a total of 395 gold medals to the American's 337 during the course of the Cold War. Many in the West believed that the Soviets gave their athletes performance-enhancing drugs to ensure a Communist victory – but this was never proved. This did not stop speculation in the Western media – who unkindly dubbed the five gold-medal-winning Press sisters 'the Press brothers'.

When the Olympics were held in Moscow in 1980, the United States refused to allow its athletes to attend, in protest against the Soviet invasion of Afghanistan. When the games were held in Los Angeles four years later, the Soviets and their satellite states refused to attend – claiming their athletes would not be safe.

Space

The ideal method of getting nuclear **warheads** to the enemy was by **ICBMs** (intercontinental ballistic missiles). In order for these missiles to deliver their deadly warheads over such huge distances, they had to leave the Earth's atmosphere before re-entry over their target. The technology necessary to achieve this led to an offshoot: the race to explore space. Khrushchev was keen to beat the Americans and show how superior Soviet technology was. Various American presidents also saw the importance of beating the Soviets into exploring beyond the atmosphere. The race was on.

Sputnik

In 1957, the Soviets won the first victory of the space race when they launched the first ever man-made **satellite** – Sputnik. It was only 22 inches in diameter and did little else than send beeps back to Earth, but it was a huge propaganda victory for the Communists. More than that, it terrified many Americans and convinced them that they were losing the Cold War. It wasn't so much the satellite that scared them, but the rocket that launched Sputnik. If it could reach space, it could carry a nuclear warhead to the US.

Source B ▼ *Sputnik – the first man-made object to be placed into the Earth's orbit.*

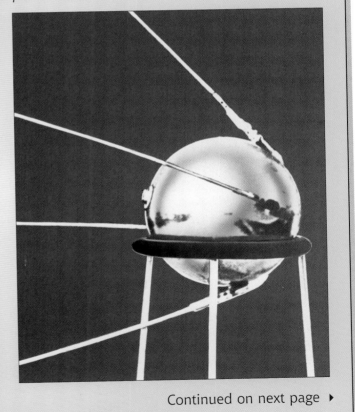

Continued on next page ▶

Space (continued)

The first space dog

Khrushchev argued that Sputnik had proven how superior the Communist way of life was. Less than a month after its launch, he got something else to brag about, as the Russians put the first mammal in space – a stray dog from the streets of Moscow named Laika. Despite Soviet claims that Laika orbited the Earth before being given a lethal injection, the dog actually died from the extreme heat shortly after leaving the atmosphere. But it was still a major propaganda victory for the Russians and yet more cause for concern in America.

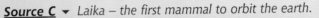

Source C ▾ *Laika – the first mammal to orbit the earth.*

The first man in space

In 1961, the Soviet victory appeared to be complete when they achieved yet another first – the first human being in space. Cosmonaut Yuri Gagarin made a 108-minute orbit of the Earth in his *Vostok 1* spacecraft.

When a fellow cosmonaut left his capsule and became the first man to perform a 'space walk', there was no doubt – the Russians were in the lead.

Source D ▾ *Yuri Gagarin, the first human in space.*

So by the early 1960s it seemed that Russia had won the space race … but the Americans soon hit back.

The US President, John F. Kennedy, responded by setting what many thought was an impossible target: 'To land a man on the moon and return him safely to earth … by 1970!' Just eight years later, on 20 July 1969, America's *Apollo 11* moon-mission triumphed and Neil Armstrong became the first man to walk on the surface of another world. Millions across earth watched the event 'live' on their TV sets. To many Americans, and other countries of the world, landing a man on the moon was more of an achievement than putting one in space – it showed the greatness of the American way of life and its superiority over the Russians.

Space continued to be a Cold War battlefield until the late 1970s.

Continued on next page ▸

Space (continued)

Source E ▾ *Landing on the moon.*

WISE UP WORDS

• warheads   ICBMs   satellite

WORK

1 **a** Explain why the chess match between Fischer and Spassky made the front page of newspapers around the world.

   b Write the opening paragraph and headline to a newspaper report on the Fischer/Spassky chess match. Write one for a US paper and another for a Soviet one.

   c In what ways are your reports different?

2 **a** Put the following statements in the order that you think were the most important reasons why the superpowers entered into a space race:

   i they wanted to prove that their technology was the best in the world;

   ii they wanted to explore outer space; or

   iii they wanted to perfect the technology that would let them send a nuclear warhead anywhere on the planet.

   b Explain why you have put them in the order you have chosen.

3 Why were the Olympic Games 'war without the hostility' during the Cold War?

America and the Communist threat

AIMS

Aim to:
- Know what the term 'containment' means;
- understand how and why the United Nations got involved in the war in Korea.

The Cold War was not just a conflict between the USA and the USSR – it was a struggle between Capitalism and Communism. The USSR supported Communist movements all over the world ... and the USA promised to fight them. In fact, the USA tried to 'contain' Communism and stop it spreading. They wanted to spread Capitalism instead ... and supported Capitalist countries all over the world.

In this section, you will look at three case studies that outline exactly how the Americans tried to contain Communism.

Case study one: The Korean War 1950–53

Background to the war

Korea had been conquered by Japan in the early 1930s. But when Japan surrendered in 1945, Korea was occupied by Soviet troops in the North and American troops in the South.

By 1950, American and Russian troops had pulled out but Korea was still divided. A Communist government (supported by Russia) occupied the North and an anti-Communist government (supported by America) occupied the South.

The United Nations

The United Nations was set up after World War II as a way for countries to sort out their arguments without going to war. It was headed by a Security Council, which at first contained three permanent members – Britain, USA and USSR. It was the Security Council's job to keep peace in the world but for any action to be taken the three permanent members all had to agree. In 1949, China went Communist and the USSR wanted them to become one of the permanent members of the Security Council. After all, China had the biggest population in the world and the Soviet Union saw the Chinese as a powerful, Communist ally. Britain and America refused and the Soviet Union stormed out in protest.

North versus South

In 1950, Communist North Korea invaded the Capitalist South. By September, the South was close to defeat. Many Capitalist countries felt they could not allow Communism to spread into South Korea and wanted the UN to do something about it. US President, Harry Truman, managed to get the UN to condemn the invasion and to send forces to help South Korea against the Communist invaders. Normally, the Russians would have defended Communist North Korea but they had left the UN Security Council and could now do nothing about it.

The war itself

Although the UN force was supposed to be international, America provided 50% of the army, 86% of the navy and 93% of the air force. The man in charge of the force was the American, General MacArthur, who took orders from Truman – not the UN.

At first, the UN invasion was very successful and they managed to push the North Korean army back. China warned MacArthur not to take his soldiers past the original dividing line between North and South Korea – known as the 38th Parallel. MacArthur ignored these warnings and orders from Truman, and took his soldiers right up to the Chinese border (see **Source A**).

Source A ▶
A map showing the North Korean maximum advance around Pusan and the sights of UN landings.

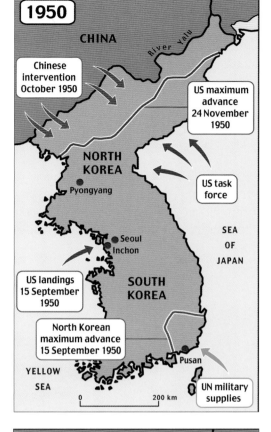

MacArthur got too close for comfort for the Chinese and, in October 1950, they launched a massive invasion of Korea that forced the UN forces right back again (see **Source B**). Truman sacked MacArthur.

With America strongly supporting UN forces on one side and the USSR and China supporting the other, the two sides were fairly evenly matched. By 1953, they had reached stalemate and a ceasefire was agreed in July of that year. North Korea remained Communist while South Korea stayed Capitalist (see **Source C**).

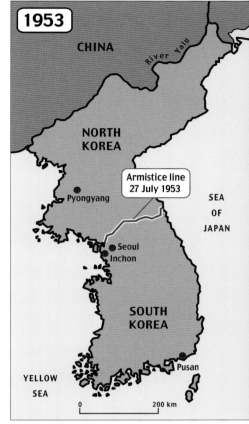

Source C ▶ *A map showing the maximum advance.*

Consequences of the war in Korea

There were both physical and political consequences of the Korean War:

- 1.5 million Koreans from the South died and 3.5 million from the North died.
- 33 000 Americans died.
- The UN's mission was to make Korea one country with free elections, supervised by the UN. The war failed to achieve this.
- The war stopped North Korea taking over the South.
- Many saw the Korean War as proof that the UN was going to take a firm hand and stand up to aggression.
- Others believed that the Americans had used the UN in its war against Communism.
- The war in Korea showed that the Cold War was now global.

Source B ▶
A map showing the maximum advance of the UN force.

Case study two, Cuba: 'A hedgehog in Uncle Sam's pants'

The closest the two enemies ever came to a full-scale war was in October 1962. For 13 days, the world faced the very real possibility of World War III. So why did this terrible situation occur? Exactly how close was a nuclear attack? And how did this crisis – and the Cold War itself – finally come to an end?

The USA and the USSR went to the brink of nuclear war over Cuba, a Caribbean island 90 miles from the American coast. In 1959, a young Communist called Fidel Castro had seized control of Cuba. The USA, fearing a Communist country so close to their own, ordered a top secret invasion of Cuba. The invasion was a total flop and a great embarrassment for the US President, John F. Kennedy. Castro, fearing another invasion, asked the new Russian leader, Khrushchev, if he wished to set up any missile bases in Cuba. The Russians gladly accepted.

On 14 October 1962, a US spy plane discovered nuclear missile bases, which were now in easy range of most major American cities – New York, Washington, Boston, Miami and Chicago.

Source D ▼ *A map showing American sites of a Russian nuclear attack from Cuba.*

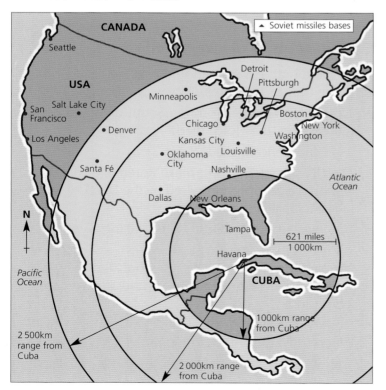

Source E ▼ *A photograph of a missile base in Cuba, taken by a US spy plane.*

US spy planes spotted more missiles on their way from the USSR to Cuba and the USA sent warships to stop the missiles reaching their destination. As the world held its breath, the two leaders – Kennedy and Khrushchev – negotiated with each other. Finally, on 27 October, an agreement was reached. The Americans promised not to invade Cuba and agreed to remove some of their own missile bases near Russia – and the Russians agreed to turn their ships around. The world breathed a huge sigh of relief when the news was announced – this was the closest the world has ever come to World War III.

Source F ▾ *Robert McNamara, one of President Kennedy's advisers, speaking in March 1988.*

"It was a beautiful fall [autumn] evening, the height of the crisis, and I went up into the open air to look and to smell it, because I thought it was the last Sunday I would ever see."

Source G ▾ *Fyodor Burlatsky, one of Khrushchev's advisers.*

"I phoned my wife and told her to drop everything and to get out of Moscow. I thought the bombers were on the way."

Consequences of the Cuban Missile Crisis

Surprisingly, the Cuban Missile Crisis led to an improvement in relations between the USA and the USSR. Both countries had come so close to nuclear war, they realised that if things were to get so bad

again, the end result may not be so peaceful. In 1963, both countries agreed to stop testing new nuclear bombs and a direct telephone line – the 'Hot Line' – was set up so they could negotiate more easily in future. Despite other situations, where America or America's allies fought the USSR's allies, never once did an American soldier fight a Russian during the whole of the Cold War. As a result of the crisis, Kennedy agreed to remove the missiles from Turkey.

Source H ▾ *Soviet leader Khrushchev, speaking in private to other Soviet leaders, in September 1962. Here, he refers to American missile bases in Turkey, which is close to the USSR. Khrushchev was eager to have his own missiles in Cuba, close to America – just as America had missiles close to Russia.*

"The American missiles in Turkey are aimed at us and scare us. Why not throw a hedgehog in Uncle Sam's pants? Our missiles in Cuba will be aimed at the USA, even though we don't have as many of them. They will still be afraid."

WORK

1 Explain why it was UN troops who fought on South Korea's side in 1950.

2 What mistake did General MacArthur make that caused Truman to sack him?

3 **a** Look at 'Consequences of the war in Korea'. Separate the consequences into positive and negative ones.

   b "The war in Korea was a success for the UN." Referring to all of the consequences, explain whether you agree with this statement or not.

4 Read **Source H**. According to this source, why did Khrushchev send Soviet nuclear missiles to Cuba?

5 Look at **Source D**. Why was Kennedy so alarmed by the placing of Soviet missiles in Cuba?

6 Read **Sources F** and **G**. Why are these sources useful in telling us how close the world came to nuclear destruction?

7 In your opinion, did the Cuban Missile Crisis have any 'winners'?

'The elephant and the grasshopper'

AIMS

- To understand:
- why France fought and lost a war in Vietnam;
- the political situation in Vietnam after France left.

What was French Indo-China?

France had ruled the countries of Cambodia, Laos and Vietnam since the late 1800s. During World War II, France was in no position to stop Japan invading these countries, known as Indo-China to the French, as they themselves had been occupied by Germany. When the Japanese surrendered in 1945, a man called Ho Chi Minh declared that his country was now free from foreign rule. He was the Communist leader of a rebel group called the League for the Independence of Vietnam – known as the Viet Minh. France was desperate to restore some pride after its humiliation in World War II. The French had no intention of allowing Vietnam to become an independent nation. War soon followed as the French sent an army over to Vietnam to defeat the rebels.

French defeat

As Ho Chi Minh was a Communist, he was supported in his battle against the French by the Soviet Union and Communist China, and was supplied with weapons and ammunition. Ho transformed his guerrilla bands into a powerful fighting force and, for the next eight years, the two sides fought each other in a struggle that he described as a comparison between an 'elephant and a grasshopper'.

The grasshopper proved to be more than a match for the French elephant and more than 90 000 Frenchmen were killed, wounded or declared missing. The final straw came at a battle in Diem Bien Phu. The French public no longer had the stomach for what they now called 'la sale guerre' – the dirty war. In 1953, at an international conference in Geneva, France agreed to withdraw permanently from South East Asia. One of the most powerful countries in the world, a former great power, had been brought to its knees by a tiny, poverty-stricken nation.

The Geneva Accords

It was agreed in Geneva that Vietnam would be divided into two separate states – the Communist North led by Ho Chi Minh and the Capitalist South led by the Catholic Ngo Dinh Diem. The United States didn't like or trust Diem but as he was anti-Communist, they backed him with money, weapons and military advisers. Diem's regime was corrupt and unpopular, meaning that many peasants in the South turned to Communism as they saw it as a fairer system. The Communists in the South were supplied with weapons from the North down what became known as the Ho Chi Minh Trail and they started attacking Diem's army. They adopted hit-and-run guerrilla tactics that were very effective and by 1962 the Viet Cong, as the Southern Communists were now called, controlled most of the countryside. If Diem's regime was going to survive, he was going to need help.

Source A ▼ *A divided Vietnam. The Communists in the south (the Viet Cong) were supplied by the north through the Ho Chi Minh Trail, which went through the countries of Laos and Cambodia.*

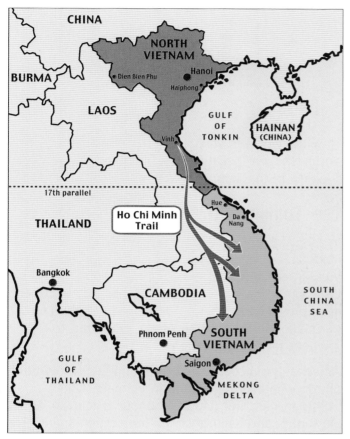

Source C ▶ *Ngo Dinh Diem, the Catholic and corrupt leader of South Vietnam.*

Source D ▼ *Dien Bien Phu fell on 7 May 1954 and the defeated French left Indo-China shortly after. Here, captured French soldiers trudge through the fields after the surrender.*

Source B ▼ *Ho Chi Minh, the leader of the Vietnamese Communists.*

WORK

1 Why did France send its army to fight in Vietnam?

2 In your own words, explain why Ho Chi Minh compared his war with France with a fight between 'an elephant and a grasshopper'.

3 Explain why America decided to support South Vietnam after France had been defeated.

4 Why do you think communism appealed to many peasants in South Vietnam?

The 'undeclared war'

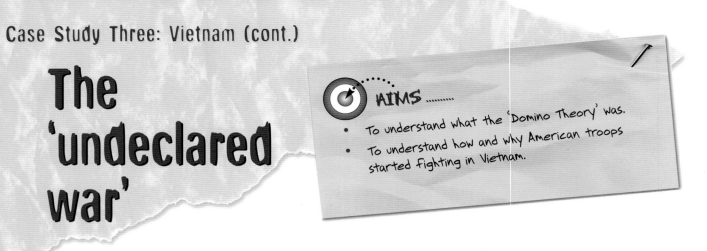

AIMS ....

- To understand what the 'Domino Theory' was.
- To understand how and why American troops started fighting in Vietnam.

For much of the 1950s and 1960s, many Americans saw the world in very simple terms. There was the Free World and there was the Communist World and both were engaged in a bitter struggle. This belief had been turned into official US policy in the Truman Doctrine.

The Domino Theory

Rather than looking at the conflict in Vietnam as a nation's struggle for independence, many Americans saw the war in terms of the 'Domino Theory' (see **Source A**). They believed that if South Vietnam fell to the Communists, then it would spread to Laos, Cambodia, Burma, Thailand and then India. This would make World Communism far stronger and threaten the security of the United States. Many Americans felt that if Communism could spread through South East Asia, then perhaps it could spread to the United States itself one day too! America had been supplying Diem's troops with ever increasing amounts of money, equipment and experts since 1954 but, by 1963, President Kennedy's advisers were deeply divided over what to do next (see Pause for thought 1). Eleven and a half thousand US military advisers were helping the South Vietnamese but no combat troops had seen action. On 22 November 1963, President John F. Kennedy was assassinated and the question of just what to do over Vietnam moved to the top of the political agenda.

A new course of action

The Vice-president, Lyndon B. Johnson (known as LBJ), was sworn in as American leader after JFK's death. LBJ had a far clearer vision of what to do in South East Asia. Just two days after Kennedy's death, before his funeral had even taken place, LBJ called a meeting with his senior advisers in which he told them he 'was not going to lose Vietnam'. His specific instruction was as clear as could be: 'Win this war.'

The Tonkin Gulf Incident

In August 1964, an American warship, the *USS Maddox*, claimed it had come under fire from North Vietnamese gunboats while in international waters. LBJ claimed he was outraged by what he described as unprovoked aggression. He asked Congress for permission to take 'all necessary measures' to 'prevent further aggression'.

American politicians voted 416–0 in favour of letting LBJ do whatever he wanted in Vietnam. One politician said 'Our national honour is at stake, and we cannot and will not shrink from defending it.' He was not alone. Opinion polls showed that 85% of Americans were in favour of taking military action. LBJ now had permission to do whatever he saw fit in South East Asia. It was the closest the United States ever came to declaring war on North Vietnam.

Source A ▾ *Many Americans believed that if one country 'fell' to Communism, it would spread to the next country. Soon, whole continents would fall like a 'row of dominoes'.*

Source B ▾ *LBJ being sworn in as President on-board 'Air Force 1' with JFK's widow, Jackie, standing beside him.*

Source C ▾ *Two graphs showing US troops and deaths in Vietnam 1960–74.*

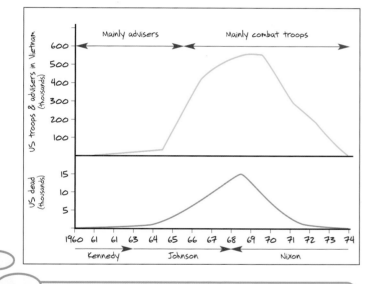

Pause for thought 2

Tonkin Gulf – a reason for war?

The *USS Maddox* was accompanying South Vietnamese boats as they attacked radar installations in North Vietnam. The Maddox didn't take part in the attack but listened to the radio traffic coming from the North. The USA claimed that the *Maddox* was in international water but the Communists claimed that the seas were theirs and sent three torpedo boats to chase the American vessel away. All three Vietnamese boats launched their torpedoes and all three missed. The *Maddox* fired back and called for an air strike, which caused the sinking of one torpedo boat and severely damaged the other two. The next day, South Vietnamese boats again attacked northern radar stations and a tropical storm blew up in the gulf. The Captain of the *Maddox* got the 'impression' he was going to be attacked and called for another air strike – but the pilots could find nothing. Nobody on board had 'actual visual sightings' of the North Vietnamese and not one sailor on the *Maddox* heard gunfire. The incident was enough, however, for LBJ to claim that 'repeated acts of violence against the armed forces of the United States' had taken place. It was enough to pass the Tonkin Gulf Resolution through Congress, which was, according to LBJ, 'like Grandma's nightshirt. It covers everything.' It was all he needed to take America to war.

Pause for thought 1

It is one of history's great questions – would America have entered the war in Vietnam if JFK had not been shot down by a sniper's bullet in down-town Dallas? Historians have argued over whether America's policy in South East Asia would have been different if Kennedy had lived – and there seems to be evidence to support both sides of the argument. In Kennedy's first speech as President, he said that he was willing to 'pay any price' and 'bear any burden' to defend South Vietnam from Communism – indicating he was willing to send US troops to war. However, Kennedy also ordered all of his senior advisers to read the book, *The Guns of August*, which tells how Europe's leaders stumbled into war in 1914. 'We are not going to bungle into war', Kennedy told his team.

WORK

1 Explain why many Americans thought that Vietenam was 'like a domino' in the 1950s and 1960s.

2 Explain how American military involvement increased in the period 1954–65.

3 In what way did the assassination of JFK affect America's policy in Vietnam?

4 "LBJ was delighted when he heard about the attack on the *USS Maddox*." Explain why this statement may be true.

Masters of war?

AIMS ....

- To understand the effect that the arrival of hundreds of thousands of American GIs had on South Vietnam.
- To understand the tactics the United States used to try to win the war.
- To be aware of the typical experiences and difficulties that GIs faced in Vietnam.

When America decided to send its own combat troops to South Vietnam, it meant the arrival of the wealthiest, most technically advanced army on the planet in the middle of a third world, tropical country. So what effect did this have on South Vietnam? How did the Americans attempt to use their wealth and hi-tech weaponry to defeat the Communists? And what was it like to fight the war from an ordinary American soldier's perspective?

The Americans arrive

South Vietnam was completely transformed by the arrival of the Americans. Giant bulldozers carved roads through the jungle, huge rivers were bridged and airfields, helicopter pads and landing strips were built. Enormous bases were built from scratch to accommodate the new arrivals from the US (see **Source A**). The average age of American soldiers in Vietnam was 19 and the majority had never been abroad before. In order to help them cope, and fight, in an alien culture, US soldiers were kept very well supplied with necessities from home. They were given beer, cigarettes and hot food, including turkey at Christmas. Post Exchanges (PXs) looked like department stores where troops could buy cameras, radios, whiskey, hair spray, aftershaves and condoms.

Death in the countryside; desperation in the towns

The Americans launched attacks from their bases, roaming above the jungle canopy in helicopters. They would 'seek and destroy' the Viet Cong in the countryside. In order to escape being caught in these attacks, millions of villagers left their homes and fled to vast shanty towns on the edge of every city. Each US base was catered for by bars, massage parlours, nightclubs and brothels. Young Vietnamese women became prostitutes and could earn as much in a week as their fathers earned from farming rice in a year.

Search and destroy

In terms of fighting the war, the Americans tried to use their vastly superior technology and firepower to their maximum advantage. Bases were built all along the coasts and borders of South Vietnam, which were used to launch 'search and destroy' missions in the countryside. At the same time, the US air force carried out a relentless heavy bombing campaign in North Vietnam and along the supply routes of the Ho Chi Minh Trail.

It soon became clear that the US armed forces were not suited to the kind of guerrilla warfare that the Viet Cong had perfected fighting the French. The Viet Cong avoided open combat at all costs, denying the Americans the opportunity to use their heavy weapons and air support. Instead, the Viet Cong would ambush the US patrols that were meant to be searching for them, before melting back into the villages or jungle. To the young, inexperienced GI it was impossible to tell the difference between an enemy soldier and an innocent civilian. As a result, they were often treated the same. Helicopter gun ships skimmed the tree tops, firing at anything they thought suspicious.

The GIs' war

The American GI faced many problems, which made fighting in Vietnam a horrific experience and badly effected America's ability to win the war.

Look at the picture of Private Al Milner (**Source A**).

The ordinary American troops were known as GIs. This is because the words 'General Issue' were stamped on the uniforms handed to every soldier.

Source A ▾ *A typical American GI.*

My name is Al Milner from Modesto, California. I'm a 20 year old private serving in the Marines, although I never wanted to. I got a letter from the government telling me I had to come to this hell-hole. Apparently, you get five years in jail if you refuse to join. My Dad fought against the Germans in World War II and my whole family wanted me to fight for my country too. I didn't really have much choice. Even if I could live with letting my family down, I couldn't live with being sent to prison, so I packed my bags and joined up. I've been here for 121 and a half days and I am just concentrating on staying alive and unhurt until I reach day 365, then I can go home. I'd quite happily see those days out without seeing the Viet Cong at all. I'm not interested in killing these people or winning this war. I don't even know what we're all here for; all I know is that this war sucks. When we're on search and destroy missions, the strain of being in constant danger, the feeling that you're being watched all the time, the knowledge that your next step could set off a booby trap, it's enough to drive you insane. I hate it when you get an officer who is desperate to find the enemy and get into a fight. You hear stories of guys 'fragging' their officers. This means blowing up the officer with a grenade when they're out on patrol where no one can see. Then, when they get back to base without having had to fight, they say the officer stepped on a booby trap. A lot of the guys take drugs to escape from the reality of this place. I've tried marijuana a couple of times but

This steel helmet is really hot but it's useful for keeping my cigarettes, matches and letters from home dry. It also comes in useful as 'butt armour' – I sit on it when riding in the helicopters.

I sometimes think this backpack is cutting the blood off to my arms and my fingers get numb when I'm out on patrol. I carry my ration packs, as much ammo as I can carry and spare socks. It means I'm hulking 90 pounds (about as heavy as my kid sister) on my back and some guys use captured VC packs instead of our ones as they say they're more comfortable.

This is the fifth uniform I've had – they just rot in the heat and the damp.

This is my M16 – supposedly the most advanced and lightweight assault rifle in the world. The stupid thing jams the minute it gets near water or mud – which is pretty much everywhere in this damn country. The number of GIs who've gone home in a body bag because of this thing is a disgrace and I just don't trust it when it comes to a firefight.

In this heat, with this weight, on patrols this long, with fire ants biting my skin, I carry as much water as I can. It all adds to the weight but no matter how much I carry, I'm always thirsty.

I got these boots after my last pair rotted away. They are nylon at the top and have drainage holes to let the water out. They also have re-enforced soles to stop 'punji spikes' - hidden, sharpened bamboo sticks - stabbing through our feet.

Smoke grenades are used to let the helicopters know where we are so they can come and get us out. I don't carry too many 'frag' grenades, the kind that explode and spray deadly red-hot fragments as I've seen guys accidentally pull pins out on the undergrowth. I don't need to tell you what happened to them.

Source B ▼ *Written by Max Hastings, a British journalist who was working in Vietnam.*

"The Americans had created a vast military society from end to end of the country, with its own barbed-wire-encrusted towns and villages, messing routines, entertainments, transport facilities and daily life, wholly divorced from those of the Vietnamese people outside the perimeters."

Source C ▼ *US soldiers getting out of helicopters to search and destroy the Viet Cong.*

Source D ▼ *One of the huge airport and supply bases built in Vietnam for US troops . These bases were communities in their own right, containing bars, sports facilities, shops and post offices. Indeed, US officials tried to make them a 'home from home'.*

Source E ▾ *A photograph of US soldiers stopping a group of Vietnamese people. Note how the soldier on the right is pointing his pistol at the men. It became increasingly difficult during the conflict for US soldiers to tell the difference between Viet Cong soldiers and civilians – which led to them being treated the same.*

WORK

1 **a** What was 'search and destroy'?

   b What effects do you think 'search and destroy' missions had on the people of South Vietnam?

2 Separate the following factors into:

   a problems the Americans made for themselves

   b problems caused by the Vietcong:

   i Many American troops took drugs.

   ii GIs' equipment was unsuitable and unreliable.

   iii The Vietcong was a hard enemy to find.

   iv It was nearly impossible to tell the Vietcong from innocent victims.

   v Many US troops had been drafted and didn't want to be there.

3 Imagine you were a government advisor out in Vietnam. Write a Top Secret report explaining the problems that ordinary soldiers face. You might comment on uniform, equipment and attitude of the soldiers, as well as the impact they may be having on the South Vietnamese.

Death from above

AIMS

- To understand the effects the bombing had on the people and country of Vietnam.
- To understand how this bombing affected the way the Viet Cong fought the war.
- To be aware of the reasons that allowed a third-world army to withstand a full-scale invasion by a superpower.

In February 1965, the United States air force launched Operation Rolling Thunder. This was an enormous bombing campaign that intended to bomb Vietnam: 'back to the stone age'. For the next eight years, giant B-52 bombers poured high explosives, napalm (burning petrol jelly) and cluster bombs on to North Vietnamese cities, army bases and supply roads. In all, the United States dropped more bombs on tiny Vietnam than had been dropped in the whole of human history. After one particularly fierce raid, an American officer said: 'We had to destroy the town in order to save it.' So what were the consequences of this incredible bombing campaign at ground level? How did the Viet Cong survive and adapt to fighting under such horrendous conditions? And how did they eventually triumph against all the odds?

Chemical warfare

As well as bombs, the United States dropped 18 million gallons of herbicide in order to kill the rainforests that the Viet Cong hid in and the rice crops that they lived off. One of the chemicals used was Agent Orange, which caused cancer and skin diseases, and took years to disappear from the ecosystem, poisoning generations of Vietnamese.

Bombing on this scale meant that ordinary Vietnamese civilians were caught up in the carnage too. The Viet Cong's strength was their ability to withstand the relentless attack from the air by adapting their 'home turf' and by blending seamlessly with the civilian population. Unfortunately for the Vietnamese people, the GIs' inability to tell the difference between an ordinary peasant and a Viet Cong soldier meant that they were often treated as the same thing by US pilots and soldiers.

The underground war

The Viet Cong quickly learned that anything visible from the air soon became a target – so they looked beneath their feet. Viet Cong bases were built in extensive underground bunkers. These were not muddy fox holes, but complex tunnel systems that stretched for over 300 kilometres under the forests of Vietnam. They contained workshops, hospitals, store houses, conference rooms and kitchens. To prevent US soldiers who found them from penetrating too deeply, they were carefully and ingeniously booby-trapped.

Cutting off supplies

The Americans had hoped to stop Russian and Chinese supplies reaching South Vietnam by relentlessly bombing the Ho Chi Minh trail. This was not very successful as, when the main form of transportation is either foot or bicycle, it is impossible to make the roads impassable. The Viet Cong always knew, or found, a way through.

In total, two million Vietnamese people died during the war. Many civilians are included in this total and many more who survived were brutally raped and tortured. The sheer volume of bombs dropped meant that entire communities and village populations fled the terror of the countryside and were broken up forever. Vietnam was never the same again.

<u>Source A</u> ▾ *A typical Viet Cong soldier.*

My name is Nguyen Quang Son. I'm 22 and come from the town of Tay Ninh in South Vietnam. I have been fighting for eight years and will not stop until I am dead or until the last American has left my country. I have killed and injured many GIs. We use our intimate knowledge of the jungle and hide in wait for the Americans who come looking for us. We often dig up the mines that they leave for us and use them ourselves to set up booby traps with bamboo spikes and crossbows. These don't kill hundreds of the enemy – but they terrify all of them! We never take the Americans head-on – we ambush and leave! Most of the GIs aren't interested in fighting anyway and if we kill these foreign invaders in ones and twos, they will all soon lose the stomach for the fight! The Americans are very rich and powerful – but if they cannot find us, then they cannot beat us. As soon as we have attacked, we disappear into the villages or tunnels. We may not drive the Americans from the battlefield, but they will never stop us from attacking them and fighting to reunite our country. Soon the price in blood will be too much for the Americans and they will have to leave. Blood is the one thing that we have got plenty of and we will pay any price to achieve freedom for our country!

We don't wear a uniform – that way the Americans can't identify us as the enemy.

This is my Russian AK-47 assault rifle. It is very simple, very reliable and very accurate. Even when it has been under water, it has never let me down.

I use this to make 'punji sticks', which I hide in pits and cover with leaves. The Americans fall into the pits and impale themselves on the bamboo spikes.

I carry a ration of rice with me and live off the jungle or donations from villagers. We travel very lightly, which lets us move quickly through the rainforest.

Source B ▼ Ingenious Viet Cong tunnel complexes enabled them to live and fight despite the horrific attack from the air.

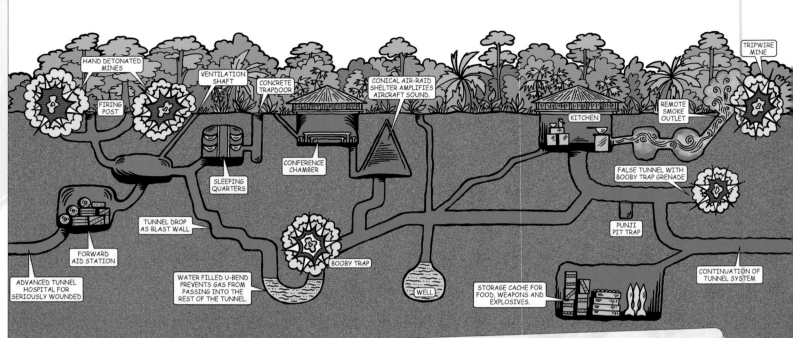

HAND DETONATED MINES

FIRING POST

VENTILATION SHAFT

CONCRETE TRAPDOOR

CONICAL AIR-RAID SHELTER AMPLIFIES AIRCRAFT SOUND.

TRIPWIRE MINE

KITCHEN

REMOTE SMOKE OUTLET

CONFERENCE CHAMBER

SLEEPING QUARTERS

FALSE TUNNEL WITH BOOBY TRAP GRENADE

TUNNEL DROP AS BLAST WALL

FORWARD AID STATION

PUNJI PIT TRAP

BOOBY TRAP

ADVANCED TUNNEL HOSPITAL FOR SERIOUSLY WOUNDED

WATER FILLED U-BEND PREVENTS GAS FROM PASSING INTO THE REST OF THE TUNNEL.

WELL

STORAGE CACHE FOR FOOD, WEAPONS AND EXPLOSIVES.

CONTINUATION OF TUNNEL SYSTEM

Source C ▶ B-52 bombers were designed to carry nuclear bombs. In Vietnam, they 'carpet bombed' large areas with conventional bombs, killing civilians as well as soldiers.

Source D ▾ *Vietnamese soldier in tunnel, holding a hatch.*

WORK

1 **a** Why did the Americans resort to the policy of 'carpet bombing'?

 b How did the Viet Cong adapt to fight under these conditions?

2 Apart from explosives, how else did the Americans target the Viet Cong from the air?

3 Why did 'Operation Rolling Thunder' fail to stop supplies reaching the Viet Cong in South Vietnam?

4 **a** Imagine that you are an American Air Force General. Separate the following factors into advantages and disadvantages of Operation Rolling Thunder:
 i American pilots are much safer from attack than GIs attacking on the ground.
 ii Attacking such large areas from very high altitude means you can't target the enemy – you have to kill everything.

 iii Constant bombing on such a huge scale disrupts the Viet Cong's preparations and movements.
 iv Dropping Agent Orange on the jungle will poison people and the land for years to come.
 v Constant bombing on such a huge scale costs millions of dollars.

 b Do you think the advantages outweigh the disadvantages?

 c Are some factors more important than others? If so, which are most important and why?

5 Look at **Source A**. List as many reasons as you can why Ngyen Quang So would be a more effective soldier than Private Al Milner (see page 261).

War in your living room

Vietnam was the first television war. The American people were served up a nightly diet of death and destruction on the evening news. In the Korean War, the footage shown on the news had been taken by official military cameramen. In Vietnam, it was filmed by TV networks who were allowed to move freely and film what they wished. Using lightweight cameras, they were flown around the war zone by army helicopters, capturing the horrors from the front in full colour and sending the pictures back to America at great speed.

But to American viewers, some of what they were being *shown* didn't match up with what they were being *told*. This caused people to question how much they could trust their government and shocking images, such as GIs 'torching' villages and Buddhist monks setting themselves on fire, caused many Americans to question whether they could really be the good guys.

Source A ▼ *By Nick Tomalin, a British journalist who covered the Vietnam War for the* Sunday Times.

"The Americans may not tell you the truth, but they provide the means for you to go and find out the truth for yourself."

On 5 August 1965, *CBS Evening News* showed a GI setting fire to the straw roof of a peasant's home with his Zippo cigarette lighter, while the villagers stood by and begged for mercy. People questioned why US soldiers had to burn down the homes of helpless peasants. What on earth was America doing in such a war?

At the beginning of 1968, the American people were told that the Viet Cong had been badly damaged by the aerial bombing and that they were on the brink of collapse. Then, during the Vietnamese Tet holiday in January, the Viet Cong launched a massive attack in more than 100 locations. Even the United States Embassy in Saigon was captured by commandos, and the battle to reclaim it, along with dead and wounded GIs, was filmed by US TV crews. The Tet Offensive was a disaster for the Viet Cong and they lost 37 000 troops but it also caused great damage to American public opinion. People questioned how an army on the brink of collapse could launch such a coordinated attack and capture the very symbol of American presence in Vietnam.

This image shows two young Vietnamese children running away after a US napalm attack. Note how the girl's clothes have been blown off — and the TV crew behind them are filming their every move.

Buddhist monks committed these horrific acts of suicide to protest against intolerance and raids in their temples by the South Vietnamese government. People questioned why America was supporting such a regime.

During the Tet Offensive, US camera crews filmed the Chief of the South Vietnamese Police, General Nguyen Ngoc Loan, holding a pistol to a Viet Cong captive's head and about to pull the trigger. The cameraman who filmed it described what he saw as 'Loan pulls out his pistol, fires at the head of the Viet Cong captive, the Viet Cong captive falls, zoom on his head, blood spewing out.' The newsmen knew they had filmed a scoop and the execution was witnessed that evening by 20 million Americans. People questioned if they were really fighting on the side of 'good'.

WORK

1 What advances in technology guaranteed that the American public at home would get a better idea of what happens in a war zone?

2 Look at the images on the TVs. For each image decide whether it would:

   a make Americans proud of their invasion of Vietnam; or

   b make Americans question whether they could trust their government; or

   c make Americans question whether they are fighting for good.

3 Read **Source A**. What point is the journalist making?

4 **a** Has America changed the way it allows the media to cover wars they are involved in? Research America's media policy in the Gulf Wars. Has it changed?

   b What lessons could the American government have learned about the media coverage of the Vietnam War?

'Hey, hey, LBJ! How many kids did you kill today?'

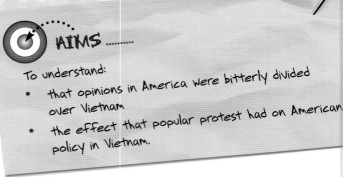

AIMS

To understand:
- that opinions in America were bitterly divided over Vietnam
- the effect that popular protest had on American policy in Vietnam.

Most Americans in the 1950s and early 1960s supported the war in Vietnam and thought that the world should be made safe from Communism. However, Americans born in the huge baby boom that followed World War II, some 30 million in total, were turning 20 years of age in the 1960s. Many of these 'baby boomers' saw the world in a very different way from their parents – and they were going to do something about it. One American professor said, 'For the first time in our history, a major social movement, shaking the nation to its bones, is being led by youngsters.' This movement could be summed up in one slogan, 'Hell no, we won't go!'

A divided nation

The war in Vietnam provided common ground on which a wide variety of young people could come together. It brought together pacifists, religious groups, students, left-wingers and those wishing to avoid being sent to Vietnam – 'draft dodgers' (see Fact box). In October 1965, there were anti-war demonstrations in more than 90 American cities, including Washington, where 80 000 people marched in protest. When Johnson increased the draft – which meant students would now be called up to fight – university campuses erupted in protest around the country. Over 500 universities had to be closed throughout the war and the army was called in to deal with protesters on numerous occasions. This led to clashes and, when unarmed students were shot dead at Kent and Jackson State Universities, anger turned to fury and American society was divided even more.

Reasons for opposition

It was not only the increase in draft that caused Americans to turn against the war. In My Lai, 300 unarmed peasant villagers, mostly women and children, were gunned down in cold blood by US soldiers. The GIs involved claimed the villagers were sheltering the Viet Cong but details of the massacre shocked the nation. The officer in charge, Lieutenant William Calley, was given a life sentence but served just three years in prison. The war became harder to justify when it was costing the lives of so many young men. By 1968, 300 Americans were dying every week, eventually reaching a total of over 50 000. But it was not only the cost in lives that caused people to question the war; it was also the cost in dollars. The war had cost $30 000 million by 1968, preventing promised reforms in the US from taking place. The types of weapon being used by the US military also caused opposition. Napalm was used extensively and many civilians fell victim to horrific burns when their villages were bombed. The knowledge that highly toxic chemicals being used to destroy the jungle were also poisoning the people went down badly 'back home'.

The silent majority

Not all Americans shared the views of the 'baby boomers'. In September 1966, three out of four Americans supported the war. These became known as the 'silent majority' and rallies were organised for them to voice their opinions. Anti-war protesters were attacked and a law was passed that made burning draft cards a crime punishable by five years in prison and a $10 000 fine. Ronald Reagan, a man destined to become president but was Governor of California during the war, summed up an anti-war protest at Berkeley University as 'Sex, drugs and treason'. When those opposed to the war started burning the stars and stripes, thousands responded by buying miniature flags to display in their windows. Posters declaring 'My country right or wrong' became a common sight across the country.

Giving up the fight

Despite the anti-war protestors being a minority, President Johnson was known to be devastated by the chants of 'Hey, hey, LBJ! How many kids did you kill today?' The first thing he asked for every day was the previous day's casualty numbers. The Tet Offensive appears to have been the final straw for LBJ, who shocked the nation by announcing live on television that 'I shall not seek, and will not accept, the nomination of my party for another term as your president.' LBJ had given up the fight.

Source A ▾ *A student anti-Vietnam demonstration in 1968.*

Source B ▾ *The 'baby boomers' took on the older generation by demonstrating at college campuses. In Kent State, this had tragic consequences.*

Source C ▶
Many of the 'silent majority' showed their support for the war by wearing badges such as these and placing flags in their windows and cars.

FACT *Conscription*

Ever since the end of World War II, young Americans had been called up to fill the gaps in the US armed forces. This was known as 'the draft'. Although this was never popular in peace time, when the Vietnam War started, the number of people trying to avoid the draft rocketed. These people were called 'draft dodgers' and caused widespread anger, especially among poor, working-class black men who found they couldn't avoid the draft. Many summed up their frustration with the phrase 'If you have the dough, you don't have to go'. Tens of thousands of those who could afford it ran off to Canada and many doctors were pressured by relatives or family friends to declare their sons 'unfit to serve'. The draft was ended in 1973 and America's armed forces have been 100% voluntary ever since.

WORK

1 Explain the term 'baby boomers'.
2 Many high school students got involved in the anti-war protests. Create an anti-war poster, including as many reasons as you can for why American troops should leave Vietnam.
3 Why do you think those who supported the war were called the 'silent majority'?
4 Look at **Source C**. Why do you think the badge that says 'No More Koreas, Win in Vietnam' means?
5 Why do you think Ronald Reagen described the anti-war protest at Berkeley University as 'Sex, drugs and treason'?
6 Why did some people think that conscription, or the draft, was unfair?

Peace with honour?

AIMS

- To understand how American troops were able to leave Vietnam.
- To decide whether they achieved peace with honour.
- To understand the consequences of the Vietnam War.

In 1968, the American people chose Richard Nixon to replace LBJ as their president. Nixon soon decided that American troops had to get out of Vietnam – but he had to find a way of doing this that did not humiliate the nation. So just how did Nixon arrange the removal of American forces? Did he avoid humiliation? And what were the consequences of America's disastrous attempts at containment in South East Asia?

Vietnamisation

From 1969 until the end of 1971, Nixon built up the South Vietnam army while steadily reducing the number of American soldiers fighting. This policy, which placed far more of the burden of fighting on the South Vietnamese, was called Vietnamisation. At the same time, Nixon pressured the leaders of South Vietnam to compromise with the North and asked China and the USSR to pressurise North Vietnam into making a deal. Nixon's secretary of state, Henry Kissinger, began talks with North Vietnam in 1969, hoping to bring about a cease-fire. In order to convince the Communists to look for peace, he also increased the heavy bombing of North Vietnam as well as on supply routes in the countries of Laos and Cambodia.

The Paris Peace Agreement

If Nixon could get a peace agreement, he could justify the removal of American troops – as there would no longer be a war to fight. In Paris, on 23 January 1973, it was agreed by the Secretary of State, Henry Kissinger, that US troops would get out of Vietnam. Le Duc Tho of North Vietnam promised that his troops would remain in their current positions and not attack the South. President Thieu, leader of South Vietnam, called the peace a 'betrayal', despite the American promise of a further $1 billion of military equipment to guarantee their safety.

A re-unified Vietnam

South Vietnam's safety was not guaranteed and the 'peace with honour' that Nixon claimed he had achieved did not last. In December 1974, North Vietnam launched an attack on the South. In April 1975, the capital of South Vietnam, Saigon, fell to the Communists and was re-named Ho Chi Minh City. Vietnam was again a complete country – a completely Communist country.

Vietnam – the aftermath

Vietnam itself came out by far the worse off from the conflict – with over two million of its citizens dead, a further 1.5 million injured and much of the country devastated or poisoned by the relentless assault from the air. Many in the South didn't want to live under the Communist regime and more than a million escaped the country between 1969 and 1990. Many of these fled on makeshift rafts (becoming known as 'boat people') and settled in the West.

America lost 58 000 soldiers but even those who survived the war had trouble re-adjusting to normal life – whether due to drug dependency or because of the horrors they had witnessed. Many Americans did not see their returning soldiers as heroes and were embarrassed by the war. These factors combined to produce over 700 000 veterans with psychological problems and caused huge numbers of suicides by 'Vietnam vets'.

America's reputation as an invincible, unstoppable superpower was greatly damaged by the war. It also damaged America's reputation as the leader of freedom and peace – if unarmed protesters could be shot at home, and war crimes such as My Lai were carried out by US soldiers, could America really be the 'land of the free'?

Vietnam also brought about the end of the Truman Doctrine. It had been proved that America could not 'contain' Communism like it had in Europe and there were Communist takeovers in Laos and Cambodia (although it didn't spread to Thailand or India).

Détente

Despite America's involvement in Vietnam angering the Soviet Union, by the time US soldiers pulled out of the war, relations between the two superpowers had improved. America had had its fingers burned in Vietnam and was looking for a period of peace. They even cut back on the amount they spent on weapons. The Soviet Union and China had fallen out and both were trying to forge better relationships with the United States. The leaders of all three countries met at numerous 'summits' and the Cold War seemed to be thawing. This period was known as the Détente.

Source A ▾ *A modern version of a 1973 cartoon showing each of the five presidents involved in the Vietnam war.*

Source B ▾ *Nguyen Phu Duc of Vietnam meets with President Nixon and Secretary of State Henry Kissinger in the White House.*

Source C ▾ *Henry Kissinger and Le Duc Tho shake hands on the streets of Paris after agreeing to stop fighting so that American troops could leave Vietnam.*

Source D ▾ *A 'Vietnam vet' at the Vietnam memorial. 58 000 US soldiers had died and many more suffered physical injuries.*

WORK

1 Explain the term 'Vietnamisation'.
2 Why did Nixon want a peace agreement before he pulled American troops out of Vietnam?
3 Nixon described the Peace Agreement as 'Peace with honour'. Thieu described it as a 'betrayal'. Which do you believe is the most accurate description and why?
4 Why do you think the communists renamed Saigon, Ho Chi Minh City?
5 Find one consequence of the Vietnam War that affected:
   i   the Cold War
   ii the people of America
   iii the people of Vietnam.

The Soviet Union and the Eastern Bloc

AIMS

Aim to:
- understand what de-Stalinisation was;
- be aware of the effects that de-Stalinisation had on the Soviet satellite states.

Joseph Stalin, the power-mad dictator of the Soviet Union, died in March 1953. He had ruled the USSR, in war and peace, for over 25 years. He had also made sure that the men in charge of Russia's satellite states – Poland, East Germany, Czechoslovakia, Hungary, Romania and Bulgaria – were totally loyal to him.

Mr Nice Guy?

For a while, after Stalin's death, Russia was ruled by a 'collective leadership', but by 1955, Nikita Khrushchev had emerged as the new leader. He wanted relations between the USSR and the USA to improve – which is exactly what many in the West wanted. He even spoke of 'peaceful co-existence' with the West because he realised that a full-scale nuclear war would be suicidal.

De-Stalinisation

In 1956, Nikita Khrushchev made an astonishing speech. He accused the former Soviet leader, Joseph Stalin, of being 'cruel and inhumane' and said he had 'completely lost touch with reality'. He even criticised Stalin's treatment of the Soviet Union's Communist neighbours (see **Source A**).

Source A ▼ A modern historian.

"While Stalin was alive, and after his death in 1953, the USSR and all the Eastern European Communist countries regarded him as almost a god. Now Khrushchev announced that this personality cult was over, and that Stalin's crimes far out-weighed any good that he had done. Under Stalin's regime, Khrushchev said Soviet citizens had 'come to fear their own shadows' and they had been terrorised by 'mass repressions and brutal acts'. This attack on Stalin had a tremendous effect on the Communist world, both inside and outside the USSR."

Khrushchev backed up his disapproval of the old regime by releasing thousands of political prisoners sent to labour camps under Stalin's regime. He went so far as to criticise Communism itself for not giving Russians what they really needed. He even proposed new economic reforms to give people more food and luxury goods. This process became known as de-Stalinisation.

Source B ▼ Part of Khrushchev's speech.

"We must help people eat well, dress well and live well. You cannot put theory in your soup or Marxism in your clothes. If, after 40 years of Communism, a person cannot have a glass of milk or a pair of shoes, he will not believe that Communism is a good thing, whatever you tell him."

Rebellion in Poland

Soon after Khrushchev's speech, there were demonstrations against food prices in Poland. Khrushchev sent in Russian troops to restore order and sensationally appointed Vladislav Gomulka as the new Polish leader. Gomulka, a very popular guy, had been imprisoned under Stalin … but now Khrushchev was putting him in charge of the country!

Soon, other Eastern Bloc countries demanded more freedom to run their own affairs – but they still didn't know just how much freedom, if any, Khrushchev would allow.

Over the next 25 years, several countries tested out the USSR to see just how tight Soviet control really was.

Study the following four case studies carefully.

Source C ▼ *Nikita Khrushchev.*

WORK

1 What do you think Khrushchev meant by the term 'peaceful co-existence'?

2 Explain what the term 'de-Stalinisation' means.

3 How did Khrushchev intend to improve the lives of the people of the Soviet Union?

4 What affects *could* the relaxation of de-Stalinisation have on the Soviet Union's relationships with the satellite states? Explain your answer.

Uprising in Hungary

AIMS

Aim to:
- understand why the 'Hungarian uprising' took place;
- be aware of how and why the Soviet Union reacted to it.

In the summer of 1956, there were widespread riots and demonstrations throughout Hungary and, in particular, the capital city of Budapest. The following series of pictures outlines what became known as the 'Hungary Uprising'.

1
Hungarian leader, Matyas Rakosi, has been chosen by the Soviet Union.

MATYAS RAKOSI

He was a harsh leader whose secret police (the AVO) carried out a terror campaign against anyone opposing government policy.

2
In the summer of 1956, ordinary citizens took to the streets of Budapest in protest against the government.

DOWN WITH AVO · WE WANT MORE FREEDOM · NO CENSORSHIP · WE WANT LAND

They were fed up with Communist control of the radio, newspapers, schools, factories and farms.

3
Demonstrators had heard the news that the people of neighbouring Poland were allowed more freedom. Many thought that they might be next.

But the protests soon turned violent.

4
After a week of rioting, Rakosi and many other government officials fled Budapest.

The Communist officials who stayed behind weren't as harsh as Rakosi. Imre Nagy was chosen as Prime Minister.

5
Nagy promised the Hungarian people just what they wanted.

I will:
* hold free elections
* get rid of the secret police
* give land back to farmers
* allow non-Communists to be part of the government
Imre Nagy
PRIME MINISTER

Amazingly, Soviet leader Khrushchev agreed to what was happening.

6
A few days later, Nagy declared that Hungary was pulling out of the Warsaw Pact, the military alliance between the USSR and the other Communist countries.

He's going a bit far now.

This was a step too far for the Soviets. They worried that rebellion would spread to the other countries of Eastern Europe, causing the total break up of the Warsaw Pact.

7
In early November, Khrushchev took decisive action. He sent in 200 000 Soviet troops and 2500 tanks into Hungary.

The aim was to remove Nagy and restore order and discipline in Hungary once more.

8
The Hungarians fought fiercely but there was little they could do against the well-trained, well-equipped Soviet troops.

Nagy called for help from the United Nations and, in particular, the USA but none came.

9

There were over 2000 Soviet casualties and around 4000 Hungarians were killed. About 200 000 fled and left Hungary altogether.

Nagy himself was arrested, sent to the Soviet Union and hanged. Around 35 000 Hungarians were arrested and 300 executed.

10

In mid-November, pro-Soviet János Kádár was appointed as leader.

Kádár remained in power for many years, but managed to introduce some of Nagy's ideas while still remaining loyal to the Soviet leadership in Moscow.

Source A ▼ *From a radio broadcast in Budapest 1956.*

"Civilised people of the world! Our ship is sinking. Light is fading. The shadows grow darker over the soil of Hungary. Hungary is dying. Help us."

Source B ▼ *From* Hungary in Revolt *by M. Orr, 1981.*

"Russian tactics were basically simple — to employ the maximum firepower against any target. If it was suspected that a sniper was hiding in the building, tank guns destroyed the building. In the last stages of the battle, the Russians used terror tactics. Queues of housewives were shot down by machine guns. Aircraft and artillery destroyed buildings. When the last 30 defenders of the Kilan Barracks surrendered, they were shot down as they emerged."

◀ **Source C** *Two Hungarians walk past dead secret policemen (AVOs). They have been dumped on a mound of Soviet propaganda leaflets.*

◀ **Source D** *Hungarian demonstrators tear down a Soviet statue of Joseph Stalin.*

WORK

1 What caused the people of Hungary to protest in the summer of 1956?

2 What did Nagy do that caused the Soviet Union to send tanks to Budapest?

3 Why do you think the USA did nothing to help the people of Hungary?

4 Read **Source B**. Give five adjectives to describe the Russian tactics in Hungary.

Why was the Berlin Wall built?

A divided nation

At the end of World War II, Germany was divided into four areas. These 'zones' were controlled by the war's major 'winners' – the USA, Britain, Russia and France. Berlin, Germany's capital, was divided into four zones too.

By the 1960s, the USA, Britain and France had merged their zones into one. It was called West Germany and they had a democratically elected government. Russia's old zone was known as East Germany – but its government was controlled by Communist Russia.

The USA, Britain and France had also joined their parts of Berlin together – but Berlin was over 100 miles *inside* Russia's old zone (now East Germany). So there was now this rather odd situation where half a city – West Berlin – had become a showpiece of the Capitalist West where workers enjoyed luxury goods and decent working conditions. And West Berlin was right in the middle of Communist East Germany – and right next to Communist East Berlin, where citizens worked long hours, endured food shortages and had a limited choice of goods (see **Source A**).

During the 1950s and 1960s, many East Germans were far from happy. For a start, there was nothing much to buy in the shops and jobs were hard to get. They resented Communist control and life seemed better – and freer – in West Germany. By 1960, over three million Germans had fled from East to West Germany. They were called **defectors**. The border between the divided nation was guarded by machine-gun towers and minefields – but people could still pass freely from East Berlin into West Berlin – and then fly out into West Germany.

A divided capital

In 1961, the Communist government of East Germany decided that too many young and skilled East Germans were defecting to the West by walking into West Berlin. Khrushchev, the Soviet leader, wanted to keep these people in East Germany so they could help to build up industry and business. So, in 1961, the route into a Capitalist lifestyle in the West was closed by the building of the Berlin Wall. By June 1961, a thousand East Germans were fleeing to the West every day.

The Wall goes up

On 13 August 1961, East German and Russian soldiers stood in a line along the border between East and West Berlin. They forced back any East Berliner who tried to get into West Berlin. The roads

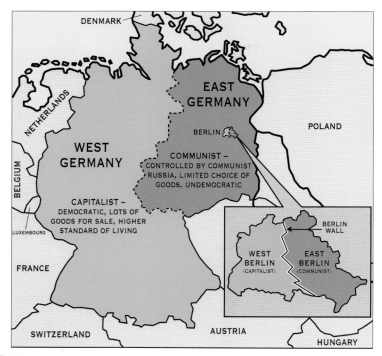

◀ **Source A** *Map showing East and West Berlin.*

were blocked too – and the trains were stopped. In seven days, a concrete wall was built around the whole of Western Berlin – right through the centre of the city and around the edge. The Wall literally divided families in two, as people in East Berlin were forbidden to visit relatives in West Berlin (see **Source B**).

Source B ▼ *A father and mother in West Berlin hold up their twin babies for their grandparents in East Berlin to see.*

So why was the Wall built?

The building of the Wall can be interpreted in two ways. The East German Communist government said the Wall was built to keep out spies from the West. They also argued that they built the Wall to stop a 'brain drain' of doctors, lawyers and teachers leaving the East for a more luxurious lifestyle in the West. Western governments, on the other hand, argued that the Wall had been built to keep East Germans in East Germany 'close to imprisonment', as one historian called it at the time. Between 1961 and 1989, 86 people were killed trying to cross the wall.

> ## WISE UP WORD
> - defectors

WORK

1 Why were many East Germans unhappy with their lives? List as many reasons as you can.

2 Why was West Berlin a problem for the Soviet government? List as many reasons as you can.

3 Look at **Source B**. Explain what is happening in the photograph.

4 **a** What is meant by the term 'brain drain'?

   b Write an article from the Soviet point of view, explaining why the Berlin Wall was built.

   c Write an article from the West's point of view, explaining why the Berlin Wall was built.

Source C ▶ *West Berliners looking over the Wall. One is holding up a newspaper that reads '10 000 DM. This is the murderer.' The photograph is of an East German policeman who shot an East Berliner escaping to the West.*

Case Study Three: Czechoslovakia, 1968

The Prague Spring

⏱ **AIMS** ·········

Aim to:
- understand why Czechoslovakia tried to escape being controlled by the USSR;
- know how the Soviet Union reacted to the 'Prague Spring' and what that meant to the rest of the Eastern Bloc and relations with the West.

The next attempt to depart from Soviet rule came from Czechoslovakia in 1968. By this time, Khrushchev had been replaced by Leonid Brezhnev as the leader of the USSR and the Czechoslovakian Communist Party had just chosen Alexander Dubček as its new President.

Dubček was aware of how the standard of living in Communist countries had fallen behind those in the West and decided to change the way the economy worked to improve things. He also knew that, after over 20 years, many people in his country were fed up with the strict Soviet system of rule and were eager for more freedom. Dubček decided to make changes here too – he wanted to keep Czechoslovakia Communist – but give it 'a human face'. These reforms took place in early 1968 and became known as the **Prague Spring** (after the capital city of Czechoslovakia). They made Dubček extremely popular within his own country, but were viewed with suspicion by Brezhnev.

Source A ▾ *Prague Spring reforms.*

Prague Spring – changes to improve the standard of living

- Less state control of economy
- Increase competition in economy
- Increase trade with Western countries

Prague Spring – changes to increase personal freedom

- Power of secret police controlled
- A free press
- Free elections
- Opposition political parties legalised
- Freedom to travel abroad

The Russian reaction

It wasn't just Brezhnev who was worried by the events in Prague – the leaders of the other Eastern European Communist countries were also concerned. They all feared that once a few freedoms were granted, people would demand more and more. This demand for freedom and reform would then spread from country to country and greatly threaten Soviet control of the whole of Eastern Europe. The leaders of the satellite states demanded that Brezhnev took action.

On the night of 20 August 1968, Russian paratroops took control of Prague airport. In the hours that followed, over half a million soldiers from Warsaw Pact countries entered Czechoslovakia. Dubček told his people to stay calm and not to fight the troops, but there were isolated incidents when civilians attacked tanks using bricks and petrol bombs (see **Source B**). Dubček was arrested and taken to Moscow. He agreed to reverse the changes he had made and allow Soviet troops to stay in his country permanently. By 1969, he had been replaced as leader of Czechoslovakia by a man fiercely loyal to Moscow. Countries in the West complained but there was nothing they could do without risking a disastrous nuclear war. The USSR had clearly shown that they were not prepared to accept change within the countries of the Warsaw Pact.

The Brezhnev Doctrine

In order to clarify exactly what was expected of Eastern European countries and to stop another Prague Spring happening, the Soviet Union issued the Brezhnev Doctrine. This stated that all Communist states must contain no political parties other than the Communist Party and all should belong to the Warsaw Pact and work together to resist any attempt by any member to abandon Communism.

Results of the Prague Spring

* Relations between East and West grew worse during the crisis but soon returned to the Détente (the gradual improvement in superpower relations happening at the time).
* The people in Eastern Europe were left in no doubt about what the Soviet Union would do if they attempted to make changes.
* Relations between the USSR and China were damaged. The Chinese were unhappy that the tanks were used against another Communist country and felt left out by the Brezhnev Doctrine.

Source B ▼ *The few Czechoslovakians that attacked the soldiers had little chance without anti-tank weapons. The Soviets re-imposed strict Communism in Czechoslovakia by force.*

Source C ▼ *This street cartoon summed up the feelings of many in Prague in 1968.*

WORK

1. Why did Dubček introduce changes in the way Czechoslovakia was run in 1968?
2. Look at the changes of the Prague Spring. Which do you think concerned Brezhev more: changes to improve the standard of living or changes to personal freedom? Give reasons for your answer.
3. Look at **Source C**. What do you think the artist is trying to say about Soviet rule?
4. What was the Brezhnev Doctrine?

Solidarity in Poland

AIMS

Aim to:
- understand the reasons why the people of Poland became unhappy with Communism;
- be aware of the 'Solidarity' movement and the role it played in Poland in the 1980s.

The next attempt to escape Soviet control came in Poland in the 1980s. Throughout Communist rule, there had been a history of strikes in Poland when food prices and unemployment levels had grown too high and these had resulted in improvements to the standard of living. But in 1980, the poor performance of the Polish economy led to calls for changes that went far further than the price of food.

The power of the Polish Pope

When Cardinal Karol Wojtyla became Pope John Paul II in 1978, he became the first Polish person to become the leader of the Catholic Church. Religion was discouraged under the Communist system but the Catholic faith was very strong in Poland. The appointment of John Paul II and the return to his homeland in June 1979 caused a surge of pride in both their country and religion. Half a million people gathered in Victory Square to hear the Pope call on God to 'renew the face of this land' and one in four of the entire population heard him speak on his nine-day tour. John Paul II was an inspiration to the people of Poland and he gave them new confidence for the struggle ahead.

The power of poverty

The Polish economy performed badly in the late 1970s and, in July 1980, the Communist Polish government increased meat prices by 100%. People walked out of their jobs in protest all over the country and, on 14 August, more than 17 000 workers walked out of the Lenin Shipyards in Gdansk.

The workers at the shipyard formed their own illegal, independent trade union called Solidarnosc (meaning Solidarity). They appointed an unemployed electrician called Lech Walesa as their leader and put forward 21 demands to the government, including the right to strike and the legalisation of trade unions. The government gave in to all of Solidarity's demands and the trade union quickly grew in size and importance. By January 1981 – just five months after it had been formed – Solidarity had an amazing 9.4 million members – 60% of all urban workers. They started to demand changes to all aspects of the way the country was run and Solidarity was now much more than a trade union – it was more like an opposition party to the Communist regime.

The USSR viewed the growth of Solidarity with alarm. They were scared that people in other Eastern Bloc countries would copy the demands Walesa was making and looked to the Polish Communists to regain control. The man in charge of Poland's army, General Wojciech Jaruzelski, was put in charge of the country. He was under pressure from the Soviets – he knew he had to act.

The power of the state

On 13 December 1981, General Jaruzelski announced that Poland was in a 'state of war'. Tanks poured onto the streets and Lech Walesa, all the leaders of Solidarity and thousands of activists were arrested. The press was closed down, strict curfews were imposed, all links with the outside world were cut and the telephone system was shut down. Solidarity had been taken completely by surprise and, with all its leaders in prison, was unable to resist the Communist clamp down and start a national uprising. By the end of December, there were no more workers on strike in Poland.

The end of Solidarity?

Jaruzelski had managed to destroy organised opposition to his government without help from the USSR. But there were real doubts over whether he could improve the economy enough to keep people happy and stop calls for change. He formed the Patriotic Movement for National Regeneration in the place of Solidarity and threatened the loss of jobs if people didn't join.

Despite the fact that he started to release Solidarity's leaders in 1983, countries in the West were not impressed with Jaruzelski's actions. Walesa and his colleagues were very popular in the USA and Western Europe and these countries were horrified by the way they were persecuted – and in some cases murdered. The West imposed trade sanctions on Poland and the effect on the Polish economy was catastrophic. Inflation reached 70% and the currency was devalued twice. Inevitably, opposition began to reappear.

Source A ▼ *Lech Walesa meets Pope John Paul II.*

Solidarity was now an illegal organisation but, by the mid-1980s, it had begun to re-establish itself and work almost openly. In 1986, it even threatened the government with a nationwide strike against price rises – and it worked! Foreign governments sent officials to meet with Walesa as if he was in charge of Poland and discussed removing the economic sanctions with him. Poland appeared to be moving away from the USSR.

But by 1986 the major threat to the Soviet rule of Eastern Europe did not come from Poland. It was in the very heart of the Communist world – Moscow.

FACT *Lech Walesa*

Lech Walesa (pronounced Lek Valensa) was born in 1943 and was the son of a farmer. When he left school, he went to work as an electrician at the shipyards in Gdansk. In 1970, he led the shipyard workers who went on strike in protest against price rises and in 1976 he was sacked from the shipyard for making malicious statements about the regime. He led strikes and was sacked from numerous jobs until, in August 1980, he helped set up and lead Solidarity. He was a highly articulate speaker and clever negotiator and his strong Catholic faith won him massive support both at home and abroad. He became the symbol of the Eastern Europeans' struggle to free themselves from Communism when he was imprisoned in 1982. He was awarded the Nobel Peace Prize in 1983 and became the first non-Communist leader of Poland since World War II in 1989.

WORK

1 How did the Pope cause a surge in national pride in Poland?

2 What incident led to nationwide strikes and the formation of Solidarity?

3 How does the Soviet reaction to Poland differ from its reaction to Hungary and Czechoslovakia?

4 It is 1989 and you are compiling a short entry for an encyclopaedia on the world's leaders. Write a report on Lech Walesa, explaining his background, his position in Solidarity and his popularity in Poland and the West.

The collapse of the Red Empire

AIMS

Aim to:
- understand why Russia's control over Eastern Europe ended so quickly;
- understand the effects this had on the Cold War and the lives of millions of people in Europe.

In 1985, Mikhail Gorbachev became the leader of the USSR. It was clear to him that the Soviet system was not working and that changes had to be made. The standard of living in the Soviet Union was much lower than that of the West and lower than most of its Eastern Bloc allies. Gorbachev knew that he couldn't keep spending a fortune on weapons when the Russian people were suffering from severe food shortages and living in poor housing.

Source A ▼ A map showing how a number of Eastern bloc countries broke away from the USA 1988–90.

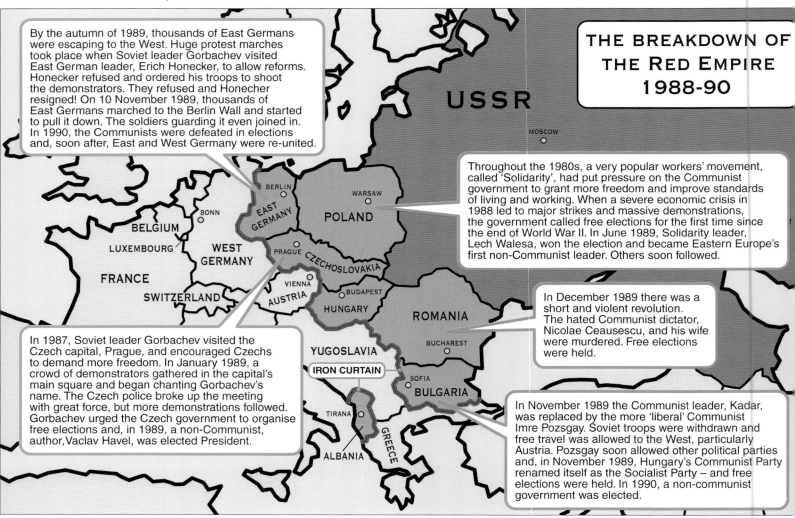

THE BREAKDOWN OF THE RED EMPIRE 1988-90

By the autumn of 1989, thousands of East Germans were escaping to the West. Huge protest marches took place when Soviet leader Gorbachev visited East German leader, Erich Honecker, to allow reforms. Honecker refused and ordered his troops to shoot the demonstrators. They refused and Honecher resigned! On 10 November 1989, thousands of East Germans marched to the Berlin Wall and started to pull it down. The soldiers guarding it even joined in. In 1990, the Communists were defeated in elections and, soon after, East and West Germany were re-united.

Throughout the 1980s, a very popular workers' movement, called 'Solidarity', had put pressure on the Communist government to grant more freedom and improve standards of living and working. When a severe economic crisis in 1988 led to major strikes and massive demonstrations, the government called free elections for the first time since the end of World War II. In June 1989, Solidarity leader, Lech Walesa, won the election and became Eastern Europe's first non-Communist leader. Others soon followed.

In December 1989 there was a short and violent revolution. The hated Communist dictator, Nicolae Ceausescu, and his wife were murdered. Free elections were held.

In 1987, Soviet leader Gorbachev visited the Czech capital, Prague, and encouraged Czechs to demand more freedom. In January 1989, a crowd of demonstrators gathered in the capital's main square and began chanting Gorbachev's name. The Czech police broke up the meeting with great force, but more demonstrations followed. Gorbachev urged the Czech government to organise free elections and, in 1989, a non-Communist, author, Vaclav Havel, was elected President.

In November 1989 the Communist leader, Kadar, was replaced by the more 'liberal' Communist Imre Pozsgay. Soviet troops were withdrawn and free travel was allowed to the West, particularly Austria. Pozsgay soon allowed other political parties and, in November 1989, Hungary's Communist Party renamed itself as the Socialist Party – and free elections were held. In 1990, a non-communist government was elected.

Radical change

Gorbachev was a life-long supporter of Communism and believed that the system could be made to work if the right changes were made. He famously called his reforms Glasnost and Perestroika.

Policy number 1: Glasnost (meaning trust or openness)

Gorbachev wanted to keep power in the hands of the Communist Party but felt that people should be more aware of the reasons for government actions. He encouraged more freedom of speech by saying that people who criticised Communism (dissidents) should not necessarily be imprisoned. He even allowed increased levels of democracy and an even more open attitude towards the West.

Policy number 2: Perestroika (meaning re-structuring)

Gorbachev knew that he had to give his people a better standard of living and more of the luxury goods that they actually wanted. For years, there had been shortages of all kinds and most citizens had to spend hours queuing for the most basic items. Under Perestroika, the Soviet economy would be changed to a more Western style economy. More goods were made that people actually wanted and profit-making businesses were encouraged. In this way, the Communist-controlled economy was gradually replaced by the free market.

Gorbachev also reduced the amount of money spent on weapons and defence. He said that the USSR should stop spending huge amounts of money interfering in other countries' affairs. He even asked Western companies to start up businesses in the USSR.

What were the results?

1. The Cold War

These changes had a huge impact both at home and abroad. To begin with, a policy of openness led to dramatically improved relations with the West and created a 'genuine friendship' with America. In two meetings between Gorbachev and US President Reagan (in Iceland in 1986 and Washington in 1987) the Cold War effectively came to an end when both leaders agreed to reduce the amounts of weapons they had.

2. The USSR

Glasnost and Perestroika had not pleased hard-line Communists. They were scared that by making changes and giving people freedom, people's expectations would be raised and more radical demands would then be made. They were right and, as the Soviet standard of living remained incredibly low, people used their freedom of speech to demand the end of Communism altogether. The people of the USSR who lived outside Russia also started to demand their independence from Moscow and, during 1990 and 1991, the 15 republics that made up the USSR won the right to rule themselves. By 1993, Russia had free speech and free elections but was suffering from enormous price rises, high crime rates and a thriving black market economy.

3. The Eastern Bloc

Glasnost had an astonishing effect on Eastern Europe. People flooded on to the streets in their thousands to demand reform and an end to Soviet rule. This time, the Soviet troops did not march in to 'restore order' and, one by one, the countries of the Eastern Bloc gained their independence from Moscow (see **Source A**).

Source B ▶
Soviet leader Mikail Gorbachev.

WORK

1 Why did Gorbachev believe that the current Soviet system was not working in the USSR?

2 In 150 words, explain how Gorbachev attempted to improve the lives of people living in Eastern Europe.

3 Look at **Source A**. 'Glasnost and Perestroika were small breaches in the dam that soon led to a huge flood.' Decide if you agree with this view. Give reasons for your answers.

Why is there conflict in the Middle East?

🎯 **AIMS** ....

Remember:
- try to understand why the area is so important to different religious groups;
- aim to remember how and why the state of Israel was established.

Look at **Source A**. This region of land is known as the Middle East. It is mainly desert but large areas of land near to rivers or by the sea are very fertile and good crops can be grown. The Middle East is also the source of 60% of the world's oil – a vital resource in today's modern society. But, for many years, this whole area has seen lots of conflict, invasion, war and terror campaigns.

So what are the causes of the problems in the Middle East?

Source A ▼ *The Middle East. It is known by other names too, most notably South East Asia.*

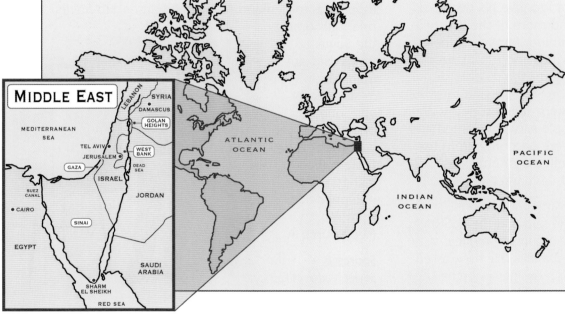

Jews versus Romans

At the time of Jesus Christ, Jews had lived in Palestine for a long time. But the area was part of the Roman Empire and was controlled by the Romans – and the Jews hated this. In fact, the Jews rebelled against the Roman rule twice (in AD66–73 and 132–135) and were defeated both times. After the second rebellion, Jews were ordered to leave Jerusalem and all Jewish religious customs were declared illegal. As a result, lots of Jews left Palestine altogether and began to settle elsewhere. However, many Jews dreamed of a return to Palestine, the place they regarded as their homeland. This belief is called **Zionism**.

Much of the conflict centres around a small, disputed territory called Palestine … or Israel, depending on who you support in the dispute. This region stretches from the Mediterranean Sea to the River Jordan and the Dead Sea (see **Source A**). It is a fertile area that contains Jerusalem – a holy city for three of the world's most important religions: Judaism, Christianity and Islam.

Here come the Christians and the Muslims

For many centuries after the Jews left, Christianity dominated the area and Jerusalem became a very important city for Christians. After all, Jesus Christ was born in nearby Bethlehem and had been killed and buried in Jerusalem.

But Jerusalem soon became a very important city for followers of Islam too. Many believe that their great leader, the prophet Mohammed, had gone up to heaven from Jerusalem and millions of his Arab Muslim followers began to settle there. As a result, both Christians and Arab Muslims wanted Jerusalem to belong to them. Indeed, during the Middle Ages, there were great battles between Arab Muslims and Christians over control of Jerusalem (remember studying the Crusades?). Gradually though, Palestine came under the control of Arab Muslims and was part of a huge Islamic empire that dominated the whole region.

Enter the Turks

But Palestine changed hands once again in the 1500s when it became part of a huge Turkish empire, ruled by Turks from Turkey. It remained under Turkish control until the 1900s. Most Arabs living there hated Turkish rule.

The British arrive

In 1918, Turkey became one of the losing nations in the Great War. Palestine was taken away from Turkey and given to Britain to look after. At this time, Palestine itself contained about 90% Arab Muslims – and 10% Jews.

Source B ▾ *An act of sabotage by fighters.*

Palestine and the Great War

Turkey was on Germany's side during the Great War … so Britain and Turkey were enemies. As a way of making trouble for the Turks in Palestine, the British encouraged the Arabs living there to rebel against Turkish rule. A British army officer, T. E. Lawrence (Lawrence of Arabia), was even sent to the region to help the Arabs to blow up trucks, destroy railway lines and generally distract the Turks from the job of trying to win the war.

A leading British politician even wrote to an Arab leader promising to support the Arab claim to control the region if the Turks were beaten during the war (see **Source C**).

Source C ▾ *Letter from Sir Henry McMahon, British Ambassador in Egypt to Sheriff Hussein, Arab leader and ruler of Mecca, October 1915.*

> *"Subject to modifications, Great Britain is prepared to support the independence of the Arabs in all the regions demanded. On the other hand, it is understood that any European advisers needed will be British."*

However, at the same time, British politicians were also making promises to Jews who hoped to return to Palestine (see **Source D**).

Source D ▾ *A letter written by the British Foreign Secretary, A. J. Balfour, in November 1917, to a leading Zionist. It is known as the Balfour Declaration. At the time, about 90% of people living in Palestine were Arab Muslims. The rest were mainly Jews who had moved back into Palestine in recent years.*

> *"The British government favours the setting up in Palestine of a national home for the Jewish people. However, you must understand that we support nothing that affects the civil and religious rights of the non-Jewish people already living there."*

British rule

After the war, the Turkish Empire was broken up and parts of it were given to other countries to look after. Palestine, part of the Turkish Empire since the 1500s, was given to Britain – so did they honour the 'promises' made to both Arabs and Jews during the war (see **Sources C** and **D**)?

Jews and Arabs in Palestine

From 1918 onwards, the British allowed Jewish immigration into Palestine, while, at the same time, promising to protect the rights of the local Arab population. In fact, between 1920 and 1930, about 100 000 Jews went to live in Palestine. And when Hitler came to power in Germany and began picking on Germany's Jews, thousands more moved into Palestine to escape the Nazis. Between 1933 and 1936, 170 000 Jews moved into Palestine.

Indeed, by 1940, 40% of Palestine's people were Jews – and now some Arabs were getting afraid of being outnumbered in what they regarded as their own country! In an attempt to prevent trouble between Jews and Arabs the British introduced a quota system, restricting Jewish immigration into Palestine.

The Holocaust

During World War II, the Nazis tried to kill as many Jews as they could, mainly in death camps dotted around Nazi-occupied Europe. By the end of the war, about six million had been killed.

When Hitler and the Nazis were defeated and the true horrors of the death camps were shown to the world, many began to think that Jews should be given their own homeland where they could be safe from persecution. Some thought that more Jews should be let into Palestine but the British stuck rigidly to the quota system. Soon tension increased in Palestine. Arabs and Jews clashed – and both blamed the British for not sorting out the problem. A terror campaign against the British even started (see **Source F**). Arabs blamed the British for letting in too many Jews while the Jews blamed the British for not letting in enough!

Source E ▼ *A photograph of death camp survivors who had been held captive in Auschwitz (Poland). When asked, many said they wanted to settle in Palestine.*

Source F ▼ *The southern wing of the King David Hotel, which was the headquarters of the British army in Palestine, was blown up by the Zionist terrorist organisation Irgun. British personnel disregarded a telephoned warning; as a consequence, 92 people died.*

In the end, the British offered talks between Jews and Arabs but both sides refused. So the British decided to let a new peacekeeping organisation, called the United Nations, decide what to do.

New nations?

The United Nations suggested separating Palestine into two countries – one Arab and one Jewish (see **Source G**).

Source G ▼ *The United Nations' plan to divide Palestine. Note that Jerusalem was to be an 'internalised' city under UN control.*

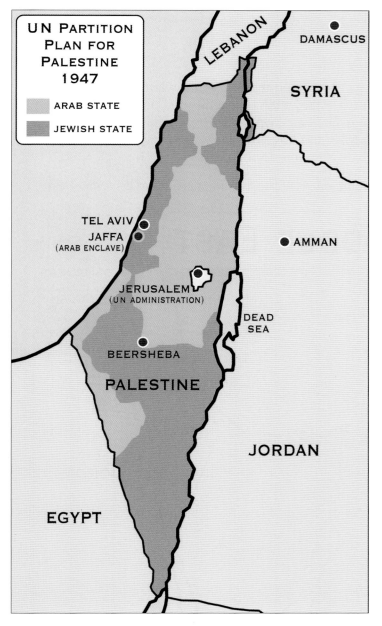

UN PARTITION PLAN FOR PALESTINE 1947

☐ ARAB STATE
▨ JEWISH STATE

LEBANON
DAMASCUS
SYRIA
TEL AVIV
JAFFA (ARAB ENCLAVE)
AMMAN
JERUSALEM (UN ADMINISTRATION)
DEAD SEA
BEERSHEBA
PALESTINE
JORDAN
EGYPT

The Arab leaders said no to the plan, arguing that the Jews had no claim at all on the land they considered their own. But the Jewish leaders accepted the plan and declared the new state of Israel. The President of the USA gave his support to the new state.

Immediately, war broke out between the new state of Israel and the Arabs. And the Palestinian Arabs were helped by their Arab neighbours – Egypt, Syria, Jordan and Iraq. Over the next 15 years, there were four wars between Israel and her neighbours!

WISE UP WORD

- Zionism

WORK

1 **a** How did the Jewish people come to be a small minority in Palestine in the years up to 1918?

   b What is 'Zionism'?

   c How did Palestine become a largely Arab Muslim country in the years up to 1918?

2 Look at **Source C**.

   a Is it clear what the British government is promising Arab Muslims?

   b How might Arabs and the British interpret this letter differently?

3 Look at **Source D**.

   a Is it clear what the British government is promising?

   b How might Zionists and the British interpret this document differently?

   c How does Balfour try to deal with the rights of people already living in Palestine?

4 **a** The British government has often been blamed for some of the problems in Palestine. It has been criticised for promising different things to different people. In your opinion, is this a fair criticism?

   b How might you defend British actions at the time?

War in the Middle East

AIMS ....

Aim to be able to:
- outline at least two of the major conflicts in the Middle East.

The Jewish state of Israel came into existence in May 1948 when the British army left the region. Immediately, a Palestinian Arab army invaded Israel because they didn't recognise the new nation. They said Jews had no claim at all on what Arabs considered to be their own land. The Arabs were helped by other Muslim nations nearby such as Egypt, Syria, Jordan and Iraq. This became known as the first Arab–Israeli war. Many other clashes were to follow.

The first Arab–Israeli war, 1948–49

The day after the state of Israel was proclaimed, on 14 May 1948, Arab armies entered Israel in an attempt to destroy it. But although Arab forces strongly outnumbered the Israelis, they were badly organised and the Jews drove the Arab armies back. By the end of the conflict, Israel controlled all of Palestine, except for two areas – the Gaza Strip that was controlled by Egyptian Arab forces and the West Bank area, which was controlled by Jordan (another Arab nation that helped the Palestinian Arabs) (see **Source A**). At the same time, hundreds of thousands of ordinary Palestinian Arabs fled the land that Israel now held and became refugees in the Gaza Strip, the West Bank or the neighbouring Muslim countries of Egypt, Jordan and Syria. Many of these people and their children have remained in refugee camps ever since.

Source A ▼ *A map to show the results of the first A–I war.*

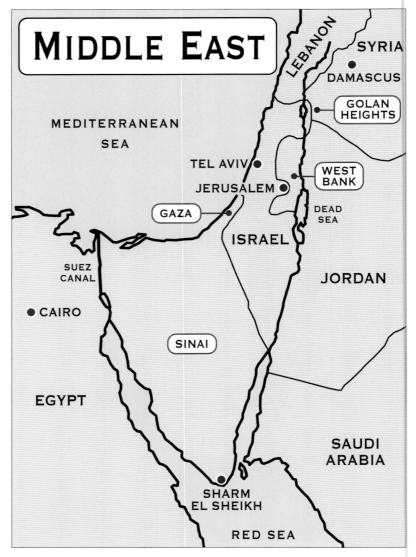

Source B ▲ *Palestinian refugees.*

The Suez Crisis

The Arab countries did not give up in their quest to destroy Israel. Egypt prevented Israeli ships from using their only port on the Red Sea and blocked Israeli ships from using the Suez Canal – a vital trade link between the Red Sea and the Mediterranean. Indeed, all Arab countries tried to stop Israel trading properly. Also, Palestinian refugees began terrorist attacks on targets across the Israeli border. But one Arab nation, Egypt, began to take a leading part in the conflict during the 1950s.

Colonel Nasser

A man called Colonel Gamal Abdel Nasser became president of Egypt in 1954 – and wanted to make Egypt the leading Arab state. His four main aims were:

- Make Egypt a strong military nation. He did this by buying weapons from Czechoslovakia and Russia.
- Bring all Arab nations together in an Arab Union.
- Restore Palestine to the Arabs. This would mean fighting Israel of course.
- Develop Egypt's land, economy and trade.

The Aswan Dam

One of Nasser's greatest schemes was to build a dam on the River Nile. He argued it was needed to generate electricity for the area and water for the whole of Egypt. The Americans promised to help to pay for it but withdrew their offer when Nasser made a military alliance with other Arab nations. The USA (where more Jews live than in any other country in the world) thought that the alliance was hostile towards Israel and decided to pull out of their deal with Egypt.

Nasser was furious at this humiliation and took control of the Suez Canal in order to use the tolls paid by ships to help finance his dam.

Tension grows

The Israelis, British and French were all frightened by Nasser. To some British politicians, Nasser's attempt to unite all Arabs and destroy Israel was similar to Hitler's attempts to unite all Germans and destroy Jews! And Britain used the Suez Canal all the time too. The Israelis were worried about Nasser's growing military strength and the French were unhappy about him helping Algerians to fight against French rule in North Africa.

Suez War

In October 1956, war broke out. The Israeli army invaded Egypt and Britain and France began bombing Egyptian military targets. Nasser blocked the Suez Canal by sinking ships across it and, the next day, British and French troops parachuted into the canal area to sieze it (see **Source C** overleaf).

But many all over the world disagreed with the attack on Egypt. The USA demanded withdrawal of the troops and Russia even threatened war. Eventually, with tension rising again, British and French troops pulled out. The Israelis withdrew to their old boundaries too – and the United Nations sent peacekeepers into the canal zone to control the area. However, the success of the Israeli armed forces meant that no Arab countries were prepared to take on Israel for many years.

Source C ▾ *The Suez Crisis. Seen from the air, the ships that were sunk to block the entrance to the Suez Canal at Port Said. Nasser became a hero throughout the Arab world after Suez – and the Russians were admired by many Arabs for supporting him.*

The Six-day War

Things remained tense between Egypt and Israel after the Suez Crisis of 1956. In early 1967, the Egyptian leader, Nasser, threatened Israel with war. The Israelis responded by launching a surprise attack on Egypt on 5 June. In six days, the Israeli air force destroyed the Egyptian air force while their ground troops seized huge amounts of territory from Egypt, Jordan and Syria (see **Source E**). This occupied land included the Gaza Strip (formerly controlled by Egypt) and the West Bank (formerly controlled by Jordan). The newly conquered lands contained a million Arabs who were now ruled by Israel – and the Israelis encouraged Jews to move into these already crowded Arab areas! Clearly, the conflict would flare up again soon.

Source D ▾ *The line up of forces for the Six-day War.*

Israel		Egypt	
Regular forces	17 000	Regular forces	190 000
Reservists	204 000	Reservists	120 000
Tanks and armour	1050	Tanks and armour	1200
Aircraft and American 'Hawk' missiles	350	Aircraft and Russian missiles	550
		Jordan	
		Forces	65 000
		Tanks	132
		Aircraft	12
		Syria	
		Forces	81 000
		Tanks	350
		Aircraft	102
		Iraq	
		Forces	82 000
		Tanks	320
		Aircraft	87
		Lebanon	
		Forces	11 000
		Aircraft	8

Source E ▾ *Maps showing the Middle East borders before and after the Six-day War, 1967.*

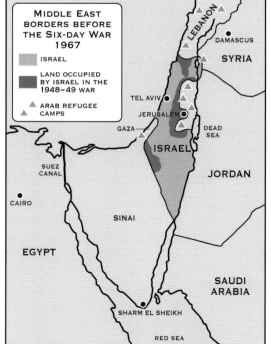

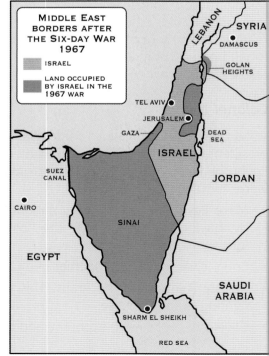

Source F ▼ *Statement by the Jewish president of Marks and Spencer, Lord Sueff.*

"We may sit comfortably in London and contemplate the threat of annihilation because it is something that is at a distance, but the people who live in Israel are genuinely afraid of being swept off the face of the earth, as the Arab leaders have said so frequently. I have relatives there, and I know their fears and how they regard this danger which confronts them. The people of Israel appear to me to be exceedingly brave. I can think of no case of a sovereign state such as Israel being eliminated by the threat of brute force exercised by its neighbours. This is not a moment when the people have to bear the brunt of threat and attack will be pleased to discuss with us the niceties of international law."

Source G ▼ *Casualty figures for the Six-day War.*

ISRAELI	Egyptian Front	Jordanian Front	Syrian Front	TOTAL
Killed	275	299	115	689
Wounded	800	1457	306	2563

ARAB	Egyptian Front	Jordanian Front	Syrian Front	TOTAL
Killed	10 000	1000	2500	13 500
Wounded	20 000	2000	5000	27 000

Yom Kippur War, 1973

On 6 October 1973, Egypt and Syria made a surprise attack on Israel. They chose to attack on Yom Kippur, a religious holiday in Israel. But after early successes, the Egyptians and Syrians were driven back when they lost a series of fierce tank battles. The Egyptians and Syrians had been supplied by Russia while Israel had bought weapons from Britain, France and the USA. During the war, the rich Arab oil-producing countries had placed a ban on selling oil to any country that helped Israel. They then increased the price of oil once the war was over. This had a disastrous effect on countries such as Britain and the USA because they depended so heavily on oil imported from the Middle East. After all, oil is vital to generate electricity, fuel transport and make plastics and fertilisers. The Yom Kippur War – and the oil crisis that followed – encouraged many Western countries, particularly the USA, to look for ways to solve the political problems in the Middle East.

WORK

1 Which side was more successful during the first Arab–Israeli war? Give reasons for your answer.

2 **a** Why was there a crises over the Suez Canal in 1956?

   b How successful was Israel during the Suez Crisis?

   c What were the consequences?

3 **a** Look at **Sources D** and **E**. Give two reasons why it would be difficult for Israel to win a war against the Arabs.

   b What evidence is there in Source E that the Six-day War was not *just* an Arab–Israeli war but a war between the USA and Russia?

4 Look at **Source F**. How does this source help explain why the Israeli army might do well in a war against the Arabs?

5 Look at **Source G**. What are the advantages and disadvantages to an historian studying the Six-day War if using casualty figures as evidence?

6 **a** How did the Yom Kippur War get its name?

   b In what ways did the Yom Kippur War affect the rest of the world?

What was Skyjack Sunday?

AIMS ....

Try to understand:
- What happened on 'Skyjack Sunday';
- Why some people turned to terrorism in order to fulfil their aims.

On Sunday 6 September 1970, a small terrorist organisation called the PFLP hijacked three passenger aeroplanes – two American and one Swiss – within a few hours of each other. Two of the planes were flown to a desert airfield called Dawson's Field in Jordan where passengers were held by PFLP terrorists. The third was flown to Egypt where it was blown up after crew and passengers had left the aircraft. On the same day, the PFLP made an unsuccessful attempt to hijack Israel's plane above England (see **Source A**). Three days later, a British plane was hijacked by the PFLP and flown to the same airfield in Jordan where the other two planes had been taken. This whole episode became known as 'Skyjack Sunday'.

So who were the PFLP? What eventually happened to the hijacked planes, the passengers ... and the hijackers? And why had some groups, like the PFLP, chosen terror as their weapon?

Source A ▼ *Leila Khaled, one of the terrorists who unsuccessfully tried to hijack an Israeli plane on 6 September. She had boarded the plane with two grenades in her pockets – but they both failed to explode. She was overpowered by security guards.*

The PFLP or **P**opular **F**ront for the **L**iberation of **P**alestine was a violent 'splinter group' linked to a larger organisation called the PLO (or **P**alestine **L**iberation **O**rganisation). It was dedicated to destroying the Jewish state of Israel and returning the land to its previous Arab Palestinian inhabitants.

The PLO was set up in 1964 by Arab governments to represent the Palestinian people. At first, it was mainly controlled by the Egyptian government. After the Six-day War of 1967, more Arab Palestinians than ever before found themselves within Israel's borders as the Israelis took over more land. For many of these people, the PLO was the only group solely out to promote the rights of Palestinians. At this time, many Palestinians fled to neighbouring Arab states such as Jordan, Egypt and Lebanon where they set up huge refugee camps. And within these wretched camps, a whole generation of Palestinians grew up who regarded land taken by Israel as their rightful home – and many turned to terror tactics to make their point! They decided they had to destroy Israel themselves – as no Arab country had managed to do it – and without a country of their own to fight from, they had to resort to terrorism. The PLO recruited thousands of young, angry Palestinians to launch attacks on Israeli military targets that bordered Israel. The PLO leader, Yasser Arafat, always officially denied any involvement in the attacks but there is little doubt that the PLO always knew about the organisations that claimed responsibility for the attacks.

These militant terror groups thought many Western nations, especially the USA, were as much to blame for the plight of the Palestinians as anyone else. The USA, they felt, was one of the main nations responsible for setting up Israel after World War II – and they continually backed them with investment and weapons. As a result, American army camps, citizens and aircraft were often targets, and one of the most spectacular attacks was 'Skyjack Sunday'.

Look carefully at **Sources B** to **H**. They outline the events of Skyjack Sunday.

Source B ▾ *Yasser Arafat, November 1974.*

"We shall never stop until we can go back home and Israel is destroyed. The goal of our struggle is the end of Israel, and there can be no compromise or mediations. We don't want peace, we want victory. Peace for us means Israel's destruction, and nothing less."

Source C ▾ *A statement adapted from guerrillas of the PFLP, 6 September 1970.*

"This action is aimed against the Middle East peace talks. It is also a blow against the American plot to liquidate the Palestinian cause by supplying arms to Israel. The Swiss airliner and its passengers will be held until the Swiss government releases the three Arabs serving long-term prison sentences in Swiss jails for the attack on an Israeli airliner at Zurich airport."

Source D ▾ *United Nations Secretary General Thant, 8 September 1970.*

"These criminal acts of hijacking planes, of detaining passengers and crew, of blowing up aircraft in transit, are most deplorable and must be condemned. It is high time that the international community, through the appropriate agencies and organisations, adopted prompt and effective measures to put a stop to this return to the law of the jungle."

Source E ▾ *Leila Khaled, PFLP hijacker.*

"I do not see how my oppressor could sit in judgement on my response to his oppressive actions against me. He is in no position to render an impartial judgement or accuse me of air piracy and hijacking when he has hijacked me and my people out of our land. My deed cannot be judged without examining the underlying causes."

Source F ▾ *The Times, 14 September.*

"Private negotiations today began to try to secure the release of 56 hostages — including eight Britons — who were still being held by the Palestinian guerrillas. The other 255 passengers from the three hijacked aircraft had left Jordan. Yesterday the guerrillas blew up the three aircraft after releasing most of the passengers."

Source G ▲ *Palestinian terrorists took over these three airliners – two American, one Swiss. They targeted American planes because they felt that the USA always helped out Israel, a country that occupies land that the Palestinians claim is their own. Palestinian terrorists argued that they have to use terrorism as they have no country to fight from. They wanted their own country – Palestine – and wanted land that Israel occupies. Terrorist acts continue in this area of the Middle East.*

Source H ▶ *From* The Times, *1 October.*

"Miss Leila Khaled, the Arab guerrilla, was flown out of Britain on her way to Cairo last night after an operation of masterly secrecy. On board the RAF Comet, she flew first to Munich where the aircraft picked up three other Arab guerrillas freed by the West German authorities.

The Comet then flew to Zurich where the three guerrillas released by Switzerland were embarked. Meanwhile the last six hostages from the airliners hijacked to Jordan were arriving in New York."

Other attacks followed after Skyjack Sunday, most notably in 1972 when 11 Israeli athletes at the Olympic Games in Munich were assassinated by a Palestinian terror group called Black September.

But the terror organisations, and the PLO, did not succeed in defeating Israel. However, they certainly kept the 'Palestinian struggle' in the news and kept Israel in a permanent state of unease. But the rise of the PLO led to tension between the Palestinians and other Arab states where they were based. In 1970, the PLO tried to take over Jordan, the country from where they had launched many of their raids on Israeli targets. The attempt failed and the PLO was forced to leave. They settled in Lebanon – and attempted a takeover in 1976 before Syria stepped in and restored order. The PLO raids from Lebanon led to an Israeli invasion of the country in 1978 in order to destroy the PLO members in the camps. The PLO army then left Lebanon for Tunisia! Indeed, by the late 1970s, it seemed as if any chance of peace in the region was a very long way off.

FACT *Lebanon*

Lebanon is an Arab country to the north of Israel. In 1970, Yasser Arafat and the PLO set up camps in the country and launched attacks on areas from there. One PLO attack on an Israeli bus in 1978 killed 34 Israeli passengers. The Israelis then invaded Lebanon and, after fierce battles around the capital city, occupied the country. The Israeli occupation was criticised by many and this criticism reached fever pitch in 1982 when the Israeli army and Lebanese Christians entered two Palestinian refugee camps and massacred over a thousand Palestinian men, women and children. When ordinary Israelis heard about the massacre, there was widespread peace demonstration in the Israeli capital, Tel Aviv. The Israelis left Lebanon in 1985.

FACT *Suicide bombers*

A suicide bomber is someone who carries explosives and then kills themselves and other people in a crowded place – a bus or market for example.

For many years, Palestinians have used suicide attacks as a way of fighting against the Israeli occupation of land they say is rightfully theirs. They argue that suicide attacks in Israeli-occupied territory in Gaza and the West Bank are launched because they cannot match the might of the Israeli army.

WORK

1 In your own words, explain what happened on 'Skyjack Sunday'. Your explanation *must* mention the following:
   - PLO
   - PFLP
   - Dawson's Field
   - Leila Khaled.

2 Look at **Source B**.
   a Who was Yasser Arafat?
   b In your own words, explain what Arafat is saying in **Source B**.

3 Look at **Source E**. What do you think Khaled meant when she said that no one had the right to judge her or accuse her of hijacking "when he has hijacked me and my people out of our land"?

4 Look at **Source G**. The three aircraft were blown up in full view of the world's press and television. Do you think the PFLP deliberately planned it this way? If so, why?

5 Look at **Source H**. In 1970 the British government released Leila Khaled and some other PFLP terrorists. Make two lists showing the argument for and against this decision.

The search for peace

AIMS

Aim to:
- remember at least two attempts to secure peace since the 1970s.

Since the 1970s, there have been many attempts to find a peaceful solution to the conflict in the Middle East. However, from the start, both sides have adopted positions that have made the search for peace a difficult quest.

In 1967, the United Nations issued an instruction that they hoped would lead to peace. They told Israel to get out of the land they occupied after winning the Six-day War – and told Arab nations to recognise the state of Israel 'and their right to live in peace within secure and recognised boundaries' (see **Source A**). But no Arab nation would accept Israel's right to exist – so Israel refused to get out of the Arab land they had occupied.

Source A ▼ *UN Resolution number 242, November 1967.*

- Israel to withdraw from territories occupied during the Six-day War.

- Recognition of the sovereignty, territory and independence of every state in the area and their right to live in peace within secure and recognised boundaries.

But, in 1977, a new government came to power in Israel. The new Prime Minister, Menachem Begin, was ready to make a deal with one of the Arab nations with which Israel had been fighting for many years – Egypt. The Egyptian president, Sadat, saw his opportunity to regain some of the land lost in the Six-day War. At the Camp David Accords in 1978, arranged by US President Jimmy Carter, Israel promised to gradually withdraw from the Egyptian territory of Sinai. However, Begin's peaceful attitude towards the Egyptians was very different from his attitude towards the Palestinians in the Israeli-occupied West Bank and Gaza Strip.

For example, Begin increased the number of Jewish settlements in the West Bank from 45 to 112 in six years. And whenever Palestinians on the West Bank opposed the Jews moving onto 'their' land, the rebellions were put down with great force. The existence of these new Jewish settlements made it harder than ever before to think about peace between Jews and Palestinians.

But a change in world opinion loomed on the horizon. From the mid-1970s, the Palestine Liberation Organisation (PLO) leader, Yasser Arafat, decided to turn to diplomacy in search for peace (see **Source B**). He was welcomed by many of the world's leading politicians who gradually began to recognise that the Palestinians had a case in their search for a homeland.

Source B ▾ *Yasser Arafat, December 1988.*

"We accept the right of all parties to exist in peace and security, including a state of Palestine, Israel and other neighbours ... We totally reject all forms of terrorism, including individual, group and state terrorism."

But Arafat's diplomatic progress was being undermined by some Palestinians now living in Lebanon. They were launching terror attacks on targets in Israel ... and the Israelis invaded to try to stop them. But world opinion, often sympathetic towards the Israelis because of the terror attacks, turned against them because of the actions of the Israeli army in Lebanon.

In 1982, for example, Israelis (or their allies) massacred Palestinian men, women and children in two huge refugee camps just across the Lebanese border. Massive anti-war demonstrations were held by an Israeli peace movement – it seemed that even ordinary Israelis were unhappy with their government.

By 1993, Israel still governed all of the Gaza Strip and the West Bank. The Palestinians still wanted them out. Eventually, after long negotiations, the two sides signed a historic agreement called the Oslo Accords with US president Bill Clinton. The idea was based on the theory of 'land for peace'. Israel also signed a peace agreement with the neighbouring Arab state of Jordan at this time.

Source C ▸ *President Clinton with Israeli PM Yitzhak Rabin and Yasser Arafat, 1993. Arafat extended his hand first, while Rabin needed some encouragement from Clinton to shake hands. Rabin was assassinated by an extremist Israeli in 1995 who thought he was an enemy of the Jewish people.*

As a result of the Oslo Accords, a Palestinian government was created, called the Palestinian Authority, to govern Palestinians living in the West Bank and the Gaza Strip.

Israel agreed to withdraw its soldiers from most of the Gaza Strip and West Bank, giving control to the new Palestinian Authority.

FACT *Young fighters*

There have been many violent uprisings in the Gaza Strip and West Bank by angry young Palestinians. They throw petrol bombs and rocks at Israeli troops who they see as an enemy on their soil. Israeli soldiers have been killed – and over 1000 young Palestinians have been killed by Israeli troops. These uprisings are known as Intifada which means 'shaking off'.

However, both sides continued to disagree on many things ... and they both distrusted each other on nearly every issue.

For example, when Yasser Arafat became the leader of the new Palestinian Authority in 1996, attacks on Israel continued by extremist Palestinian terror groups. After two suicide attacks in 2001, the Israelis responded by surrounding Yasser Arafat's headquarters in Ramallah and virtually 'grounded' him for the rest of his life (he died in 2004).

When Palestinians voted for their new government in 2006 – and elected the terrorist group Hamas – it seemed as if the conflict was no nearer to being solved than ever before. The USA and Israel refused to negotiate with the new government, despite it being democratically elected, because Hamas refused to recognise the state of Israel and wished to destroy it.

Source D ▾ *Edwards Said, a Palestinian-American historian.*

"Conditions in the occupied territories

Jabalya Camp in Gaza is the most appalling place I have ever seen. There is no sewer system, the stench tears at your gut, and everywhere you look you see masses of people falling over each other, poorly dressed, glumly making their way from one seemingly hopeless task to the other. The Gaza Strip is made up of several towns, of refugee camps and, most offensive, of a number of affluent-looking Israeli settlements, whose spacious lawns and swimming pools are far removed in appearance from the squalor all around.

The events of the Intifada

Since the Intifada [uprisings against Israeli rule] began in late 1987 until the end of June 1991, 983 have been killed by the Israeli military (that is three times the number of black [people] killed by South African troops under apartheid during the same length of time); more than 120 000 wounded and beaten and 15 000 prisoners, most of them without benefit of a trial. More than 1882 houses have been punitively [as a punishment] demolished. Many schools and universities were closed, so determined has Israel been to criminalise [make criminal] Palestinian education. Literally thousands of days of total 24-hour curfew confined almost two million unarmed and essentially defenceless civilians to their houses."

Source E ▾ *Martin Gilbert, a Jewish historian sympathetic towards Israel. This account is from 1993.*

"Conditions in the occupied territory

Despite their desire for independence, and dislike of Israeli occupation, the Palestinians living in the West Bank and Gaza benefited from the general social and economic policies of Israel. Before 1967, there were no universities; six were established after 1967.

Some improvements since the Israeli occupation

	Before 1967	After 1989
Clinics and hospitals	113	378
Mother and child centres	23	135
Villages with mains water	12	200
Malaria still a problem		
Eliminates infant deaths per 1000 births	86	20.4
School teachers	5316	17 373
Teacher training colleges	0	5
Vocational colleges	0	14

The events of the Intifada

On 9 December 1987, an uprising, known as the Intifada, began in Gaza and spread throughout the Arab-populated areas of the West Bank. Israeli soldiers were attacked, mostly with rocks, but increasingly with knives, petrol bombs and even grenades. Many Arab villages sought to block the entry of Israeli soldiers, and Arab schoolchildren were encouraged by their elders to hurl stones and abuse. The Israeli army sought to regain control by the use of tear gas, rubber and plastic bullets and (when under extreme provocation) live ammunition. Excesses took place, and several Israeli soldiers were found guilty by Israeli courts for abuse of their powers. In 1991, stabbings of Jews became more frequent in Jewish urban areas. So too did the murder and maiming of Arabs by their fellow-Arabs, accused of 'collaboration with the authorities'."

Source F ▾ *Nice Israeli homes contrast with poor homes in the Gaza Strip.*

Source G ▾ *Tony Blair, former British Prime Minister, speaking on BBC radio, March 2007.*

"What I hear most people saying is that they want a peace process to deliver two states that live side by side. Now, there are some extremists that say that they don't want a state of Israel at all but I don't think that's the view of the majority of Palestinians I speak to. Most of them would be perfectly happy to live in peace with the Israelis provided they have their own state, with a proper functioning democracy and a chance of prosperity."

WORK

1 a What was UN Resolution 242?

   b What was the attitude of Arab nations and Israel to the proposal?

2 Which two Middle-Eastern countries made peace with each other at Camp David?

3 What was agreed at Oslo in 1993?

4 Look at **Sources D** and **E**.

   a What is Intifada?

   b What differences are there between the two countries?

   c Can you think of different reasons to explain these different interpretations?

Have you been learning?

Task 1 An exercise in propaganda

a Write a full detailed definition of the word 'propaganda'.

b Read the propaganda stories below about alleged German atrocities (cruel acts that broke the 'rules' of war) during World War II.

> French children were machine-gunned by German soldiers when they conquered France. Their mothers were killed too.

> German prison camp guards refused to give captured and wounded soldiers any medical treatment or water.

> Germans used the corpses of Allied soldiers. The fat was turned into oil and the bones were mixed up with rotten vegetables for the pigs to eat.

> Thousands of innocent civilians were killed when German submarines sank passenger ships early in the war.

> Priestd all over Belgium and Holland, who refused to ring their church bells to celebrate the Germans taking their town, were killed and hung on the bells.

> German bomber planes deliberately targeted schools and hospitals on their bombing raids over Britain.

i Despite there being little proof of any of these atrocities actually being committed, some of these stories appeared in British newspapers during World War II. Why do you think the British government was so keen to advertise these allegations?

ii Imagine you work for the government as their official propaganda war artist. Using a plain sheet of A3 or A4 paper, design a propaganda poster to suit one of the above six stories that could be displayed in a British newspaper during the war.

Task 2 The beginnings of the Cold War

Read **Sources A** and **B** very carefully. They illustrate the contrast between American and Soviet opinion at the end of World War II.

Source A ▾ *US Department of State memorandum: 'The threat of International communism to Europe and the United States', June 2 1945.*

> "To a communist, Europe today politically and economically represents a perfect situation. Europe is emerging from probably the most devastating war in its history. The Red Army's exploits have been so well advertised that the majority of Europeans regard them as their liberators. Even in the West the Red Army receives the lion's share of the credit, thanks to the publicity given it by the communist press. The excesses of the Nazi regime and the fear of a rejuvenated Germany force must force Europeans to gravitate toward the strongest remaining power in Europe –the Soviet Union."

Source B ▾ *From a speech by Soviet Foreign Minister V. M. Molotov at the Paris Peace Conference, 10 October 1946.*

> "It cannot be said that the USA is one of those states which suffered serious material damage in the war. We are glad this did not happen to our ally, though we ourselves have had to go through trying times, the results of which will take us long years to heal.
>
> Now that you know the facts, place side by side Romania, weakened by the war. It (USA) would buy up the local industries, take over the more

attractive Romanian, Yugoslav and other businesses, and become masters in these small countries. It would, in practice, mean the economic enslavement of the small countries and their rule by strong rich foreign firms, banks and industrial companies. Was this what we fought for when we battled against the fascist invaders, the Hitlerite and Japanese imperialists?"

a List four reasons suggested in the sources why the USSR perhaps stood a better chance than the USA of gaining more power and influence in Europe at the end of the war. Try to write in your own words, rather than just copying from the text.

b **Source B** is a political speech. What problems might there be for an historian in using political speeches as evidence?

Task 3 How did Stalin change the Soviet Union?

So was Stalin a monster or a necessary evil?

Years after Stalin's death, a German writer asked Russians what they felt about Stalin. This is what four of them said:

- "He was a blood sucker! Just think of the number of people whose lives he ruined."

- "Who won the war for us? Who raised this country from a backward nation to the most powerful state in the world?"

- "Of course some bad things happened – but there were a hell of a lot more good things."

- "He murdered our best people because he was obsessed with total control."

Clearly people's thoughts about Stalin were divided. Now look back through all the information on Stalin's Soviet Union and find evidence that supports **one** of the following interpretations:

i Stalin was a necessary evil – he was cruel, but a genius who was needed to modernise Russia.

ii Stalin was a monster. He achieved little and murdered millions.

There will be evidence for *both* of these views, but try to form an opinion – and an argument – that supports one of them. You might want to work with a partner on this, taking an interpretation each.

You should be thinking about Stalin's impact on the Soviet Union, how people were affected by his changes, and whether Stalin was a good thing ('a necessary evil' perhaps) or a bad thing ('a monster') for the Soviet Union.

Task 4 Question time

Look at these genuine GCSE questions carefully. Why not try to complete one, two or even all of them as a revision exercise?

- Why did Japan invade Manchuria in 1931?

- Explain why Italy invaded Abyssinia in 1935.

- Why did Hitler invade Austria?

- In what ways did Hitler increase the strength of Germany's armed forces in the 1930s?

- Explain why the British government appeased Germany in the 1930s.

- Explain what was agreed at the Munich Conference in 1938?

- Explain why Germany and the Soviet Union signed the Nazi–Soviet Pact in 1939.

- Explain why the League of Nations failed in the 1930s.

- Explain why the USA introduced the Marshall Plan.

- What was the Berlin Wall?

- Explain why the Berlin Wall was built.

- What was the Prague Spring of 1968?

- Who were the Viet Cong?

- Explain why the USA became involved in Vietnam.

- Explain how the following together contributed to the USA's failure to win the Vietnam War:

- The military tactics of the North Vietnamese

- The failure of the US bombing campaign

- Public opinion in the USA.

Glossary

AAA One of FDR's 'alphabet agencies', set up to help farmers.

Abdicate To give up the throne of a country.

Absolutists People who refuse to have anything at all to do with war.

Alliances Agreements between countries.

Alphabet agencies The nickname given to the organisations and agencies set up as part of the New Deal.

Anarchist A person who believes that countries should not be ruled by governments with set laws and rules. Instead, there is a system of cooperation where everyone rules themselves.

Anti-Saloon League A Christian organisation that campaigned for a ban on alcohol.

Appeasement The policy of giving someone what they want in the hope that their demands will stop.

Area bombing Whole towns or cities bombed in an attempt to make sure everything is destroyed.

Aryan A person of German or Scandinavian origin, usually fair-haired and blue eyed. The Nazis believed that Aryans were superior to all other races.

Assassination The murder of an important or well known person.

Assembly line A system for making goods in a factory; the product is put together stage by stage.

Attrition Gradually wearing down.

Austerity A British government policy from the 1950s. It meant strict controls over industry and people.

Beer Act A 1933 government act that made the manufacture and sale of alcohol legal again.

Billboards Huge roadside and city-centre display boards carrying adverts for consumer goods.

Black Friday 15 April 1921. The day when transport workers and railwaymen decided to end their support of the miners, leaving them to fight on alone.

Black Thursday Thursday 24 October 1924 – the first day of the Wall Street Crash, when share prices fell faster and lower than at any other time before or since.

Blitz A sudden air attack.

Bolsheviks Members of a larger group (led by Lenin), which was formed after the split of the Soviet Democratic Party in 1903. They believed in violent revolution.

Bootleg Alcohol brought in illegally from another country.

Bootlegger A person who brings in alcohol illegally from another country.

Brain Trust A group of men and women with fresh and exciting new ideas who worked for President Roosevelt.

Breadline A long queue that waits for free bread, soup or blankets.

CCC One of FDR's 'alphabet agencies', set up to help young people.

Ceasefire An agreement that stops two sides fighting each other.

Censorship The cutting out or banning of books, plays, films, newspapers or anything that a government does not wish to have expressed.

Chaperone Older person who accompanies and supervises a young person on a day (or night) out.

Cheka Russian secret police, set up by the Communists in 1918. Have also been called OGPU, MVD, NKVD and KGB.

Civilians People not in the army, navy or air force.

Clauses Sections of a document.

Collective farms A group of small farms in Russia, each one having been taken away from its peasant owner.

Collective security A way of avoiding war by which a number of countries agree to protect another if any one country is attacked.

Communism A political system where all property is owned by the government.

Communists People who lives in a country where the government follows the political system known as Communism.

Congress The law-making body, or parliament, of the USA.

Conscientious objectors People who are against war and refuse to help the armed forces.

Conscription The policy of forcing men to join the army, navy or air force.

Constitution The rules by which a country is governed.

Consumer goods Products available to buy by the vast majority of ordinary people, such as watches, vacuum cleaners, cars, radios and so on.

Covenant A promise to do something.

Crazes Short-lived fashion for an item of clothing, a leisure activity or similar. Sometimes called a 'fad'.

CWA The Civil Work's Administration was set up to create jobs during the Great Depression.

Dawes Plan An agreement between the USA and European countries in 1924 (drawn up in America by Charles Dawes). The plan organised for US loans to be given to European countries, especially Germany, in order for them to build factories, roads and so on.

Defectors People who change their alliance with one group to another.

Dekulakisation The process of wiping out approximately five million kulaks.

Demilitarised An area where military activity is not permitted.

Democracies Countries that are run by governments that are chosen by the public.

Democratic Party One of the two main political parties in America. Seen as more sympathetic to the problems of the poor.

Democratic republic A system of running a country in which all adults have the right to vote for the government they want.

Depression A period when trade is poor, factories close and unemployment is high.

Dictator A person with complete control over others.

Dictatorships Countries ruled by a dictator.

Diktat The nickname given to the hated Treaty of Versailles. Translates as 'dictated peace'.

Disarmament To reduce the size of your armed forces.

Dividend Payment from the profits of a company to those who have shares in it.

Dual government Period in 1917 when both the Provisional government and the City Soviets ran Russia.

Duma The Russian parliament.

Dust bowl A large area of farmland in which the soil is too dry and exhausted to grow good quality crops. Terrible dust storms hit this part of America as well, forcing many to leave their farms.

Economy Act A 1933 government act that cut spending on government wages.

Emergency Banking Act A 1933 government act that closed down all banks and only allowed the well-run ones to reopen.

Enabling law A law introduced by Hitler in March 1933, which gave him the power to pass laws without the consent of the German parliament.

Eugenics The study of methods of improving the human race.

Evacuation Being taken from a high-risk area to somewhere safer.

Fascism A system of government that is against democracy and personal freedom and supports a strong, aggressive army, navy and air force.

Fascists People who are against democracy and believe in rule by one powerful leader, supported by a strong army, navy and air force.

FCA One of FDR's 'alphabet agencies', set up to help farmers.

FERA Federal Emergency Relief Administration: the name given to an organisation set up to reduce adult unemployment.

Final Solution The Nazi name given to the attempt to wipe out Europe's Jews between 1942 and 1945.

Fireside chats The nickname given to President Roosevelt's radio broadcasts in the 1930s.

Firestorm A 'super-heated' fire where winds reach speeds of 120 miles per hour.

Flappers Usually richer, younger women who shocked older Americans with their independent behaviour.

Free Corps A group of ex-soldiers in Germany who joined with the government in 1919 to fight the Spartacus League (Communists).

Fürher German word for 'leader', used by Hitler as leader of Nazi Germany.

Gangsters A member of a criminal gang.

German–Anglo Naval Agreement An agreement made between Britain and Germany, to limit the size of the German navy.

Gestapo German secret police.

Ghetto A small, sealed-off section of a town or a city in which Jews were forced to live.

Great Depression The very serious economic crisis that hit America after the Wall Street Crash. Too many goods were produced, not enough people bought them and millions lost their jobs. It lasated for most of the 1930s.

Hereditary Passed on genetically from one generation to another.

HOLC Homeowners' Loan Corporation, established in 1933, by Franklin Roosevelt, to help people keep their homes by providing them with extra loans up to 30 years long.

Holocaust Usually used to describe the murder by millions of Jews by the Nazis during World War II.

Hooverville A shanty town made from old rubbish, where homeless people lived.

Hyperinflation A sudden, dramatic rise in prices.

ICBMs Intercontinental ballistic missiles, long-range missiles, designed for nuclear weapons delivery.

Ideologies Ways of thinking.

Immigrants People coming from abroad to live in a country.

Import duties Taxes or charges put on goods imported (brought in) from foreign countries.

Incendiary Bombs specially designed to start fires.

Indoctrinated Another word for 'brainwashed' – someone who has been taught to accept a belief without question.

Industrialise A process where society is changed into an industrial, factory-based one.

Infamous Well known for something bad.

Investors A person who buys shares in a company hoping to make a profit.

Isolationism The idea that Americans should not play an important role in European problems and concentrate on what is happening in their own country.

Jazz A type of music, started by black Americans, with an exciting rhythm. It often involves improvisation.

Kamikaze Japanese suicide pilots.

Kapp Putsch The violent attempt to take over Germany in 1920, led by Wolfgang Kapp.

Kellogg–Briand Pact A 1928 deal signed by 65 countries promising not to attack each other.

Kolkhoz A farm in a collective farm.

Kulaks The better-off peasants in Russia.

Laissez faire A policy of non-interference by the government in industry and society.

League of Nations An international peace-keeping organisation set up at the end of the Great War.

Lebensraum Living space. The Nazis believed that the German people needed and deserved more land.

Left wing Believing in (or a belief in) ideas closely associated with Communism.

Limitation A set limit.

Locarno Pact A deal signed in 1925 between Germany, Britain, France, Belgium and Italy where they promised not to invade each other.

Majority The greater proportion.

Mandates Countries governed by another country, appointed to do so by the League of Nations in 1920.

Manifesto A statement of what a political party will do if elected.

Mass produce Make goods in large numbers, usually on a production line.

Mass rallies Huge meetings.

Mein Kampf A book written by Hitler containing his views.

Mensheviks Members of one of the groups formed after the start of the Social-Democratic Party in 1903. They didn't think Russia was ready for revolution.

Militant Aggressive or violent in support of a cause.

Moonshine Home made alcohol, often very poisonous!

Munitions Materials used in war, such as guns, bullets and shells.

Mutiny A rebellion by soldiers and sailors who refuse to take orders.

National Insurance A system organised by the government to insure people against sickness, injury and so on.

Nationalisation A policy which means that a country's major industries are taken over and run by the state.

Nationalise When the state takes over and runs the country's major industries.

Nazi–Soviet Pact A 1939 deal between Germany and Soviet Russia which said that both countries would not fight against each other. A secret part of the deal agreed to split Poland between them if (and when) Germany invaded.

Neutrality Taking neither side in a war or dispute.

NRA One of FDR's 'alphabet agencies', set up to help industry and workers.

October Manifesto The document that gave Russians basic civil rights, such as freedom of speech and the right to form political parties.

Organised crime Groups of people, often called gangsters, working together to break the law.

Overproducing Producing too many goods.

Pact of Steel An agreement between Nazi Germany and Fascist Italy, which reinforced trust and cooperation between these countries.

Passive resistance To protect against government, law and so on by non-violent acts.

Polish guarantee Britain's promise, in the late 1930s, to defend Poland if attacked by Germany.

Precision bombing The bombing of specific targets without causing damage to other buildings.

Prefabs Temporary houses.

'Priming the pump' The idea that the government spends money to create jobs that, in turn, means people have more money to spend. Eventually, the government gets some of the money back by taxing wages.

Prohibition The nickname for the ban on making and selling alcohol in America. In force from 1920 to 1933.

Propaganda Information that is spread by a government to influence people's opinions.

Proportional Representation A system of elections in which the number of politicians elected for a particular party is in proportion to the number of votes the party receives. PR can lead to lots of small parties gaining seats and an unstable government.

Purge To get rid of many opponents by arrest, imprisonment and execution.

PWA The Public Works Administration, set up to improve public work, by spending 3.3 billion dollars on improving equipment.

Racketeering An illegal activity in which gangsters demand a payment from a businessman or a shopkeeper on return for protection (and a promise not to smash up their shop).

Rationing Giving every person a fixed amount of certain sorts of food, fuel or clothing when they are in short supply.

Red Friday 31 July 1925. The day when the government gave money to coal owners so they could pay miners and avoid them going on strike.

Red Terror A civil war terror campaign, during which opponents of the Bolsheviks were shot.

Reforms Changes made usually for the better.

Reich Church A new Church set up by the Nazis in an attempt to pull worshippers away from traditional places of worship.

Reparations Payments made by Germany to the winning nations after the Great War to compensate for the damage done.

Repeal To annul a law.

Republican Party One of the two main political parties in America. Seen as more sympathetic to wealthy people.

Retaliate To hit back.

Retreat To pull back.

Rioting Unruly, mob behaviour, usually out in the street.

Satellite An object put into space by man, often used as a weapon or for tracking.

Satellite States The East European countries that remained under Soviet rule after Potsdam.

Self-determination The ability of small countries to rule themselves.

Shareholders People who own a share of a company in the hope of making a profit.

Socialism A belief that economic activity (factories, farms, transport, banking and so on) should be owned and run by the government for the benefit of everyone, and that wealth should be divided equally.

Spartacus League Communist Party in Germany who wanted a revolution similar to the one that had taken place in Russia in 1917.

Speakeasies Illegal bars during the prohibition era.

Star system Nickname for the system by which movie companies worked hard to publicise the celebrity lifestyle of the star, not just the film itself, in the hope of big box office receipts.

Sterilised Stopped from having children.

Stock market The place where shares are bought and sold.

Stockpiling Building up a large quantity of something for future use.

Storm troopers A Nazi organisation that attacked opponents.

Suffragettes Campaigners for the right of women to vote; often prepared to use violence to get their message across.

Suffragists Campaigners for the right of women to vote; less militant than the suffragettes.

Supremacy The belief that white people are better or superior to all other races.

Superpowers Powerful countries.

Swastika The crooked cross symbol adopted by the Nazi Party as their emblem.

Tariffs A charge or tax put on goods coming in from another country. Tariffs on foreign-made goods make them more expensive – so people usually buy home-produced goods.

The Red Scare Fear of Communism in America, in the 1920s.

Theory of evolution An idea that humans developed slowly from single-cell creatures over millions of years. Opposite to the 'creation theory', which proposes that God made the world.

Total war A phrase introduced by Goebbels during World War II. He called for all Germans, civilians and soldiers to take an active part in the war.

Treaty of Versailles An agreement that the German government signed at the end of the Great War which outlined Germany's punishments.

Triple Alliance Military union between Germany, Austria–Hungary and Italy in 1914.

Triple Entente Military union between Great Britain, France and Russia in 1914.

Tsar Russian king or emperor.

Volstead Act Set out punishments for breaking Prohibition laws and defined 'intoxicating liquor' as liquid containing more than half a percent of alcohol.

War Communism Period during the Civil War, when the Communist government took over all factories and supplies of food.

Warheads The explosives in weapons.

Weimar Republic The name given to Germany's democratic system between 1919 and 1933.

Welfare state A system by which the government looks after the well-being of the nation, particularly those who cannot help themselves, such as the old, children, the sick, unemployed and so on.

White Rose An anti-Nazi youth group.

Whites Any opposition group fighting the Reds during the Civil War.

Women's Land Army Name given to the organisation that put women to work on farms during World War II.

WPA One of FDR's 'alphabet agencies'.

Young Plan Reduced Germany's reparations payments.

Zeppelin German airships, used as observation decks and then bombers in World War I.

Zionism The movement to set up an independent state of Israel.

Index

A

abdicate   89, 95, 163, 170

absolutists   45

advertising   10, 32, 34, 134, 157

air raids   64, 207, 208, 209, 223, 228

aircraft   15, 60, 59, 215, 217, 243, 294–295

alcohol   11, 144–145, 156,

alliances   18, 36, 40, 42, 121, 172, 201, 238, 243, 276, 291

alphabet agencies   156–157, 158–159

American Constitution   131

American independence   130–131

anarchists   142, 143

Anschluss (Germany and Austria)   194–196, 205

appeasement   197, 198

Arafat, Yasser   295, 297, 298–299

area bombing   228–231

Aryans   110, 113

Asquith, Herbert   15, 17, 59

assembly line   6, 133, 163

atomic bombs   see nuclear bombs

attrition   52

Austria–Hungary   39, 40, 41, 42–43, 54, 62, 63, 65, 74–75, 95, 100

B

Baldwin, Stanley   18, 24

Balkans   39, 40, 62

Battle of Britain   125

Battle of Jutland   55, 62

Battle of Midway   209

Battle of Stalingrad   209

Battle of the Atlantic   226–227

Battle of the Somme   52, 56–57

Belgium   36, 41, 43, 46, 48, 63, 64, 67, 86, 102, 107, 206–207

Berlin   91, 94–95, 97, 101, 102, 107, 122, 124, 210, 223

Berlin Wall   278–279

Beveridge, William   26, 30

Big Three   66–69, 72

Bill of Rights   130–131

Black Friday   18

blackout   222

Blitz   25, 207, 208, 220

Blitzkrieg   206–207

Boer War   9

Bolsheviks   169, 172, 175, 177, 178–179, 180–181, 182, 185

bombs/bombing   6, 14, 31, 42, 48, 53, 60, 119, 124–125, 145, 152, 163, 168, 197, 240, 244–246, 291, 297, 299

Bonus Army   152–153

Booth, Charles   4, 9

bootleggers   144–145

Brezhnev, Leonid   280–281

British Empire   35, 67, 129, 130, 204

British Union of Fascists (BUF)   25

Bulgaria   39, 65, 74–75, 83, 85, 87, 95, 100

C

cars   6, 11, 22, 23, 42, 76, 133, 134, 148, 150, 154

Cat and Mouse Act   14

ceasefire   55, 94, 253, 272

censorship   115

Chamberlain, Neville   25, 33, 121

Chaplin, Charlie   7, 139

chemical weapons   43, 264, 270

chess   248

Children's Charter   10

church   19, 99, 119, 141, 180, 282

Churchill, Winston   26, 28, 34, 54, 69, 209, 212, 213, 217, 223, 226, 230, 239, 241

cinema   7, 32, 33, 34, 94, 107, 115, 134, 139, 146, 186

Clemenceau, George   66–67, 72

Cold War   238–241, 249, 250, 252–253, 254–255, 273, 285

collective farms   183

collective security   81

Communists/Communism   66, 77, 78, 79, 119, 25, 110, 112, 115, 117, 119, 142, 159, 168–169, 175, 176–177, 178, 179, 180–181, 183, 185–186, 201

concentration/death camps   116, 118, 195

conscientious objectors   45

conscription   44, 45, 120, 192, 271

Conservative Party   17, 26

consumer goods   7, 26

Cuba   245, 254–255

D

D-Day   206, 210

Dad's Army   224

Dawes Plan   86, 106, 107

democracy   13, 19, 76–79, 128, 285

Democratic Party   99, 131, 155

dictatorship   76–79, 177

diktat   72, 101

disarmament   67, 86, 88, 93, 198, 199

Domino Theory   258

Dresden   124

Dual Government   171

Dubček, Alexander   280

Duma   166–167, 171

Dunkirk   207, 212–213

E

Ebert, Friedrich   94, 96–97, 101

education   26, 32, 76, 78, 79, 128

El Alamein   209

electricity   5, 19, 30, 34, 101, 125, 94

Emergency Banking Act   156

empires   6, 35, 37, 38, 89, 91, 164, 180, 182, 202, 207

Ethiopia   91

eugenics   113

evacuation   122, 207, 213, 218, 221

F

factories   6, 8, 12, 15, 23–22, 31, 38, 49, 59, 64, 65, 107, 111, 117, 118, 119, 150, 157, 132–133, 228, 165, 170, 176–177, 179, 180, 184, 186

farmers/farms   58, 64, 65, 66, 78, 97, 118, 135, 150–152, 157, 177, 183, 210, 220, 276, 283

Fascists/Fascism   25, 77, 79

Ferdinand, Franz   42–43

'Final Solution'   122–123

flappers   136–137

food shortages/famine   94, 124, 129, 179, 180, 183, 284, 278

Ford, Henry   6

Free Corps   96, 97, 101

G

Gallipoli   54, 62

gangsters   145

gas   19, 31, 30, 34, 53, 55, 94, 125, 135, 232

general strike   18–20

German–Anglo Naval Agreement   192, 197

German Workers' Party   99, 109

Germany and rearmament   120, 191

Germany and the peace settlement   70–73

Gestapo   112, 116, 118

Glasnost   285

Goebbels, Joseph   115, 117, 124

Gorbachov, Mikail   284–285

Great Depression   22–25

Great War   *see World War I*

guerrilla warfare   256, 266

H

Haig, Sir Douglas   56–57

Hardie, Keir   16–17

Harris, Sir Arthur   228, 231

health programmes   80

Himmler, Heinrich   116

Hitler, Adolf   22, 92, 108–109, 110, 111, 117, 190–197

and the young 113–114

and women 114

assassination attempts on 119

death of 210

'hate list' 112, 122

invasions by 125

'Holocaust' 122, 123

Hoover, Herbert 146–147, 150–152, 154–155

Hungary Uprising 276–277

hunger strikes 14

hyperinflation 102–103, 105, 106, 107

I

immigration 142

Independent Labour Party (ILP) 16–17

indoctrination 113

industrial power 6, 9, 38, 180, 184

Iron Curtain 241

isolationism 82, 162–163

Italy and Fascism 79, 193

J

Japan 22, 62, 86, 88–89, 163, 166, 193, 208–209, 210–211, 232–235, 238, 240, 252, 256

Jarrow March 24–25

jazz music 137, 138–139

Jerusalem 286, 287, 289

Jews 25, 190, 195, 286, 289

Johnson, Lyndon B. 258, 270–271

K

Kaiser Wilhelm II 37, 55

kamikaze pilots 233

Kapp Putsch 101

Kellogg–Briand Pact 86, 107

Kennedy, John F. 245, 250, 254–255, 258–259

Korean War 252–253, 268–269

Ku Klux Klan (KKK) 140–141

L

Labour Exchanges 11

Labour Party 16–17, 26, 28, 30

laissez faire 154, 159

League of Nations 67, 69, 88–93, 107, 120, 191, 192, 196, 205

Lebensraum (living space) 120

Lenin, Vladimir 169, 172–175, 176–181, 182, 186

Liberal Party 9, 11, 16, 17

Lloyd George, David 9, 11

Locarno Pact 86, 107

London 214, 217, 228

and the Blitz 207, 208, 223

and the general strike 19

and the Great Depression 24

poverty in 9

Luftwaffe 214, 223

M

MacDonald, Ramsey 17

Marshall Plan 241

Marx, Karl 78, 168–169, 175, 177

mass rallies 110, 117

Means Test 24

media 19, 29, 139

Mein Kampf 78, 191

Mensheviks 168–169

Military Service Act 58

miners 16, 18, 19, 20, 23, 135, 184

'Monkey Trial' 141

Moseley, Oswald 25

Mussolini, Benito 78–79, 84, 89, 91, 193, 194, 204, 210

mutiny 94, 179, 180

N

National Health Insurance 11

National Health Service (NHS) 26, 28–29, 31

nationalisation 30

NATO (North Atlantic Treaty Organisation) 243

Navy 38, 58, 60, 65, 93, 94, 132, 155, 156, 163, 259, 100, 118, 120

Nazi–Soviet Pact 121, 200–202, 239

Nazis 25, 107, 110–111, 162, 182, 193

origins of 109, 111

propaganda 204

neutrality 162–163

New Deal 155, 156–161

New Economic Policy 180

Nixon, Richard 272–273

no man's land 48, 51, 53

nuclear bombs 210–211, 232–235

O

October Manifesto 166

Operation Sealion 214–217

organised crime 145

overproduction 148

P

Pact of Steel 201

Palestine 294, 296, 299

Pals Battalions 44

Pankhurst, Emmeline 13

Paris Peace Conference/peace treaty 66

passive resistance 103, 118

Pearl Harbor 163, 232–234

peasants 164–165, 169, 171, 172, 177, 180, 183

pensions 4, 9, 10, 26–27, 105, 152, 160, 177

People's Budget 11

Perestroika 285

Poland 22, 75, 120, 121, 123, 129, 176, 190, 201–202, 206

Polish guarantee 201

Pope John Paul II 282–283

Potsdam Conference 239–240

poverty line 5, 9, 135

Prague Spring 280–281

prefabs 31

Princip, Gavrilo 42–43

Prohibition 144–145, 156

propaganda 44, 115, 117, 177, 181, 248, 249, 250, 277

Proportional Representation 98

purges 185

R

racketeering 145

radio 32–34, 115, 117, 133, 134, 137, 138, 146, 148, 154, 156, 186

Rakos, Matyas 276–277

rationing 60

rearmament 120, 191

Red Army/Guards 178–179

Red Empire 284–285

Red Friday 18

Reich Church 119

Reichstag 88, 94, 112

religion 76–77, 96, 119, 128–129, 137, 177, 194, 237, 282, 286

Rentenmark 106

reparations 74, 86, 100, 106

repeal 144–145

Representation of the People Act 17

Republican Party 131, 146, 154, 159

Rhineland 100, 120, 190, 193, 196

rich and poor, gap between 4–5, 16–17

Roosevelt, Franklin Delano (FDR) 145, 156–159, 163, 164

Rowntree, Seebohm 4, 5, 9

Ruhr 97, 102–104, 106

Russia 22, 39, 41, 43, 46, 63, 65, 66, 96, 97, 124, 128, 132, 162

and Communism 159, 168–169

forming of the Soviet Union 180

population of 164

Russian Civil War 178, 179

Russian Empire 164, 180, 182

Russian Revolution (1905) 166–167

Russian Revolution (1917) 170–171

Russo–Japanese War 166

S

Schlieffen Plan 38, 40, 46–47

Serbia 39, 42, 43, 62, 74

shares 22, 31, 146–149, 150

shipbuilding 11, 24

Six-day War 292

snipers 36

social classes 4, 169

socialism 16–17

Solidarity 282–283

space travel 249

Spartacus League 96–97

speakeasies 144–145

sport 7, 24, 79, 137, 159, 237, 248, 249

SS (Schutzstaffel) 116

stalemate 47, 48, 52, 54

Stalin, Joseph 174, 180–181, 182–187

sterilisation 113

stock market 146–149

stockpiling 244

storm troopers 110

Strategic Arms Limitation Talks (SALT) 247

Stresemann, Gustav 104, 106–107

strikes 19–20, 79, 101, 102–104, 118, 162, 166, 171

submarines 55, 62, 70, 110, 120

Sudetenland 120–121

suffragette 13–14

suffragist 12

Suez War 291–296

superpowers 182, 273, 238–239, 281

swastika 110

T

tanks 54, 56, 70, 91, 100, 110, 115, 120, 124, 152, 162, 191, 193, 206, 213, 231, 179, 276, 280–281, 282

taxes 11, 24, 26, 150, 155, 156, 159, 130–131, 134, 164

telephone 7, 22, 30, 116, 133, 148, 154, 174

television 32–34

Tennessee Valley Authority (TVA) 158–159

terrorists 294, 296, 300–301

three-tier system 32

total war 124

Trade Union Congress (TUC) 19–20

trade unions 16, 17, 19, 76, 112, 118, 119, 157, 159, 160

transport developments 6

Treaty of Brest–Litovsk 65

Treaty of Lausanne 74

Treaty of Sèvres 74

Treaty of St Germain 74–75

Treaty of Trianon 74–75

Treaty of Versailles 70–72, 92, 100–101, 110, 120

trenches 46–47, 48, 94, 108, 109

Triple Alliance 18

Triple Entente 40, 41, 42

Trotsky, Leon 186, 172–174, 177, 178–179, 180–181

Truman, Harry S. 211, 233, 234

Tsar 63, 165, 166, 168–169, 170–171, 173, 178, 182

Turkey 39, 54, 62, 65, 74, 75, 95, 100

U

U-boats *see submarines*

unemployment 8, 79, 150–151, 158, 162–163, 177

benefits/payments 11

United Nations 236–237

V

Vietnam 245, 256–257, 258–259, 260–263, 264–267, 268–269

Volstead Act 144

Voting 95, 98, 107, 112

for women 12, 58–59

W

Walesa, Lech 283

Wall Street 146–149, 150–153

War Communism 178–180

Warsaw Pact 243, 276, 280–281

warships 7, 19, 39, 43, 55, 86, 162–163

Weimar Constitution 98–99

Weimar Republic 96–99, 103

welfare reforms/state 11, 26–27, 28, 31

White armies 178–179

White Feather Campaign 44–45

White Rose group 119

Wilkinson, Ellen 24

Wilson, Woodrow 66–67, 80–81

women and war 15, 94

Women's Land Army 58

working classes 4, 8, 16–17, 25, 99

world trade 22, 24, 111

World War I 18, 62

causes of 202

end of 235

World War II 33

causes/start of 190, 200–202

cost of 211

end of 210, 232–235

impact on civilians of 222–225

numbers of deaths in 228, 211

surrender 209, 210

Wright brothers 6–7

Y

Yom Kippur War 293

Young Plan 86, 106

Yugoslavia 73, 74

Z

Zeppelin airships 60

Zionism 286